To Buddhist friends in dialogue

Contents

Wednesday

Pure Land Friday

Boxes, Figures, and Maps

BOXES

FIGURES

MAPS

Acknowledgments

During my first decade teaching Buddhism, I focused my research primarily on the Indian traditions. In terms of this early study, I am grateful to Kenneth K. Inada (SUNY, Buffalo), David J. Kalupahana (University of Hawaii), Hajime Nakamura (Tokyo University), and Frederick J. Streng (Southern Methodist University). At that time, I also pursued a secondary interest in Chinese Buddhism, for which I am grateful to Chung-yuan Chang and Chung-ying Cheng at the University of Hawaii.

In the early 1980s, I began to work in the field of interreligious studies, and contacts with other scholars led me to broaden my study. In this regard, I am very grateful to the following people: Keiji Nishitani (Kyoto University); Masao Abe (Nara University); Geshin Tokiwa (Hanazono University, Kyoto); Heinrich Dumoulin (Sophia University, Tokyo); Taitetsu Unno (Smith College); Ryusei Takeda (Ryukoku University, Kyoto); Alfred Bloom (University of Hawaii); Kenneth K. Tanaka (Musashino Joshi University, Tokyo); David W. Chappell (University of Hawaii); Francis H. Cook (University of California at Riverside); Sallie B. King (James Madison University); Sung Bae Park (SUNY, Stony Brook); Ven. Dr. Hamalawa Saddhatissa and Ven. Dr. Pandith M. Vajiragnana, both scholars at the London Buddhist Vihāra; Judith Simmer-Brown and Reginald Ray of the Naropa University; Jeffrey Hopkins (University of Virginia); Rita M. Gross (University of Wisconsin–Eau Clare); Ven. Geshe Lhundup Sopa (University of Wisconsin); and Ven. Geshe Lobsang Tenzin (Emory University).

Many of these Buddhist scholars also introduced me to the living traditions of Buddhism East and West. This encounter was an invaluable aid in writing the final two chapters of this book. In regard to this encounter with contemporary Buddhism, I would also like to thank A. T. Ariyaratne; Sulak Sivaraksa; Chatsumarn Kabilsingh (Tammasat University, Bangkok); Ven. Dr. Havanpola Ratanasara; Samu Sunim; Jinwol Sunim; monastics of Dharma Drum Mountain; monastics of Fo Guang Shan Buddhist Order; the Tzu Chi Compassion Relief Association; members of Won Buddhism; members of Risshō Kōesi-kai, especially Michio Shinozaki; members of Sōka Gakkai International, especially Virginia Straus; members of the Insight Meditation movement, especially Joseph Goldstein and Sharon Saltzberg; as well such Zen Buddhists leaders as Robert Aitken, Norman Fischer, Blanche Hartman, and Stephanie Kaza.

For help in preparing the manuscript of this book, I would like to thank the following persons for their assistance and critical advice with the text: Paul J. Griffiths (University of Illinois, Chicago), Sallie B. King, George Bond (Northwestern University), David J. Kalupahana, Bryan Phillips (University of Virginia), David W. Chappell, John Keenan (Middlebury College), Robert E. Busswell, Jr. (University of California at Los Angeles), Taitetsu Unno, and Steven Heine (Florida International University). For help with the photographs, I would especially like to thank Johanna Becker, O.S.B. (College of St. Benedict), for her many hours selecting and preparing most of the photographs from her own collection. For other individual photographs, I would like to thank Mary Grell, O.S.B.; Mary Margaret Funk, O.S.B., and Monastic Interreligious Dialogue; Jigme Norbu; Robert Aitken; the Risshō Kōsei-kai; the nuns of Hsi Lai Temple; and the Korean National Tourism Organization. Special thanks to those who helped prepare the photographs: Catherine Wallace (College of St. Benedict) and Mary Jo Corso (Purdue University).

As for the translations, in order to maintain consistency throughout the book, I have given my own versions of the texts drawing on multiple translations and checking the originals when possible. Many translations consulted are in the selecting readings. In a few cases, there is only one English translation to consult. In this regard I would like to thank John T. Davenport for his translation of Sakya Pandita's text and Robert E. Busswell, Jr., for his translation of Chinul's texts. For maps, I consulted Ninian Smart, ed., *Atlas of the World's Religions* (New York: Oxford University Press, 1999).

I would also like to thank all the persons who contributed essays for the boxes placed in the text. These boxes are intended to give the reader a glimpse into what the topics being addressed in the text can actually mean in a person's experience today. Two of these essays were also published elsewhere. The essay by His Holiness the Dalai Lama is published in Donald W. Mitchell and James Wiseman, O.S.B., eds., *The Gethsemani Encounter: A Dialogue on the Spiritual Life by Buddhist and Christian Monastics* (New York: Continuum, 1996). The essay by Jeffrey Hopkins is published in Jeffrey Hopkins, *Cultivating Compassion* (New York: Broadway Books, 2001).

Finally, I would like to thank my students, who for over thirty years have pushed me to deepen my understanding of Buddhism and to present it more clearly. I would especially like to thank the members of a seminar on Buddhism offered in the fall of 1997. I would also like to thank Shin Kim for his advice, Elaine Klemme and Ann Mitchell for their help with the manuscript, and my editors at Oxford University Press, Robert Miller and Liam Dalzell.

Donald W. Mitchell
Purdue University

Pronunciation Guide

Although most of the Buddhist texts from India were written in either Pali or Sanskrit (or rather Buddhist Hybrid Sanskrit), I have preferred always to use the Sanskrit version of Indian Buddhist terms for the sake of consistency throughout this book. Where particular terms play important roles in Theravāda Buddhism, which relies on Pali, I have placed the Pali equivalents in parentheses. Since both Pali and Sanskrit have more than twenty-six letters, to write them in the Roman alphabet necessitates the use of diacritical marks. However, where terms have become part of the English language, I have left them unitalicized and without diacritical marks. For Chinese terms, I have used the Wade-Giles system. The following are a few guidelines to aid in pronunciation for these and other languages.

SANSKRIT AND PALI

Unmarked vowels:
a as in "hut"
i as in "bit"
u as in "put"
e as in "bed"
o as in "boat"

Marked vowels:
ā as in "father"
ī as in "beat"
ū as in "rule"

Unmarked consonants:
c as in "cheap"
ph as in "cup-handle"

Marked consonants:
ś or **ṣ** as in "ship"
ṛ as in "rip"
ñ as in "canyon"
ṃ as *ng* in "sing"

CHINESE

Initial consonants:
ch or **ch'** as in "cheap"
hs as in "she"

Vowels:
a as in "father"
e as in "change"

ts/tz or **ts'/tz'** as in "its"   **i** as in "sing"

o as in "dong"
u as in "lung"
ai as in "high"
ao as in "how"
ei as in "they"
ou as in "go"
u as in "good"
ui as "way"

KOREAN

ae as in "ape"   **ŏ** as in "soap"
ai as in "gap"   **ŭ** as in "soup"
e as in "let"   **ŭi** as in "movie"

JAPANESE

Vowels with macrons, **ō** or **ū**, are simply sounded longer than those without macrons.

INTRODUCTION

Buddhism, one of the great religions of the world, is a diverse complex of doctrines and institutions, as well as ritual, moral, devotional, and meditative practices, spanning 2500 years of history in numerous cultures throughout Asia. From its beginning in fifth century B.C.E. India, with the Awakening of Gautama Buddha, Buddhism has focused on the realization of enlightenment. It has placed a high value on developing spiritualities that lead to enlightened insight through cultivation of morality, meditation, and wisdom. While the vast array of Buddhist religious cultural forms define the breadth of the experience of Buddhism, its profound spiritual quest for enlightenment—and its wealth of teachings about this quest and its goal—define the depth of Buddhist experience.

Given the extent of this breadth and depth, one is faced with many choices in writing an introductory textbook on Buddhism. On the one hand, a writer needs to introduce the reader to the richness and diversity of the historical and cultural forms of Buddhism in a balanced way. On the other hand, one needs also to introduce the reader to the more fundamental depths of Buddhist experiences as they are articulated in those many forms. If one emphasizes the diversity of Buddhism too much, the danger is that a little is said about many things and the textbook becomes a catalog of people and sects, practices and ideas, dates and places, rites and customs, and art and literature. If one emphasizes the depth of the Buddhist experience too much, the danger is that so much is said about only spiritual matters that Buddhism becomes a kind of abstract and idealized religious entity without any correspondence to social, historical reality.

What this textbook does is to focus on introducing something of the depth of Buddhist experience as evidenced in both thought and practice within the context of telling the story of its historical development. There are good reasons, both from without and within the Buddhist tradition, to introduce Buddhism in this way. First, from without, one could argue that the fundamental

1

ideas and practices that express and generate the experiences of Buddhism are the foundations of the religion. Whatever the cultural shapes and textures that Buddhism has taken in popular practice, monastic life, art, literature, and so on, below this diverse landscape one finds these foundations of thought and practice. Second, one could point out that only in recent centuries has the term *Buddhism* been used to name this religion. This name was coined by Western scholars and eventually became accepted by Buddhists themselves. Previously, the religion was often referred to as the Buddha's *teaching* or *message* and the Buddha's *way* or *path* of attainment. These words used within the tradition itself indicate the central importance of doctrine and practice to define the experience of what we now call Buddhism.

Other pedagogical issues should be taken into consideration in making choices as to what to present in an introduction to Buddhism textbook. For example, students who take courses that introduce Buddhism are most often fascinated by the Buddha, his experience of Awakening, and the fact that Buddhists practice spiritualities that lead to a realization of that Awakening in their own experience. These students are happy to study the history of Buddhism in its many cultural contexts, but they want the narrative to emphasize the particular ways in which the paths to, and attainment and nature of, Awakening are understood in the varieties of Buddhist experience. Also, when Buddhist guests speak to classes, no matter what the topic of the lecture may be, they often begin by introducing foundational teachings and practices of the tradition. Before speaking, for example, about Japanese rock gardens, Buddhist guests often feel that it is important for the students to understand the Zen experience of which rock gardens are artistic expressions. The patterns of thought and spirituality that are emphasized in this textbook seem to be of special interest to students, as well as of central importance to the Buddhists about whose religion this book is written.

One final consideration in this regard has to do with the fact that in today's academic world, courses on Buddhism are often taught in departments of philosophy as well as departments of religious studies. In a course on Asian philosophy, for example, it is not enough just to mention in passing the names and a few major concepts of the various schools of Buddhist thought in India, Tibet, and East and Southeast Asia. Therefore, this book intends to introduce in at least some detail the reflective and critical thought of Buddhism as it articulates Buddhist experience in a variety of cultures.

Fundamental to the variety of Buddhist traditions is the classical opinion that to be a Buddhist means to take the Three Refuges or to take refuge in the Three Jewels: the Buddha, the Dharma, and the Saṅgha. In this story of Buddhism, we will examine the life of the historical Buddha, the viewpoint that posits a host of Buddhas at all times and places, and what is considered the essence of Buddhahood as it is experienced in various traditions. We will explore the Dharma (Teaching) of the historical Buddha as it is recorded in the early texts and the Dharma as it is explicated in different ways during the history of Buddhism. We will also introduce the institutional forms, schools, and sects that have defined the Saṅgha (Community), and their diverse practices in pursuit of the ideals of Nirvana and Buddha-hood. In short, we will focus attention on the diversity of Buddhist experience, the different teachings that define these experiences, and the many spiritualities that seek ultimate transformation in light of such experiences. In doing so, other aspects of Buddhism will be mentioned, but not pursued in great depth. For those wishing to explore these other aspects of Buddhism, as well as the various topics covered in this book, there are suggestions for further reading at the end of each chapter. These selected readings are not intended to be complete scholarly bibliographies, but should help students begin to find further information about different aspects of Buddhism.

Drawing on recent scholarship, the first five chapters of this book cover the history of Buddhism in India. The emphasis on Indian Buddhism is important because it is the root experience from which all other forms of Buddhism have grown. These chapters explore the fundamental ideas and practices that in India formed a common heritage for the Buddhist traditions which emerged in other parts of Asia. We will also see that as Buddhism traveled outside of India, it adapted to different Asian cultures. For example, Theravāda spread into Sri Lanka and parts of Southeast Asia, preserving a classic branch of Indian Buddhism. In Chapter 3, we introduce this tradition in what is called "southern Buddhism." We will see that the popular practice of southern Buddhism is not pure Theravāda, but includes worship and rites associated with both pre-Buddhist spirit-religiosity and Hinduism.

In Chapter 6, we introduce what is called "northern Buddhism" as it took shape in Tibet based on the Mahāyāna teachings and Tantric traditions of India. Here we find that the Tibetan schools of northern Buddhism, influenced by their experience of indigenous shamanism, emphasized the mystical and powerful techniques of Tantra, which entail the yogic experience of familiarization with the essence and qualities of Buddhist deities.

While the Chinese were at first interested in the "wonderworking" element of later Indian Buddhism, what is called "eastern Buddhism" is the product of inculturation influenced by Confucian and Taoist strains of classical Chinese culture. While Indian Buddhism was informed more by an interest in intricate analysis and spiritual transcendence, we see in Chapter 7 that the Chinese stressed the experience of Awakening here and now through practical methods that emphasize simplicity, naturalness, and the realization of the interrelatedness of life in ways that contribute both to social harmony and a sagelike "free and easy wandering" through life. This Chinese experience of the Buddhist vision was also central to the inculturation of eastern Buddhism in the rest of East Asia, and from there into Vietnam. In Chapter 8, we see that in Korea, where harmony and unity were so highly valued, Buddhist inculturation integrated in practical ways the diversity of Buddhism that had grown up in China. In Chapter 9, we introduce a number of select single-practice traditions that in Japan gave a variety of avenues to realize and live the Dharma in daily life.

What one might call "western Buddhism" is today beginning to take shape as more Westerners seek enlightenment by adopting and adapting Asian

forms of Buddhism. As this new phenomenon is taking place, Asian Buddhism is also changing in order to engage the modern world that in Asia is
so influenced by Westernization. Indeed, modern Buddhism in Asia and the
West is orienting itself to address the pressing global needs of society and
the natural environment. As we see in Chapter 10, Buddhist responses to
these needs in Asia have produced a number of new Buddhist movements.
These movements balance the seeking of Awakening in traditional ways
with new forms of social engagement and new institutional changes that,
for example, allow women a more equal role in the community and its work.
In Chapter 11, we introduce the ways in which Buddhism has come to the
West from the Asian countries discussed in the previous chapters. We also
discuss what recent scholarship identifies as the important issues emerging
in the founding of western Buddhism, issues that, given globalization at the
beginning of the third millennium, will help define how the story of Buddhism is written in the future.

   With these general comments in mind, we should mention some of the
particular features of this book that are intended to give focus to the text in
the ways described above. What is introduced in Chapters 1 and 2, on the
life and teachings of the Buddha, is based on early Buddhist writings preserved primarily in the Pali texts. In terms of the story of the life of the Buddha, references are also made to some of the legends presented in later famous biographies, which expand on what the tradition came to consider the
experience of the historical Buddha. In Chapter 2, emphasis is given to the
major teachings of the historical Buddha, which explain his experience of
the condition of human existence, as well as the path to and the state of Nirvana. In so doing, the reader is guided through a translation of what is referred to as the Buddha's First Sermon. In both chapters, the early texts are
quoted extensively in order to let the tradition speak for itself and to help
familiarize the reader with the language of the early Indian tradition.

   In Chapter 3, Theravāda Buddhism, which emerged from the time of the
early Buddhist councils, is introduced. Theravāda went on to form the core
of southern Buddhism. Having in Chapter 2 already covered many of the
early teachings of Buddhism that are central to Theravāda, in this chapter
the developed Theravāda "Path of Purification" that defines monastic spirituality is discussed in more depth. To be concrete in this regard, a good
part the chapter is devoted to guiding the reader through some of the salient
passages of Buddhaghosa's classic Theravāda text, *The Path of Purification*.
In this way, one can appreciate the dynamic of growth in the experience of
Theravāda Buddhism. The chapter concludes with a discussion of the history of Theravāda in Sri Lanka and Southeast Asia and its place in both
monastic and lay Buddhist life.

   Chapter 4 introduces Mahāyāna Buddhism, both in terms of theory and
practice. Selections are quoted from some of the major *sūtras* that characterize aspects of Mahāyāna experience. The full text of the *Heart Sūtra* is
quoted and discussed to help the reader appreciate the new kind of language that Mahāyāna introduces into the Buddhist tradition. The practices

of the Six and Ten Perfections as well as the Ten Stages of the Bodhisattva Path are introduced. To be concrete, passages from the *Daśabhūmika Sūtra* are used to guide the reader through each of the Ten Stages. In this way, the reader can better understand what the tradition is itself saying about the experience of the bodhisattva journey to Buddhahood.

Chapter 5 is devoted primarily to the Buddhist philosophies of India. The focus here is on the major philosophies of Mahāyāna Buddhism, primarily Mādhyamika and Yogācāra, given their importance to both northern and eastern Buddhism. Much time is devoted to an explication of philosophical positions concerning emptiness, consciousness, and the *Tathāgata-garbha* in ways that are intended to clarify Indian Mahāyāna Buddhist experience as well as prepare a basis for introducing northern and eastern Buddhism. Since the philosophical texts are quite technical, not as many quotations are given as in the previous chapters. The Tantric tradition of practice in India is also introduced. As we see in Chapter 6, Tantra is especially important in forming the esoteric experience of Tibetan Buddhism.

Chapter 6 treats the Tibetan Buddhist experience. Besides introducing the disseminations of Buddhism in Tibet and the history of the traditions that have molded Tibetan culture, a good deal of time is spent discussing Tantra. This introduction includes Tantra's theoretical grounding in the Mahāyāna *sūtras* and Tantras, the types of Tantric experience, the particular practices that are common to all of its forms, and some of the unique practices found in each of the schools of Tibetan Buddhism. One will hopefully gain some understanding of the process of spiritual growth that Tantra is said to provide. Also, passages are quoted from such writers as Atīśa and Tsong Khapa to indicate how Tantra builds on a foundation that includes practice of the early discipline of Indian Buddhism, as well as certain Mahāyāna practices that generate *bodhicitta*, the thought of, or aspiration for, Awakening in order to benefit all living beings.

Chapter 7 gives attention to how the Chinese Buddhist schools have defined the experience of Eastern Buddhism. First, emphasis is given to the ideas of the T'ien-t'ai and Hua-yen schools, helping the reader understand the latter by quoting a series of passages from the famous *Treatise on the Golden Lion*. Second, the more intuitive experiences of Ch'an (Zen) Buddhism are discussed, with quotations from the *Platform Sūtra*. Third, the devotional experiences of Pure Land Buddhism are introduced, with a quotation from the *Parable of the White Path*. The chapter concludes with an introduction to Buddhism's interaction with aspects of Chinese society and culture in recent history.

Chapter 8 looks at the Korean experience of Buddhism. Less time is spent on the Korean Buddhist schools, since most are versions of Chinese schools introduced in the previous chapter. Instead, focus is given to the major Buddhist figures who are responsible for the unique approach to Buddhism in Korea. Perhaps the most important of these figures is Chinul, the great Korean reformer. Quotations from a number of his writings concerning his three spiritual attainments introduce the reader to the particular flavor of the Korean Buddhist experience.

Chapter 9 treats the Japanese experience of Buddhism. This chapter presents both Tendai and Shingon Buddhism in some detail, supplemented with quotations, since both schools are foundational for the innovations of the Kamakura reformers. In terms of the latter, there are lengthy selections from Hōnen, Shinran, Dōgen, and Nichiren, letting these great Japanese innovators speak for themselves about their own experiences. Similar to the chapter on China, there are sections devoted to Buddhism and Japanese society and culture in the post-Kamakura periods.

While there are many different kinds of developments in modern Asian Buddhism, there has been significant recent scholarship on socially engaged Buddhist movements throughout Asia. Chapter 10 seeks to introduce these important forms of modern Buddhism by going back over all the areas of Asia introduced in the previous chapters to see what types of new Buddhist movements are developing in each area. Here, the thought and activities of some of the most influential Buddhist leaders during the past century are introduced. Quotations from their writings are added so that the reader can sense the quality of their experiences. Millions of persons in Asia and around the world are followers of these movements, presenting a fascinating and influential face of modern Buddhism. The chapter ends with a treatment of how the inclusion of women into the structures of many of these new movements has challenged the role of women in the more traditional forms of Buddhism in Asia.

Finally, Chapter 11 presents Buddhism as it has come to, and taken form in, the West. This concluding chapter is, in a way, a new beginning. Two approaches to the topic are made in this chapter, one historical and the other thematic. First, the ways that various types of Buddhism introduced in previous chapters are now being formed and re-formed in the West are described. In this description, many of the influential Buddhist leaders who are involved in this process are also introduced. It is of interest to note here that this book features a number of boxes containing essays in which Buddhist leaders and scholars share their experience about how the topics being covered in the body of the text relate to their own lives. Many of these essays are written by some of the influential Buddhist figures mentioned in Chapters 10 and 11. Second, Chapter 11 also provides a discussion of some of the important themes that have arisen in the experience of Buddhism in the West, including gender, ethnicity, identity, authority, ecumenism, interfaith dialogue, and social engagement. As we examine these aspects of Buddhist experience in the West, as well as the Asian experience introduced in Chapter 10, we gain a glimpse into how future chapters of the story of Buddhism may eventually be written.

SUGGESTIONS FOR FURTHER READING

Bechert, Heinz and Richard Gombrich, eds. *The World of Buddhism: Monks and Nuns in Society and Culture.* London: Thames and Hudson, 1984.

Buswell, Robert E., Jr., and Robert M. Gimello, eds. *Paths to Liberation: The Mārga and Its Transformations in Buddhist Thought*. Honolulu: University of Hawaii Press, 1992.

Conze, Edward. *Buddhist Texts through the Ages*. New York: Harper & Row, 1964.

de Bary, Wm. Theodore, ed. *The Buddhist Tradition in India, China, and Japan*. New York: Random House, 1972.

Gethin, Rupert. *The Foundations of Buddhism*. Oxford: Oxford University Press, 1998.

Harvey, Peter. *An Introduction to Buddhist Ethics: Foundations, Values and Issues*. Cambridge: Cambridge University Press, 2000.

Kalupahana, David J. *A History of Buddhist Philosophy: Continuities and Discontinuities*. Honolulu: University of Hawaii Press, 1992.

Kitagawa, Joseph, and Mark Cummings, eds. *Buddhism in Asian History*. New York: Macmillan, 1989.

LaFleur, William R. *Buddhism: A Cultural Perspective*. New York: Prentice Hall, 1997.

Lopez, Donald S., Jr., ed. *Buddhist Hermeneutics*. Honolulu: University of Hawaii Press, 1992.

———, ed. *Buddhism in Practice*. Princeton, NJ: Princeton University Press, 1995.

Reynolds, Frank E., and Jason A. Carebine, eds. *The Life of Buddhism*. Berkeley, CA: University of California Press, 2000.

Silk, Jonathan A. *Wisdom, Compassion, and the Search for Understanding: A Buddhist Studies Legacy*. Honolulu: University of Hawaii Press, 2000.

Strong, John S. *The Experience of Buddhism: Sources and Interpretations*. Belmont, CA: Wadsworth Publishing Co., 1995.

Takeuchi, Yoshinori, ed. *Buddhist Spirituality I: Indian, Southeast Asian, Tibetan, Early Chinese*. New York: Crossroad, 1995.

———, ed. *Buddhist Spirituality II: Later China, Korea, Japan and the Modern World*. New York: Crossroad, 1999.

Tsomo, Karma Lekshe. *Buddhist Women Across Cultures: Realizations*. Albany, NY: SUNY Press, 1999.

ONE

THE LIFE OF GAUTAMA BUDDHA

Siddhārtha Gautama (Pali: Siddhattha Gotama) is the person the world has come to know as the *Buddha*, the "Awakened One." Gautama was born during a historical epoch when the Indian culture was open to his religious message of enlightenment, compassion, and peace. The sixth century B.C.E. in India was a time of social and religious change. New monarchies were established as empires were carved out by ambitious warrior kings. There was a growth of new and larger cities that replaced smaller tribal societies. Increase in trade also led to a richer money economy and the emergence of a well-to-do and powerful merchant class. With these changes, not only were the older social structures and cultural customs coming under question, but also the traditional religious viewpoints and institutions that were associated with them.

In this questioning intellectual environment, numerous schools of religious thought and practice emerged. Some religious leaders were emphasizing the mystical ideas of the more recently composed Upaniṣads rather than the ritual practices extolled by the older Vedic tradition. This Vedic tradition was the product of the Āryans who began to invade the Indian subcontinent around 2000 B.C.E. The Vedas contained hymns to the gods (*devas*) along with religious materials and teachings used in ritual sacrifices and in daily life. The earlier Upaniṣads, on the other hand, were being composed by spiritual masters, many of whom preferred yogic practice to Vedic ritualism.

While the earlier Vedas had emphasized the ritual worship of many gods, the Upaniṣads presented the more mystical belief in a universal and unitary spiritual Reality, called Brahman, which is the true essence, or Ātman (Self), of all things. It was believed that the personal realization of this divine essence through insight, matured in the depths of meditation, would lead one to spiritual liberation, or *mokṣa*. Liberation was understood to be release from karma (Pali: *kamma*) and rebirth. Karma was thought to be a subtle form of moral energy that results from one's good and evil actions. This karmic energy was believed to determine what kind of rebirth one will experience after death. To gain liberation, according to the Upaniṣads, it is not enough to worship the gods; one has to destroy one's karma and attain spiritual realization of the divine in all things in order to escape the rounds of rebirth. Only by the practice of spiritual discipline can one's true Self, the eternal Ātman, find liberation from rebirth by merging with the divine Brahman.

This spiritual ideal not only challenged the value the Vedas gave to religious ritual but also clashed with the materialism found in the large cities and enjoyed by the newly rich merchant class. Moreover, while some people were disillusioned by the Vedic ritualism and urban materialism and were attracted to the ideal of liberation, they were also suspicious of the spiritual integrity of the learned priests and sages. These religious leaders were, for the most part, married and making a living from their teaching and ritual celebrations. People were therefore open to new religious movements that were formed as seekers for liberation left the cities and resided in the forests. Members of these new religious communities were called śramaṇa (Pali: samaṇa), or "strivers" for liberation and contentment. They often were wandering ascetics who lived in poverty and begged for what they needed. Among these śramaṇa communities were the Jains, the Ājīvakas, the Materialists, and the Skeptics.

Jainism was founded around the time of Siddhārtha Gautama by Vardhamāna Jnātṛputra, known as *Mahāvīra*, the "Great Hero." This group taught that all beings have a "life principle" (*jīva*). This *jīva* is like an individual soul that is bound by karma and rebirth to the material world. The only way that one can free the *jīva* from this bondage is by severe asceticism. The Ājīvakas believed in rebirth, but not in the power of karma to effect the condition of one's rebirth. One's life is determined by fate, not by any moral or spiritual striving. Each life is fated as to how it will work itself out. One can find peace by accepting one's life in whatever form it might take. The Materialists denied both karma and rebirth. Since for them there is nothing besides matter, when one dies, one's self is annihilated. Therefore, the Materialists taught that contentment can only be found in the pleasures of a balanced life that includes enjoyable relationships with others. Finally, the Skeptics avoided the confusion that was caused by all these different viewpoints by simply withholding judgment. In this skeptical avoidance of the problems that so concerned others, they found a certain peace of mind.

As we shall see, on his spiritual quest Gautama joined a small group of śramaṇas for a time. However in his teachings after his Awakening, he rebuked the shortcomings of the views and practices of the śramaṇa groups. He was opposed to the Jains' rather mechanical notion of karma and their extreme asceticism. He felt that the Ājīvakas' fatalism discouraged the vigor and effort needed to attain Awakening. The Materialists, he believed, were deluded in thinking that lasting happiness can be found in temporary enjoyments. And the Skeptics were simply wrong in doubting all views since some viewpoints can be proven true by meditative insight. Gautama also thought that one needs a certain "faith" that the spiritual life can lead to liberation in order to have the necessary commitment to attain that liberation.

THE EARLY LIFE OF SIDDHĀRTHA GAUTAMA

It was into this world of religious and cultural transition that Siddhārtha Gautama was born. The exact date of his birth is a matter of contention among scholars. Different Buddhist sources claim that Gautama died either 100 years or 218 years before the consecration of King Aśoka. Since that consecration can be plausibly dated anywhere between 280 and 267 B.C.E., and since Gautama is said in all Buddhist sources to have lived for eighty years, the date of his birth using these sources could be put between 578 and 447 B.C.E. On the other hand, scholars point out that the 100- and 218-year figures can also be seen as ideal numbers, hence the lack of consensus. Until recently, most modern scholars have accepted the earlier dating for Gautama's life. But today, many scholars place his life fully in the fifth century B.C.E.

Scholars also point out that not only the date of Gautama's birth but also stories about his life must be questioned in terms of historical accuracy. The complete biographies of Gautama's life were written hundreds of years after his death and include legends not found in earlier texts. These later biographies include the *Mahāvastu* ("Great Story") from the first century C.E.; the *Lalitavistara* ("Graceful Description"), also from the first century C.E., and the famous *Buddhacarita* ("Acts of the Buddha") written by Aśvaghoṣa in the second century C.E. The older sections of Buddhist scriptures, called the *Nikāyas* or *Āgamas*, do not contain a full biography of his life, but only fragmentary references. Also, scholars point out that we have no historical evidence concerning the Buddha's life to use in order to judge the value of even these earlier writings. However, it seems reasonable at least to tell the story of the Buddha's life based on the earlier writings, with occasional mention of the more popular legends that appear in the later biographies. For sites related to the life of Gautama Buddha, see Map 1 in Chapter 3.

Birth

The earlier Buddhist scriptures say that the historical Buddha was born to the warrior-caste Gautama family of the Śākya clan in the state of Kosala. *Gautama,* meaning "most excellent cow," should be understood in the context of cow veneration that was a custom in Indian culture. *Śākya* means "one who possesses power." In the later tradition, the Buddha is given the title "Śākyamuni," or "sage of the Śākya clan." A personal name for the Buddha was not given in the earlier texts, but appears in later texts as *Siddhārtha,* meaning "one who has achieved his goal." In early texts, Gautama's father is named *Śuddhodana,* meaning "pure rice." This seems appropriate since the Śākya clan resided between the Ganges plains and the foothills of the Himalayas, a region in which rice is cultivated. Śuddhodana is referred to in the earlier texts as one of the council of rulers of the Śākya clan and leader of the town of Kapilavastu where the family lived. Later biographies of the Buddha claim that Śuddhodana was actually a king.

Early texts report that Gautama's mother, Māyā, was in the garden of Lumbinī near Kapilavastu when she gave birth to her son. Buddhists celebrate the birth of Siddhārtha Gautama on the full moon of Vaiśākha (April–May), which is the fourth month of the Indian calendar. An early text records a prophecy made by a hermit named Asita at the time of Gautama's birth:

> Holding the bull child of the Śākya tribe, he . . . examined him, and with joy in his mind raised his voice saying, "This is the supreme man, foremost among men. . . . This prince will reach the heights of true Awakening; he will see the utmost purity and benefit many because of his compassion; he will turn the wheel of the Dhamma [Teaching] and his pure actions will be widely spread. (*Sutta-nipāta*, 679–700)

Later biographies relate the tragic story that seven days after giving birth to Gautama, Māyā died. In this account, Śuddhodana later married Māyā's younger sister, whose name was said to be Mahāprajāpatī. Mahāprajāpatī is also said in this story to have raised Gautama along with his half-brother, Nanda.

Youth

All Buddhist texts agree that Gautama grew up enjoying the luxuries of an aristocratic life. Reflecting on those days, he is reported in an earlier text to have said:

> I was comfortable, extremely comfortable, incomparably comfortable. My father's mansion had lotus pools of blue, red and white all for my benefit. . . . Day and night a white canopy was held over me to protect me from the cold, heat, dust, chaff or dew. I had three palaces, one for winter, one for summer and one for the rainy season. During the rainy season, I was at the palace suited for the rains surrounded by female entertainers, and was never left alone. (*Anguttara-nikāya*, I, 145 ff.)

In later biographies, this luxury was explained with a legend concerning the conception of Gautama. In that legend, it is said that when he was conceived, his mother dreamed that a white elephant with a white lotus in his trunk entered her body. The astrologers interpreted this dream to mean that if Gautama married and remained a householder, he would be a great warrior and perhaps unite all of India, something that had not been accomplished up until that time. However, if he would leave the householder state and retreat into the forest like the *śramaṇa* were doing, he would be a great religious leader. Śuddhodana, who was certainly influenced by the fact that during his day many nobles were creating great empires throughout India,

Figure 1.1. Māyā's dream; *stūpa* railing bas relief detail, Amarāvatī; second century B.C.E., India. Government Museum, Madras, India.

told the astrologers that he wanted Gautama to remain a warrior and not to wander off to follow the religious life. They responded that to ensure that Gautama would not pursue the religious life, his father should surround him with sensual pleasures and hide from him anything that might make him dissatisfied with his householder life. This story is important to Buddhists today because it defines the major distractions in daily life that keep a person from undertaking the spiritual quest: attachment to worldly pleasures and the security that wealth seems to offer.

Despite the many pleasures and luxuries enjoyed in his youth, Gautama was disturbed by certain negative aspects of the human condition that he could not avoid. After giving the above-quoted description of his comfortable life, the Buddha goes on to say that he could not help "observing old age in another person." And when he would observe old persons as well as diseased persons and even corpses, he would feel "annoyed, ashamed and disgusted." In other words, these sights would disturb the enjoyment of his riches and pleasures. However, this feeling of annoyance led him to feel ashamed because all persons, including himself, share the weaknesses of the human condition. In the end, he felt disgusted and despondent about his being subject to, and about his reaction to, human suffering and finitude.

Another early text indicates that once Gautama did happen upon a possible spiritual avenue to a deeper form of peace and happiness that is neither dependent on fleeting pleasures nor limited by the suffering human condition:

> I remember well when my father was performing his duties and I sat under the shade of the Jambu tree along the path to the field. Separated from desires and from unwholesome affairs, I achieved the first stage of meditation. This entailed the joy produced by these separations, and is accompanied by initial and discursive thought. I believed that certainly this was the way to Awakening. (*Majjhima-nikāya*, I, 246)

In due time, Siddhārtha Gautama married a young woman named Yaśodharā, and eventually they had a son, who was named Rāhula; the name *Rāhula* means "fetter." Some interpret this name to mean that Gautama considered the birth of his son to be an obstacle to his pursuit of the religious life. Others point out that while this may be true, there is every indication in the texts that Gautama loved his family very much. So, Rāhula was not so much an unwanted responsibility for Gautama, but was the cause of another bond of love to his family. In any case, the naming of Rāhula certainly indicates that Gautama was struggling with his love for home and family on the one hand, and the spiritual impulse to the religious life on the other. In the end, this latter impulse to find Awakening and answers to his questions about life became so strong that at the age of twenty-nine, he decided he must follow this impulse by leaving home and family to undertake a spiritual quest. Reflecting back, he would later say, "In this spring of my life, despite the tears shed by my parents, I shaved my head, put on robes, renounced my home, and became a homeless monk" (*Majjhima-nikāya*, I, 163).

The Four Sights

Gautama's struggle with the householder life and the religious quest noted in the early texts would later be woven into the story of the Four Sights. In this legend, as he approached his thirtieth birthday, Gautama found himself in the grips of a very painful struggle between his attachment to his "home," with everything his family meant to him, and his attraction to the "homeless" religious life, with its spiritual quest. This crisis was said to have been precipitated by Four Sights. It seems that one day while on a chariot ride, he passed beyond the area around his home that was secured by his father from anything upsetting. It is said that for the first time he saw a decrepit old man. When he asked his charioteer about this person's sad condition, the charioteer answered that the ills of old age are the fate of all people. Returning to the palace, Gautama fell into melancholy and could no longer find any enjoyment in the pleasures of his princely life.

On a second ride, it is said that for the first time Gautama saw a severely diseased man, and he understood more deeply that disease is not kept at bay by worldly power. Returning to the palace, Gautama's melancholy deepened. On his third trip, for the first time he saw a corpse, and again he was faced with the ultimate fate of all humankind from which no amount of worldly security can keep one safe. Deeply depressed about the plight of the human condition, Gautama set off on a fourth trip and saw a religious hermit practicing meditation. The charioteer told Gautama that this person had left the material comforts of the householder life to seek spiritual liberation from the ills of the human condition.

Through these Four Sights, it is said that Gautama understood that the impermanent pleasures he had been enjoying were passing, that they could not provide a permanent happiness that the ills of life, represented by old age, illness, and death, could not destroy. He also understood that if he wanted to find that kind of lasting inner peace, he must follow the religious life. This is a lesson that all Buddhists are taught to apply to their own lives. As with Gautama, the nature of our shared suffering human condition, when faced with honesty and courage, presents one with a fundamental reason for following the religious journey to spiritual freedom and peace. In Gautama's case, his despondency is said to have lifted as he realized in the sight of a religious hermit that there is a solution to the dissatisfaction he found with his ordinary life.

The story then goes on poignantly to recount the deeply emotional parting of Gautama from his beloved family and home when he finally made the decision to pursue the religious quest for liberation. In the middle of the night, with firm resolve and motivated by a higher spiritual sense of duty, Gautama gazed for one last time at his cherished wife and son. Then with his charioteer, he left the city on horseback. Reaching the banks of a river, Gautama dismounted, shaved his head, and exchanged clothes with a passerby. Finally, it is said that Gautama sent his charioteer back to his father with a message explaining his actions, and then he set off on his spiritual quest called the "Great Renunciation."

THE GREAT RENUNCIATION

It is important to view the story of Siddhārtha Gautama's departure from his home in the social context of the sixth century. We must take into account that at that time the extended family, especially a well-to-do family like Gautama's, shared the responsibility of caring for all family members. So when Gautama set off on his pilgrimage to liberation, his wife and child would be cared for by his extended family. This certainly is not to deny the sense of loss that each member of the family must have felt because of Gautama's departure. However, his decision was not taken lightly, and he surely felt the pain of separation as he traveled on foot away from his home and loved ones. But, he believed firmly that he was responding to a higher spiritual calling—a calling that he could no longer resist. He had to go out to meet his destiny with total commitment.

According to the early scriptures, Siddhārtha Gautama journeyed south from Kapilavastu, across the Ganges River to the city of Rājagṛha, the capital of the state of Magadha. Magadha was south of the state of Kosala where Gautama had lived. It is said that in Rājagṛha, Gautama begged for alms and inquired as to where the religious seekers in the area were living. Being told that they resided in the eastern foothills of Mt. Paṇḍava, he went and stayed there for some time. While there, he is said to have been visited by King Bimbisāra, who tried to persuade him to give up his spiritual quest and return to the worldly life. Some scholars say that perhaps King Bimbisāra was seeking an alliance with the Śākya clan against Kosala, Magadha's rival state. In any case, Gautama restated his decision to pursue Awakening and lasting peace, and later left the Rājagṛha area.

Spiritual Teachers

In what is referred to in some of the later texts as "a short distance away," Gautama found some ascetics and joined them for a time. However, he decided that they were "practicing a wrong path," and then went to the hermitage of Ārāḍa Kālāma, a teacher of meditation. The early texts say that Ārāḍa taught his disciples how to attain "the state of non-existence" in meditation. Gautama attained this state, and was even asked by Ārāḍa to help him teach in his community. However, Gautama responded, "This Dharma (Teaching) does not lead to avoidance, to separation from desire, to cessation, to peace, to wisdom, to true Awakening, to Nirvana (Pali: *nibbāna*). It merely makes us attain the state of non-existence" (*Majjhima-nikāya*, I, 165). In other words, the meditation taught by Ārāḍa produced a high state of absorption in which all forms of existence disappear. But when one emerges from that trancelike state, his or her life is still lacking in peace, wisdom, selflessness, and true Awakening.

After Gautama studied with Ārāḍa, he went to stay with Udraka Rāmaputra, another teacher of meditation. Udraka taught Gautama the attainment of "neither perception nor non-perception." Again, Gautama reached this highest state of meditative absorption, but found that it too did not produce the freedom from desires, inner peace, wisdom, Awakening, and Nirvana that were the goals of his spiritual quest. Although Gautama left Udraka as he had Ārāḍa, it seems that he was influenced by both of these teachers. Early Buddhism included both of these types of formless absorbing meditation among its practices to foster an encouraging meditative "taste" of Nirvana.

Asceticism

After leaving Udraka, Gautama journeyed east to the area of Uruvelā. Early texts state that Gautama practiced asceticism in that area for many years, during which time he seems to have struggled with Māra, a tempter spirit who seeks to entrap spiritual seekers in order to keep them in this world where he can influence their lives. In an ancient account of these temptations, Māra is said to have suggested that Gautama turn from his more spiritual "endeavor" and pursue doing good works along with making Vedic sacrificial offerings in order to accumulate good karma. In fact, this was a temptation to give up the search for Awakening because, in Buddhist thinking, moral behavior and ritual actions alone cannot produce the state of Awakening and Nirvana. Another early passage suggests that during his ascetic period, Gautama had to combat certain inner states of mind that are not conducive to the attainment of Nirvana, and also physical conditions that discourage spiritual advance. The text attributes these temptations and trials to Māra: "Your first army is desire, your second army is discontent, your third army is hunger and thirst, your fourth army is ceaseless clinging. Your fifth army is laziness and sleep, your sixth army is fear, your seventh army is doubt, your eighth army is pretense and stubbornness" (*Sutta-nipāta*, 436, 437).

The early texts state that it was at this time that five ascetics joined Gautama because they were so impressed with the degree to which he practiced self-mortification in hopes of spiritual freedom and Awakening. However, after several years of ascetic practice, Gautama was still unable to attain Awakening and Nirvana. He finally realized that the ascetic path was not the true way to the spiritual life he was seeking and decided to give it up. But what was the true way?

Facing this question, Gautama remembered the meditative state he had entered when he was a young boy sitting under a shady tree while his father was working. In that tranquil repose, his mind had attained a deep state of meditation that brought him a great joy and freedom from worldly desires and immoral thoughts. Overcoming his ascetic aversion to anything pleasant, Gautama considered turning to a more moderate way of spiritual practice that naturally welled up within him. Later, he would call this path the "Middle Way" because on the one hand it rejects the sensual indulgence he had enjoyed as a young man, and on the other hand it rejects the mortification of the flesh that he had practiced as an ascetic. The former ignores the spiritual journey, and the latter inhibits its progress by destroying the organic mind-body unity that is important for spiritual advancement.

Since his extreme fasting had left him emaciated, Gautama accepted some milk offered by a village girl, thus abandoning his extreme asceticism. But when his five companions saw that he had given up his fasting, they concluded that he had also abandoned his striving endeavor, and so they left his company in disgust. However, Gautama with renewed resolve then sat under what is called the *Bodhi* Tree ("Tree of Awakening") near Bodhgāya, vowing to remain in that place until he attained Awakening. Later legends state that when Gautama gave up his asceticism, he sat under a sacred tree. While he was sitting there, a woman named Sujāta arrived at the tree and gave him a bowl of rice and milk. Sujāta, honoring a vow, had come to the sacred tree intending to place an offering under it.

THE AWAKENING OF THE BUDDHA

After regaining his strength, Gautama remained in seclusion on the banks of the Nairañjana River near Bodhgāya. The opposite shore was a popular place for ritual practices and ascetic sacrifices offered by both priests and ascetics. Symbolically turning his attention away from both of those types of religious activities, Gautama began practicing meditation in order to seek liberation within himself. He sat under the *Bodhi* Tree, faced east, and vowed not to move from that place until he attained Awakening.

In later biographies, it is said that it was at this point that Māra appeared and presented Gautama with his temptations. According to these stories, Māra sends his armies that include such trials in the spiritual life as sensuality, discontent, doubt, fear, and so on. In some accounts, Māra sends his three daughters—Discontent, Delight, and Desire—to tempt Gautama. It is also said that when these temptations failed, Māra then questioned Gautama's merit to become the Buddha, the Awakened One. While Gautama was protected from this temptation of self-doubt by his great merit, he had no one with him to witness to this fact. So, Gautama touched the earth asking for its witness that he was indeed worthy to become the Buddha. This action is represented by the earth-witnessing posture of the Buddha often depicted in Buddhist art. In response to Gautama's request, there was an earthquake and the earth goddess appeared. This goddess wrung a flood of water from her hair that had accumulated when Gautama had done ritual water-pouring after doing meritorious deeds in past lives. With the earthquake and flood, and as the sun was setting, Māra and his armies fled.

Buddhists see an important lesson in this legend; namely, that when one makes a sincere commitment to the true path of spirituality, there arise certain trials that test one's resolve. There are trials that cause fear; one fears what might lie ahead in the journey, for example. There are trials of self-doubt wherein one feels unable to go ahead or unworthy of the ideal one is seeking. And there are the temptations that arise from one's attachments to the world and the many sensual pleasures one finds in that world. One must have the faith or confidence to go ahead in the holy path despite these obstacles.

Enlightenment

Sitting under the *Bodhi* Tree at Bodhgāya on the night of the full moon during the month of Vaiśākha, Gautama attained Awakening. The early texts say that he did so by ascending what are called the Four Meditations (*dhyāna*; Pali: *jhāna*). The first meditation is one of concentration free from sensual pleasure and base thoughts but with discursive reflection, elation, and deep joy. This is what he had experienced in his youth. The second meditation sets aside any discursive reflection for a deeper and more unified mental tranquillity. The third meditation negates emotional elation, which is a hindrance to equanimity and clarity of mind. The fourth meditation transcends even joy so that its opposite, dejection or sorrow, is also transcended into a complete state of mindful equanimity. The mind, being purified at this point, is said to become stable, yet "soft and workable."

Having reached this state of meditative clarity, Gautama chose not to "work" his mind into the higher meditative absorptions that he had learned from Ārāḍa and Udraka. Rather, he purposely focused his contemplation into a penetrating insight into the truth about existence itself. In this manner, he is said to have ascended to the highest level of Awakening (*bodhi*) through three stages. During the first watch of the night (evening), Gautama saw all of his own previous lives, one by one. During the second watch of the night (midnight), he saw the rebirth of others according to their karma, and the whole of existence appeared to him "as if in a mirror." During the third watch (late night), he destroyed all mental and emotional impurities, selfish desires, false views, and ignorance. With pure and penetrating insight, some early passages say, he realized the dependent arising (*pratītya-samutpāda*) of all existence, how all things dependently come to be what they are. Other passages say that he was able to realize (1) the dissatisfactory nature of existence (*duḥkha*), (2) the cause of its arising, (3) the cessation of its arising, (4) and the path that leads to that cessation. Later, Gautama would call these the Four Noble Truths. By dawn, all ignorance had been extinguished, as Gautama's Awakening was complete. He was now Gautama Buddha, Gautama the Awakened One.

With this description of his Awakening, we can better understand an early text's presentation of the following words attributed to Gautama Buddha:

> I truly made effort and endeavor, my thought was firm and undistracted, my body was tranquil and passive, and my mind was concentrated. I was free of desires and unwholesome thoughts, and though I still had initial thought and discursive thought, I had arrived at the first meditation with the joy created by such a separation. . . . [Having attained the second, third and fourth meditations,] in this manner my mind became concentrated, purified, cleansed, without defilement, pliable, flexible, established and immovable. I then directed my mind to wisdom raising the recollections of my past lives . . . recalling numerous past lives along with each individual appearance and detailed conditions. . . . This was the first light of wisdom attained during the early part of the night. . . . I then directed my mind towards the knowledge of the birth and death of all living beings. . . . I observed living beings die and be born . . . following the results of their karma. . . . This was the second light of wisdom attained during the middle of the night. . . . Then, I directed my mind towards the knowledge of the wisdom that eliminates ignorance. At that time, I realized [the truth about] the dissatisfactory condition of life [its nature, cause, cessation and path to its cessation]. . . . When I realized this, my mind was freed from the defilement of desire, my mind was freed from the defilement of ignorance, and as I became free, I realized that I was free. . . . This was the third wisdom attained at the end of the night. (*Majjhima-nikāya*, I, 21ff.)

Nirvana

According to the early texts, the Buddha engaged in deepest meditation for four or more weeks in the vicinity of the *Bodhi* Tree. There, he enjoyed the

Nirvana that he had attained by his Awakening. During that time, two merchants, Trapuśa and Bhallika, came from a nearby village and venerated him. After this offering, they asked to be received as lay followers, and the Buddha accepted them. However in this case, the Buddha did not preach the Dharma (Pali: Dhamma), or his Teaching, to them. In fact, the Buddha wondered if humankind, given its attachment to the worldly life, could ever understand what he had realized. In one early account, it is said that he reflected: "How can I teach what I have realized through painful toil? For those who suffer from craving and ignorance, this Dharma is not easy to understand. It is contrary to the current of this world, profound and exceedingly subtle. . . . [I]t will be impossible to be seen by those clinging to greed and covered with ignorance" (*Saṃyutta-nikāya*, I, 136).

In response to this hesitation of the Buddha, Sahampatī Brahmā, said to be the most important god worshiped at that time, came to the Buddha and asked him to teach the Dharma to the world. He told the Buddha: "With eyes of wisdom . . . observe the people who are submerged in the sorrow of birth and death. Please teach the Dharma, there will be some who can become Awakened" (*Saṃyutta-nikāya*, I, 137). So, with his wisdom eyes, the Buddha surveyed the entire world, and saw that in fact there were some people who would understand his teaching. Out of compassion, he decided to preach the Dharma to the world. Then, the Buddha is said to have used his eyes of wisdom to determine whom he should teach. At first, he thought of his teachers, Ārāḍa and Udraka. But then he realized by his spiritual vision that they had both died. Next, he turned his vision toward the group of five ascetics with whom he had lived, and discovered that they were residing at Deer Park at Sārnāth near the city of Benares. The Buddha then realized that they had the discipline necessary to understand the Dharma. So he left Bodhgāya and traveled 130 miles to Sārnāth.

THE MISSION OF THE BUDDHA

By all accounts, the Buddha found his former companions in the Deer Park at Sārnāth. At first the five ascetics resolved to shun him because he had abandoned their severe ascetic life. However, when the Buddha approached them, given his appearance, "they were unable to follow their own agreement." The Buddha was then able to convince them that he had not returned to a lavish lifestyle, and the five ascetics decided to listen to his words. In the earlier texts, it is said that the Buddha taught them for a period of time. He would teach some of the ascetics while the others begged for alms. Eventually, the five came to understand the hindrances to Awakening and peace that are associated with this transient world. Then searching for emancipation from all hindrances, they found wisdom, Awakening, and Nirvana. Early texts record what has become known as the Buddha's First Sermon. This First Sermon, as presented in the early texts, is most likely a formalized presentation of the kinds of things the Buddha did teach to his first disciples. We will look at these teachings in detail in the next chapter. For now it is enough to note that whatever the Buddha taught his five new disciples, it brought them all to the attainment of Awakening and Nirvana. The Buddha referred both to himself and to these enlightened disciples as *arhats* (Pali: *arahats*), meaning "worthy ones."

The Three Refuges

Through the Buddha's instruction, the five ascetics attained enlightenment and received admission as celibate monks (*bhikṣu*; Pali: *bhikkhu*) into the Buddha's new spiritual order, which he referred to as the *Saṅgha*, or "Community." It is said that from the beginning of the Saṅgha, those who entered it as celibate members and those who associated with it as lay followers all took what came to be called the "Three Refuges." A Buddhist takes "refuge" in (1) the Buddha, (2) the Dharma, and (3) the Saṅgha. These Three Refuges are also called the "Three Jewels," since by seeking refuge in the Buddha, Dharma, and Saṅgha, one receives these three treasured gifts. The Saṅgha, in the "conventional" sense, includes just the ordained celibate monastics. However in the "pure" sense, the Saṅgha consists of all, including lay followers, who take the Three Refuges and have penetrated and lived the Dharma to the point that they can teach it to others.

In the Indian culture at the time of the Buddha, taking refuge was a formal act of submission to a person or god. One promised with this action to be a faithful follower of a being who could offer protection and benefits. The formal words of refuge-taking in Buddhism are: "I go for refuge to the Buddha. I go for refuge to the Dharma. I go for refuge to the Saṅgha." So the word "refuge" here also carries the connotation of protection and help. In other words, in taking these refuges, one shows confidence that the Buddha, Dharma, and Saṅgha can protect one from the dissatisfactory human condition of life and can help one reach the truly satisfactory attainment of Nirvana. In the words attributed to the Buddha by an early text, by taking the Three Refuges, one professes "clear confidence in the Buddha . . . the Fully Awakened One . . . perfect in knowledge and conduct . . . clear confidence in the Dharma taught by the Exalted One . . . that brings one near that which should be known by the wise . . . clear confidence in the Saṅgha of the followers of the Exalted One on the direct right path . . . without defects, which brings freedom" (*Dīgha-nikāya*, II, 93). Elsewhere in the same text, the Buddha makes clear that turning to him for refuge and help implies living in conformity with his Dharma: "He who, having entered on the course, lives in conformity with the Dharma . . . pays reverence to the Tathāgata [a title for the Buddha]" (*Dīgha-nikāya*, II, 138). It is also this living together of the Dharma that is at the heart of true refuge in the Saṅgha.

Important Conversions

According to the early texts, the next convert to the Saṅgha after the five ascetics was a wealthy young man from Benares named Yaśa. Yaśa, "disillu-

BOX 1.1

The Authenticity of the Buddha

Buddhism is a religion which does not insist on rituals; and being a Buddhist means something much more than participating in rituals. This is something I had to learn over time.

The very first ceremony I went through as a Buddhist was taking the Three Refuges. I was about eight years old and in the third grade. In my class, there were thirty-seven students, all of whom were Buddhists. The school arranged for us to attend this ceremony at one of the well-known temples in Bangkok.

We arrived at the temple in the afternoon and were guided to the hall with the main shrine. I remember the chief monk led us to recite the Three Refuges three times.

I take refuge in the Buddha.
I take refuge in the Dhamma.
I take refuge in the Saṅgha.

This ceremony was a public pronouncement that I am a Buddhist. But, I never bothered to think what it really meant to take the Buddha as my refuge until much later in life.

The Buddha was born in sixth century B.C.E. to a princely clan in an area which is now Nepal. He was brought up in a luxurious lifestyle, but when confronted with the problems of old age, sickness, and death, he was concerned and wanted to know how we as human beings can get rid of this cycle of suffering. When a son was born to him, he decided to leave the worldly life and began a serious search for spiritual freedom.

At the age of thirty-five, after six years of practice, he was enlightened and came to be known as the Buddha . . . the fully enlightened one. The truth he discovered was simple yet profound: Life is full of suffering, there is a cause to this suffering, there is a cessation to this suffering, and there is a path leading anyone to freedom from this suffering. During the forty-five years after his enlightenment, the Buddha founded a group of followers (Saṅgha), first consisting of monks and later of nuns.

When I took refuge in the Buddha, how could that historical person truly be my refuge? The historical Buddha passed away some 2500 years ago, so he cannot really be of any help to me today. But over time, I understood that the Buddha could be meaningful to my life and spiritual salvation because he discovered the Truth that frees one from human bondage. More important than that, he made known his spiritual discovery as well as the path leading to it. That Truth was real for him, and it is real for me also. That salvation was possible for him, and also for me.

With this understanding, I committed myself to putting the Buddha's teachings into practice, and that is how I really became a Buddhist. The authenticity of the Buddha does not lie just in his life, but in the enlightenment which made Prince Siddhārtha the Buddha. That enlightenment is accessible to everyone. It depends on our effort to make it a reality for our lives.

CHATSUMARN KABILSINGH

Professor Emerita
Thammasat University, Bangkok
Now Buddhist nun, Dhammananda Samaneri

sioned" with his luxuries and his indulgence in sensual entertainment, came to the place where the Buddha was staying. Later, Yaśa's father, missing his son, came in search of him. The Buddha consoled Yaśa's father, and in the end the father took the Three Refuges. Hearing the instruction the Buddha gave his father, Yaśa attained Awakening. Thus, Yaśa became the sixth ordained disciple of the Buddha, and his father became his first official lay disciple. The two merchants who gave homage to the Buddha at Bodhgāya did not receive the Dharma, or enter the Saṅgha. Yaśa's mother and wife, who also came in search of him, both took the Three Refuges and thereby became the first women lay followers of the Buddha. Lay followers of the Buddha, both men and women, did not want to enter the celibate Saṅgha, but sought to benefit spiritually from the Buddha and his teachings by their association with the community of monks. Also, it is said that fifty-four of Yaśa's friends were converted and attained Awakening under the guidance of the Buddha. This brought the number of enlightened members of the monastic Saṅgha to sixty-one, including the Buddha himself. Once the Buddha had these sixty disciples, he sent them out to preach the Dharma.

After living in nearby Benares for some time, early texts say that the Buddha returned to the Uruvelā area where he had attained his own Awakening. Then he is said to have gone to Rājagṛha, where he converted King Bimbisāra of Magadha. This was an important event since it led to many people in the Magadha area joining the Buddha. Also while the Buddha was in Rājagṛha, another major event in the early Saṅgha took place when two of the disciples of a noted Skeptic converted to the Buddha and brought with them 250 of their followers. These two converts were Śāriputra and Maudgalyāyana, who became two principle disciples. Śāriputra was known for his wisdom and ability to teach the Dharma. Maudgalyāyana was known for his psychic powers developed in meditation. There were other stories of how not just individuals, but whole groups of religious seekers joined the Buddha's Saṅgha. Later biographies relate that it was also at the time the Buddha resided at Rājagṛha that he converted Mahākāśyapa. Mahākāśyapa was known for his attainment in meditation, and he appears in the later legends of Zen Buddhism. He was also said to be the person who convened the First Buddhist Council when the Buddha died and who was responsible for organizing the memorization of the Buddha's teachings and precepts.

The later biographies also say that the Buddha went from Rājagṛha to his home town of Kapilavastu. There, he met with his father, stepmother, wife, and son Rāhula. While the rest of the family accepted him and even pledged homage to him, his son and his half-brother, Nanda, actually became ordained monks. It was also during this visit that Upāli became a monk. Among the Buddha's close disciples, Upāli had the greatest memory of the precepts, and is said to have recited them at the First Buddhist Council. The Buddha's cousin, Ānanda, became a monk at this time, and went on to be the closest companion of the Buddha. Given his extraordinary memory and constant proximity to the Buddha, Ānanda was said to have recited the dialogues and teachings of the Buddha at the First Buddhist Council.

Figure 1.2. The Buddha begs alms from his son; painting, Ajaṇṭā Cave 17, Gupta Period; fifth century C.E., India.

Monasticism

While the early texts do not mention Sudatta, a wealthy merchant from Śrāvastī, the capital of Kosala, later biographies stress the importance of his conversion to Buddhism. It is said that he became a follower of the Buddha when he was in Rājagṛha on business. Later, he bought and donated the Jeta Grove in Śrāvastī to the Buddhist Saṅgha. It was here that Sudatta built the famous Jeta Monastery. From the time of his residing with the five ascetics at Sārnāth, the Buddha had spent the rainy seasons each year in retreat with his followers. For those early years, the biographies relate, the monsoon retreats were held in houses. The Jeta Monastery provided an adequate facility for the retreat gatherings of monks during the rainy seasons. This monastic site would become a model for the building of other Buddhist monasteries.

During the Buddha's life, it became a custom for the monks not to travel and preach the Dharma during the rainy season, but they would instead remain together in spiritual retreat. This custom was institutionalized by the establishment of monasteries that would eventually become centers of Buddhist religion and culture. As monasteries developed, the monastic Sangha became a model of ethical, cultural, intellectual, and spiritual life for the larger society. Eventually, Buddhist monasticism provided an extraordinary standard for humankind that was always an ideal for both personal and social fulfillment. For Buddhist monastics, monasteries became a haven for pursuing the spiritual life by being formed in the teachings and discipline of the Buddha. For Buddhist laypeople, the monasteries were oases of peace and goodness, communities that modeled what the enlightened life would be like if it were attained and lived by all society. The monasteries also provided places for moral and spiritual guidance, teaching, and the possibility for merit-making for the laity.

In administering the monastic Sangha, the Buddha shared many responsibilities with his enlightened followers. While traditional Indian religious sects reserved their teachings for an elite few, and their teachers retained personal control over their members, the Buddha allowed his representatives to ordain new members and entrusted his local monastic communities to manage their own affairs. The Buddha had great confidence in his enlightened followers and often recognized their expertise in teaching the Dharma. While the Buddha taught a number of "rules of discipline" to the monastic members of the Sangha, some of the minor precepts were open to changes and even to being revoked if need be. The members of the Sangha were seen as equals, and the governing of the communities was democratic.

Social Concern

The Buddha not only founded his own religious communities but also spoke out about the broader social and political conditions of his time. According to the early texts, he often denounced the injustices of the caste system, and the Sangha was open to persons of all castes. The Buddha taught that respect should be earned by moral deeds and spiritual attainment, not given on the basis of one's birth. In terms of social violence, in one early text, after telling a story of a king who did not care for the poor, the Buddha says, "Thus, from not giving to the needy, poverty spreads; from the growth of poverty, stealing increases; when theft becomes more and more common, there is an increased use of weapons; when this happens, there is a greater loss of life" (*Dīgha-nikāya*, III, 68). Elsewhere in that text, there is another story in which a king is advised as to how to deal with such social conflict:

> If your majesty were to increase taxes, that would be the wrong thing to do. If your majesty were to try to get rid of this problem by executions and imprisonment . . . the problem would not be ended. . . . However, with the fol-

---

BOX 1.2

THE GIFTS OF THE BUDDHA

Becoming a Buddhist was a slow process for me that began first with the intellect and only gradually shifted to a personal practice.

Lacking belief and facing death and rational absurdity in my early twenties, I only found consolation in nature, an abiding natural order of existence. Living with this intellectual sense of nature for several years, and supported by the nurturing presence of being part of nature, softened my expectations and judgments.

This experience was confirmed and supported by the Buddhist practice of emptying oneself of false hopes and rigid ideas and the Buddhist patient acceptance of our dependent arising with all things. The Buddha's teaching emphasized that misery is created by ourselves and that we need to become aware of the way emotions arise based on how we interpret what is happening to us. Calming ourselves and noticing the interpretations we are giving to events and what expectations are thus being frustrated give a certain distance from our misery and empower us. New and more positive interpretations and emotional responses arise by noticing alternative interpretations and responses. Just by taking time out to notice our emotions and alternative interpretations became a constant source of relief and positive thinking.

Another way that Buddhism has permeated my life has been its method of social reform. As a child of the social gospel and the 1960s, I was eager to save the world but was messed up emotionally. Buddhism taught methods of inner transformation as a basis for changing my sense of the world, and also gave gentler and more inclusive ways to act in the world. Gautama Buddha was a social activist, but he practiced dialogue and compassion, without stridency or righteous indignation. The easy temptation to condemn others, to demonize enemies, and to feel righteous in our militancy was completely absent from the Buddha.

Instead, stories about the Buddha's life show the capacity to find goodness in those who are different from us and to emphasize our interconnections. Until recently, Buddhism has had a weak social gospel. But on looking at the forty-five years that the Buddha taught, one can find many practical ways in which he tried to bring about reform. Even though emperors and kings may have domesticated Buddhism into a passive monastic life, in the stories of Gautama Buddha we find a busy and effective social activist.

The gifts of the Buddha to the world are many. Formally, being a Buddhist means to take refuge in the "Three Jewels": the Buddha, the Dharma, and the Saṅgha. Gautama Buddha is the founder of the Dharma (teaching) that I have found most true and most nurturing, and his life is a model for living this Dharma in compassionate and effective ways. His Saṅgha, the Buddhist community on which I rely, consists, I believe, of people from all religions and cultures who are filled with modesty, compassion, good humor, and appreciation for others, especially for those who are most different from them. And finally this Saṅgha, Dharma, and Buddha become just other names for the infinite mystery of the secret connectedness of all things in the midst of our dying and living.

DAVID W. CHAPPELL

Professor Emeritus, Department of Religion
University of Hawaii

lowing policy, you can completely eliminate this problem. To those who are engaged in farming and raising livestock, let your majesty distribute needed grain and fodder. To those engaged in trade, give them the capital they need. To those in government service, assign them a living wage to meet their needs. Then all of those people will be intent on pursuing their occupations, and they will not harm anyone. (*Dīgha-nikāya*, I, 135)

This attitude of compassionate concern for those in need was modeled by the Buddha himself in dealing with people outside and inside the Saṅgha. One story in a later text tells of the Buddha's intervention on behalf of five hundred bandits who were awaiting execution. The Buddha secured their release and gave them, by his teaching, what they really wanted, namely, spiritual as well as physical freedom. Another later story tells how the Buddha tended personally to one of his monks who was suffering from an advanced skin disease. Out of fear of contracting this disease, this person's fellow monks had avoided any contact with him. One day when the Buddha was visiting their community, he discovered the man's plight. Along with his disciple Ānanda, the Buddha took a basin of water and a towel and washed the monk himself. Then he instructed the other monks with these words: "Monks, you do not have a mother or a father here who can tend to you. If you, monks, do not tend to one another, who is there to take care of you? Remember that whoever tends a sick person, as it were, tends me" (*Mahāvagga*, VIII, 26).

Women's Ordination

One issue that arose in regard to the monastic life was that of allowing women into the fully ordained monastic Saṅgha. From the beginning, women were welcome as members of the lay community that was associated with the monastic Saṅgha. Then, according to later biographies, five years after his enlightenment the Buddha was visited by his foster mother, Mahāprajāpatī, who was accompanied by a large group of women. They asked to be ordained into the monastic Saṅgha. The Buddha is said to have rejected their request. But after more pleading, and with the intervention of Ānanda, the Buddha accepted the women into the Saṅgha as ordained nuns (*bhikṣuṇī*; Pali: *bhikkhuṇī*).

In his discussions with Ānanda about this issue, the Buddha made it clear that women could attain all the goals of his religion including full Awakening. So why his initial reluctance to admit women into the celibate Saṅgha? Scholars today surmise that one concern may have been that the relationship between the men and women in the monastic community would have made things more complicated. The men's order needed time to become fully established and mature. Another concern may have had to do with the fact that many non-Buddhists did not like the practice of the celibate life for young men, and such a life for young women seemed even more unconventional and difficult to accept by the broader Indian society. So it would seem that any sudden influx of women into the communities at an early stage of their development would have caused problems both within those communities themselves as well as with the general population. Therefore, according to this interpretation, the Buddha took a cautious approach. Only when he felt that the time was right, when Indian society had accepted the Saṅgha as a valid religious entity, and when the community, represented by Ānanda, was ready for this radical change, did he admit women into the monastic Saṅgha.

The Buddha gave the women monastics special rules resulting in a certain gender hierarchy. For example, the Saṅgha hierarchy is determined by how long one has been ordained, not by merit or personal attainment. However, in the case of nuns, they must treat all monks as seniors, even those who were ordained after them. Also, while any monk can reprove a nun, no nun can reprove a monk. On the other hand, since this hierarchy has nothing to do with attainment, its subordination of women does not indicate spiritual inferiority. Also, in order to prevent the monks from using the hierarchy to take advantage of the nuns, the Buddha instituted certain rules that safeguard the dignity and independence of the nuns. The monks could not demand work or service from nuns, and the nuns were not to be given any inferior spiritual instructions or ethical rules.

A text entitled *The Verses of the Women Elders* (*Therīgāthā*) records in seventy-three poems the lives and Awakening of early nuns in the Saṅgha. There are also early records of the Buddha giving high praise to certain nuns. Besides Mahāprajāpatī, who was the senior nun, Uppalavaṇṇā was considered one of the Buddha's chief disciples. Khemā, the former queen of King Bimbisāra, was also respected as a chief disciple of the Buddha. Bhaddā Kapilāni was pledged by her family in marriage to Mahākāśyapa, who became a leading monk in the Saṅgha. Later, Bhaddā Kapilāni became a nun and distinguished herself by her awakened memory of her past lives.

The Rebellion of Devadatta

Another issue addressed by the Buddha was brought about by his cousin, Devadatta, who had joined the Saṅgha. Early texts indicate only that Devadatta was lazy and annoyed the Buddha in various ways. However, in later stories, it is said that Devadatta, stimulated with ambition, wanted to gain control of the Saṅgha when the Buddha had grown older. He, along with an accomplice, actually tried to kill the Buddha, but the Buddha escaped each attempt on his life. For example, a rock intended to crush the Buddha is deflected by mountain peaks, and a wild elephant charging down a narrow street toward the Buddha turns around tamely because of the Buddha's friendly thought. In each case, it is said that the Buddha dealt with Devadatta with gentleness, exhibiting his view that hatred is not deterred by hatred, but by loving kindness.

Later texts that were concerned about distinguishing Buddhism from extreme asceticism claim that Devadatta tried to gain control of the Saṅgha in another way. He attempted to make the precepts of the community more ascetically rigorous. Devadatta was said to have proposed five severe ascetic rules: Monks should dwell all their life in the forest, they should live only on alms that they beg, they should only wear robes made from gathered rags, they should dwell only at the foot of trees, and they should not eat fish or meat. The breaking of any of these rules would lead to expulsion from the Saṅgha. It is said that in the spirit of tolerance, the Buddha decided that all of these rules suggested by Devadatta would be permissible, but not compulsory. He only insisted that the monks not sleep under trees during the rainy season. Devadatta is said then to have tried to draw the monks away from the Buddha to follow his reform movement. However, in the end this attempt to gain leadership by producing a schism in the Saṅgha also failed. Again, throughout these trials brought upon the Buddha, his Dharma, and the Saṅgha, the Buddha maintained an attitude of compassion and loving kindness toward Devadatta.

THE LAST DAYS OF GAUTAMA BUDDHA

Because of his sense of mission to preach the Dharma, the Buddha spent much of his time in or around the towns and cities that were appearing on the Indian landscape. He is said by the early texts to have often resided in or around Śrāvastī in Kosala and Rājagṛha and Vaiśālī in Magadha. One early text tells a rather detailed story about the last days of the Buddha's life. It states that near the end of the Buddha's life, he was residing in the suburbs of Vaiśālī. As the rainy season was approaching, he went to a nearby village where he made his final monsoon retreat with a few of his disciples. During the retreat, the Buddha was struck by an extremely painful illness. In response to Ānanda's concern, the Buddha said, "I have grown old . . . and have traveled down the road of life being in my eightieth year. [I am like] an old cart that can barely manage to hold itself together without the help of leather straps" (*Dīgha-nikāya*, II, 100).

One day after begging alms in Vaiśālī, the Buddha took his midday rest at a sacred tree. There, the story goes, he was visited by Māra, who encouraged him to end his life and attain final Nirvana (*parinirvāṇa*). The text indicates that the Buddha had not wanted to pass away until he had monks, nuns, and male and female disciples who were accomplished in the Dharma, who walked in the path of the Dharma, and who could teach the Dharma to others. Now that this holy life was well established, the Buddha responded to Māra that his passing would come in just three months. The Buddha is said to have at that time renounced his vital "life principle." When this final renunciation occurred, there was a great earthquake accompanied by thunder.

Some time later, taking a final look at Vaiśālī, the Buddha departed and journeyed to the town of Pāvā, where he stopped at the mango grove of a blacksmith named Cunda. The Buddha instructed Cunda in the Dharma, and then took the food Cunda offered to him. The text says that after eating, the Buddha was struck by a severe illness that produced much pain.

From the textual description of the illness, scholars conclude that he contracted food poisoning from eating either pork or a mushroom dish. However, the Buddha was able to rise from his illness and even walk to the village of Kuśinagara some distance away. At one point, he stepped off the road and sat under a tree to rest. Ānanda, at the request of the Buddha, brought him some water to drink. At that moment, it is said that a pupil of Ārāda Kālāma named Pukkusa approached the Buddha. He engaged the Buddha in conversation about the "lofty powers" of Ārāda, and in the end, Pukkusa accepted the Buddha and became his lay follower.

Then the Buddha, along with a number of his monks, went into a nearby river to bathe and drink water. Emerging from the river, the Buddha lay down to rest and spoke to Ānanda about Cunda the blacksmith. The Buddha was concerned that Cunda would feel that it was his fault the Buddha died. So he instructed Ānanda as to what to say to console him. Then the Buddha traveled to another place nearby where he lay down between two sāla trees. The Buddha lay on his right side, with his head to the north and one foot on top of the other. It is said that the trees burst into blossom and sprinkled the blossoms down onto the Buddha. As this happened, the text says that music and song was heard from the sky, and later even the gods gathered weeping over the Buddha's passing. The Buddha acknowledged this homage, but noted that "supreme homage" is given to the Buddha when a disciple practices the Dharma properly.

At this point, the early story goes, Ānanda discussed with the Buddha what to do with his remains. Following this discussion, Ānanda went off some distance and wept with grief. The Buddha called for Ānanda to join him and consoled his grief. He reminded Ānanda, "Have I not already told you that all things . . . are subject to change . . . subject to decay—so how could it be Ānanda that anything should not pass away?" (*Dīgha-nikāya*, II, 144). The Buddha then compassionately praised Ānanda for the loving kindness and wholehearted care Ānanda had always shown to him. He concluded his words to Ānanda by encouraging him to continue to follow the path so that soon he could gain the freedom he was seeking. In his presence, the Buddha also praised Ānanda to the whole assembly of monks for his "remarkable and wonderful qualities," noting that in the past, all Buddhas had such a remarkable chief attendant.

Some of the people from Kuśinagara came out of the town to pay their respects to the Buddha. One person who came to see the Buddha was a wandering religious person named Subhadra. At first, Ānanda would not let Subhadra speak to the Buddha because of concern for the Buddha's condition. However, the Buddha compassionately requested that Subhadra be permitted to speak to him. Subhadra asked the Buddha about the attainment of other famous teachers, but the Buddha would not make such judgments about others. Instead, he taught Subhadra the Dharma. Subhadra converted and became his "last personal disciple." When he finished instructing Subhadra, the Buddha turned to Ānanda and said, "You may think, 'The teacher's instruction has ceased, now we do not have a teacher!' But it should not be seen like this, Ānanda. For what I have taught and explained to you as the Dharma and the discipline will, at my passing, be your teacher" (*Dīgha-nikāya*, II, 154).

Finally, the Buddha asked his monks if they had any doubts or uncertainties about the Buddha, Dharma, or Saṅgha: "Ask monks! Do not later feel remorse thinking 'The teacher was right there before us and we did not ask him face to face' " (*Dīgha-nikāya*, II, 154–155). When no one asked a question, the Buddha spoke his last words: "Now, monks, I declare that all the conditioned things of the world are passing. Attain your liberation with diligence!" (*Dīgha-nikāya*, II, 156). Following these words, the Buddha entered into meditation and passed away.

After the Buddha had died, members of the Malla clan from Kuśinagara wrapped his body in new cloth and held six days of mourning. On the seventh day, they cremated the Buddha's body. It is said that messengers from seven clans, including the Buddha's own Śākya clan, asked for relics. The Malla clan also requested relics. Those who received relics took them home and built *stūpas* (memorial mounds) for them. The bowl that collected the ashes, along with the ashes themselves, were placed under two other *stūpas*. These *stūpas* became centers for devotion to the Buddha. The Buddha himself is said to have proclaimed shortly before he died, "Whoever lays wreaths of flowers, or puts perfumes, or adds color [to the *stūpas*] with a devout heart will reap benefit and happiness for a long time" (*Dīgha-nikāya*, II, 142). There is also a legend that centuries later, King Aśoka unearthed these relics and further divided them, enshrining them in 84,000 *stūpas* throughout his empire in India.

As we can see, much of the Buddha's time for the forty-five years after his Awakening was devoted to teaching the Dharma, founding the Saṅgha, and forming his disciples in the path of the discipline. Even during the very moments before his death, the Buddha was carrying out these tasks compassionately for the good of others. Many people in India during the sixth and fifth centuries B.C.E. were looking for new ideals to guide their lives, new ideas and practices that promised personal transformation, and new social forms of community life. The Buddha offered to the world his own spiritual experience, and he modeled that enlightened and nirvanic ideal with joy, loving kindness, and compassion. His Dharma offered others a path to attain the experience of Awakening and Nirvana and a way of living this ideal in daily life. His Saṅgha provided the spiritual guidance and social support necessary to achieve this ideal and to live out its freedom and peace as a witness to what is possible in human relationships. In the following chapter, we examine the experience of this path and ideal as they are presented in the teachings of the Buddha.

SUGGESTIONS FOR FURTHER READING

Aśvaghoṣa. *The Acts of the Buddha (Buddhacarita)*. Translated by Edward H. Johnston. Delhi: Motilal Banarsidass, 1978.

Carrithers, Michael. *The Buddha*. Oxford: Oxford University Press, 1983.

Cook, Elizabeth, ed. *The Holy Places of the Buddha*. Berkeley, CA: Dharma Publishing, 1994.

Cowell, E. B., trans. *The Jātaka or Stories of the Buddha's Former Births*. 3 vols. London: Luzac, 1969.

Jones, John Garrett. *Tales and Teachings of the Buddha: The Jātaka Stories in Relation to the Pali Canon*. London: George Allen & Unwin, 1979.

Murcott, Susan. *The First Buddhist Women*. San Francisco: Parallax Press, 1991.

Nakamura, Hajime. *Gotama Buddha*. Tokyo and Los Angeles: Buddhist Books International, 1977.

Nyanaponika Thera, and Hellmuth Hecker. *Great Disciples of the Buddha: Their Lives, Their Works, Their Legacy*. Boston: Wisdom Publications, 1997.

Schelling, Andrew, and Anne Waldman. *Songs of the Sons and Daughters of the Buddha: Versus of the* Theragāthā *and* Therīgāthā. Boston: Shambhala Publications, 1996.

TWO

THE TEACHINGS OF
THE BUDDHA

An early text relates the story of a Buddhist monk who was especially fond of speculative religious discussions that seem to be never-ending. Once, he approached the Buddha intending to get him to resolve his speculative questions. He asked if the world was eternal or created, if the world was finite or infinite, if the body and soul are the same or different, and whether the *arhat* exists after death or not. The monk even threatened to leave the Saṅgha and become a layperson if the Buddha did not answer his questions. The Buddha responded that one does not enter the Saṅgha in order to answer these kinds of philosophical questions. If one does so, one can spend all his or her time pondering these questions and never have time for religious practice, namely, for following the path that leads to Awakening and Nirvana. In fact, the Buddha added, a person would not live long enough for the Buddha to explain the truth concerning all of these speculative matters.

To illustrate his point, the Buddha used the following metaphor:

> It is as if . . . a man had been wounded by an arrow thickly smeared with poison, and his friends and companions, his relatives and kinsfolk, were to procure a physician or surgeon for him. And the sick man would then say, "I will not have this arrow removed until I have learned whether the man who wounded me belonged to the warrior caste, or to the priestly caste, or to the agricultural or menial castes." Or he would say, "I will not have this arrow removed until I have learned the name of the man . . . the clan to which he belongs . . . whether he is tall or short . . . the town from which he comes . . . what kind of bow . . . bowstring . . . arrow shaft . . . arrow feathers . . . and arrowhead . . . he used." That man will die without ever having learned all these things. (*Majjhima-nikāya*, I, 428)

After giving this metaphor, the Buddha went on to say that no matter what particular answers one might learn concerning the philosophical questions the monk had raised, the dissatisfactory condition of ordinary, unenlightened life would remain like a poisoned arrow. So, the Buddha concluded his reply by saying that there were some questions he would leave unanswered, namely, those that do not lead to religious edification. Therefore, he would only teach about those matters that "tend to aversion, absence of passion, cessation, quiescence, knowledge, supreme wisdom and Nirvana."

The point of this story is that the Buddha did not want to become involved in abstract discussions about religious issues that do not advance spiritual transformation. Some scholars conclude that the questions themselves were ill formed, such that no sufficient answers could ever be given. Others claim that the Buddha only wanted to teach about what directly impacts the existential wounded condition of humankind. Seeing himself as a kind of spiritual physician, the Buddha was concerned with helping humanity understand the nature and causes of its dissatisfactory condition and the path that leads to liberation from this condition. This kind of existential concern determined what the Buddha taught and what the way of life was that he asked his disciples to follow. As for his specific teachings, scholars have always debated about what the Buddha actually taught, since even the earliest texts that record his teachings were written down hundreds of years after his death. However, scholars usually agree that there are certain basic teachings, which, since they are presented in so many places throughout the early texts, must represent at least the kinds of things the Buddha actually taught. In this chapter, we will examine some of these basic teachings that can help us understand more clearly the experience of the Buddha and of early Buddhism.

THE THREE CHARACTERISTICS

One early text quotes the Buddha as saying

> Whether Buddhas arise, O monks, or whether Buddhas do not arise, it remains a fact that . . . all [the world's] constituents are [1] transitory . . . that all its constituents are [2] dissatisfactory . . . that all its constituents are [3] lacking a permanent self. (*Anguttara-nikāya*, III, 134)

Here, the Buddha is teaching the Three Characteristics of what he calls *saṃsāra*. *Saṃsāra*, literally, "wandering on," refers to the phenomenal world in which one is born, dies, and wanders on to be reborn. All of the world's "constituents," even the constituents of its heavenly realms, are "impermanent" (*anitya*, Pali: *anicca*), are ultimately "dissatisfactory" (*duḥkha*; Pali: *dukkha*), and contain no permanent inner substance or "self" (*anātman*; Pali: *anattā*). Given the earlier answer of the Buddha to the monk's speculative questions, we can assume that understanding the nature of the impermanence, dissatisfactoriness, and selflessness of life "tends to" Awakening and Nirvana. Let us look at each of these characteristics one at a time.

Impermanence

The first characteristic of life's constituents is impermanence. For the Buddha, everything except for Nirvana is in constant flux and change. Material

---

BOX 2.1

IMPERMANENCE

Ever since inheriting the Lamp of the Dharma and becoming President of Risshō Kōsei-kai, I have wanted more than ever to be a genuine Buddhist and inherit Śākyamuni's enlightenment.

Through studying and learning what has been handed down from the teachings of the Buddha and others, I finally came to understand the "teaching of impermanence." I became confident that this is the supreme and most fundamental of the Buddha's teachings, the basic essence of Śākyamuni's enlightenment.

With this realization, I was released from all clinging and delusion, and felt indescribably refreshed. It was as though a cloud of fog hanging over me had suddenly disappeared in the rays of the sun.

In the second chapter of the *Lotus Sūtra* we find, "It is for this great cause alone that Buddhas, the world-honored ones, appear in the world. . . . The Buddhas, the world-honored ones, appear in the world because they want living beings to open themselves to the Buddha's knowledge and insight, and thus gain a kind of purity." In short, the one "great cause" means that Buddhas appear in the world for one purpose only, to open us to Buddha-knowledge.

Buddha-knowledge is the Buddha's wisdom. Given this knowledge, how do we see this world and human life? We see that all things in this world are dependently arisen, never stopping for a moment, always changing. In short, to open ourselves to Buddha-knowledge is to become aware of the teaching of impermanence.

By opening ourselves to Buddha-knowledge, that is, by being aware of the teaching of impermanence, we can become aware of the importance of living here and now, become mindful of the value of today, and be filled with a sense of dedication. We can spontaneously become joyfully full of life and energy through getting along with others, while giving full play to our individual natural abilities. The infinitely continuous creation of our lives can be developed.

Thus, I have realized that we can be reborn by becoming aware of the teaching of transience, this most precious Buddhist doctrine. I have continued to this day to keep a vow to spread this truth, this Dharma.

PRESIDENT NICHIKO NIWANO

Risshō Kōsei-kai
Tokyo, Japan

---

things undergo obvious changes, and one's mental-emotional life is also constantly changing. Even the gods, according to the Buddha, are born, experience change, and eventually die only to be reborn in another state of existence. According to one early text, "All compounded things are impermanent, prone to arise and fall" (*Dīgha-nikāya*, II, 157). The implication here is that all things are impermanent because they are "compounded" by constituents that arise together and then, in time, fall apart. One is reminded of the Buddha's statement near the time of his passing that he felt like an old cart that needed to be held together by leather straps.

Impermanence, as the arising and passing away of the things of life, is sometimes described in the early texts as taking place in three stages. The elements of an object come together so that it "arises" into existence. Then, the arisen object is subject to "decay." This means that once an object has come into being, it changes over time. Finally, the elements of an object change to such an extent that the thing passes away. In this manner, all things are impermanent in two senses: They arise and pass away, and while existing they are in a state of constant change.

Dissatisfactoriness

This characterization of impermanence leads to the second characteristic of phenomena, namely, "dissatisfactoriness" (duḥkha). Duḥkha has often been translated as "suffering." But that term does not capture the rich meaning of this important notion. The term duḥkha connotes the dissatisfactory condition caused by an axle hole that is not properly made. Whether the hole is too big or too small, it causes the axle to wobble or rub in a way that is dissatisfactory. Since the Buddha taught that all the phenomena of this world are also made in ways that produce dissatisfactoriness, the question is, in what ways are things made such that we experience dissatisfactoriness, or duḥkha? And what is the dissatisfactoriness that things produce? The Buddha taught that there are three qualities of things that account for duḥkha in life. First, physical phenomena are constituted such that they can produce suffering. In the early texts, giving birth, getting sick, growing old, and dying are given as examples of the suffering that one experiences because of how the physical world is constituted. These sufferings, and many others as well, are associated with the changing conditions of physical life.

A second way in which things are dissatisfactory has to do with their impermanence and humanity's search for happiness. The Buddha did not deny that one can find some happiness in the enjoyments of this life. In the early texts, the Buddha mentions the happiness that comes from such things as family life, life in the Saṅgha, and meditative attainments. However, he also points out that these enjoyments are "impermanent, duḥkha, and subject to change" (Majjhima-nikāya, I, 90). That is, they are dissatisfactory because they cannot provide the lasting happiness that humanity ultimately seeks. In other words, since all things in life must pass away—given their impermanence—so must all the pleasures these things provide be fleeting. Since humanity ordinarily seeks a lasting happiness in things that do not last, or a permanent satisfaction in impermanent things, these things are said to be characterized by duḥkha. They leave one with a sense of lack, a feeling that something is still missing that would provide lasting happiness.

A third way in which things are said to produce dissatisfactoriness has to do with the manner in which the human mind is constituted. We have seen that things are characterized as dissatisfactory because they are physically constituted in ways that produce suffering and do not provide permanent happiness. The Buddha also taught that the changing states of human consciousness are constituted such that they produce both personal and social *duḥkha*. Just as an improperly made axle hole functions in a dissatisfactory way, so too the different constituents of one's mind generate such unwholesome states as hatred, anger, greed, and delusion. These unwholesome states of mind, in turn, produce *duḥkha* for oneself and, when acted upon, for others as well. These harmful actions also contribute to such social *duḥkha* as war, poverty, and political repression.

No-Self

Many of the spiritual teachers at the time of the Buddha would have agreed that the world and human nature are constituted in ways that produce suffering and that the true and lasting happiness sought by humankind is not to be found in the fleeting pleasures of the world. However, the Upaniṣadic teachers of the time held that lasting happiness (*ānanda*) could, in fact, be found deep within one's self. They called this inner, permanent, and divine reality the "Self" (Ātman). The Buddha, on the other hand, presented a third characteristic of existence that rejects any such permanent Self. He said that all phenomena lack any underlying and permanent substance; they all have the characteristic of "no-self." This also means that within human nature, there is no permanent self or soul.

The Buddha always affirmed that persons have an empirical selfhood constituted by a body and a mind. But he also claimed that the various constituents of this conventional selfhood are characterized by impermanence and *duḥkha*; they are always changing, and they ordinarily produce mental and physical processes that are experienced as ultimately dissatisfactory. The Buddha also taught that when one examines these constituents of conventional selfhood, one does not find any permanent substance. Impermanence is not just a characteristic of the phenomena of the external world; it applies to oneself. The Buddha's notion of no-self expresses humankind's radical finitude. It was also the Buddha's view that the belief in a permanent substantial self is not only false, but also leads to selfishness and egoism, which, in turn, make the world so dissatisfactory for everyone. The Buddha found in his own Awakening that the realization of the absence of such a permanent self leads to selfless loving kindness and compassion for others.

In discussing his no-self doctrine, the Buddha did not just deny the existence of a substantial and permanent self behind or within the various constituents of human nature. He also described these constituents and, in so doing, showed that none of them could be considered a permanent substance or self. These constituents of selfhood were called by the Buddha the Five Aggregates (*skandha*: Pali: *khandha*). To understand more clearly just what the Buddha meant by no-self, let us see what these Five Aggregates entail.

THE FIVE AGGREGATES

The first of the Five Aggregates that constitute ordinary human selfhood is material "form" (*rūpa*), or the body that is made up of impermanent material elements. These material elements are said ultimately to be produced by impermanent atoms of different types. The other four aggregates are the mental constituents of the functional self. The second aggregate is "sensation" (*vedanā*), which includes sensations associated with the body as well as feelings. These sensations of felt experience are categorized as pleasant, unpleasant, or neutral. The third aggregate is "perception" (*saṃjñā*; Pali: *saññā*), which includes the cognition and recognition of physical objects and of mental phenomena (ideas or thoughts). The fourth aggregate is "mental formations" (*saṃskāra*; Pali: *saṃkhāra*), which include the various mental states, attitudes, and dispositions that form the character of one's life. These are especially important mental factors because they include all the willful states of mind (*cetanā*) that move one to do good and bad actions, and therefore result in good and bad karma. The fifth aggregate is "consciousness" (*vijñāna*; Pali: *viññāna*), which includes mental awareness and discrimination.

Of all the aggregates, the best candidate for a permanent self or soul would seem to be this last aggregate of consciousness. Indeed, the Upaniṣadic tradition claimed that consciousness is of the essence of the Ātman. However, the Buddha taught that consciousness only arises when one of the six sense faculties (*āyatana*) experiences a sense object. For the Buddha, there are six sense faculties, which include the eye, ear, nose, tongue, body, and mind. By mind here, the Buddha means a mental faculty that engages mental objects like thoughts and ideas. When any of these six faculties engages its object (visible form, sound, odor, taste, tangible objects, and mental phenomena), a form of consciousness arises. For example, the Buddha gives, in an early text, the following description of the arising of visual consciousness: "Consciousness takes its name according to the conditions in which it arises: on account of the eye and visible forms, it arises and is called visual consciousness" (*Majjhima-nikāya*, I, 250). In the Buddha's view, then, consciousness does not indicate a permanent substance. It simply arises in different forms depending on different factors, so that it is just as impermanent as any other kind of phenomenon.

Since these Five Aggregates are constantly changing mental or physical states or processes, none of them can be considered as a permanent metaphysical self or soul. Therefore, in his Second Sermon, the Buddha said that one is not able to point to any constituent within his or her self and say, "This is mine, this I am, this is my self" (*Saṃyutta-nikāya*, II, 68). Another early text explains this idea by using the simile of a chariot for the self. In a dialogue between a Buddhist nun named Vajira and Māra the tempter, the question arises about the nature of the self. Vajira says,

> There is no "being" found here [within oneself], only a heap of karmic constituents. Just as the word "chariot" is used when we come across a combina-

tion of parts, so we speak conventionally of a [human] being when the Five Aggregates are present. (*Saṃyutta-nikāya*, I, 135)

A later text uses this same simile in a dialogue between the monk Nāgasena and King Milinda. After describing in some detail how the word "chariot" designates the combination of parts that makes it up, Nāgasena concludes that the word "self" is simply a name that designates the Five Aggregates. Therefore, Nāgasena concludes, "In the final analysis, in the ultimate sense, there is no [permanent] self to be found [within the Five Aggregates]" (*Milindapañha*, 27).

DEPENDENT ARISING

The Five Aggregates give a static view of the conventional self; that is, they describe the various parts that constitute the self. The Buddha also taught the notion of dependent arising (*pratītya-samutpāda*; Pali: *paṭicca-samuppāda*), which gives one a dynamic picture of how these parts interact in ways that generate *duḥkha*, and also bring about the cessation of *duḥkha*. This notion of dependent arising is so important that when the Buddha spoke of his Awakening experience, he said, "I have attained the Dharma, profound and difficult to see. . . . Difficult to see is this: contingent or dependent arising. Also difficult to see is this: the quiescence of all composite conditions . . . cessation, Nirvana" (*Majjhima-nikāya*, I, 211–212). The Dharma, or teaching, of the Buddha constantly presents the notion of dependent arising as essential to comprehending the awakened Buddhist experience of life. It is through this teaching that one can understand the way in which *duḥkha* arises in the functioning of the Five Aggregates, as well as how it can be brought to cessation.

Here is how the Buddha described dependent arising in general: "That being, this comes to be; from the arising of that, this arises. That being absent, this is not; from the cessation of that, this ceases" (*Saṃyutta-nikāya*, II, 28). This general principle of conditionality simply states that all things arise and pass away due to certain conditions. When necessary conditions are present to support a thing's existence, it comes to be. As those conditions change and new conditions appear, the thing changes. When the conditions for the thing's existence are finally removed, the thing ceases to be. This principle applies not only to the existence of phenomena but also to the quality of things. For example, the Buddha said that when certain conditions are present, *duḥkha* arises. When those conditions change, *duḥkha* is modified. And when the conditions for *duḥkha* are removed, *duḥkha* itself ceases.

In fact, the Buddha applied this general principle of conditionality to the human condition in order to explain the arising and cessation of *duḥkha*. That is, he taught a more specific version of dependent arising in order to explain how certain impermanent constituents of human experience arise such that *duḥkha* itself arises, and also how those constituents can be modified to reduce *duḥkha* until they are fully removed and *duḥkha* ceases. This specific version of the notion of dependent arising can be called the "twelve links (*nidāna*) of conditionality." The twelve conditioning links that produce *duḥkha* include: (1) ignorance, (2) mental formations, (3) consciousness, (4) mind and body, (5) senses, (6) contact, (7) sensation, (8) craving, (9) attachment, (10) becoming, (11) birth, and (12) the whole mass of *duḥkha*. Let us look at these twelve links one at a time.

The following verses from a teaching by the Buddha about these twelve links state how they arise conditionally according to the general formulation of dependent arising, namely, "That being, this comes to be; from the arising of that, this arises:"

> On [1] ignorance depends [2] mental formations; on mental formations depends [3] consciousness; on consciousness depends [4] mind and body; on mind and body depends [5] senses; on senses depends [6] contact; on sense contact depends [7] sensation, on sensation depends [8] craving; on craving depends [9] attachment; on attachment depends [10] becoming; on becoming depends [11] birth; on birth depends [12] old age and death, sorrow, lamentation, misery, grief and despair. Thus does this entire mass of *duḥkha* arise. (*Saṃyutta-nikāya*, II, 90)

With this concrete pattern of dependent arising in mind, we will first look at the individual links as they contribute to the arising *duḥkha*. Then, we will look briefly at how the Buddha says this process can be modified such that *duḥkha* itself ceases. Indeed, most of the rest of this chapter will be devoted to the Buddha's teachings on overcoming *duḥkha*.

The first link, *ignorance*, is defined as being ignorant of the Four Noble Truths that we will discuss in detail below. In brief, these four truths concern (1) the nature of *duḥkha*, (2) the various causes of *duḥkha*, (3) the possible cessation of *duḥkha*, and (4) the spiritual path that leads to the cessation of *duḥkha*. Ignorance concerning these truths about the dissatisfactory condition of life will condition the second link, namely, one's *mental formations*. These mental formations, as we have seen, are the fourth of the Five Aggregates. While the Buddha taught that the mind is essentially pure and luminous, he explained that it is also defiled by certain mental states that are formed by the mind and that arise dependent ultimately on ignorance. In other words, ignorance conditions negative mental formations, or unwholesome mental states or attitudes. For example, if a person believes that he or she can be satisfied by the passing things of the world, that person will form unwholesome, pleasure-seeking mental states like greed or lust.

The third link is *consciousness*. Its placement at this point means that mental formations condition the state of one's consciousness. For example, if one is always getting angry at people, anger can become a general disposition of one's consciousness. And that disposition of ill will can affect what one is conscious of in others. One may only be conscious of the faults of others, and not their positive qualities. The Buddha also taught that it is this intentional consciousness that, due to karma, continues for a time after death until it sparks a new conscious life, "like one flame lighting another" (*Milin-dapañha*, 40). Thus the positive and negative qualities of consciousness follow a person into his or her next life.

The fourth link is *mind and body*, literally, "name and form" (*nāma-rūpa*). That is, the status of one's mind and body, including one's health, is conditioned by the state of one's consciousness. At this point, the body becomes more involved in this process of dependent arising in that one's mental and physical state conditions the fifth link, namely, the orientation of one's *senses* to the world around one. For example, the senses of one's body are drawn toward certain persons and things depending on the orientation of one's mind and body. When one walks into a room, one notices some people and not others because of one's sense orientation toward the people in the room. In this way, one's senses condition the kind of *contact*, which is the sixth link, one has with the world.

Then, because of the positive or negative qualities of this contact, certain *sensations/feelings*, the seventh link, arise. If one contacts something one takes to be positive, one begins to entertain pleasant sensations or feelings. If, on the other hand, one encounters something one takes to be negative, unpleasant sensations or feelings arise. It is based on these emotional responses to persons, things, and events that there is the arising of the eighth link, namely, *craving*. Craving is either a self-centered desire to prolong the enjoyment of a pleasurable feeling or a self-centered desire to get rid of an unenjoyable feeling. This craving conditions the arising of the ninth link, *attachment*. In fact, cravings evolve into attachments. That is, the prior links of ignorance, unwholesome mental formations, and negative orientations toward life all intensify cravings to the point that they give rise to attachments.

An attachment is an active, decision-based clinging to the things of this world, to the pleasures derived from these things, or to an aversion to things one does not enjoy. It is these kinds of attachments that condition the *becoming* of one's life, the tenth link in the process of dependent arising. In other words, one's attachments in life condition the continuing unwholesome process of existence that has arisen from ignorance, negative mental formations, self-centered orientations, and craving. This continuing process of becoming, marked by one's personality-forming attachments, conditions one's *birth*, the eleventh link. This link means how one is reborn after death. However, it can also mean that the way one lives his or her life "gives birth," as it were, to one's personal identity—the kind of person one is. Finally, this birth or identity, because it arises dependent on attachments that are based ultimately on ignorance, conditions the final link, namely, "the entire mass of *duḥkha*."

An example of how these twelve links of conditionality might actually work themselves out in a particular life process would be the following. If we take a person who is born into an abusive situation, because of that person's (1) ignorance, he or she may not understand what is causing the *duḥkha* of that situation. Based on this ignorance, he or she might develop certain unwholesome (2) mental formations, or attitudes, about his or her self, other persons, and the world in general. These attitudes could affect his or her states of (3) consciousness, and thereby his or her (4) mental and physical well-being. This unhealthy condition of mind and body could then affect what he or she (5) senses, (6) contacts, (7) feels, and (8) craves in life. Some of these cravings may develop into unhelpful (9) attachments to people or things that simply continue negative (10) becoming, or patterns of affectivity and behavior. These patterns give (11) birth to the person's identity in ways that produce (12) *duḥkha* for himself or herself and others.

We can see from this example why Buddhists claim that these twelve links of dependent arising should be seen as forming a circle. That is, the conditions of *duḥkha* that a person produces for himself or herself and for others simply contribute to the arising of more ignorance in one's life. Thereby, the circle of negative conditionality continues and deepens. Buddhist art depicts this circle of conditionality as a twelve-spoked Wheel of Life. However, this is not a pessimistic doctrine about life; the Wheel of Life can be broken by the attainment of Awakening and Nirvana. The Buddha expresses this hope by presenting the twelve links in terms of their cessation:

> On the complete fading away and cessation of [1] ignorance ceases [2] mental formations; on the cessation of mental formations ceases [3] consciousness; on the cessation of consciousness ceases [4] mind and body; on the cessation of mind and body ceases [5] senses; on the cessation of senses ceases [6] contact; on the cessation of contact ceases [7] sensation; on the cessation of sensation ceases [8] craving; on the cessation of craving ceases [9] attachment; on the cessation of attachment ceases [10] becoming; on the cessation of becoming ceases [11] birth; on the cessation of birth ceases [12] old age and death, sorrow, lamentation, misery, grief and despair. Thus does the entire mass of *duḥkha* cease. (*Saṃyutta-nikāya*, II, 90)

What is implied here is that the process of dependent arising can also be a process of dependent cessation. We are brought back to the second part of the abstract formulation of dependent arising, namely, "That being absent, this is not; from the cessation of that, this ceases." As we shall see below, the Buddha teaches an Eightfold Path whereby one brings to awareness, pacifies, and even eradicates the ignorance, unwholesome attitudes, craving, and attachments that produce *duḥkha*. The "complete fading away and cessation" of these negative conditioning factors and their resultant *duḥkha* is Nirvana.

KARMA AND REBIRTH

In the center of some of the artistic renderings of the Wheel of Life are pictures of the various realms in which living beings can be reborn through karma. Karma, according to the Buddha, is the result of willful intention: "It is will [*cetanā*], O monks, that I call karma; for having willed, one acts through body, speech or mind" (*Aṅguttara-nikāya*, III, 415). In other words, the good or bad willful intentions that motivate the doing of good or bad actions are what result in karmic fruition. Accidental or unintended good or bad actions, like nonmoral actions, do not result in karma. However, all intentional moral or immoral acts condition or mold one's consciousness in ways that, in turn, condition one's life in the future, and ultimately one's rebirth. Remember that it is consciousness, which, like a flame in this life, lights the flame of one's next life. In this regard, good or bad rebirths are not to be seen simply as rewards or punishments, but as the resulting effect of one's conscious character molded by lives of good and bad actions that reflect how one ultimately chooses to live.

In defining good and bad actions, the Buddha spoke of wholesome (*kuśala*) and unwholesome (*akuśala*) acts. A wholesome action is one that produces a positive condition of mind and body for the actor and for those affected by the action. A positive condition is one that is ultimately conducive to the attainment of Nirvana. An unwholesome action is one that produces harmful effects and is not ultimately conducive to attaining Nirvana. The Buddha taught that there are three fundamental motivations, or "root causes," of unwholesome actions: greed (*rāga*; Pali: *lobha*), hate (*dveṣa*; Pali: *dosa*), and delusion (*moha*). These are known as the Three Root Evils. Being motivated by greed can mean allowing one's actions to be rooted in longing for something or someone or in more strong desires like avarice or lust. This kind of motivation can also involve clinging to dogmatic views in ways that are not uplifting for oneself or others. Being motivated by hatred can involve irritation with something or someone or strong feelings of aversion, anger, or even wrath. Delusion as a motivation means pursuing actions that result from an active distortion of, or hiding from, the truth in certain matters or from being unclear or full of doubts about things one should make the effort to understand.

On the other hand, the Buddha also taught that one should be motivated by the opposites of these Three Root Evils. Then, one's actions will be wholesome for oneself and others and will contribute to conditions that are conducive to the attainment of Nirvana. For example, motivation from non-greed (*alobha*) implies the positive intentions of generosity or renunciation for the benefit of others. Non-hate (*adosa*) motivations include friendliness, patience, loving kindness, and compassion for others. Non-delusion (*amoha*) motivations include clarity of mind and insight into reality.

Good and bad karma, resulting from these and other positive and negative motivations, determine one's rebirth in the cycle of *saṃsāra*. The world is said to have gone through incalculable eons—more, it is said, than the grains of sand in the Ganges River. The world itself at any given time is made up of countless systems or realms wherein beings are born, live, die, and are reborn. The early texts describe numerous realms in which rebirth takes place. These realms are classified into three basic types: the realms of sense desire (*kāma-loka*), the realms of form (*rūpa-loka*), and the formless realms (*arūpa-loka*).

The realms of sense desire are the lower of the three realms. They include the hell realms, the realms of the hungry ghosts (*preta*; Pali: *peta*), of animals, of humans, and of the lower gods (*deva*). In the hells, everything is repulsive, and one constantly experiences painful states of mind and body. Since no rebirth is for eternity, when the karma that brought one to such an unfortunate state is used up, one is reborn into another realm. The realm of the hungry ghosts is a state that overlaps the human world. Ghosts are so attached to earthly conditions that they are reborn on earth with a body of "subtle matter" such that they are normally unseen by humans. They haunt this world tormented by their unsatisfied attachments. The animal realm is where beings, because of their karma, have to undergo certain sufferings associated with animal conditions. The human realm is the first sense-desire realm that is seen as a reward for good karma. This is because the human realm is where moral virtue and wisdom can be cultivated, since one's will is not overwhelmed by the pains of the lower states or the pleasures of the higher heavenly states.

The last status in the realms of sense desire is that of certain gods. Sometimes, proud and fiercesome celestial beings (*asuras*) are mentioned as also existing on this level. They are said to be in opposition to the gods. In any case, the gods reside in six levels of existence. In the lowest of these six levels, the gods are more like spirits that inhabit the earth's surface and atmosphere. Often mentioned in the early texts in this regard are the *grand-harvas*, spirits associated with fertility. Among the higher celestial levels are found the World-Protectors, the gods of the Vedic religion, and the Tuṣita Heaven from where persons are reborn as human Buddhas. It is believed that the next human Buddha after Gautama will be Maitreya, who now resides in the Tuṣita Heaven.

The heavenly realms of form are inhabited by higher gods, referred to as *Brahmā* deities, who reside in sixteen celestial levels of progressive calmness and purity. The top five levels are attainable by humans who have almost reached Nirvana. In those levels, one will, in fact, complete the path and achieve Nirvana. The other eleven levels are related to the Four Meditations (*dhyānas*) that were practiced by the Buddha in achieving Awakening and have been practiced in Buddhism since the earliest Saṅgha. It is said that these meditations attune the consciousness to such refined states and help one to be reborn in them. In these heavenly realms, the deities are said to have pure forms and to lack the desires that characterize the gods in the realms of desire.

The formless realms consist of the four highest levels of celestial rebirth possible. Here, the *Brahmā* deities have no desire, shape, or form, only pure mental existence. The four formless realms correspond to the Four Formless Meditations. While these meditations have been practiced in Buddhism from the beginning of the Saṅgha as part of the path to Nirvana, they can also lead to rebirth into the formless realms. Rebirth into any of the *Brahmā* realms requires not just meditative attainment, but also moral discipline especially perfection of the virtues called the Four Divine Abodes, or, literally, "*Brahmā* abodes" (*Brahmā-vihāras*). These four virtues include loving kindness, compassion, sympathetic joy, and equanimity. We will discuss these meditative and moral practices later. But, it is interesting to note that Sahampatī Brahmā, the deity who came down to convince the Buddha to teach the Dharma, was from the *Brahmā* realms. Also, one should note that the Buddha did not teach that one should worship these celestial deities. However, the early texts indicate that the Buddha and the Saṅgha respected their karmic attainment.

THE FOUR NOBLE TRUTHS

We can see from the teachings of the Buddha discussed above that for him, the Five Aggregates, namely the five impermanent factors of one's existence, are always changing in certain patterns of dependent arising. No matter what realm one is born into, the patterns of this conditioning process are always in some ways dissatisfactory (*duḥkha*). To seek for a kind of permanent Self (Ātman), as some Upaniṣadic teachers were proposing, was for the Buddha a mistake. There simply is no permanent substantial self behind or within the mental and physical elements or processes of life. Instead, one should attend to the changing twelve-linked patterns of dependent arising in order to see how it is that one's life is ultimately dissatisfying. One should examine what the patterns of perceiving and thinking, of decision making and mental formation, of sensing and feeling are like that make life dissatisfactory. Then one should see what the causes of these unwholesome patterns are and how they can be changed and ultimately eliminated all together.

To make his point, the Buddha taught that all the factors of one's life are "on fire":

> All things, O monks, are on fire. And what, O monks, are all these things that are on fire? The eye, O monks, is on fire. Visible forms . . . eye consciousness . . . impressions received by the eye . . . whatever sensations, pleasant, unpleasant, or indifferent that arise dependent on impressions received by the eye are on fire. With what are these on fire? With the fire of passion, with the fire of hatred, with the fire of infatuation, with the [whole mass of *duḥkha*] are they on fire. (*Mahāvagga*, I, 21)

The Buddha goes on to repeat this claim in regard to the other five senses (including the mind). His point is that all aspects of one's experience are "burning" from an inner "fire" that one must discover and extinguish. Since the word *Nirvana* means "to blow out" or "to extinguish," in order to realize Nirvana, one must discover the hidden "fire" that burns one's life with dissatisfaction and then extinguish it. In his Awakening, the Buddha understood the "fire" causing *duḥkha*. He also discovered how to get rid of that fire in order to extinguish *duḥkha* and to attain what he called the "coolness" of Nirvana. Moved by compassion for humankind's suffering from the burning of *duḥkha*, it is said that the Buddha sought out the five ascetics with whom he had been friends and delivered to them his First Sermon at Deer Park.

Figure 2.1. Dharma Cakra (Wheel of the Dharma) on the hand of the enthroned Buddha; fourth century C.E., India. The Art Institute of Chicago.

This First Sermon was the "turning of the wheel of the Dharma" that presented what are called the Four Noble Truths. These Holy Truths are about the dissatisfactory human condition, its cause, its possible end, and the path that leads to this release. These are called "noble" truths because they are morally and spiritually fruitful: When they are realized in a person's experience, they lead to the achievement of Nirvana. They are also noble because it takes a noble person, a person of courage, honesty, and insight, to realize them. It is not easy to face the dissatisfactory conditions of one's own life. In fact, people often do whatever they can to avoid these unpleasant facts. They sometimes turn to worldly diversions, immerse themselves in studies or work, or even lose themselves in mind-dulling drugs or alcohol. But the teaching of the Buddha is that if one truly and courageously faces reality and sees the truth about his or her life, indeed about life itself, with time and guidance, one can find the cause of the discontent, heal it, and realize a new and truly satisfactory life.

The Middle Way

Let us look, then, at the First Sermon of the Buddha (*Saṃyutta-nikāya*, V, 420 ff.) to see what these Four Noble Truths entail. The Buddha begins his sermon by addressing the ascetics' concern that he had given up the rigors of the spiritual life to return to a life of self-indulgence:

> These two extremes, O monks, are not to be practiced by one who has gone forth from the world. What are these two extremes? That one which is joined with the

passions, low and vulgar, common, ignoble and useless. And also that one which is joined with self-torture and pain, ignoble and useless. Avoiding those two extremes, the [Buddha] has gained the knowledge of the Middle Way, which gives sight and knowledge, tends to calm, to insight, to Awakening and Nirvana. What, O monks, is the Middle Way . . . ? It is the Noble Eightfold Path, namely, Right Understanding, Right Thought, Right Speech, Right Action, Right Livelihood, Right Effort, Right Mindfulness, and Right Concentration. . . .

The Buddha makes it clear that his Middle Way avoids the pursuit of sensual pleasures on the one hand and the pursuit of ascetic self-torment on the other. He had experienced both the way of life-attachment and life-denial, and found them lacking. What did lead to Awakening and Nirvana was a Middle Way of moral discipline, meditation practice, and penetrating insight that can be found through following the Noble Eightfold Path. It is only after proposing this path that the Buddha goes on to present the Four Noble Truths. In this way, he subordinates conceptions about the truth to moral and spiritual transformation.

The First Noble Truth: Life Is Duḥkha

What are these Four Noble Truths that put one in touch with the reality of the human condition and present one with a religious path that can transform one's life? In the next lines of the Buddha's First Sermon, the first truth is stated:

Now this, O monks, is the noble truth of *duḥkha*. Birth is *duḥkha*, old age is *duḥkha*, sickness is *duḥkha*, and death is *duḥkha*. Sorrow, lamentation, dejection, and despair are *duḥkha*. Contact with unpleasant things is *duḥkha*, and separation from what one wishes is *duḥkha*. In short, the Five Aggregates onto which one grasps are *duḥkha*.

This First Noble Truth, the truth of *duḥkha*, proclaims that life as ordinarily lived is dissatisfactory. We have already seen what *duḥkha* means when we discussed the Three Characteristics. In this sermon, it is said that *duḥkha* is found in at least four kinds of situations that arise in ordinary life. First are the dissatisfactory conditions associated with physical processes such as old age, sickness, and death. Second are the dissatisfactory conditions, such as sorrow and dejection, that are associated with mental-emotional processes. Third is the particular dissatisfaction one finds with unpleasant things. Fourth is the dissatisfaction one finds in not possessing the things one wants or needs. Finally, the Buddha says that all of these kinds of situations that characterize the human condition point to a simple fact. This fact is that when one "grasps" for lasting happiness in the impermanent physical things and mental processes of ordinary life, distinguished here by the Five Aggregates, one will only find dissatisfaction.

As we saw before, the Buddha is not denying that there is any happiness in life. But, since all elements of life are subject to change, such happiness is not lasting, and therefore not fully satisfying. Certainly most people find some degree of happiness in life, but when one looks around at the world or within oneself, one often finds that things are just not fully satisfactory. Reading this statement of the Buddha into our own times, how many people are living in desperate situations with little or no hope of relief? Even for those who are not directly affected by great tragedies, who is without the experience of "sorrow, lamentation, dejection, and despair?" The Buddha taught that given the dissatisfactory conditions of human life, even in times of relative happiness, within every person there is a sense of lack, a sense that something is missing, a sense of *duḥkha*. *Duḥkha* is not an abstract idea; every person has his or her personal *duḥkha*. It takes a noble person to realize this fact and to seek the cause of this unfortunate condition shared by all humanity, as well as a possible remedy.

The Second Noble Truth: The Cause of Duḥkha

The Second Noble Truth is the truth about the cause (*samudaya*) of *duḥkha*. Here is how the Buddha describes the cause of *duḥkha* in the next verses of his First Sermon:

> Now this, O monks, is the noble truth of the cause of *duḥkha*: that craving which leads to rebirth, combined with pleasure and passion, finding pleasure here and there. This is the craving for sensual pleasure, the craving for continued becoming, and the craving for non-becoming.

The word we translate as "craving" is *tṛṣṇā* (Pali: *taṇhā*), which literally means "thirst." This thirst includes the many forms of desire that seek self-gratification in order to find happiness. In this sermon, the Buddha presents what he calls elsewhere the "Three Forms of Thirst." The most obvious form of such thirst is the desire for "sensual pleasure." Since all sensual objects of desire are impermanent, the self-gratification that one obtains from possessing them obviously cannot give one lasting happiness. To try to find such happiness in these sensual pleasures only leads to frustration and dissatisfaction, which, in turn, fuel the craving from more pleasures. Also, the search for happiness in the enjoyment of pleasures motivates one to relate to others in self-centered ways that result in negative karma and unhappy rebirths. Here is also a psychological basis for social conflict, injustice, violence, and war.

The second form of thirst is the desire for "becoming." We have already seen in the twelve links of conditionality that craving (or thirst) conditions attachments, which condition becoming, meaning the continuing process of one's life. So, this second type of thirst includes the desires to defend or protect oneself and one's possessions and pleasures, to advance one's own life, to enhance one's ego and social status, to gain more power and prestige. On the other hand, the thirst for "non-becoming" includes desires for self-denial in the ascetic life, for the removal of unpleasant people or things from one's life, for self-destructive habits or patterns of behavior. We can see from these Three Forms of Thirst, that, for the Buddha, craving is not just a single phenomenon; it has multiple and even conflicting forms.

It is also clear from the twelve links of conditionality that thirst is not the first cause of *duḥkha*. It is conditioned by a deeper source, namely, the ignorance that is referred to as the first of the twelve links. What is this fundamental ignorance? It is a lack of realizing the Buddha's Dharma concerning the real nature of self and world. Using the metaphor from the Buddha's Fire Sermon quoted above, the ignorance of such realities as impermanence, no-self, and *duḥkha* produces a very subtle yet powerful self-awareness that is self-centered and burns one's life with craving or thirst. To use another metaphor, this self-awareness is like a "field" in which everything that one experiences is analyzed and judged from a self-centered and ultimately ignorant point of view. It is from this ignorance, this lack of clear insight into the Four Noble Truths about life, that "seeds" of *duḥkha* grow.

In this First Sermon, the craving that causes *duḥkha* implies an ignorant view of the self as an ongoing possessor and enjoyer of the things of life. People are thirsting to be and to possess, to become and to acquire, in ways that produce a dissatisfactory life for themselves and others. This unwholesome lifestyle is based on people's view of themselves as "controllers" or "possessors" and the world as being made up of people and things to be controlled or possessed in ways that cause *duḥkha*. It seems that this inner self-centered vision of self and world "solidifies," as it were, into the kinds of thirsting and often self-destructive states of mind that the Buddha identifies as the causes of *duḥkha*.

Also, this ignorant view of self and world is related to another form of thirst that the Buddha mentions in other sermons, namely, a craving to be right that leads to an attachment to ideas, views, theories, or beliefs. This kind of attachment produces dogmatism, prejudice, and intolerance. When one puts this kind of dogmatic attitude together with the thirst to obtain personal happiness, the thirst to advance one's life (including one's views) by the use of power, and the thirst for self-destructive actions, one finds causes for everything from "verbal wrangling" to ideological warfare. When the Buddha spoke out about the social, economic, and political issues of his day, he taught that these problems that bring about so much *duḥkha* in people's lives are ultimately rooted in the human mind. It is there, in ignorance and unwholesome mental formations, that the root of humankind's *duḥkha* must, in the final analysis, be addressed. For the Buddha, only a deep, insightful penetration into how unwholesome dispositions, attitudes, feelings, and thoughts are produced from ignorance and thirst can enable a person to stop fueling the inner fire that produces the burning of *duḥkha*.

❦ *The Third Noble Truth: The Cessation of* Duḥkha

The Third Noble Truth concerns the cessation (*nirodha*) of *duḥkha*. In his First Sermon, the Buddha states it in just a few words: "Now this, O monks, is the noble truth of the cessation of *duḥkha*. It is the complete cessation of that very craving, giving it up, renouncing it, release from it, detachment from it." Although in this particular sermon he does not use the word, the cessation he is speaking about here is Nirvana. As we have seen, Nirvana literally means "blowing out" or "extinguishing" and was used to describe the cessation of a fire. In this sermon, the Buddha is saying that the cessation of *duḥkha* is brought about by the extinction of craving or thirst. When craving ceases, its effect, namely *duḥkha*, ceases and the result is Nirvana.

One thing that is interesting about the Buddha's statement of the Third Noble Truth is the few words he uses in comparison to the number used in stating the other three truths. Perhaps the reason is that the Buddha never spoke very much about what Nirvana ultimately is. Up to this point we have been looking at teachings of the Buddha that he explicates at some length. Therefore, there is not a great deal of disagreement among scholars about what those teachings entail. However, this is not the case with Nirvana. In fact, volumes have been written in which scholars have tried to answer the question, "What is Nirvana?" Some claim that it is an absolute Truth. Others say it is a transcendent metaphysical Reality. Still others argue that it is a supermundane experience, or a supreme and pure state of mind.

At the conclusion of this chapter, we discuss why the Buddha did not speak about Nirvana in any great detail and also present an interpretation of Nirvana based just on the early texts. Here, it is enough to say that no matter how Nirvana is interpreted, in the Third Noble Truth it refers to the cessation of *duḥkha* brought about by the letting go of craving. In other teachings by the Buddha, Nirvana is said to entail the cessation of defilements or the cessation of the Three Root Evils of greed, hate, and delusion. However, one should not conclude from these statements that Nirvana is something that is "caused" by the cessation of craving. Nirvana is not produced by anything, and so it is called "unconditioned" (*asaṃskṛta*; Pali: *asaṃkhata*). On the other hand, Nirvana is "realized" by following the Eightfold Path that is proclaimed in the Fourth Noble Truth. That is, the Eightfold Path does not cause or produce Nirvana, but leads one to it like a path that leads to a place that is already there to be discovered.

The Fourth Noble Truth: The Eightfold Path to the Cessation of Duḥkha

The Buddha presents the Fourth Noble Truth, about the Path (*mārga*; Pali: *magga*) that leads to the cessation of *duḥkha*, in the next lines of his First Sermon:

> Now this, O monks, is the noble truth of the way that leads to the cessation of *duḥkha*. This is the Noble Eightfold Path, namely, Right Understanding, Right Thought, Right Speech, Right Action, Right Livelihood, Right Effort, Right Mindfulness, and Right Concentration. . . .

In the Four Noble Truths, we can see a method of medical treatment that was popular at the time of the Buddha. First, there is the identification of the disease. Second, there is an analysis of the cause of the disease. Third, this analysis is followed by defining the desired cure that will remove the cause of the disease, and thereby the disease itself, thus producing renewed health. Fourth, there is a specific method prescribed for curing the disease. In the Eightfold Path, the Buddha gave a prescription that will "cure" the dissatisfactory condition of human existence. This Fourth Noble Truth provides a path for the journey from ordinary human living, characterized by *duḥkha*, to a life characterized by freedom, peace, and happiness, namely, to the Nirvana proclaimed in the Third Noble Truth. It is the Middle Way of moral and religious practice that the Buddha mentioned in the introductory passages to this First Sermon.

In the naming of each of these eight steps, we find the word "right" (*samyak*; Pali: *sammā*) being used as an adjective. This word is not used by the Buddha to indicate a command. The Buddha is not demanding that his disciples follow these steps as a religious or moral duty. Rather, the word "right" means "skillful." In other words, these eight steps will skillfully help one advance in the religious way that leads to Nirvana. Therefore, the Buddha said that one should not follow these steps simply because he taught them. One should try them in his or her own experience to see if they do indeed lead to Awakening and Nirvana. Also, these steps are not intended to be taken one after the other in the order they appear in the Buddha's listing of them. Rather, they are to be developed more or less together so that they reinforce each other in one's spiritual life. In the next section of this chapter, we will look at each of these steps to see how they skillfully advance one's life in the direction of Awakening and Nirvana.

Awakening

In the conclusion to his First Sermon, the Buddha says:

> As long as I did not perceive with knowledge and insight . . . these noble truths, so long, O monks, in this world . . . had I not attained the highest and complete Awakening. But, when I perceived with knowledge and insight . . . these noble truths, then, O monks, in this world . . . I attained the highest and complete Awakening. Thus I knew; knowledge arose in me, insight arose that the emancipation of my mind is unmovable. This is my last existence; now there is no more rebirth.

In complete Awakening, one realizes the end of *duḥkha*. Ignorance, as first in the twelve links of conditionality, is said to entail not knowing the Four Noble Truths. In this passage, Awakening is said to entail knowing these truths with penetrating insight. Thus, the ignorance that conditions the arising of craving is extinguished. By Awakening, achieved through the Eightfold Path, one can find release from the unwholesome factors of mind that produce the dissatisfactory state of ordinary human existence. In short, the Buddha teaches that true "emancipation" from rebirth is Nirvana, and this lasting happiness and peace can be found by attaining Awakening through

Figure 2.2. Seated Buddha; c. 475 C.E., India. Museum of Archaeology, Sārnāth, India.

following the Eightfold Path. At this point, then, let us look more carefully at this path to Nirvana.

THE EIGHTFOLD PATH

The steps of the Eightfold Path are arranged under three categories. The first two steps (Right Understanding and Right Thought) fall under the category of "proper view"; they present a perspective and way of thinking that orient one skillfully on the path to Awakening and Nirvana. The next three steps (Right Speech, Right Action, and Right Livelihood) fall under the category of "proper conduct"; they define what is required to walk the path in terms of moral purification and living. The last three steps (Right Effort, Right Mindfulness, and Right Concentration) fall under the category of "proper practice"; these practices deepen proper view into the wisdom of Awakening and deepen proper conduct into an awakened life.

These three divisions of the Eightfold Path are also labeled in another way by the Buddha. Proper view is called "wisdom" (*prajñā*; Pali: *paññā*), since its two steps provide the wisdom necessary for Awakening. Proper conduct is called "morality" (*śīla*; Pali: sīla), since its three steps define the moral precepts of the Buddhist path. Finally, proper practice is called "concentration" (*samādhi*), since its three steps advance the concentrated states of mind necessary for inner spiritual purification and the attainment of Nirvana. With these general remarks about the Eightfold Path in mind, let us now turn to an introduction of each step on this Holy Path.

Right Understanding

Right Understanding means a "clarity" of understanding that skillfully leads one along the path to Awakening. It involves a clear understanding of the impermanent process of life, the unsatisfactory condition of this process, and the dependently arisen factors of life that make it so dissatisfying. It also entails understanding rightly how the conception of a substantial and permanent self influences one's self-centered dispositions, attitudes, and other mental formations that bind one to this process of dissatisfactory living. On the other hand, it also means to understand well the positive qualities of mind and moral living that can heal this condition and to understand clearly the steps one needs to take to cultivate these satisfactory qualities of thought, word, and action. Right Understanding, in short, means to understand skillfully the Dharma of the Buddha in a way that develops into, to use the words from the Buddha's First Sermon, "knowledge and insight" into the true nature of all things, of how they really are (*yathābhūtaṃ*). In this sense, it is the "seed" of a wisdom that destroys ignorance and becomes complete in the attainment of Awakening and Nirvana.

Right Thought

While Right Understanding entails a "clarity" of insight into the truth about life, Right Thought entails a "purity" of thinking about life. It entails the development of freedom from unwholesome states of mind like thoughts of greed, harm, violence, or ill will toward others. In the development of this freedom, pure or wholesome states of mind such as thoughts of selflessness, good will toward others, and compassion are cultivated. These Right Thoughts will, in turn, be expressed in the next steps on the path that have to do with moral treatment of other persons. Without developing wholesome thoughts and attitudes of mind toward others, one's moral actions will only be motivated by an external sense of duty rather than an inner caring attitude. This second step also involves the willingness to relinquish any state of mind that obstructs one's progress on the path. So it includes the right kinds of aspirations for oneself and for others, seeking what is good for all living beings. Therefore, this step is sometimes called "Right Aspiration." It entails thoughts of compassionate aspiration for the well-being of all, tender thoughts of concern for all who are suffering, and the desire to bring goodness and freedom to all living beings.

Right Speech

With the right mental attitudes and aspirations, one can then use his or her speech skillfully for the benefit of all beings. Also, since people speak what they think, Right Speech follows Right Thought. For the Buddha, this third step means that one should refrain from four types of wrong speech: falsehood, slander, harsh words, and idle gossip. Note that besides *refraining* from these forms of wrong speech, one is also asked by the Buddha to *cultivate* forms of Right Speech. For example, one should refrain from telling lies, and instead develop the virtue of truthfulness expressed in what one says. Since slander breaks fellowship with other persons and does violence to their reputation, one should always speak in ways that defend and affirm the dignity of other persons. While harsh words issue from an unkind heart, gentle words, by contrast, issue from a kind and compassionate heart. To engage in harsh language only hardens one's heart and drives out the compassionate virtues of enlightened living. Idle gossip disturbs others in ways that are beneficial neither to the one who is listening nor to the one about whom one is speaking. Such gossip works against peacefulness in relationships and society. Like slander and harsh words, gossip expresses the unwholesome thoughts of ill will and cruelty toward others. One should instead use words that sow the seeds of peace in all relationships. In this regard, the Buddha also advised that if one cannot say anything useful in a situation, one should keep a "noble silence."

Right Action

Right Thought is also expressed in moral actions. The Buddha often presented Right Action in terms of the Five Precepts. Note that just as with Right Speech, while each precept presents what one *should not* do, the Buddha also taught what one *should* do. For example, the first precept is "not to kill." The Buddha, in discussing this virtue, says:

> In what ways . . . is a monk perfected in morality? Forsaking the taking of life, he refrains from killing. Having given up stick or sword, he is careful and compassionate, showing concern for the welfare of all living beings. Thus, he is accomplished in morality. (*Dīgha-nikāya*, I, 63)

In other words, one should not only *not* kill any living being, but should also carefully practice compassion with a sincere concern for all. The second precept is "not to steal." Here, too, one should not take what belongs to others, and should practice charity, respect, and generosity in all relationships. The third precept is "not to commit sexual misconduct." Here, one is advised to practice self-control in order to live a life of purity in relationship to others. The fourth precept is "not to lie." Instead of telling falsehoods, one is asked to practice sincerity and honesty in what one says. Finally, the fifth precept is "not to partake of intoxicating drinks or drugs." Here, restraint is practiced in order to better cultivate one's freedom and develop one's mindfulness. The Five Precepts ask people to preserve life, respect others, develop self-control, express the truth, and attain freedom. To act in these ways deepens compassion, love, and respect for oneself and for others. Acting in ways that destroy life, disrespect others, increase irresponsibility, hide or distort the truth, and lead to addiction decrease one's freedom, enlightenment, and compassionate living.

Right Livelihood

A person who practices Right Action is naturally drawn to a Right Livelihood. This is a step designed for laypersons because the Buddha's monastic disciples relied exclusively on alms. Right Livelihood means that the layperson should only pursue a living that will not cause harm or injustice to others. The Buddha gave as examples of wrong livelihoods the sale of arms and lethal weapons, the slaughter of animals and human beings, and the production of intoxicating drinks and poisons. In pursuing any acceptable form of work, the Buddha cautioned that a layperson's motivation should not be to make more money than one needs. Work should not be done in order to make money for the enjoyment of luxuries. If work is done for this purpose, then it is a wrong way of making one's livelihood in that it only deepens one's craving for, and attachments to, the pleasures of life. Further, if one is motivated by the desire to become rich for one's own benefit, one may become willing to use deceit or to exploit others to get ahead. If this happens, then any form of livelihood—even an honorable one—becomes a detriment to moral and spiritual living. By working in this "wrong" way, one is becoming more and more bound to what will be a dissatisfactory lifestyle for oneself while harming other persons at the same time. On the other hand, by working in the "right" way, one's work can itself be a vehicle for the development of compassion and loving kindness for others. One will then have the satisfaction of making a living for oneself and one's family, serving humankind, and personally advancing toward spiritual freedom all at the same time.

Right Effort

It certainly takes a great amount of effort to translate one's understanding, thinking, and aspirations into wholesome and skillful forms of speech, action, and work. In doing so, one needs to rid oneself of any unwholesome states of mind that unskillfully compromise one's spiritual journey to Awakening and Nirvana. One also needs to develop wholesome states of mind that skillfully advance that journey. Therefore, there are four types of Right Effort. First is the effort to "prevent" unwholesome states of mind from arising. Second is the effort to "abandon" unwholesome mental states that have already arisen. Third is the effort to "produce" wholesome states of mind. Fourth is the effort to "cultivate" wholesome mental states that are already part of one's mentality. Finally, it should also be noted that Right Effort not only builds a moral foundation for a wholesome life but also aids in cultivating the higher spiritual life. Right Effort can also be used to sustain the spiritual practices of mindfulness and meditation. In short, by Right Effort one's energy can be channeled into the skillful development of all aspects of the Buddhist life.

An example of Right Effort can be seen in the Buddha's advice concerning how to deal with temptations. If one is confronted with unwholesome mental states, such as evil desires, one should practice the second type of Right Effort, namely, the effort to abandon those states of mind. To do so, one should first be mindful of the particular object that is causing those desires. Then one should practice the third type of Right Effort by picturing to oneself, or turning one's attention toward, another object that will produce an opposite mental state, such as loving kindness. This is because the more one focuses on the object of temptation, the worse the temptation becomes. One should simply abandon the tempting object of desire for something that produces wholesome mental states. If the temptation still persists, one should make the effort to look at the broader situation and to visualize the painful consequences to oneself and to others that will happen if one pursues the temptation. If all this fails, one should practice another version of the third type of Right Effort, that is, one should make the effort to change one's environment so that new and more positive sensory input is produced.

Right Mindfulness

Right Mindfulness involves a state of keen awareness with regard to (1) one's body, what one is doing at a particular moment; (2) one's sensations, feelings, thoughts, and impulses at a particular time; (3) one's ideas or views; and (4) the true nature of things, namely, their transience, nonsubstantiality, and dissatisfactory nature. We will discuss the actual practice of mindfulness in the next chapter. However, what is essential to mindfulness in all cases is a bare and nonprejudiced awareness that gives one a clear picture of one's dependently arisen mental, emotional, and physical processes and states that are occurring in the present moment. In one case, mindfulness may expose the truth about the impermanent process of one's experience. In another case, it may uncover the sensory, mental, or emotional factors that are interweaving in this process in ways that are either wholesome, unwholesome, or neutral.

The development of mindfulness prevents the person from being led astray in the spiritual journey by bodily sensations or by feelings, desires, thoughts, and ideas that play through the mind. In this sense, being mindful of what one is thinking and feeling can help one know where to direct Right Effort. For example, if one is mindfully aware of a certain desire—say, the desire for vengeance—and is aware of its unwholesome nature and possible consequences, one can see clearly where to use one's Right Effort in order to free oneself from this negative state of mind. In this way, mindfulness can contribute to one's Right Effort to free oneself from what are discerned to be unwholesome patterns of thought and behavior and from wrong or unjust situations in the world. Not to be mindful of one's own condition is to be moved unreflectively by inner thoughts, emotions, and desires like a puppet on strings. Not to be mindful of the dissatisfactory conditions of the world is not to be aware of how one should live responsibly and compassionately in particular situations. The clarity of mindfulness provides the mental awareness of self and world needed for skillfully changing oneself for the better and for skillfully contributing to bettering the world in which one lives.

Mindfulness practice is also directed toward one's ideas or views. The Buddha taught that the views one uses to understand life can themselves distort one's awareness of how things really are. We have already seen how the Buddha taught that if one believes in a substantial self that must be gratified for it to be happy, that view will blind one to what will, in fact, bring real and lasting happiness. Also, one can misread the facts of a certain situation in an effort to force them to fit one's political or religious ideology. Mindfulness of the conceptual lenses that one uses in viewing oneself and the world can help one see oneself and the world in a clearer, less judgmental, and more compassionate way. Finally, mindfulness practice involves focusing the mind on an object, thus contributing to the next step, namely, Right Concentration.

Right Concentration

By Right Concentration (*samādhi*), the Buddha meant a "one-pointedness of mind" (*cittasyaikāgratā*). It was this concentrated state of mind that helped the Buddha to his full realization of Awakening. His perfect wisdom, arising within the deepest state of concentration, illuminated the true nature of all things such that he realized the Four Noble Truths. Therefore, Right Concentration involves something more than just thinking hard about something. It involves a focused state of mind that supports penetrating insight leading to Awakening. This state of mental concentration also contributes to the healing and integrating of the various aspects of one's being into a pure and unified wholeness leading to Nirvana. Right Concentration achieves these transformative effects by stilling and focusing the mind, by pacifying distracting thoughts, and by purifying unruly emotions and inordinate desires that create *duḥkha*. It thereby brings about mental-emotional

---

BOX 2.2

EXPERIENCING WHAT THE BUDDHA TAUGHT

After several years of Zen Buddhist meditation practice, I became curious about the relationship between meditation and the seemingly complex teachings on the self, suffering and the cause of suffering, and dependent arising. I knew from my study that the lists and categories of the early teachings were composed in atmospheres of deep meditation and contemplative investigation, and I was anxious to make this personal link as well.

I arranged to do a monthlong retreat in a Tibetan Buddhist retreat center, under the supervision of the resident lama and his students. I found myself in a simple, quiet room under a rule of silence, solitude, and structured practice. Most of the day was devoted to sitting meditation, a simple mindfulness of breathing, which calmed and settled my mind and brought me into the present moment. Several hours of each day I studied the classical texts of the Tibetan Abhidharma, the "Higher Dharma" which comprises these teachings on impermanence, selflessness, and dissatisfactoriness. The lama then suggested structured contemplations in which I would quietly label thoughts as they arose and passed away, identifying how they were painful and looking into their impermanent and selfless aspects. Periodically, he or one of his students met with me, inquiring about my experience.

While I had been familiar with group practice settings, *sesshins* in the Zen tradition, this was my first solitary retreat. The long periods of mindful breathing were simple, naked, and grounding. But I was not prepared for the power of the contemplations, which the lama had given me. I watched the torrent of thoughts, emotions, and sense perceptions rush through my mind and despaired at being able to label them at all. Eventually, the torrent slowed to a river, and I was able to distinguish between thoughts and emotions, between emotions and sense perceptions. Yet they quickly raced by, constantly changing. As I experimented with ways of focusing my mind and labeling, I became more adept at the practice and continued for weeks of focused contemplation.

By the end of the retreat I was astonished—the relevance of the teaching of the Five Aggregates (*skandhas*) came alive! I could no longer regard my concerns, obsessions, and subconscious gossip as weighty and convincing. Instead, I experienced the insubstantiality and constantly changing quality of my experience and felt "myself" dissolve as well. What remained was a constant flow of fleeting vivid moments laced with luminous awareness and steady calm. The liberating message of the Buddha became one of inexpressible simplicity instead of endless numerical lists, compassionate method instead of metaphysics. It is clear why the "Enlightened One" placed so much emphasis upon personal experience in meditation rather than upon intellectual learning.

JUDITH SIMMER-BROWN

Chair, Religious Studies Department
Naropa University

"equanimity," "peacefulness," and "harmony," which, in turn, foster the wisdom and mental-emotional integration needed to realize Awakening and Nirvana. The process of transformation achieved through Right Concentration is called "mental culture" (*bhāvanā*).

The Buddha taught specific practices that could be used to cultivate Right Concentration. In the next chapter, we explore a number of these techniques as we examine the original form of Buddhism based on the Buddha's teachings. For now, it is enough to indicate that there are two principle types of mental culture taught by the Buddha. First is "tranquillity" (*śamatha*; Pali: *samatha*) meditation, which is used to develop one-pointed mental concentration. A metaphor for this kind of calming meditation is cleaning a mirror. The ordinary mind is like a mirror covered by dust, in that its inherent clarity is "covered" with mental activity, and therefore cannot reflect reality clearly. With a mind that is made tranquil by meditation, persons can see more clearly what is real about themselves and the world. Tranquillity meditation quiets discursive thoughts and unruly emotions. While the resulting stillness of mind has a healing and integrating effect in and of itself, it also brings forth an inherent inner luminosity that can, in turn, be the basis for deeper penetrating insight into reality. Tranquillity practice also leads to the development of other forms of absorbing meditation, which we discuss in the next chapter.

The second principle type of meditation directly cultivates penetrating insight, and therefore is called "insight" (*vipaśyanā*; Pali: *vipassanā*) meditation. Right Concentration implies not only the concentrating and calming of the mind, but also focusing insight into the dependently arisen factors of experience that contribute to, or bring the cessation of, *duḥkha*. For the Buddha, concentration involves turning one's mental focus onto the inner states of mind and processes of life in a manner that brings insight into the real nature of things. It is this insight that builds on mindfulness and cleanses the mind of defilements—of unwholesome states of mind such as worries and anxieties, doubts and craving, hatred and delusion. Insight also aids in cultivating wholesome mental qualities like awareness and knowledge, confidence and joy, leading ultimately to freedom and the wisdom that bring about Awakening and Nirvana. With the clarity of penetrating insight, and with the freedom it brings, one is better able to live in wise and compassionate ways that are of benefit to oneself and others.

In concluding this introduction to the Eightfold Path, we should note two other things. First, the practice of these eight steps takes place at different levels. The beginner practices the eight steps at a more elementary level in which he or she works on certain issues that will only be fully dealt with later by practicing at the advanced level. For example, a beginner may practice Right Understanding of the Four Noble Truths at a more intellectual level of insight. But a more advanced practitioner may practice Right Understanding at the level of more direct and profound wisdom. The highest practice of the eight steps is engaged in by the Buddha and the *arhats*. Second, it should now be more evident that the eight steps all reinforce each

other in the journey to Awakening and Nirvana. For example, Right Mindfulness and Right Effort contribute to Right Concentration. Right Concentration contributes to Right Understanding and Right Thought. Right Speech,
Right Action, and Right Livelihood give form to Right Thought and also
contribute a firm foundation for Right Mindfulness and Right Concentration. All these steps together ultimately lead to the attainment of Nirvana.

NIRVANA

As mentioned earlier, since the Buddha himself did not describe Nirvana in
any detail, many theories about it have been put forward over the centuries.
In what follows, we will not try to present a developed theory about the nature of Nirvana. We will only describe what, according to the early texts, its
attainment entails in human experience. In most cases, this attainment is described in terms of what is brought to an end, of what ceases or is extinguished in the "blowing out" of Nirvana. For example, the Buddha says that
Nirvana is "the complete cessation of craving (thirst), letting it go, renouncing it, being free from it, detachment from it" (*Samyutta-nikāya*, I, 136).
Or elsewhere, a disciple of the Buddha, when asked about Nirvana, replied:
"Whatever . . . is the cessation of greed, hatred and delusion, this is called
Nirvana" (*Samyutta-nikāya*, IV, 251). We know from the Second Noble Truth
that craving, and other negative mental formations like the Three Root Evils
of greed, hatred, and delusion, are the cause of *duḥkha*. So in simplest terms,
Nirvana is that freedom from *duḥkha* that one realizes when the causes of
duḥkha are extinguished.

The term "detachment," used in the above quotation, often appears in the
Buddha's description of Nirvana. For example, "If a monk is freed by turning away, by detachment in regard to things . . . it is fitting to call him a
monk who has attained Nirvana here and now" (*Samyutta-nikāya*, III, 164).
Detachment from things entails freedom from craving for, or clinging to, the
things of this world in ways that keep one locked into unwholesome patterns of living. However, this kind of detachment does not mean that a person who enjoys the status of Nirvana does not care about others or about
the suffering conditions of the world. Rather, while the Buddha refers to
Nirvana as personally "secure" and "peaceful," when he describes the way
a nirvanic person relates to others, he often mentions the Four Divine
Abodes. Again, these four virtues are the wholesome relational attitudes of
compassion, loving kindness, sympathetic joy, and equanimity. The virtue
of equanimity means that one lives the virtues of loving kindness, compassion, and joyful affirmation of others equally with everyone, friend and foe
alike. So it is clear that when a person is detached, he or she is *free from* reacting to others in unwholesome ways and is thereby *free to* respond to others in wholesome ways. It is said that when a person enjoys the freedom of
Nirvana, he or she is like a lotus flower that rises out of the muddy waters.
Detached from the unwholesome (muddy) states of mind, a nirvanic person's life flowers with the beauty of wholesomeness.

Besides living the Four Divine Abodes, the person who attains Nirvana is also said to live the Six Perfections that are cultivated in Buddhist spirituality. These ideals are (1) selfless *generosity*, or charity; (2) benevolent *morality*; (3) *patient endurance* of the difficulties in life that cannot be changed; (4) *energy* to change what one can for the better; (5) the single-pointedness and equanimity of *meditation*; and (6) *wisdom* insight into the truth about existence. Such virtues flow naturally from the mind and heart of the enlightened person enjoying Nirvana. He or she does not have to "struggle" or "toil" to cultivate them anymore.

Note that the last perfection in this list is wisdom. Nirvana thus also entails the cessation of ignorance. In terms of the fire metaphor, the flames of negative states of mind that cause the burning of *duḥkha* are fully extinguished when the fuel that ultimately creates these fires, namely, ignorance, is eradicated. It is because of the cessation of ignorance in the attainment of Nirvana that the Buddha refers to Nirvana as an attainment of "absolute Truth" (*satya*; Pali: *sacca*).

Therefore, with inner freedom, detachment from things, care for all beings, the perfection of virtues, and wisdom realizing the Truth, one is finally free from *duḥkha* and attains the peaceful status of Nirvana. This status of peace and freedom is said by the Buddha to be "unmoved" by the events of life that ordinarily "move" one to negative and unwholesome states of mind. It is said that the person who enjoys this Nirvana is free from any "disturbance" or "oppression" that might limit or compromise his or her nirvanic status. While the nirvanic person is not immune to such things as sickness, the problems of old age, and even death, in facing these ills one's mind is always "unmoved," "at rest," "peaceful and calm." And one continues to live kindly and compassionately for the good of all beings.

Nirvana is said by the Buddha to be more than just a moral attainment or an insight into the Truth. It is said to be a "supreme status" that is "holy." This supreme holiness, the Buddha said, is a "full consummation," or a "final end," that brings into human experience the "blessedness" of the "highest good." When one reads descriptive terms such as these, one can see that Nirvana is ultimately a sublime religious status. Since our words and concepts are derived from ordinary experience and reflection, language cannot fully convey this sublime status. Nirvana is a blessedness that is ultimately beyond ordinary conceptual understanding and description. Since this is so, the Buddha sometimes used a type of *via negativa* to help people understand something about Nirvana by saying what it is not.

Three negative words he often used are "unborn," "unconditioned," and "deathless." For example, in one text we read, "That monk who here is devoid of craving and passion attains to deathlessness, peace and the unchanging state of Nirvana" (*Sutta-nipāta*, 204). In another text, there is a famous definition of Nirvana:

There is, O monks, an unborn, not-become, unproduced, not-compounded. Were it not, O monks, for this unborn, not-become, unproduced, not-compounded, no escape from the born, become, produced and compounded would be known. But, O monks, since there is an unborn, not-become, unproduced, not-compounded, there is an escape from the born, become, produced and compounded. (*Udāna*, 81)

That Nirvana is "unborn," "not become," or "unproduced" means that it is not the result of anything; it is not dependently arisen, or "born," like all worldly phenomena. Therefore, it also cannot be produced by the Eightfold Path or even the attainment of Awakening. It is a status that always is—one simply has to realize it in one's own experience. To say that Nirvana is "unchanging," "unconditioned," or "not-compounded" means that it is not like the phenomena of ordinary experience. As we have seen, all such worldly phenomena are dependently arisen, compounded, conditioned, and constantly changing. Only Nirvana is unchanging, uncompounded, unarisen, and not conditioned or moved by any factors of existence.

Finally, to say that Nirvana is "deathless" means that even death cannot condition it or bring it to an end. In this regard, it is important to note that the Buddha spoke of two types of Nirvana. First is Nirvana "with remainder" (*sopadhiśeṣa*), which means Nirvana with the Five Aggregates. This is the Nirvana that is attainable in this present existence. The Buddha himself is said to have lived this type of Nirvana for the last forty-five years of his life. The second type is Nirvana "without remainder" (*anupadhiśeṣa*), which is Nirvana without the Five Aggregates. This Nirvana is also called "Final Nirvana" (*parinirvāṇa*). It is the destiny of the Buddha or *arhat* because he or she, having attained full Awakening and Nirvana in this life, has no more karma to produce a new rebirth. Since this ultimate nirvanic status is "without remainder" of all elements of human experience, what actually happens to such a person after death is one of the questions necessarily left unanswered by the Buddha.

SUGGESTIONS FOR FURTHER READING

Anderson, Carol. *Pain and Its Ending: The Four Noble Truths in the Theravada Buddhist Canon*. Richmond, UK: Curzon Press, 1999.

Bodhi, Bhikkhu and Nyanaponika Thera, trans. *Numerical Discourses of the Buddha: An Anthology of Suttas from the Anguattara Nikāya*. Lanham, MD: Rowman & Littlefield Publishers, 2000.

Dhamma, Rewata. *The First Discourse of the Buddha*. Boston: Wisdom Publications, 1997.

Jayatilleke, K. N. *The Message of the Buddha*. New York: Free Press, 1976.

Nanamoli, Bhikkhu, and Bhikkhu Bodhi, trans. *The Middle Length Discourses of the Buddha: A New Translation of the Majjhima Nikāya*. Boston: Wisdom Publications, 1995.

Payutto, Phra Prayudh. *Buddhadhamma: Natural Laws and Values for Life*. Translated by Grant A. Olson. Albany, NY: SUNY Press, 1995.

Pérez-Remón, Joaquín. *Self and Non-Self in Early Buddhism*. The Hague: Mouton, 1980.

Rahula, Walpola. *What the Buddha Taught*. New York: Grove Press, 1962.

Saddhatissa, Hammalawa. *Buddhist Ethics: The Path to Nirvana*. London: Wisdom Publications, 1987.

Sīlānanda, U. *Four Foundations of Mindfulness*. Boston: Wisdom Publications, 1990.

Walshe, Maurice, trans. *The Long Discourses of the Buddha: A Translation of the Dīgha Nikāya*. Boston: Wisdom Publications, 1995.

Warren, Henry Clarke. *Buddhism in Translations*. New York: Antheneum, 1963.

THREE

THE WAY OF THE ELDERS

The Buddha said that after his passing, his followers would be guided by the Dharma and the *Vinaya*. This meant being guided by the "teachings" of the Buddha and by the particular "discipline" of the monastic community. Therefore, at the time of the first three-month retreat after the passing of the Buddha, the First Council of Buddhism was held at Rājagṛha to establish the authentic teachings and discipline. Chronicles of this "first recitation of the community" state that five hundred *arhats* assembled to standardize an accepted oral record of what the Buddha said about both doctrine and moral and spiritual living.

THE THREE BASKETS

In what scholars consider an idealized version, it is said that the Venerable Mahākāśyapa, who had called for the council, first questioned the elder Upāli about the rules of discipline taught by the Buddha. Upāli is said to have stated when and under what circumstances the Buddha taught each of the rules for the monastic order. Then Mahākāśyapa turned to Ānanda and questioned him about the many discourses of the Buddha. As a result of this council, what was recited by the community was said to have been memorized, establishing an oral tradition that was passed down for several centuries before being committed to writing. This oral tradition was divided into two collections, or "Baskets" (*Piṭakas*), that became the earliest form of Buddhist scripture. The collection of discourses of the Buddha make up the "Basket of Discourses," *Sūtra* (Pali: *Sutta*) *Piṭaka*; the collection of the Buddha's rules for the monastic community is known as the "Basket of Discipline," *Vinaya Piṭaka*.

A third collection of canonical teachings concerning the Dharma, called the "Higher Teachings," *Abhidharma* (Pali: *Abhidhamma*) *Piṭaka*, was also said by the tradition to have been recited by Ānanda at the First Council. However, this collection is actually the result of centuries of philosophical systemization based on lists and summaries of topics for discussion that may well have originated with the Buddha and may have been recited at the First

Council. The Buddha's original teachings in the *Sūtra Piṭaka* were given in stories, illustrations, anecdotes, and so on, and were not an attempt to present a complete philosophical system. As the early Buddhists explained and defended their views, there developed certain philosophical viewpoints that were more formally and systematically presented in the *Abhidharma Piṭaka*. Centuries after the Buddha's passing, the emerging Buddhist sects added this later scriptural material, thereby producing the more fully developed "Three Baskets" (*Tripiṭaka*; Pali: *Tipiṭaka*), which was the authoritative scripture for much of early Buddhism.

The *Tripiṭaka* is preserved in the Pali language as well as later in Chinese and Tibetan. The Pali canon is traditionally said to have been brought to Sri Lanka from northern India in the third century B.C.E., and was written down in the first century B.C.E. Scholars are skeptical that what we have today is the same as what was originally brought to Sri Lanka. What we do have today are a number of Pali texts divided into the three *Piṭakas*. The earliest of these Pali texts include the four primary *Nikāyas* ("Collections") of the Buddha's discourses (*sūtras*), as well as the *Vinaya* texts. The *Nikāya* material as found in the Chinese *Tripiṭaka* is referred to as the *Āgamas* ("Traditions").

The Sūtra Piṭaka

The *Sūtra Piṭaka* consists of the *Nikāya* material. Using their Pali titles, the older four *Nikāyas* include the *Long* (*Dīgha*), *Middle-length* (*Majjhima*), *Grouped* (*Saṃyutta*), and *Numbered* (*Aṅguttara*) *Nikāyas*. It is these four *Nikāyas* that we referred to in the previous two chapters as the "earlier texts." A fifth *Nikāya*, the *Minor* (*Khuddaka*) *Nikāya*, contains some famous writings of a somewhat later date. Included here are the *Dhammapada*, a well-known anthology of Buddhist wisdom, and the verses of the *Jātaka*, 547 popular stories about Gautama Buddha's previous lives. In the first two chapters of this volume, we have already presented an introduction to the life and teachings of the Buddha based on the older parts of the *Sūtra Piṭaka*. Here we introduce the *Vinaya* and *Abhidharma Piṭakas*.

The Vinaya Piṭaka

The *Vinaya*, which is divided into two sections, presents the Buddha's teachings on personal morality and social comportment, the precepts of the monastic orders (both men's and women's), institutional rules for the governance of the Saṅgha, and the consequences for breaking the precepts of the orders. Taking up the precepts of the *Vinaya* is done in two stages. From the age of eight, a child can take a lower, or novice, ordination. These persons undertake the Ten Precepts and are placed under the care of senior monastics, who become their mentors in the monastic life. The relationship between mentor and student should be, according to the *Vinaya*, like that of father to son or mother to daughter. The following is the typical formula for novice ordination. It includes the Three Refuges repeated three times and the Ten Precepts:

> Praise to the Blessed One, the *arhat*, the completely awakened One. I take refuge in the Buddha. I take refuge in the Dharma. I take refuge in the Saṅgha. . . . I take up the precept to refrain from taking life. I take up the precept to refrain from taking what is not given [stealing]. I take up the precept to refrain from sexual intercourse. I take up the precept to refrain from lying. I take up the precept to refrain from intoxicating drinks, which result in heedlessness. I take up the precept to refrain from eating at the wrong time [i.e., after noon]. I take up the precept to refrain from attending events where there is dancing, singing, music, or shows. I take up the precept to refrain from wearing garlands, perfumes, ointments, ornaments, or cosmetics. I take up the precept to refrain from using high or broad beds. I take up the precept to refrain from accepting gold or silver [i.e., money]. (*Khuddaka Patha*, 1, 2)

At the age of twenty, a person can take full ordination and become a monk, *bhikṣu* (Pali: *bhikkhu*), or a nun, *bhikṣunī* (Pali: *bhikkhunī*), literally, "almsman," or "almswoman." If one enters the Saṅgha as an adult, he or she must begin monastic life as a novice for a short time prior to full ordination. With this full ordination, the monastic takes on full responsibility for following what is perhaps the most important part of the *Vinaya*, namely, the *Prātimokṣa* (Pali: *Pāṭimokkha*), or "Code of Discipline." As a development of the Ten Precepts, these rules promote an ordered and peaceful way of life that is conducive to the attainment of Awakening and Nirvana and inspires confidence among the laity. In the Pali canon, there are 227 rules for men, 311 for women.

The *Prātimokṣa* is supposed to be chanted twice a month at a ceremony attended by every monastic living in community. If a monastic has broken a rule, he or she is to confess to the assembly. If not, one is to maintain silence as a sign of purity. If one is ill and cannot attend the ceremony, he or she is to send notice of his or her purity. The prelude to the chanting is as follows:

> Now, I will recite the *Prātimokṣa*. Everyone should listen and pay close attention. If anyone has broken one of these rules, he should disclose it. Those who have not broken any of these rules should remain silent. . . . A monk who remembers breaking one of the rules but does not disclose it . . . is guilty of deliberately lying. Deliberate lying, Venerable Ones, has been declared by [the Buddha] to be an impediment to progressing on the path. Therefore, a monk who remembers breaking a rule and desires purification, should disclose it; for disclosing it will be beneficial to him. (*Mahāvagga*, II, 3, 1–3)

The actual rules themselves are arranged into categories according to the degree of seriousness. The first four are the most serious rules, which if broken, lead to expulsion from the Saṅgha: intentional sexual intercourse, theft of something of value, murder of a human being, and false claims to the laity concerning one's attainments. Next are thirteen rules that require the

Saṅgha to meet formally to deal with any infractions and to proscribe probation. These rules deal with sexual misconduct other than intercourse, the place and size of one's dwelling, causing or supporting a schism, and having a bad influence on the laity. Then, there are two more rules having to do with proper contact with women. The next thirty rules, which deal with such things as handling money (something that is not permitted) or obtaining articles of value, require confession and possible forfeiture. These are followed by ninety-two rules that only require confession if broken. They deal with issues like lying, verbal abuse, harming living beings, destroying plant life, and drinking liquor. Next are seventy-five rules of deportment that are followed by novices as well as fully ordained monastics. These rules help the members of the Saṅgha cultivate a graceful and dignified presence through the way they walk, beg alms, eat, and so on. Finally, the last few rules outline procedures for resolving disputes.

The Abhidharma Piṭaka

While the precepts given in the *Vinaya Piṭaka* formed the discipline of the Saṅgha, the *Abhidharma Piṭaka* evolved in ways that helped to form the philosophy of the Saṅgha. These more philosophical texts were likely beginning to be composed by the fourth century B.C.E. In the fully developed Pali canon, the *Abhidharma Piṭaka* consists of seven texts. Some of the texts, such as *The Enumeration of* Dharmas (*Dhammasaṅgaṇi*), examine the "factors" (*dharmas*: Pali: *dhammas*) that constitute the physical world and mental experience, and the various mental and physical processes that are produced by them. The many factors of existence analyzed in these texts are refinements of such concepts as the Five Aggregates that were taught by the Buddha. Other texts discuss the process of perception, the working of the mind, the psychology of spiritual attainment, and the types of causal relationships entailed in dependent arising.

We introduce some of these *Abhidharma* ideas later in this chapter and in Chapter 5, where we also present various types of Buddhist philosophy in India. But here, it may be instructive to quote some passages from at least one text, namely, *The Enumeration of* Dharmas. These passages show how a "good thought" can, given dependent arising, generate a series of wholesome mental states (*dharmas*). Here, we will just mention a series of ten of those states that result in Right Concentration, the eighth step in the Eightfold Path. First, the text lists the ten mental states, and then defines each one:

When a good thought concerning the sense-desire realm has arisen, accompanied by gladness and knowledge, and has as its object a visible form, or a sound, smell, touch, mental state, or whatever [the object of the thought] might be, then there is [1] contact, [2] sensation, [3] perception, [4] volition, [5] thought, [6] application of thought, [7] sustained thought, [8] zest, [9] ease, and [10] self-collectedness.

Born of [1] contact is . . . [2] pleasurable and easeful sensation, pleasurable and easeful feeling. . . . Also born of contact is [3] perceiving with an appropriate element of representative cognition. . . . The [4] volition that is [then] born is purposeful. . . . The [5] thought on that occasion forms ideas in the mind and heart which are clear.

On that occasion, there is [6] an application, fixing, focusing of the mind. . . . [7] Sustained thought is the process, the sustained procedure, the progress and access [of the mind] which on this occasion is the [continuous] adjusting and focusing of thought.

[8] Zest on this occasion is joy, rejoicing at, rejoicing over, mirth and merriment, felicity, exultation, and the transport of the mind. . . . [9] Ease is the mental pleasure, the mental ease, which on this occasion is a pleasant and easeful experience.

[10] Self-collectedness then is the stability, solidity, absorbed steadfastness of thought. Here, there is an absence of distraction, balance, unperturbed mental processes, quiet, the faculty and power of concentration, of Right Concentration. (*Dhammasaṅgaṇi*, 1–11)

The text goes on to show how other wholesome states of mind arise from Right Concentration in this process of consciousness. Those wholesome states include faith, mindfulness, insight, right views, and the absence of the Three Root Evils, namely, hate, greed, and delusion. Here we see one of the central teachings of the *Abhidharma*, namely, that the cultivation of moral thoughts lays the foundation for Right Concentration, which in turn furthers one's advancement on the path to Awakening and Nirvana.

THE SECOND AND THIRD COUNCILS

About one hundred years after the Buddha's death, a Second Council was held at Vaiśālī. The council was called because of a disagreement over certain rules in the *Vinaya*. However, problems did not end with this "second recitation" of the tradition. Scholars debate about what the points of dispute were that continued after the Second Council. Most recent scholarship suggests that there was continuing disagreement concerning the *Vinaya* rules. Doctrinal issues, many scholars claim, were not as important at that time, and differences in opinion about them would most likely not have led to schism. In any case, eventually there was a formal division in the Saṅgha. On one hand were the *sthaviras* (Pali: *theras*), or "elders"; on the other hand was the *mahāsaṅghika*, or "great community." The school of the elders is referred to as *Sthaviravāda* (Pali: *Theravāda*), meaning the "Way of the Elders." In the next chapter we look at the Mahāsaṅghika School. In this chapter we focus on the Way of the Elders and its subsect of the same name that would eventually become the primary form of Buddhism in Sri Lanka and Southeast Asia.

As the *Abhidharma Piṭaka* was taking shape during the centuries after the Second Council, the Way of the Elders was also producing different viewpoints about the Dharma. These differences did become important and resulted in a second group splitting off from the Sthaviravādins. This group was called the Pudgalavāda ("Personalist School"). They believed that associated with the Five Aggregates, but not separate from them or identified with them, is an ongoing form of "personhood" (*pudgala*). They felt that the impersonal analysis of the self, in terms of the many *dharmas*, could not account for the full experience of personhood, the unique identity of oneself as a person. On the other hand, the Sthaviravādins believed that by positing something called a "person," the Pudgalavādins were compromising the Buddha's teaching about no-self (*anātman*).

Another group to leave the Sthaviravādin fold was the Sarvāstivāda ("All-Exists School"). In particular the two factions had conflicting ways of understanding the nature of the *dharmas*, the factors of existence discussed in the *Abhidharma Piṭaka*. On the one hand in this debate was the Sthaviravādin sect, the Vibhajyavādin ("Distinctionist School"), and on the other hand was the Sarvāstivādins. The Sarvāstivādins claimed that the factors of existence not only exist in the present, but also in the future and the past. They exist in "all" times: past, present, and future. The Vibhajyavādins claimed that the factors of existence only arise and exist in the present, distinct from the past and future. We examine these views in more detail in Chapter 5. But for now it is important to note that eventually many of the Sarvāstivādins moved to the west and north of India. There, they founded centers that influenced Buddhist thought and practice in India and Central Asia for centuries to come.

The early tradition records that at about 250 B.C.E., King Aśoka called for a Third Council to be held at Pāṭaliputra to resolve another debate that had arisen among the Sthaviravādins. Scholars today are trying to discern what exactly was involved in this debate. Early scholarship taught that the differences had to do with the breaking away of the Sarvāstivādins. But most scholars today believe the debate had to do with another disagreement about the *Vinaya*. In any case, the council seems to have decided in favor of the Vibhajyavāda position within the Sthaviravāda fold.

With this support, backed by King Aśoka, the Vibhajyavādins carried on the Way of the Elders in the Ganges Valley area. At the time of the Third Council, one of its sects was becoming established in Sri Lanka. This sect kept the Pali name for "Way of the Elders," namely, *Theravāda*. Theravāda became the main religion of Sri Lanka and later spread throughout Southeast Asia. It still flourishes there today. Theravāda has preserved the Way of the Elders over the centuries and has remained one of the major branches of Buddhism in the world. In introducing Theravāda, we need to begin with the person who was most responsible for its emergence onto the world scene, King Aśoka.

KING AŚOKA

In 268 B.C.E., King Aśoka inherited the Magadhan empire, which covered most of the Indian subcontinent, except for the far south. Some years later, it is said that he converted to Buddhism, but was only a nominal follower.

Map 1. Buddhism in India and Sri Lanka: c. third century B.C.E.–first century C.E.

Then eight years into his reign, after the bloody conquest of Kaliṅga in the northeast of India, King Aśoka began to appreciate the true implications of the Buddhist religion. The carnage and destruction of Kaliṅga filled him with remorse, and he began to take the Dharma of the Buddha seriously. King Aśoka recorded his experience in the following edict:

> When [King Aśoka] had been consecrated eight years, Kaliṅga was conquered with 150,000 people deported, 100,000 killed, and many times that number dead. But after that conquest of Kaliṅga, [King Aśoka] began to follow the Dharma, to love the Dharma, and to teach the Dharma. Now, the king feels sorrow over the conquest of Kaliṅga. . . . [He] is depressed even more because among the inhabitants were Brahmins, ascetics, adherents of other sects, and lay people, all of whom were obedient to elders, parents and teachers, who treated [others] . . . with respect, and were firm in their faith. All of these persons were injured, or killed, or separated from loved ones. . . . The fact that all people share in this suffering is grievous to [King Aśoka]. . . . Indeed, [he] desires safety, self-control, calmness of mind, and gentleness for all beings. For, [King Aśoka] considers Dharma-conquest to be the greatest form of conquest. This kind of conquest he has won here [in India] and in all the borderlands up to 600 leagues away. . . . I had this inscription about the Dharma engraved so that all my sons and grandsons may not seek to gain new [military] conquests . . . that they may consider the only true conquest to be the conquest of the Dharma, which is of value both in this world and the next; and that their only pleasure may be in the Dharma. (*The Thirteenth Rock Edict*)

We can see from these words that based on his study of the Buddha's teachings, King Aśoka began to change his personal life and the way he governed the empire. Instead of conquering and ruling by physical force, he began to "conquer" and "rule" by the force of the Dharma. "Dharma-conquest" meant not only preaching Dharma in India, but also sending proclaimers of the Dharma to other kingdoms. Some of King Aśoka's envoys were said to have been sent to the rulers of Syria, Egypt, and Macedonia to the west and Sri Lanka and Southeast Asia to the south. Tradition has it that around 250 B.C.E., he sent his own daughter and son—Saṅghamittā and Mahinda—to Sri Lanka. They went as nun and monk and succeeded in converting the whole country to Buddhism.

"Dharma-rule," for King Aśoka, meant to govern in a way that protected and cared for his subjects and also elevated them morally and spiritually according the Dharma. In fact, he believed that by providing for the physical needs of his subjects, he was laying a foundation for them to follow the moral and spiritual life taught by the Buddha. King Aśoka became famous for his public works, which included providing wells and rest houses for travelers, hospitals for people and animals, care for orphans and the elderly, schools for children, and equal justice for all people. The supreme moral value he preached was *ahiṁsā*, or nonviolence, which he taught by example. He replaced his hunting trips with pilgrimages to Buddhist sites, made his large royal household vegetarian, banned animal sacrifices, and protected

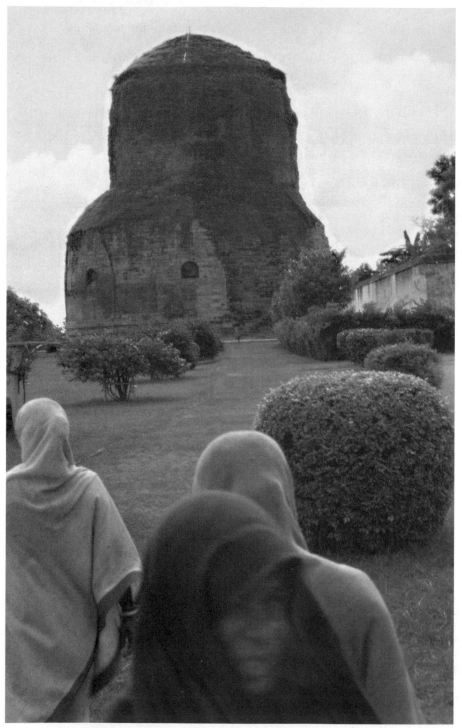

Figure 3.1. *Stūpa* commemorating the Dharma; c. 500 C.E., Sārnāth, India.

nonfood animals. Other values like generosity, mercy, truthfulness, respect for elders and teachers, and chastity were all virtues of the *Vinaya* that he tried to live himself and taught to his subjects.

In his support of Buddhism, King Aśoka convened the Third Council to restore harmony to the Saṅgha. He is said by later legends to have opened the original ten *stūpas,* and then to have distributed the relics of the Buddha to 84,000 new *stūpas* throughout India. In this way, he may have helped popularize devotion to the Buddha in *stūpa* rituals. Also, by using the ideology of Buddhism to support a national sense of righteousness, King Aśoka contributed to the unity of the empire as well as the well-being of his subjects. King Aśoka had his edicts relating to the Dharma, like the one just quoted, engraved on rocks and monolithic pillars around his kingdom.

These activities on behalf of Buddhism did not mean that King Aśoka failed to support other religions. In fact, he tended to the needs of Jain, Brahmin, and Ājīvaka communities in his empire. He believed that all religions contribute to the righteousness of the people and should be respected in the spirit of religious toleration. His views were expressed in the following rock edict:

> [King Aśoka] honors members of all religious sects, whether ascetics or lay, by gifts and honors. But more important than gifts and honors is his support of the essential message of all sects. The essential message varies from sect to sect . . . [so] one should keep in check praising one's own sect and criticizing another's sect. . . . By doing so, one strengthens one's own sect and helps others too. By doing otherwise, one harms one's own sect, and does a disservice to the others. Whoever honors his own sect and disparages another's, whether from blind loyalty or intending to show his sect in a more favorable light, does the greatest harm to his own sect. Concord is best, where each person listens to and respects the teachings of others. . . . [T]he result is the progress of one's own sect, and the illumination of the Dharma. (*The Twelfth Rock Edict*)

THERAVĀDA'S PATH OF PURIFICATION

Theravāda, or the Way of the Elders that King Aśoka is said to have introduced into Sri Lanka and Southeast Asia, is based on the original teachings of the Buddha presented in the Pali texts and discussed in the previous chapter. There, we saw that Buddhist monastic experience involves an inner purification of the whole person through moral discipline, the practice of meditation, and the cultivation of wisdom. To appreciate Theravāda's practice of this threefold purification, this Way of the Elders that leads to Awakening and Nirvana, we need to see what it is that they feel requires purification. In other words, we need to understand the Theravāda view of the human condition.

In the previous chapter, we saw that the Buddha taught the Three Characteristics of existence—impermanence, dissatisfactoriness, and the lack of any permanent self. Further, for the Buddha, life is a continuous process of dependent arising in which each aspect of the world and conventional selfhood (the Five Aggregates) arises, develops, and ceases interdependently. We saw an example of this view in the Buddha's teaching about the twelve links of conditionality. We have also seen in this chapter that the *Abhidharma Piṭaka* presents a more detailed analysis of the processes of life. Based on these ideas, Theravāda teaches that human existence is constituted by numerous, dependently arisen, and constantly changing physical and mental factors (*dharmas*).

For Theravāda, this dynamic view of the human person as constituted by changing, interrelated mental and physical factors is not just an abstract theory. In Theravāda experience, the practices of mindfulness and meditation give one an awareness into the changing processes of life and into the various factors that constitute the mental-physical continuum. What one discovers thereby, Theravāda claims, is that these physical and mental factors ordinarily arise and pass away in a manner that is experienced as *duḥkha*, dissatisfactory. Every person's life is in some way dissatisfactory and needs a healing purification of those factors that are causing this condition of life. For Theravāda, the Way of the Elders is a Path of Purification (*visuddhimagga*) that is not only healing, but ultimately leads to Awakening and Nirvana.

The greatest systematizer of the Way of the Elders, the fifth-century C.E. monk named Buddhaghosa, composed the classic Theravāda text entitled *The Path of Purification (Visuddhimagga)*. This book has helped define the Way of the Elders over the centuries in Theravāda countries. At the beginning of that text, Buddhaghosa says, "Purity should be understood as Nirvana, which is devoid of all stains, is utterly pure. The Path of Purification is the path to this purity [of Nirvana]" (*Visuddhimagga*, I, 5). Buddhaghosa goes on to situate each of the three divisions of the Eightfold Path in the following order. First is "morality" (*śīla*), which includes Right Speech, Right Action, and Right Livelihood. Second is "concentration" (*samādhi*), which includes Right Mindfulness, Right Effort, and Right Concentration. Finally is "wisdom" (*prajñā*; Pali: *paññā*), which includes Right Understanding and Right Thought. The following is Buddhaghosa's rational for this ordering:

> [One] should, having become well established in morality, develop the serenity and insight that are described as concentration and wisdom. This is how the Blessed One teaches the Path of Purification under the headings of morality, concentration and wisdom. . . . Here the training of higher virtue is shown by morality; the training of higher consciousness by concentration; and the training of higher understanding by wisdom. The system's goodness in the beginning is shown by morality. . . . Its goodness in the middle is shown by concentration. . . . Its goodness in the end is shown by wisdom. (*Visuddhimagga*, I, 8, 10)

Let us look at each of these three aspects this Path of Purification as discussed by Buddhaghosa one at a time in order to introduce the moral, meditative, and wisdom dimensions of the Way of the Elders, of the Theravāda Buddhist experience.

Morality

Theravāda Buddhism provides its monastics and laity with high ethical standards. Today, scholars discuss the ways in which these standards for personal moral behavior may have informed social ethics in Theravāda countries. However, here we are not so interested in examining standards for moral and social behavior. Rather, we want to look at how morality plays a part in a purification of consciousness that, in turn, leads to the purity of Nirvana. In this sense, morality is part of the process of mental culture. It is primarily concerned with the inner inclinations, volitions, dispositions, and attitudes that motivate people to perform good or bad actions. The actions that define moral living are the result of ethical choices that are influenced by these motivating dispositions and attitudes. So moral purification, Theravāda teaches, is not just a matter of changing the way one behaves; one must also purify the interior attitudes that motivate one's actions. Therefore, the core of Theravāda morality is, "Refrain from doing evil deeds, perfect good deeds, and purify the mind; that is the teaching of the Buddha" (*Dhammapada*, 183). It is precisely this purifying of the mind that brings the inner freedom and wholesomeness needed truly to refrain from evil and perfect goodness.

Buddhaghosa emphasizes the importance of this inner moral purification in his ranking of the four ways in which morality is understood in Theravāda:

> [1] Morality as a matter of volition has to do with the kind of volition present in the one who . . . fulfills the practice of the precepts. . . . [2] Morality as a condition of consciousness is the mental states of non-greed, non-hate, and non-delusion. . . . [3] Morality as restraint should be understood as restraining oneself in five ways: restraint by the precepts, restraint by mindfulness, restraint by knowledge, restraint patience, and restraint by energy. . . . [4] Morality as non-transgression is the non-transgression, by body or speech, of the precepts that have been taken. (*Visuddhimagga*, I, 17, 18)

Buddhaghosa has ranked these four meanings of morality in a descending order of importance. At a minimum, morality means to follow the precepts with one's body and speech. More important is to develop an inner moral restraint from doing evil by observing the precepts, by mindfulness and knowledge, and by patience and energetic effort. Even more important is to remove the Three Root Evils of greed, hatred, and delusion from one's consciousness and to replace them with the virtues that are their opposites. Finally, most important is the ultimate moral purification of one's will that is entangled in desires that lead to *duḥkha*. As Buddhaghosa says, "a network of craving . . . arises again and again, up and down among the states of consciousness. . . . [Thus] this order of living beings is entangled in a network of craving, intertwined, interlaced by it" (*Visuddhimagga*, I, 2). Morality, in its deepest sense in Theravāda, seeks "to disentangle this tangle" by purifying the will (*cetanā*) that determines what one desires in life. With a pure will, one's desire will not be for evil, but for the purity and goodness of Nirvana.

Moral culture at all of these four levels progresses gradually and in ordered stages through Theravāda practice. On the level of moral behavior, lay Buddhists follow at least the Five Precepts taught by the Buddha; the monastic Buddhists add the precepts of the *Prātimokṣa*. As these moral precepts are lived in the context of mental culture, they become internalized. That is, since they are rules that define what one is not supposed to do, as they are lived with "mindfulness and knowledge, patience and energy," they gradually generate inner moral "restraints," which is the second meaning of morality according to Buddhaghosa.

In the last chapter, we saw that the precepts not only define what one should not do, but also define the virtuous ways one should live. So, as the precepts are internalized as inner restraints, one is also developing moral virtues, or wholesome states of consciousness. Here we are at Buddhaghosa's third level of morality, where one's consciousness is purified of unwholesome states of mind, like the Three Root Evils, and wholesome states are cultivated. In the words of Buddhaghosa, "[Morality] is an upholding, meaning a basis that serves as a foundation for profitable states of mind. . . . The abandoning of an [unprofitable state] upholds a profitable state in the sense of providing a foundation for it" (*Visuddhimagga*, I, 19). An example of this purification of consciousness by morality is when the precept of "not killing" is internalized as a spiritual attitude of compassion for all living beings.

We can now see that in Theravāda, the gradual purification of moral consciousness has two sides to it. On the one hand, the Buddhist begins to let go of unwholesome attitudes or dispositions. On the other hand, he or she begins to cultivate wholesome attitudes or dispositions. What is happening in this transformation of moral consciousness affects one's will, one's power of volition. At this fourth and deepest level of morality, one more and more wills the goodness that these wholesome states of consciousness embody. One therefore not only chooses good thoughts, deeds, and words with a purer mind and heart, but also wills to pursue more fully the ultimate goodness of Nirvana.

In speaking about volition or the will, we should make it clear that moral purification is ultimately not achieved by just a willful suppression of negative desires and unhealthy states of mind. Rather, in the practice of morality there is a gradual pacification of these unwholesome states through a process of self-understanding and releasement. For example, as one is able to gain insight into why it is that a certain negative desire arises in particular situations—and one is able to see the unfortunate effects that acting on it has on oneself and others—then one finds within oneself a stronger volition not to be controlled by this desire. Also, as one cultivates a virtue that is the opposite of the negative desire—and sees its effect on oneself and others in those same situations—then one develops a stronger volition to live in this more wholesome way. With this strengthened positive volition, there is a pacification of the power of the desire over one's will. That is, gradually with clearer insight, one's will is no longer controlled or "tangled" by the desire, but is released from its grip. One freely wills to live in a wholesome way that benefits oneself and others. On the other hand, this does not

---

BOX 3.1

A MESSAGE FOR EVERYONE

I noticed a young man making his way toward me through the crowd at a Sunday night Meet-Your-Neighbors party at a ski condominium a few years ago.

"My parents just met you," he said, nodding in the direction of a couple I'd talked with earlier, "and they said you were a Buddhist teacher. I'm studying Buddhism in my World Religions class. What kind of Buddhist are you?"

"I teach at Spirit Rock Meditation Center," I replied. "The program there is based on mindfulness and *metta*, loving kindness, the principal meditation practices described by the Buddha in the Pali Canon."

"Oh, I see," he said, "that's Theravāda Buddhism, isn't it?"

"Yes it is," I replied.

"Is it true," he asked, "that those were the selfish Buddhists who were only interested in their own enlightenment and not in the liberation of all beings?"

I hope I did not wince at what I recognized as a not uncommon survey textbook, shorthand differentiation of Hīnayāna and Mahāyāna traditions. It is true that the Buddha was a monk and—in keeping with the culture of his time, which considered the renunciate path as ideal for spiritual seekers—he did encourage people to "go forth into homelessness" as a support to their practice. It is also true that he taught laypeople, ordinary householders as well as kings. His message of liberation for "all beings" is that craving is the cause of suffering, that the end of suffering is possible, that peace is possible in this very life, that insight leads to wisdom, which manifests as compassion on behalf of all beings. This message that Theravāda proclaims has remained central to Buddhism for the 2500 years of its evolution through different cultures and different times.

SYLVIA BOORSTEIN

Spirit Rock Meditation Center
Marin County, California

---

mean that the Theravādin does not have to make difficult moral choices, and even painful sacrifices. As Buddhaghosa said, restraint is an important part of morality. While pacification develops through gradual growth in insight, there is always need for renunciation.

The purity of the wholesome, disentangled moral will and consciousness then becomes a basis for the next two aspects of the Way of the Elders, namely, the practice of concentration and the attainment of wisdom. In this way, morality's contribution to the Path of Purification produces not only growth in virtue and freedom of the will, but also a necessary foundation for spiritual practice. In this regard, Buddhaghosa says,

> Once one's morality is perfected, one's mind then seeks nothing else than the perfection of Nirvana, the state of utter peace. Such is the blessed fruit of morality. . . . So, let the wise person know it well, this root of all the branches of perfection. (*Visuddhimagga*, I, 159)

Since the status of Nirvana includes perfected morality, the practice of morality in Theravāda generates a deep seeking for Nirvana, which can only be
found by further progress in the Path of Purification. With this questing
spirit, one is more inspired to practice concentration and attain wisdom.

Concentration

Buddhaghosa begins his comments on this second aspect of the Path of Purification by saying,

> Concentration is . . . a profitable single-pointedness of the mind. . . . It is con-
> centration in the sense that it entails the act of concentrating the mind . . . the
> centering of consciousness and the factors of consciousness evenly and rightly
> on a single object. . . . It is the state, in virtue of which, consciousness and its
> many factors remain evenly and rightly on a single object undistracted and
> unscattered. (*Visuddhimagga*, III, 2, 3)

Buddhaghosa then goes on to discuss the traditional forty objects on which
one can concentrate in meditation. First are the ten *kṛtsnas* (Pali: *kasiṇas*), or
objects and concepts used to calm and focus the mind in meditation. These
include earth, water, air, and fire, as well as forms of color, light, and a limited space. Second are the ten types of bodily decay used in meditation in
order to develop detachment to material existence. Third are the ten recol-
lections of positive qualities associated with the spiritual life, namely, the
qualities of the Buddha, Dharma, and Saṅgha; morality and generosity; faithfulness and peace; and mindfulness of the body, death, and breathing. Fourth
are the Four Divine Abodes that also need to be cultivated in meditation.
Fifth are the states to be attained in the Four Formless Meditations. And finally, there are certain nutriments and elements that can also be used in
meditation practice.

   One example of these concentrating meditations is mindfulness of body
and breathing. Actually, the teaching on mindfulness that is most revered
by Theravāda Buddhism down to today is contained in an early Buddhist
text, *The Establishment of Mindfulness* (*Satipaṭṭhāna Sutta*), which is said to be
taught by the Buddha. This text describes not only mindfulness of body and
breathing but also other forms of mindfulness that contribute to concentration, Awakening, and Nirvana. The following are passages from that text
concerning mindfulness in the pursuit of purification:

> There is, O monks, this particular way for purifying beings, for overcoming
> sorrow and distress, for the extinguishing of pain and sadness . . . for the at-
> tainment of Nirvana: The Four Foundations of Mindfulness. What are these
> four? Contemplating the body as body . . . sensations as sensations . . . the
> mind as the mind . . . and mental objects as mental objects. . . .
>   How, O monks, does one contemplate the body as body? Having gone into
> the forest, or to the foot of a tree, or to a lonely place, a monk sits down cross-
> legged, holding erect his body and establishes himself in mindfulness. Mind-

fully he breaths in, and mindfully he breaths out. Breathing in a long breath, he knows that it is a long breath; and breathing out a long breath, he knows it is a long breath. . . . Breathing in a short breath, he knows it is a short breath; and breathing out a short breath, he knows it is a short breath. . . . He trains himself by thinking, "I will breathe in, being conscious of my whole body. . . . I will breathe out, being conscious of my whole body. . . . I will breathe in, calming my whole body. . . . I will breathe out, calming my whole body."

And how is it, O monks, that one abides contemplating sensations as sensations [or feelings as feelings]? When a monk experiences a pleasant sensation [or feeling], he knows that it is pleasant. Then, experiencing an unpleasant sensation, he knows that it is unpleasant. . . . He abides contemplating the arising of sensory [or emotional] states, and their passing away. . . . In this mindfulness, he has only a bare awareness of the sensations.

And how is it, O monks, that one abides contemplating the mind as mind? When a monk has a greedy mind, he knows it is greedy; when it is free from greed, he knows it to be so. When a monk has a hating mind, he knows it is hating; when it is free from hatred, he knows it to be so. When a monk has a deluded mind, he knows it is deluded; when it is free from delusion, he knows it to be so. . . . He abides contemplating the arising of mental phenomena, and their passing away. . . . In this mindfulness, he has only a bare awareness that there is mind. (*Dīgha-nikāya*, II, 290–292, 298–300)

After presenting the mind with its Three Root Evils of greed, hate, and delusion, the text goes on to discuss the arising and passing away of other mental phenomena, both positive and negative, including forms of craving, the experience of the Five Aggregates, various mental factors leading to Awakening, and the Four Noble Truths. The point is clearly made that mindfulness concentrates the mind in a "bare awareness" of the dependent arising of physical, emotional, sensory, and other mental states, as well as the ideas and views one entertains. One gains, thereby, a clearer understanding of oneself and the world as they really are (*yathābhūtam*). Therefore, through mindfulness practice, one can begin to uncover what is often hidden from one's awareness: the dispositions and attitudes that affect moral and spiritual life. This mindful concentration can contribute to purifying one's mind and body of discerned unwholesome patterns of thought and action. Finally, it is important to note that in this mindfulness practice, one is not trying to alter any of the negative states one uncovers, but just to observe them and to gain insight into their nature and effect on one's life. While there are other techniques to alter one's mental-emotional life, the Four Divine Abodes for example, the assumption behind mindfulness is that awareness naturally produces alteration.

A second example of the forty objects of concentration are the Four Divine Abodes—loving kindness, compassion, sympathetic joy, and equanimity. Loving kindness is an attitude of pure goodwill toward self and others that always seeks the welfare and happiness of all beings. In loving-kindness meditation, one learns to develop this attitude and to extend it to all living beings. Compassion, an attitude of pity or empathy for oneself and others who are suffering, contains the desire to free all beings from pain.

Again in compassion meditation, one develops and extends this attitude to all living beings. Sympathetic joy is an attitude of joyful affirmation of the dignity and value of oneself and others. Here too, in meditation, one learns to develop such joyful sympathy and extend it to all living beings. Finally, equanimity meditation breaks down barriers between oneself and others and generates an attitude of universal embracement of all beings. This type of meditation helps one share the same degree of loving kindness, compassion, and sympathetic joy with all persons, those who are lovable and those who are not, both friends and enemies.

As we saw when we discussed morality earlier, Theravāda teaches that the negative attitudes or dispositions of the human heart, which result in unwholesome thoughts, words, and actions, are gradually pacified with the cultivation of their opposites. Therefore, the development of the Four Divine Abodes is seen as an aid to overcoming such unwholesome states of mind as the Three Root Evils of greed, hatred, and delusion. Buddhaghosa described how loving-kindness meditation can overcome hatred:

> One should seat oneself comfortably on a well-prepared seat in a secluded place. Then one should contemplate the dangers of hate. . . . Thereupon, one should begin to develop loving kindness in order to rid the mind of hate. . . . First of all, loving kindness should be developed only toward oneself by repeatedly thinking, "May I be happy and free from suffering. May I keep free from enmity, affliction, and anxiety, and live happily." . . .
>
> But, does not this attitude conflict with the [teachings of the Buddha]? It does not, because in it one is referring to oneself as an example. . . . One should develop this attitude in this way, "I am happy. And just as I want to be happy and dread pain and death, so too do other beings." Then with one's happiness as an example of what others want, the desire for others' well-being and happiness will arise in oneself. This method was indicated when the Blessed One said, "I visited all parts of my mind, and found none dearer than myself. The self of every other person is likewise dear to them. Who loves oneself will never harm another." . . .
>
> So, one should first, as an example, pervade oneself with loving kindness. Next, in order to proceed easily, one should recollect the kindnesses . . . that inspire love . . . given by a teacher or equivalent . . . thereby developing loving kindness toward that person. . . . If a monk is not content with just that much loving kindness, and wants to break down more barriers, he should develop loving kindness toward a beloved friend . . . then toward neural person . . . then toward an enemy. If resentment arises when one applies loving kindness toward an enemy, because one remembers wrongs done by that person, one should get rid of that resentment in the following way. Enter repeatedly into the loving kindness for one of the first mentioned persons, and then each time direct that loving kindness toward the enemy. (*Visuddhimagga*, IX, 1–3, 8–12, 14)

After giving more ways of overcoming resentment and hatred, Buddhaghosa says that if one can enter a certain level of meditative concentration, then one should practice the following kind of loving-kindness meditation as taught by the Buddha in *Dīgha-nikāya*, I (250):

> Now it is by means of . . . meditation that one "dwells focused on one direction [of the compass] pervading it with loving kindness from one's heart. Likewise, one should do the same in the second direction, the third direction, above, below, and all around. Everywhere and equally one dwells pervading the entire world with loving kindness from the heart, abundant, exalted, measureless, free from enmity, and free from all afflictions." (*Visuddhimagga*, IX, 44)

Besides mindfulness and the Four Divine Abodes, concentration on the Path of Purification also includes the Four Meditations (*dhyānas*; Pali: *jhānas*), which the Buddha himself used in attaining his Awakening. The first of these four calming meditations achieves an inner peacefulness, free of bother by passions and evil states of mind, while one continues to think discursively, to be joyful, and to feel deep happiness. The second brings about the cessation of discursive thought, while the third brings joyfulness to an end, leaving only happiness or a sense of well-being. In the fourth of these meditations, even happiness is transcended, thus bringing its opposite (unhappiness) also to an end. In this deep state of meditative peace, there is only pure and clear equanimity of mind.

Since this concentrated state of mind is one of equanimity, in this meditation one can understand all things with equal clarity and penetrating insight. Thereby, one is better able to understand the true nature of all life. This is what the Buddha did at the time of his Awakening. The lesson we learn from the fact that the Buddha did not just remain in the quiet peace of this fourth meditation is that such inner absorption is not the final goal of the Theravāda Buddhist quest. The real goal is awakening to the full Truth and the attainment thereby of Nirvana. Therefore, Theravāda continues to use these Four Meditations in order to calm and integrate the mind, pacify unruly mental-emotional states, and purify one's awareness with luminous equanimity so that one can see reality more clearly.

Among the forty objects for meditation are also the objects of the Four Formless Meditations. The objects of these "higher" meditations are (1) boundless space, (2) boundless consciousness, (3) nothingness, and (4) neither perception nor nonperception. In the first of these Formless Meditations, according to Buddhaghosa, one moves from an awareness of a spatial object to spatiality as such. In the second, one lets go of any awareness of spatiality and gives attention to consciousness as such. In the third, one lets go of any awareness of spatiality or consciousness, so that one is aware of nothing at all. Buddhaghosa explains this third Formless Meditation with the following metaphor: "Suppose a person sees a community of monks gathered together in a meeting hall. . . . Then at the conclusion of their business, they all depart. The man then returns and stands in the doorway seeing the room as empty" (*Visuddhimagga*, X, 35). In the same way, Buddhaghosa says, one finds in the third Formless Meditation that boundless consciousness and space have simply "disappeared."

In the fourth Formless Meditation, there is no perception in the ordinary sense, but only a very subtle perception. Buddhaghosa explains:

> By "neither perception" is meant that perception is not capable of performing its [ordinary] function of perceiving. By "nor nonperception" is meant that perception is still present, but in a very subtle form, as a kind of residual form." (*Visuddhimagga*, X, 52)

Buddhaghosa says that this very subtle awareness includes not only perception, but also all the other states of mind. In other words, this is the highest meditative state of subtle, pure, clear, peaceful, one-pointedness awareness. The value of this meditative experience is that its refined purity, clarity, and subtle peacefulness are a "taste" of the "flavor" of Nirvana.

However, this formless meditative taste is not the same as Nirvana itself because the latter is a permanent condition enjoyed in the midst of the world, not just in a meditative state. Also, Nirvana includes not only peacefulness and purity, but also compassion, joy, and loving kindness in relationship to all living beings. On the other hand, this refined meditative state encourages one to continue on the Path of Purification because its subtle awareness gives one an appreciation for the beauty, freedom, and goodness of Nirvana. The Buddha also pointed out that these Four Formless Meditations are impermanent, just like anything else in life. Therefore, those who practice them can gain a better appreciation of the truth of impermanence and the need for nonattachment even to spiritual attainments.

Associated with these higher mediation practices are five types of supernormal abilities (*siddhi*; Pali: *iddhi*) that can occur in the lives of advanced practitioners. First are certain supernormal powers such as being invisible, walking through solid objects or on water, traveling through the air, and so on. Second is an ability, called "divine ears," by which one can hear both human and divine beings who are far away. Third is the ability to know what is in the hearts and minds of other persons. Fourth is the ability to recall one's past lives. Fifth is an ability, called "divine eyes," by which one can see the passing away and rebirth of beings due to their karma. These abilities are not understood as gifts bestowed by a divine being, but as potentials that all persons could realize if their minds were developed adequately through meditation. Thus these abilities are *not* signs of holiness and are *not* essential to the attainment of Nirvana.

In fact, while these powers can be used to help others, they can also be hindrances to one's liberation if one becomes attached to them or prides oneself on possessing them. In this regard, we should remember that one of the reasons for expulsion of a monastic from the Saṅgha is boasting about spiritual attainments. This warning about supernatural powers reinforces the Theravāda view that the primary goal of the meditative experience in Buddhism is the fostering of a pure moral consciousness on the one hand, and

---
BOX 3.2

INNER PEACE, OUTER HARMONY

I was born into a Buddhist family in a Buddhist country and have spent about sixty years of my life as an ordained monk. Theravāda Buddhist culture is, therefore, deeply ingrained in my being. But I have lived now thirty-three years in the West in countries where Buddhism is either completely unknown or at best a minority faith practiced by a few. Part of my work has been to spread knowledge of the teachings to a wider audience. This has given me the opportunity to assess what it is about Buddhism, and especially about Theravāda Buddhism, which appeals to people who have not been born and brought up with it.

I see one of the key features of the Theravāda tradition as being relatively free of complicated rites and rituals. Its approach is refreshingly simple and straightforward. For laypeople, there are Five Precepts, accepted voluntarily and to be followed in daily life. This establishes a moral platform which gives spiritual meaning to everything Buddhists do and say. Meditation then helps them to develop their characters and personalities and leads them toward contentment and joy.

It is only too easy to allow ourselves to cultivate a frenzied state of mind. This destroys any possibility of being either peaceful or happy and gives rise to further *duḥkha*. Meditation can help anyone who wants to live a life free from tension, anxiety, and the other forms of contemporary misery. It enables us to experience a life of peace and joy, filled with the kind of understanding which will allow us to observe events as they happen without reacting to them in a way which generates negative thoughts and emotional turmoil.

Meditation ultimately purifies the heart of all its negative emotions, and it encourages a state of mind in the individual in which selfishness is transformed into generosity, hatred into love, cruelty into compassion, and so on. It also deepens the individual's ability to develop warm and meaningful relationships, thereby leading to personal contentment and happiness.

Out of the development of such inner peace and outer harmony, the individual begins to see human existence as it really is. He or she sees not only how suffering is created in the mind of the sufferer but also how that suffering can be overcome and transformed. For Buddhism, wisdom includes the many insights that meditation brings about whereby persons see how they create suffering for themselves and others. It is this wisdom that is at the very core of Buddhism: "Meditation is impossible for one who lacks wisdom, wisdom is impossible for one who does not meditate. One that both meditates and possesses wisdom is near Nirvana" (*Dhammapada*, 327).

I am utterly convinced of the relevance of Theravāda Buddhist teachings to the problems of everyday life in the modern world, and it is my hope that more and more people will come to benefit from hearing the Dharma.

MOST VEN. DR. M. VAJIRAGNANA

Head, London Buddhist Vihara

a penetrating clarity of insight on the other. In Buddhaghosa's words, concentration "cleans the defiling stains and their [moral] pollution" and "provides the benefit of insight by serving as the proximate cause of such insight" (*Visuddhimagga*, XI, 121, 125). Concentration thereby deepens both the moral and wisdom aspects of the Path of Purification.

From this introduction of concentration on the Path of Purification, one can see that various types of meditation seek to produce either tranquillity (*śamatha*; Pali: *samatha*) or insight (*vipaśyanā*; Pali: *vipassanā*). Some of the forty objects of meditation, for example, are used to center, unify, purify, and still the mind in calm abiding or tranquillity. A kind of meditation that produces these results is called "tranquillity meditation." It produces the serene mind that is needed for mental culture, especially for the development of insight that untangles the unwholesome patterns of thought, speech, and action. Insight does so by uncovering and pacifying the negative attitudes and dispositions that cause these afflictive patterns. Meditation practice that generates insight is called "insight meditation."

Insight meditation not only gives one a deeper realization of the source of one's own *duḥkha*, but also gives one a more profound awareness of the true nature of life itself. One gains insight into the impermanence of life, its dependent arising, and the fact that all phenomena in the process of life are lacking in independent and permanent selfhood. Here, we can see that Buddhist insight meditation links concentration and the final aspect of this path, namely, wisdom. As insight gradually evolves into wisdom, there is greater clarity concerning the Dharma, and the purification of mind and heart continues to grow toward full Awakening. Theravāda teaches that this growth is possible because the original nature of the mind is pure luminosity. So, when ignorance is removed from the mind by the penetrating insight of wisdom, its nature as pure luminosity becomes the basis of Awakening and Nirvana. Thus, we reach the third and final aspect of the Theravāda Path of Purification, wisdom.

Wisdom

The wisdom aspect of the Path of Purification presents us with the core of enlightened Theravāda Buddhist experience. Here, insight meditation becomes the dominate form of meditative practice. Buddhaghosa says,

> Wisdom has the characteristic of penetrating insight into the essential nature of phenomena. Its function is the abolishing of the darkness of delusion, which conceals the essential nature of phenomena. . . .
>
> How is wisdom developed? Such things as the Five Aggregates, the bases, elements and faculties [of experience], the Four Noble Truths, dependent arising, etc. are the soil of wisdom. The purification of morality and concentration are the roots of wisdom. The Five Purifications . . . are the trunk of wisdom. After one performs morality and concentration as the roots of wisdom, then one should fortify wisdom by learning and questioning about those things that are the soil of wisdom. Then one can develop the Five Purifications that are the trunk of wisdom. (*Visuddhimagga*, XIV, 7, 32)

What is meant here is that by practicing the first two aspects of the Path of Purification—namely, morality and concentration—one is establishing the "roots" of wisdom. Then, one can examine the "soil" of wisdom, namely, those things that give nourishment to wisdom's growth. These include the many factors of existence, like the Five Aggregates and dependent arising, that one will need to understand with penetrating insight in order for wisdom to develop. Finally, the Five Purifications, which we introduce below, can then be used to actually develop wisdom, like the growing of a tree trunk.

After preparing the "roots" of wisdom by morality and concentration, the first step in the direct practice of wisdom is learning, in some depth, about its "soil." In particular, this means learning about the nature of the Five Aggregates, the factors and faculties that account for human experience, the Four Noble Truths, and the dependent arising of existence. When one's learning about these realities, which we have already discussed in the previous chapter, has reached a certain degree, then one can develop the first of the Five Purifications. This is called "Purification of View." It entails the clarification, by penetrating insight, of the views one has learned about all the various mental and material aspects of life. Next, one develops "Purification by Overcoming Doubt." This involves the purification, again by penetrating insight, of any doubts one might have about what one has learned concerning the cause and effect processes that account for the conditionality of life. In particular it involves insight into the dependent arising of the Five Aggregates in the past, present, and future as influenced by karma. Third, one develops "Purification by Knowledge and Insight of What Is the Path, and What Is Not the Path." Here, one's penetrating insight is focused on what one has learned about the path that leads to Nirvana. In so doing, one is able to abandon any false views or misunderstanding about what leads one to Nirvana.

In the fourth purification, "Purification by Knowledge and Insight of the Way," one develops a deeper wisdom about all of life by moving through a spiritual crisis. One first contemplates the "rise and fall" of the mental and physical elements of life. In so doing, one deepens his or her insight into the Three Characteristics of existence—the impermanence, dissatisfactory nature, and nonsubstantiality of all phenomena. When one focuses one's insight onto the "breaking up" of all phenomena, one is gripped by a "great terror." One experiences the fear over the dissolution of one's own mind and body and cannot find any consolation in the things of this world, because they too will pass away. Thus, one feels a desire to escape from this situation, the desire for freedom from the rising and falling of this impermanent life. Through this desire, one becomes detached from the world; with this dispassionate mind, one again looks at the Three Characteristics of life. Now one's insight meditation is more clear and stable, there is a deeper calm-awareness of life, along with renewed energy, strength, and determination to attain Nirvana. It is said that by this new and more profound wisdom, one enters the "gateway" to liberation.

Four Stages are essential path to enlightenment in Theravada Buddhism as believed by Buddha himself

Finally, one reaches the fifth purification, "Purification by Knowledge and Insight." In the Way of the Elders, the Purification by Knowledge and Insight is the final step on the Path of Purification. In the First Sermon of the Buddha, which we read in Chapter 2, it is said that it was with "knowledge and insight" that the Buddha attained his Awakening. Theravāda claims that this awakening knowledge and insight can be attained through a Purification by Knowledge and Insight that entails what are called the Four Paths. Here again are Buddhaghosa's words:

Next comes a change-of-lineage consciousness. . . . Purification by Knowledge and Insight consists of knowledge of the Four Paths, that is, the path of the Streamwinner, the path of the Once-returner, the path of the Never-returner, and the path of the *arhat*. . . . The thick murkiness that hides the truth has been dispelled. . . . Then when knowledge's repetition [of the aspects of life] has ended, the change-of-lineage consciousness arises which has as its object the signless, unborn, unconditioned, cessation, Nirvana. . . . As one enters into this cessation, Nirvana, one's [consciousness] lineage changes. . . . So is the knowledge associated with the path of the Streamwinner. . . .

A Streamwinner makes it his task to reach the second plane by reducing both sensual desire and ill-will. . . . He works the field of mental formations with the knowledge that they are impermanent, dissatisfactory, and lacking in any permanent self. Thus he embarks on a progressive series of insights. . . . The knowledge associated with this is the knowledge of the path of the Once-returner. . . .

A Once-returner makes it his task to reach the third plane by abandoning, without any remainder, both sensual desire and ill-will. . . . He works over and turns up the same field of mental formations with the knowledge that they are impermanent, dissatisfactory, and lacking in any permanent self. Thus he embarks on a progressive series of insights. . . . The knowledge associated with this is the knowledge of the path of the Never-returner. . . .

A Never-returner makes it his task to reach the fourth plane by abandoning, without remainder, craving for existence in the form-realms, craving for existence in the formless-realms, pride, restlessness and ignorance. He works over and turns up the same field of mental formations with the knowledge that they are impermanent, dissatisfactory, and lacking in any permanent self. Thus he embarks on a progressive series of insights. . . . The knowledge associated with this is the knowledge of the path of the *arhat*. . . .

At this point, this *arhat* . . . is one of the Great Ones with all cankers destroyed. He bears his last body, he has laid down the burden, reached the goal and destroyed the fetters of becoming, he is rightly liberated with final knowledge, and is worthy of the highest offerings of the world and its deities. (*Visuddhimagga*, XXII, 1–2, 4–5, 22–23, 25–26, 28–30)

These Four Paths were said, by even the early Buddhist texts, to have been taught by the Buddha. The first of the Four Paths is that of the Streamwinner, whose "stream" or "lineage" of consciousness changes radically as one gains direct knowledge of Nirvana. Buddhaghosa says that this knowledge is not full Nirvana, but more like a "glimpse" of Nirvana because certain defilements still "cloud" the Streamwinner's mind. However, even in this glimpse of insight, the person has destroyed three of the Ten Fetters, namely, *doubt* concerning the Buddha and his teachings, *belief* in the saving power of rites and ceremonies, and *delusion* concerning the impermanence of selfhood. One who has attained this state will not be reborn in a lower realm, such as the hells, the animal realm, or the realm of the hungry ghosts. Also, one is assured of attaining Nirvana in, at most, seven more lifetimes.

As a Streamwinner, one continues to deepen his or her insight, and reduce thereby the other fetters that still obscure full Awakening and Nirvana. Insight, Buddhaghosa says, is focused on mental formations, especially those that are unwholesome. When one's insight develops to the point that two more fetters (*sensual desire* and *ill will*) are reduced enough, one is reborn on the second of the Four Paths, as a Once-returner. A Once-returner will be reborn only one more time as a human or in the realms of the *devas*. Any other rebirth will be in the *Brahmā* realms. The Once-returner continues to "turn over" the "soil" of his or her mental formations, with deeper insight into their impermanence, dissatisfactory nature, and lack of substantial selfhood.

When the Once-returner has, by insight, destroyed completely the fetters of sensual desire and ill will, he or she will attain the path of the Never-returner. On this third of the Four Paths, the Never-returner directs his or her attention to destroying the remaining five fetters by gaining the necessary insight. These five fetters are *craving* for existence in the realms of form, *craving* for existence in the formless realms, *pride, restlessness*, and finally *ignorance*—the last and most entangling of the Ten Fetters. If the Never-returner is successful in destroying these fetters and attaining full Awakening in his or her lifetime, he or she will enter the last of the Four Paths and become an *arhat*. If not, the Never-returner will be reborn in the one of the highest *Brahmā* realms of pure form. There, he or she will mature in insight until becoming an *arhat*.

The *arhat*, or saint, is the person who has finally completed the Path of Purification, who has been made a "worthy one" in the Way of the Elders by following in the footsteps of the Buddha. In the above quotation, Buddhaghosa says that the *arhat* has completely destroyed not only the Ten Fetters but also the cankers (*āsrava*; Pali: *āsava*). These include sensual desire, desire for the continuing process of life, and ignorance. Sometimes a fourth canker is mentioned—holding views that are not liberating. Being free from all such hindrances and defilements, one's attainment of Awakening is complete, and one realizes Nirvana. One's task is finished, one's burden is put down, the final goal of the Path of Purification is reached, and with one's death, he or she attains Nirvana "without-remainder."

As a footnote, we should add that Theravāda Buddhism does not call such a person a "Buddha." This is because human Buddhas, according to Theravāda, have not followed a humanly established spiritual path, but have discovered Awakening and Nirvana by themselves. An *arhat*, instead, follows the path taught by a Buddha. Finally, it is also recognized that there may be people who make this attainment without following a path taught by someone else, but do not communicate this attainment in the form of a teaching. Such a person is called a "Solitary Buddha" (*pratyekabuddha*).

THERAVĀDA BUDDHISM IN SRI LANKA AND SOUTHEAST ASIA

Given the support of King Aśoka, Buddhism became more widely known in India and was proclaimed by missionaries in other countries as well. The first historical account of Buddhism being presented south of India is of King Aśoka's missionaries reaching Sri Lanka around 250 B.C.E. Theravāda Buddhism was quickly accepted in Sri Lanka, and centuries later it became the major religion of much of Southeast Asia. Theravāda continues to this day to be the dominant religion of both Sri Lanka and Southeast Asia. The very early acceptance of Theravāda Buddhism has given Sri Lankans a strong sense of responsibility for the Way of the Elders in the Buddhist world.

Sri Lanka

Tradition states that King Tissa of Sri Lanka, converted by King Aśoka's son and daughter, helped to spread the Dharma throughout the island. He also built the Mahāvihāra, a huge monastery complex in his capital at Anuradhapura. As Buddhism became the state religion, the monastics of Mahāvihāra took on the role of preserving the orthodox practice of Theravāda, especially in the face of early Mahāyāna developments in India (see next chapter). But in the first century B.C.E., a new monastic community formed in Anuradhapura, the Abhayagiri-vihāra. Faced with this division, Mahāvihāra scholars committed the Pali canon and commentaries to writing. However, its final structure was not established until the fifth century C.E.

In the third century C.E., the Jetavana monastic center was established as a third branch of the Saṅgha. It is not completely clear as to how these three traditions differed. Past scholarship proposed that the Mahāvihāra opposed Mahāyāna developments in the other two sects. These scholars also saw this as the main reason that the Pali texts were committed to writing. However, recent scholarship has shown this view to be somewhat problematic. In any case, during the following centuries, Anuradhapura gained a reputation for scholarship in the Theravāda tradition, and many Indian monastics came to Sri Lanka to study. One such person in the fifth century was Buddhaghosa, whose ideas we have introduced in this chapter.

Sri Lanka was conquered by the Hindu Tamils in the early eleventh century, and the Saṅgha was severely disrupted. Indeed, it seems that the women's order in Sri Lanka died out at that time. Then in the middle of the eleventh century, King Vijayabahu of Sri Lanka, with the aid of Burma, drove out the Tamil forces. The king decided to reestablish Theravāda Buddhism from his new capital in Polonnaruva; this meant that the monastic ordination lineage had to be reestablished. Instead of turning to India, for obvious reasons, the king brought monks and Pali texts from Burma. Unfortunately, the nun's lineage was not reestablished in Sri Lanka. But the new relation-

Map 2. The spread of Buddhism into Southeast Asia: c. first century B.C.E.–tenth century C.E.

ship between Sri Lanka and Burma forged a connection in the faith between Sri Lanka and Southeast Asia that remains strong today. Then, during the twelfth century, King Parākrama Bahu I unified the Saṅgha in Sri Lanka under the Mahāvihāra Order. For the next three centuries, a golden age of Theravāda and Pali scholarship in Sri Lanka blossomed.

In 1505, Portuguese colonists arrived in Sri Lanka and controlled the lowland coastal regions. The Sri Lankan kings ruled what they could and supported Buddhism from their new capital at Kandy in the interior mountains. The Portuguese were replaced by the Dutch in 1658, and finally the British in 1798. The British conquered Kandy in 1815 to rule the whole island. After this defeat, the Saṅgha was weakened significantly. This unfortunate condition of the Saṅgha had also been worsened by the introduction of Western education that replaced the monastic-based education system and by the Christian missions that portrayed Buddhism as backward and superstitious.

In the later half of the 1800s, a movement arose within the Buddhist community to debate Christians and to renew the Buddhist discipline and teachings in ways that were relevant to the modern world. This movement was supported, and in some ways guided, by founding members of the Theosophical Society, Helena Blavatsky and Henry Steel Olcott. In fact, both Blavatsky and Olcott went to Sri Lanka and proclaimed themselves to be Buddhists. When independence was gained after World War II, this spirit of renewal increased and produced a vital and influential Saṅgha along with lay movements dedicated to social reform. We introduce one such movement, the Sarvodaya Shramadana Movement, in Chapter 10. The government has continued to support Buddhism and founded the World Buddhist Fellowship in 1950. The Sri Lankan Saṅgha now sends monastics around the world to introduce the Dharma and teach the practice of meditation.

Southeast Asia

King Aśoka is said to have sent missionaries to the area of Southeast Asia that is now part of southern Burma (Myanmar) and central Thailand. This may have been true. However, many scholars argue that Theravāda was more likely introduced into that region from Sri Lanka in the early centuries C.E. In any case, by the fifth century C.E. in the northern part of Burma, it is certain that there was a coexistence of Hinduism, different forms of Buddhism, and the indigenous worship of local spirits. In southern Burma, Theravāda was the dominant form of religion. When the northern Burmese King Anawratha (1040–1077) unified the country, he made Theravāda from the south the main religion of all Burma. It was also this king of Burma who sent monks and Pali texts to Sri Lanka in order to help reestablish the Theravāda lineage in 1065. Over the centuries, since the time of King Anawratha, Sri Lanka and Burma have enjoyed a close religious collaboration in supporting Theravāda in their two countries.

This Theravādin collaboration was later joined by Thailand. From the eleventh century, Theravāda missions were sent into Thailand from Burma, and the religion enjoyed support from the Thai people. When the Thais won independence from their Cambodian Khmer rulers in the fourteenth century, Theravāda became the official religion of Thailand. At that time, religious connections with Sri Lanka were also established; these ties remain strong today. During the nineteenth century, a number of reforms were made within the Thai Saṅgha; under King Rāma V (ruled 1868–1910), all the Theravāda sects were united under the Mahānikāya (Great Sect). In this century, there have been influential Theravādin leaders in Thailand, such as the Venerable Buddhadāsa (1906–1993), whom we discuss in Chapter 10.

It is said that different forms of Buddhism were brought to Cambodia in the second century C.E. It is certain that by the sixth century, Mahāyāna and Hinduism were joined together in a popular syncretistic form of religion. In the eighth century, Cambodia, along with most of the rest of Southeast Asia, was under the rule of Java. Buddhism had been already introduced down the Malay peninsula and into the islands of Sumatra and Java in the fourth and fifth centuries. During the Java empire, around 800 C.E., a huge *stūpa* was build in Borobudur, Java. It remains the largest in the Southern Hemisphere. A Cambodian prince named Jayavarman was a hostage in Java at the time. When he returned home, he proclaimed Cambodian independence and went on to build the Khmer empire covering most of Cambodia, Laos, Thailand, and Vietnam.

It was during this Khmer empire that the great temples and mausoleums were built at Angkor. At first, the complex of buildings were dedicated to Hindu deities. However, in the twelfth century, Burmese missions to the empire won many converts to Theravāda Buddhism, and Buddhist elements

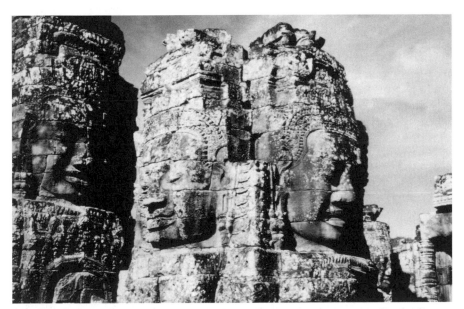

Figure 3.2. Towers of Bayon, Angkor Thom; thirteenth century C.E., Cambodia.

began to appear in the Angkor temples. In the fourteenth century, the Cambodian royalty accepted Theravāda, and it has remained a strong tradition in Cambodia ever since. Also, because of Cambodia's influence on Laos, Theravāda became the official religion of that country around 1350. The Khmer empire lasted until the Thais gained independence in 1431.

Mahāyāna Buddhism reached northern Vietnam from both India and China as early as the third century C.E. However, the north of Vietnam was most strongly influenced culturally and religiously by neighboring China. Thus Chinese forms of Pure Land and Thien (Zen) Buddhism were popular from the ninth century on and enjoyed state support from the tenth century. In the south of Vietnam, Hinduism and Mahāyāna were also introduced by the third century. After an invasion from the north in the fifteenth century, the Chinese forms of Mahāyāna Buddhism became the dominant religion throughout Vietnam. Although Theravāda Buddhism continued to exist in the south in areas near Cambodia, Vietnamese Buddhism has been most strongly formed by the Chinese Mahāyāna traditions.

Theravāda Monastic and Lay Experience

The Path of Purification, which we introduced earlier in this chapter, has traditionally been seen in Theravāda as a way to Nirvana that normally requires being a monastic. Some early Buddhist texts indicate that the Four Paths could be reached by laypersons. But the Theravāda experience was that such a feat would be almost impossible because of the lack of time necessary for proper learning and practice. Recently, however, this view has been reconsidered as lay practice in Theravāda countries has been on the increase. For example, during the twentieth century, Myanmar centers for the lay practice of mindfulness and insight meditation were founded. These centers have developed techniques that have influenced modern Buddhist practice in other Theravādin countries as well as in the West. Some persons who use these techniques believe that given this training, and the time that certain laypeople have today for extended retreats, the higher levels of the Path of Purification can be reached by lay practitioners. On the other hand, over the centuries traditional practice of Theravāda Buddhism by the laity has been more focused on moral living, the attainment of this-worldly benefits, and merit for a better rebirth.

As for moral living, the monastic communities of Theravāda in Sri Lanka and Southeast Asia have preached ethical teachings and have provided moral guidance to the laity. We should note that in Theravāda, city monasteries focus on the study of the Dharma, performing rituals, and ministering to the needs of the lay community. Forest monasteries focus on the meditative attainment of their monastics, but sometimes also offer the laity meditative guidance and retreats under the direction of a skilled teacher. The city monasteries have been mainly responsible for providing the teaching of the Dharma and the moral discipline to the larger lay community. More than this, these monastic communities have provided models of moral living for society in general. In their monastic way of life, the monks and nuns present a social ideal for all Buddhists: a community of persons living together such moral virtues as generosity, forgiveness, loving kindness, and compassion. The monastic Saṅgha gives an example of how people can live together in peace and harmony, with all individuals treated equally and honored not for wealth or power, but for moral and spiritual achievement. Indeed, monasticism has always been at the very heart of the Theravāda Buddhist world.

To carry out their role as moral and spiritual guides for the laity, Theravāda monasteries, especially in cities, contain a complex of halls in which the laity can be educated and can participate in religious ceremonies. There are also monastery schools for children and shrines where statues or paintings of Buddha images are kept for offerings of flowers, food, incense, and the lighting of candles. These offerings are said to bring merit to the laity and to reinforce the values that lay Buddhists try to live in daily life. There may also be *stūpas* where objects for veneration are kept. In fact, Theravāda provides the laity with numerous opportunities for merit-making. Other examples of merit-making possibilities include attending certain rituals, presenting food to monastics when they beg for a meal, listening to a Dharma talk or to monks chanting, making general donations to the Saṅgha, repeating and listening to passages in the Pali texts, and calming the mind in meditation. These and other actions can, Theravādins believe, produce merit that will benefit one in this life and bring a more fortunate rebirth. Therefore, the laity sees the monastic community as a source of growth in the Dharma and moral life as well as a source of good merit that can be obtained, shared with others, and even channeled to the larger society for the benefit of all persons.

Since Hinduism spread south from India along with Buddhism, very early on there were no clear boundaries between these religions. Thus, there developed a popular blending of these religions in Sri Lanka and Southeast Asia that has had a continuing influence on the religiosity of Theravādin laypeople. For example, in Sri Lanka sometimes Buddhist and Hindu religious leaders interacted so closely that they lived in different quarters on a shared religious site. Lay people consulted the Buddhist monastics about matters having to do with morality, understanding the higher truth about life, and release from the rounds of rebirth. These same people also asked the Hindu priests to pray to the Hindu and local gods for this-worldly benefits such as good fortune, prosperity, and health. Even today, shrines are provided in many Buddhist sites for the worship of both Hindu and local gods. When a young person leaves home, his or her parents may give the following traditional blessing: "May you have the refuge of the Buddha, and the protection of the gods." Another example of this kind of religious interaction is found in Burma, where the ancient belief in local spirits (*nats*) led to accepting Buddhist spirituality along with shamanistic practices, especially for healing sickness. The rational for this kind of interaction is that the Buddha did not deny the existence of deities that may be interested in helping humans with their needs and may have the powers to do so. He only denied that rites and ceremonies to the gods would aid one in the ultimate journey to Nirvana.

From this we can see that the Theravāda religion has not only provided its monastics in Sri Lanka and Southeast Asia with a spiritual path to follow to the highest state of Nirvanic freedom, but has also given its lay members concrete guidance on how to live certain moral values and spiritual qualities taught by the Buddha. Theravāda monasticism has helped to form the values of its societies and has produced an impressive Buddhist culture with art and literature that express the ideals taught by the Buddha. The Theravāda experience of Buddhism has provided a wellspring for the moral, social, intellectual, and cultural life of Sri Lanka and Southeast Asia, while also preserving the Way of the Elders leading to Awakening and Nirvana.

SUGGESTIONS FOR FURTHER READING

Buddhaghosa. *The Path of Purification (Visuddhimagga)*. Translated by Nanamoli Thera. Berkeley, CA: Shambhala Publications, 1976.

Bunnag, J. *Buddhist Monk, Buddhist Layman: A Study of Buddhist Monastic Organization in Central Thailand*. Cambridge: Cambridge University Press, 1973.

Carrithers, Michael. *The Forest Monks of Sri Lanka*. Delhi: Oxford University Press, 1983.

Carter, John Ross. *On Understanding Buddhists: Essays on the Theravāda Tradition in Sri Lanka*. Albany, NY: SUNY Press, 1993.

Chakravarti, Uma. *The Social Dimensions of Early Buddhism*. Delhi: Oxford University Press, 1987.

Gombrich, Richard F. *Theravāda Buddhism: A Social History from Ancient Benares to Modern Colombo*. London: Routledge & Kegan Paul, 1988.

Gunaratana, Henepola. *The Path of Serenity and Insight: An Explanation of the Buddhist Jhānas*. Delhi: Motilal Banarsidass, 1985.

Harvey, Peter. *The Selfless Mind: Personality, Consciousness, and Nirvana in Early Buddhism*. Richmond, UK: Curzon Press, 1995.

Hoffman, Frank, and Deegalle Mahinda, eds. *Pali Buddhism*. Richmond, UK: Curzon Press, 1996.

Kalupahana, David J. *Ethics in Early Buddhism*. Honolulu: University of Hawaii Press, 1995.

Mannikka, Eleanor. *Angkor Wat: Time, Space, and Kingship*. Honolulu: University of Hawaii Press, 1996.

Miksic, John. *Borobudur: Golden Tales of the Buddha*. Boston: Charles E. Tuttle, 1995.

Snodgrass, A. *The Symbolism of the Stūpa*. Ithaca, NY: Cornell University Press, 1985.

Strong, John. *The Legend of King Aśoka*. Princeton, NJ: Princeton University Press, 1983.

Swearer, Donald K. *The Buddhist World of Southeast Asia*. Albany, NY: SUNY Press, 1995.

Wijayaratne, Mohan. *Buddhist Monastic Life According to the Texts of the Theravāda Tradition*. Translated by Claude Grangier and Steven Collins. Cambridge: Cambridge University Press, 1990.

FOUR

THE GREAT VEHICLE

In the Pali texts, there is a story about a person named Sumedha, who lived eons ago and during his lifetime met a Buddha named Dīpaṃkara. Sumedha decided not to become a disciple of Dīpaṃkara and strive to be an *arhat*. Rather, he decided to follow what is called the Path of the Bodhisattva ("a being who is to become Awakened") in order to become a Buddha like Dīpaṃkara. This Bodhisattva Path entails cultivating what are called "perfections" (*pāramitās*) for many eons in order to attain full Buddhahood. In this way, instead of being an *arhat*, who would disappear from *saṃsāra* at the end of his lifetime, Sumedha could devote all his bodhisattva lifetimes and his life as a Buddha to helping others gain Awakening. The story goes that Sumedha was successful and eventually became Gautama Buddha.

The early schools of Buddhism that we introduced in the previous chapter recognize this bodhisattva ideal, but taught that it is a heroic path for only the very few. Therefore, it is best to follow the shorter path to Arhatship and Nirvana, rather then the long and arduous path to full Buddhahood. But as time went on and the Buddhist literature tended to exalt the status of the Buddha, it seems that there developed an interest in the Saṅgha to explore the option of the bodhisattva.

Eventually, at about the time of the beginning of the Christian era, new *sūtras* began to appear that claimed to be discourses of the Buddha. From these *sūtras* came the opinion that the Bodhisattva Path leading to Buddhahood and the spiritual qualities gained thereby are superior to the path leading to Arhatship and its degree of spiritual attainment. The Bodhisattva Path was therefore named the *Mahāyāna*, meaning "Great Vehicle," "Great Course," or "Great Journey." The path to Arhatship taught by the original schools of Buddhism was referred to as *Hīnayāna*, or "Lesser Vehicle," since it does not lead all the way to full Buddhahood.

Until recently, many modern scholars following certain Buddhist sources have taught that this Mahāyāna movement emerged from the Mahāsaṅghika School. The doctrines of Mahāsaṅghika stressed the transcendent nature of the Buddha and questioned the spiritual status of the *arhats*. They also taught that the early scriptures are not the sole authority in deciding what the Buddha's teachings are. Therefore, one would think that Mahāsaṅghika would be more open to the Mahāyāna *sūtras*. Also, earlier scholarship has seen Mahāyāna as being inspired by lay devotion and *stūpa* worship, and it seems that Mahāsaṅghika was quite accepting of a fuller participation of the laity than some of the other ancient schools were.

However, more recent scholarship has noted that perhaps the Mahāyāna writings and practices actually influenced Mahāsaṅghika positions. In fact, there is evidence that Mahāyāna was not originally associated with just one sect but was a kind of "esoteric" spirituality of interest to persons in many schools. There is also evidence that devotion was practiced by lay and monastic members of the Saṅgha alike, and many scholars believe that instead of originating from the laity, Mahāyāna may have actually originated within the spirituality of the monastics. In any case, it is known that for centuries the monastics who practiced Mahāyāna lived in the monasteries of different schools alongside monastics who were not interested in their new form of religiosity.

The task for early Mahāyāna was, therefore, to define their Great Vehicle, or the Great Course/Journey that leads to Buddhahood. They did so in the Mahāyāna *sūtras*, considered by Mahāyāna to be a new "turning of the wheel of the Dharma." Presented as teachings delivered by the Buddha, the Mahāyāna *sūtras* were said to have been kept secret until the Saṅgha had matured to the point where it was capable of understanding their deeper message. In any case, the new *sūtras* were written anonymously mainly in Sanskrit from around the first century C.E. up until the eighth century.

While the different *sūtras* contribute a variety of ideas to Mahāyāna, there are some characteristic ideas that have become associated with the tradition, especially as it spread to Tibet, East Asia, and Vietnam. Here, we mention four that are discussed in some detail in this and in the next chapter. The first characteristic notion found in developed Mahāyāna is the view that a Buddha, rather than an *arhat*, is the person who can be of most help to people who are suffering and in need of liberation. To achieve this condition of Buddhahood, one needs to follow the Bodhisattva Path. This bodhisattva life begins with what is called the "arising of the thought of Awakening," or *bodhicitta*. This *bodhicitta* is really the altruistic desire, or heartfelt aspiration, to attain Buddhahood so that one can help others gain freedom from suffering. What this means concretely is that one aspires to follow the Bodhisattva Path, or the "Great Journey," rather than the path leading to Arhatship. In fact, Mahāyāna was called the *Bodhisattvayāna*, or "Bodhisattva Vehicle" bringing one to Buddhahood, in distinction from the *Śrāvakayāna*, or "Disciple Vehicle" bringing one to Arhatship. Early Mahāyāna taught the Six Perfections that advance this bodhisattva journey to Buddhahood. Later Mahāyāna introduced Ten Stages on the Bodhisattva Path and added four other perfections so that each stage has a particular perfection associated with it. We introduce this path in some detail later in this chapter.

A second characteristic of Mahāyāna teaching is the notion of a "higher wisdom" (*prajñāpāramitā*) realizing "emptiness" (*śūnyatā*). This notion has to do with the awakened experience of the Buddhas and bodhisattvas. For Mahāyāna, what one experiences with awakened consciousness is that all the "factors of existence" (*dharmas*), which we have seen were so carefully ana-lyzed in the *Abhidharma Piṭaka*, are "empty" (*śūnya*) of existing independently, or "on their own." In the language of Mahāyāna, all aspects of existence are "*svabhāva-śūnya*," that is, "empty of own-being." This means that nothing can exist on its own. In other words, all things in the world, the elementary fac-tors of life and the particular beings that these factors constitute, are seen by a higher wisdom to have this fundamental characteristic of emptiness.

The term *śūnya*, which we translate as "empty," can mean in Sanskrit "hol-low," as in something that looks solid but is in fact hollow inside. So, "empty of own-being" means that while things seem to ordinary experience as if they are independent entities, deeper insight shows that they are really empty, or hollow, of that independence. This is another way of saying what the Buddha himself taught, namely, that all things arise dependently. To ex-perience this dependently arisen nature of things—their "emptiness" of in-dependence—is the core of wisdom experience according to Mahāyāna. It is this profound Mahāyāna experience of penetrating insight into the empti-ness of all things by the awakened consciousness that brings one freedom. It is this profound wisdom realizing emptiness that, coupled with a com-passionate motivation to save all living beings, furthers one's Great Journey to the goal of Buddhahood.

A third characteristic of Mahāyāna teaching concerns the nature of con-sciousness. We have seen that one view of consciousness found in early Bud-dhist texts teaches that the mind is naturally pure and clear, having been stained by mental defilements. While in Mahāyāna there are many and some-times conflicting notions concerning consciousness, we find a similar strand of thought. It claims that consciousness, prior to being affected by defile-ments, is the luminous clarity and nirvanic status of enlightened Buddha-hood. This pure luminosity as the true essence of consciousness gives peo-ple the potential for Buddhahood. But ordinary conscious life generates conceptualizations and other mental formations that frustrate this potential. In the end, it is the mind that enslaves people in a life that is untrue and un-satisfying (*duḥkha*); and it is also the mind that can set people free.

Finally, the fourth characteristic notion has to do with the nature of Bud-dhahood, the goal of the Bodhisattva Path. While the early Buddhist texts claim that the cosmos includes realms of hells, ghosts, gods, and *Brahmā* be-ings, Mahāyāna expanded this vision of the cosmos by claiming that it also contains countless Buddhas residing in Buddha realms. In following the Bod-hisattva Path, one can be reborn in one of these realms, where one can progress toward Buddhahood under the guidance and with the blessings of the Buddha of that realm. When one attains Buddhahood, one will also cre-ate a Buddha realm from where one will help others throughout the cos-mos. In the meantime, one can receive guidance and blessings in this world, as well as visualize these "celestial" Buddhas and their realms and the ad-vanced bodhisattvas that abide in them in ways that are spiritually transforming. These Buddhas and advanced bodhisattvas develop special skill-ful means (*upāya*) that they use to appear in the many world systems of the cosmos in order to help other beings become free from suffering and progress in the journey to Awakening and Buddhahood.

As we noted earlier, for many centuries after the beginning of the Mahāyāna movement, indeed perhaps up until the seventh century C.E., members of this newer tradition lived in monasteries side-by-side with Bud-dhists who chose to follow the original teachings of the Three *Piṭakas*. How-ever, as time passed and some of the *sūtras* became more polemical as they stressed the "superiority" of the Mahāyāna over the older tradition, Mahāyānins began to separate from the other schools. We have seen that the Theravādins spread into Sri Lanka and Southeast Asia. Mahāyāna flour-ished in various places in India from where it eventually spread into other parts of Asia, especially Central and East Asia. It became the primary form of Buddhism in such countries as Tibet, China, Korea, Japan, and Vietnam. So, with these general comments about Mahāyāna and its teachings, we can now look at some of the individual *sūtras* that have been especially impor-tant in defining the Mahāyāna experience of Buddhism.

THE MAHĀYĀNA *SŪTRAS*

The Mahāyāna *sūtras* were written to teach the experiences of Mahāyāna in following the Bodhisattva Path to Buddhahood. The following are some of the major Mahāyāna *sūtras* that introduce the kinds of teachings we have al-ready outlined. We include some selections from these *sūtras* that present the notions of wisdom and emptiness, the nature of consciousness, the tran-scendent nature of the Buddha, and the existence of Buddha realms. In the next section, we introduce the Bodhisattva Path and its stages and perfec-tions in some detail.

The Perfection of Wisdom Sūtras

Among the earliest of the Mahāyāna *sūtras* are the *Perfection of Wisdom Sūtras* (*Prajñāpāramitā-Sūtras*). These *sūtras* began to be written in the first century C.E. Longer versions were written during the next two hundred years; more condensed *sūtras* were written from 300 to 700 C.E. These condensed ver-sions include the famous *Diamond Sūtra* and *Heart Sūtra*. Within some of the Wisdom Literature, the journey of the bodhisattva is defined by the Six Per-fections (giving, morality, patience, vigor, meditation, and wisdom). This Bodhisattva Path is lived compassionately for the benefit of others because one's practice of it is motivated by *bodhicitta*, the aspiration to attain Bud-dhahood in order to save all living beings. This altruistic attitude leads the Mahāyāna Buddhist to renounce any personal attainment of Arhatship and Final Nirvana so as to continue to help others in need. In this regard, the *Perfection of Wisdom Sūtras* depict the *arhats* as selfishly leaving society be-hind to enjoy the quiescence of Final Nirvana after death.

In following this compassionate path, bodhisattvas can eventually be re-born in celestial Buddha realms where they can gain the powers and skill-ful means necessary to become Buddhas and help others do the same. As a celestial bodhisattva, and eventually as a celestial Buddha with one's own Buddha realm in the heavens of the cosmos, one will be a more universally active source of blessings for all living beings. Mahāyāna taught that these blessings are possible because of "merit transfer." Since karmic merit can be transferred from one person to another, celestial bodhisattvas and Bud-dhas—who have accumulated great merit during eons of practicing the Per-fections—can transfer that merit to needy sentient beings.

Besides the compassion of the bodhisattva and its implications for reli-gious practice, the *Perfection of Wisdom Sūtras* also expound the wisdom of the bodhisattva. Through the ordinary use of perception and language, one experiences the many things of the world as being separate and distinct en-tities. But the wisdom of the bodhisattva brings one to the realization that the things of the world are not independent; they lack their seeming inher-ent existence. Things as normally seen are said to be "like a dream." This does not mean that they do not exist but that they exist like a dream de-pending on a dreamer. In other words, the many things of the world appear as if they are independent entities; but this appearance of independence de-pends on one's perception of them and is not how they really exist. One term often used in the *Perfection of Wisdom Sūtras* to describe this condition of things is "non-arising" (*anutpāda*). That is, the things one sees as so sep-arate from oneself and other beings have "not arisen" in such an independent manner.

When one experiences the real status of things, claims the Wisdom Liter-ature, one beholds "emptiness." As we mentioned earlier, emptiness is not a thing in its own right, but is precisely the way all things are in their de-pendent arising, namely, "empty of own-being" (*svabhāva-śūnya*). This means that emptiness is not some ultimate reality beyond the forms of existence themselves; rather, the myriad forms of existence are emptiness—they are empty of own-being. An analogy that is used to help one understand this notion of emptiness is a flower that always needs sunlight, water, soil, nu-trients, and so on to live. In a similar way, Mahāyāna is saying that each be-ing needs the full matrix of life to be what it truly is. Wisdom is the insight of the enlightened consciousness that penetrates this matrix of life, this emptiness of things. This experience of wisdom insight into the true nature of things reveals what is called, in many Mahāyāna *sūtras*, "suchness" (*tathatā*). To experience the suchness of things means to experience things "such as they are," without superimposing views about them. That is, while one ordinarily views things as independent entities, experiencing the such-ness of things is to see the emptiness of this independence, to see things as they are dependently arisen.

With wisdom insight into suchness, into the empty nature of all beings, there is a liberating effect on the person of wisdom. In experiencing the emptiness of all things, one's attachments to the things of the world are loosened, defilements are brought to an end, and delusion is dispersed. The state of mind that one realizes with this freedom is Nirvana. But since Nirvana is also experienced as empty—as not an independent state separate from the ordinary *saṃsāric* world—one is also free from attachment to this spiritual status. With freedom from the world of *saṃsāra* on the one hand and from Nirvana on the other, one "courses" in the Middle Way. This means that one is free from any attachment to either *saṃsāra* or Nirvana; and therefore one is free to embrace all things as they are in their suchness, while responding to their needs out of selfless compassion. As we shall see in the next chapter, these ideas about wisdom and emptiness presented in the *Perfection of Wisdom Sūtras* became the inspiration for Mādhyamika, one of the major schools of Indian Mahāyāna Buddhist philosophy, as well as many of the schools of Mahāyāna Buddhism in other parts of Asia.

With these remarks in mind, let us now look at the *Heart Sūtra*, which is said to capture in a few words the "heart," of the Perfection of Wisdom. This is one of the best-known *Perfection of Wisdom Sūtras* in East Asia. Its teaching is given to Śāriputra, one of the Buddha's chief disciples. Note that the first part of the text begins by saying that the famous celestial bodhisattva named Avalokiteśvara, while engaged in the Great Journey, looks down at the world with his perfection of wisdom. From that vantage point, he sees that the Five Aggregates are "empty of own-being" and that emptiness is not different from the Five Aggregates. Emptiness is their true nature. Avalokiteśvara then sees that all the *dharmas*, analyzed and categorized so carefully by the earlier *Abhidharma* texts, are also empty of own-being. Therefore, from the point of view of emptiness, the *dharmas* are not produced as discrete entities to be characterized by the categories of the *Abhidharma*—they are all the same in that they are all characterized by emptiness.

> Om! Praise to the blessed and noble perfection of wisdom! The noble Avalokiteśvara Bodhisattva was moving in the deep journey of the perfection of wisdom. When he looked down at the Five Aggregates, he saw that they are empty of own-being.
>
> Here, O Śāriputra, form is emptiness, emptiness is form. Form is not different from emptiness, emptiness is not different from form. What is form is emptiness, what is emptiness is form. The same is true for sensations, perceptions, mental formations and consciousness.
>
> Here, O Śāriputra, all *dharmas* are characterized by emptiness; they are neither produced nor cease, they are neither defiled nor pure, they are neither deficient nor complete.

In the next part of the text, it is said that the perfection of wisdom realizing emptiness looks over the Five Aggregates, the six senses and their objects, the eighteen elements that constitute conscious experience, the twelve links of dependent arising, the Four Noble Truths, and the knowledge and attainment, or lack thereof, associated with the *arhat*. In fact, these factors and processes of existence are the ones that Buddhaghosa says are the "soil" to be "turned over" with knowledge and insight in order to become an *arhat*.

However, the *Heart Sūtra* says that when Avalokiteśvara looks at these factors of existence with his higher bodhisattva wisdom, he sees that they do not exist as ordinarily conceived because they are all empty of own-being.

> Therefore, O Śāriputra, in emptiness, there is no form, sensation, perception, mental formation, or consciousness; no eye, ear, nose, tongue, body or mind; no forms, sounds, odors, tastes, objects of touch, or objects of the mind; no eye-element and so on up to no mind-consciousness element; there is neither ignorance nor cessation of ignorance and so on up to neither old age and death nor cessation of old age and death. There is no *duḥkha*, no origination of *duḥkha*, no cessation of *duḥkha*, no path to the cessation of *duḥkha*. There is no knowledge, no attainment, no nonattainment.

The text goes on to say that with this higher insight into the emptiness of all things including the attainment of Nirvana, the bodhisattva is indifferent not only to worldly things but also to any attainment of Final Nirvana apart from this world. Instead, like all the Buddhas of all periods of time, he or she relies on the perfection of wisdom to be free of any obstacles to becoming a Buddha, and in the end actually realizes Nirvana in this world. The text ends with the great *mantra* that is spoken, as it were, by a personification of the perfection of wisdom. It is implied that while ordinary *mantras* can soothe some *duḥkha*, the perfection of wisdom, like a great *mantra*, conveys the power to bring about a cessation of all *duḥkha* through Awakening inspiring joyfulness. The text concludes with an actual *mantra* in praise of the perfection of wisdom that goes beyond everything to the full Awakening of Buddhahood.

> Therefore, O Śāriputra, because of being indifferent to attainment, a bodhisattva relies on the perfection of wisdom and remains thereby free from mental hindrances. Being free from mental hindrances, he or she is not afraid, overcomes erroneous views, and in the end attains Nirvana. All Buddhas of all times have attained the highest and perfect Awakening by relying on the perfection of wisdom.
>
> Therefore, one should know the great *mantra* of the perfection of wisdom, the *mantra* of great knowledge, the unsurpassed and unequaled *mantra*, the *mantra* that allays all *duḥkha*—it is true, for there is nothing lacking in it. By the perfection of wisdom is this *mantra* spoken. It is the following: Gone, gone, gone beyond, utterly gone beyond; Awakening; O joy! (*Prajñāpāramitā-Hṛdaya-Sūtra*)

The Vimalakīrti Sūtra

Another important Mahāyāna *sūtra* is the *Sūtra Expounded by Vimalakīrti* (*Vimalakīrti-Nirdeśa-Sūtra*). Composed in the first century C.E., this *sūtra* tells the story of Vimalakīrti, a rich layman living in Vaiśālī, whose understanding of the Buddha's teaching was so deep that he was accepted as a bodhisattva. Indeed, Vimalakīrti's wisdom was so profound that it surpassed not only the insight of the *arhats*, but even of some of the great bodhisattvas who had come down to visit from their celestial realms. Thus, the Mahāyāna point is made that the attainment of the bodhisattva is greater than that of the *arhat*, and it is not only for monastics but is also open to laypersons.

In this *sūtra*, as in the Wisdom Literature, the doctrine of the emptiness of things is presented. Here, it is said that because of emptiness, the world appears in ordinary experience. However, this does not mean that emptiness is an imperceptible causal force—like a God—that is apart from the things one perceives. Emptiness is instead the hidden "suchness" of all the things one ordinarily experiences with a discriminating mind. In the words of the *sūtra*, emptiness is the "baseless base" of all discriminated things. This emptiness, or suchness, or baseless-base of existence is hidden from view by the "dualities" of the discriminating mind. By dualities are meant the perceived differences between self and other, between the senses and objects of sense, between purity and defilement, and, ultimately, between *saṃsāra* and Nirvana. When asked what the nondual condition of life is like, Vimalakīrti "kept silent without saying a word," because words cannot describe it. True understanding of this nondual reality of emptiness must be realized in the direct experience of full Awakening.

In the *sūtra*, there is an instructive dialogue between a goddess taught by Vimalakīrti, and Śāriputra, who represents those who follow the older path of the disciples. This discussion is about how the discriminations emphasized in that earlier tradition, between, for example, wholesome and unwholesome things, cannot capture the real suchness of things. The discriminating mind cannot see the reality that lies beyond its discriminations:

> A goddess . . . listening to the Dharma in Vimalakīrti's room, appeared in bodily form and showered flowers on the bodhisattvas and chief disciples of the Buddha who were present. The flowers that landed on the bodhisattvas fell off and onto the ground. But those that landed on the disciples stuck to their bodies and did not fall off despite all their efforts to shake them off.
>
> Thereupon, the goddess asked Śāriputra why he tried to shake off the flowers. Śāriputra replied, "I want to shake off these flowers because they are not of the status of suchness." The goddess said, "Do not say that these flowers are not of the status of suchness . . . because it is you who gives rise to such a discrimination. . . . But if you no longer make such discriminations, this all will be of the status of suchness. Look at the bodhisattvas whose bodies do not hold the flowers. That is because they have put an end to such discrimination."
> (*Vimalakīrti-Nirdeśa-Sūtra*, VIII)

As is said in the *Heart Sūtra*, it is by going beyond the discriminations of ordinary experience that one finds emptiness, and the freedom it brings from things "sticking" to one in ways that hinder one's spiritual journey to Awakening. However, it seems that Śāriputra did not understand the goddess's words because later he asks her to change her female body into the form of a man. He is discriminating a man's body as superior to a woman's. The goddess again teaches that in their suchness, all forms are the same in that they are in reality empty of their discriminated characteristics, including those of gender. The goddess points out Śāriputra's attachment to the male gender and chides him for not realizing that the suchness of all forms is the same. Awakening to this truth about the ultimate "sameness" of all things is—the story implies—open to everyone, male and female, lay and monastic.

> Śāriputra asked, "Why do not you change your female form?" The goddess replied, "For the last twelve years, I have been looking in vain for a female form. So, what is it that you want me to change?"
>
> Thereupon, she used her supernatural powers to change Śāriputra into a celestial goddess, and to change herself into a man similar to Śāriputra. She then asked him, "Why do not you change your female form?"
>
> The goddess said, "Like Śāriputra, who is not a woman but only appears in female form, all women are the same. Though they appear in female form, they are ultimately not women. Hence the Buddha said, 'All things [ultimately] are neither male or female.'" (*Vimalakīrti-Nirdeśa-Sūtra*, VIII)

The Laṅkāvatāra Sūtra

While the previous two *sūtras* focus more on emptiness, the *Laṅkāvatāra Sūtra* examines the nature of consciousness, its production of ordinary experience, and its potential for Awakening and Buddhahood. The *Sūtra on the Descent into Lanka* (*Laṅkāvatāra Sūtra*) is said by scholars to have been composed around the fourth century C.E. We have seen in the *Perfection of Wisdom Sūtras* and *Vimalakīrti Sūtra* that ordinary consciousness has a role in discriminating people's mistaken experience of independent selfhood and independent objects. The *Laṅkāvatāra Sūtra* explores how the mind creates this false dualistic experience of self and world and how the mind can also escape this misperception of things and attain Awakening and Buddhahood.

The *Laṅkāvatāra Sūtra* stresses the need for an inward journey of meditation to overcome the ordinary workings of the mind, which produce mental discriminations that result in an unsatisfactory life. One's ordinary mental functioning dualistically objectifies an independent self and a world of independent objects in a fashion that leads to unwholesome attachment to things and, thereby, unhappiness. By turning one's meditative attention into the inner field of consciousness itself, one discovers that one's misperception of reality is based in a deeper mental phenomenon, what the *sūtra* calls the "storehouse-consciousness" (*ālaya-vijñāna*). It is this foundation of consciousness that is the ultimate cause of both one's subjective experience of selfhood and one's objective experience of the world. This depth of consciousness is said to create both one's subjective and objective experience like the deep ocean creates waves on its surface. One's experience of oneself and the world—like waves produced by the force of the ocean—is created by the force of the storehouse consciousness. As the *sūtra* says,

> At that time, the [Buddha] recited these verses: "Like waves that rise on the ocean when stirred by the wind, dancing without interruption, in a similar

way the storehouse-ocean is constantly stirred by the winds of objectivity such that the multiple waves of consciousness are seen dancing about.

"As the waves in all their variety are stirred on the surface of the ocean, so in the storehouse the variety of what is known as consciousness is produced. The mind and its [variety of] consciousness are discriminated as regards their form; [but] the [variety of] consciousness is not separate from the mind. . . . Just as there is no distinction between the ocean and its waves, so in the mind there is no evolution of the variety of consciousness.

"The visible world is discriminated by the [variety of] consciousness. . . . Form with characteristics and status are presented to our consciousnesses as such; they are seen as evolving in the same way as waves." (*Laṅkāvatāra Sūtra*, 46–47)

While the Wisdom Literature and the *Vimalakīrti Sūtra* call for the bodhisattva to experience emptiness, the *Laṅkāvatāra Sūtra* calls for an experience of this ocean of consciousness below the waves of experience. The *sūtra* proposes this experience of the very foundation of consciousness because it recognizes that its storehouse produces not only the experience of selfhood and the world but of Buddhahood as well. How is this possible? The *Laṅkāvatāra* says that if one realizes a "reversion of the foundation of the mind," one can discover its clear, pure luminosity that is the very essence of Buddhahood. Therefore, the storehouse-consciousness is also called the "Womb of the *Tathāgata*" (*tathāgata-garbha*). The term *Tathāgata*—meaning "Thus come" or Thus gone"—is a title given to Gautama Buddha. It indicates that the historical Buddha was one in a series of Buddhas who have come into the world and gone. The word *garbha* means either "womb" or "embryo." So to say that consciousness is like a womb or embryo of the *Tathāgata* means that all people can be part of this series of Buddhas because each person's innermost consciousness is like a womb that holds the embryo of Buddhahood. Here again are the words of the *sūtra*:

Nirvana is the storehouse-consciousness where a reversion takes place by self-realization. . . . When a reversion takes place in the practitioner of yoga, the [varieties of] consciousness cast off discrimination between [subject and object] in what is realized as the [nature of] mind itself. Here, one enters the *Tathāgata* stage, attaining the realization of noble wisdom; and in this stage, there is no thought of existence or nonexistence. . . . When all these [varieties of consciousness] go through a reversion, I and all the other Buddhas declare that there is Nirvana. The mode and nature of this Nirvana is emptiness, which is the status of reality. . . . [This is because the storehouse-consciousness] is like a great ocean in which waves roll on constantly, but the [depths] subsist unaffected, free from the faults of impermanence . . . thoroughly pure in its essence. . . . The storehouse-consciousness is [thus] known by the name of the *Tathāgata-garbha* (*Laṅkāvatāra Sūtra*, 62, 93, 99, 220–221)

This inner essence of the mind is the original pure, luminous, and nirvanic nature of the storehouse-consciousness that is beyond the dualistic discrimination of its ordinary mental functioning. With this inner realization, the embryo of Buddhahood begins to develop. In the light of the wisdom of developing Buddhahood, one experiences that all forms in emptiness display this luminous essence of the consciousness that produces them like an ocean producing waves. As we shall see in the next chapter, this understanding of consciousness is developed in the Indian Yogācāra School of Buddhist philosophy, which in turn influences many Mahāyāna schools in East Asia.

The Lotus Sūtra

Another *sūtra* that is one of the most revered in East Asia is the *Sūtra on the Lotus of the True Dharma* (*Saddharmapuṇḍarīka-Sūtra*) written around 200 C.E. Like other Mahāyāna texts, the *Lotus Sūtra*, as it is better known, emphasizes the Bodhisattva Path entailing the practice of the Six Perfections leading in the Great Journey to Buddhahood. It also presents the perfection of wisdom's vision of the entire universe, "the world of the triple sphere in all its ten directions," as empty of own-being. In lauding this Mahāyāna experience, the *Lotus Sūtra* also holds out hope that eventually even the *arhats* will reach this higher goal of Buddhahood.

The *Lotus Sūtra* has a speical teaching about what it considers the transcendent Buddha. The *sūtra* claims to have been preached at Vulture Peak by a dramatically transfigured Gautama Buddha, who reveals that in reality he had attained his Awakening incalculable, limitless, myriads of eons ago, and resides forever present to the world like a father preaching the Dharma. His human form as Gautama Buddha is a skillful means (*upāya*) to give people confidence that they can attain Nirvana. To display his transcendent power, as the *sūtra* opens, Gautama Buddha enters deep meditation and produces the following effect on his listeners that fills them with awe:

> At that moment, a ray issued from within the circle of hair between the Lord's eyebrows. It extended over eighteen-hundred thousand Buddha realms . . . so that all those Buddha realms were illuminated by its radiance. . . . Likewise, the noble Buddhas staying and living in those Buddha realms all became visible, and the Dharma being preached by them could be entirely heard by all beings. The monks, nuns and men and women lay devotees, practitioners of yoga, those who had attained fruition and those who had not, all became visible. The bodhisattvas, the great beings, in those Buddha realms who follow the bodhisattva's journey with ability due to their earnest faith in many kinds of lessons and ideas became visible too. . . . Then there arose this thought in the mind of the great being, Maitreya Bodhisattva, "O how great a wonder does the Tathāgata display!" (*Saddharmapuṇḍarīka-Sūtra*, I)

Gautama Buddha goes on in the *sūtra* to say that all Buddhas preach the Dharma of one Buddha-vehicle (*Buddha-yāna*). But since there are different kinds of people in various states of openness to this Buddha-vehicle, Buddhas use different skillful means to reach them. Therefore, there are three vehicles being taught, that of the *arhat*, the *pratyekabuddha*, and the bod-

Figure 4.1. Mahāyāna Buddhism's spread to Japan: fan-shaped *Lotus Sūtra*; twelfth century C.E., Hōryu-ji Temple, Nara, Japan. Exhibited at Japan House Gallery, New York.

hisattva. All who follow these will eventually attain supreme Awakening and become Buddhas. To explain skillful means, Gautama Buddha tells the following parable to Śāriputra. In it, he uses the analogy of three carts for the three vehicles of Buddhism.

> Let us suppose the following, Śāriputra. In a certain village . . . there was a great householder, old . . . and yet wealthy . . . with a grand house that is high and spacious, but built along time ago and now old. . . . The house has but one door . . . and all of a sudden it is being consumed on all sides by a mass of fire.
>
> Let us suppose that the man had many children . . . and that he had come out of the house. Now, Śāriputra, that man upon seeing the house being enwrapped in fire became greatly concerned . . . and made the following reflection, "I myself am able to come out from the burning house through the door . . . but my children are staying in the burning house absorbed in their playing and amusing themselves. . . . They do not perceive that the house is on fire . . . so they are not afraid and have no wish to escape. . . . Therefore, I will warn them."
>
> With this resolution, he calls to his children, "Come, my children, the house is burning with a mass of fire. . . . " But the ignorant children do not believe him . . . for they are not afraid . . . nor understand the word "burning." On the contrary, they run around, walk about, and repeatedly glance out at their father, all because they are so ignorant.
>
> Then the man reflects . . . "Let me use some skillful means to get my children out of the house." The man knows the disposition of the children, and . . . the man says to them, "My children, your toys which are so pretty and

precious . . . goat carts, deer carts, and bullock carts . . . are outside the door
of the house for you to play with. So, come out of the house, and I will give
each of you what you want." And the children, upon hearing the names of the
playthings they like, because they suit their desires, eagerly, pushing and running against each other, quickly rush out from the burning house. . . .

The children each go up to their father and say, "Father, give us those toys
to play with that you promised, those goat carts, deer carts, and bullock carts."
Then, Śāriputra, the man gives each of his children equally . . . bullock carts
only. They are made of seven precious substances, provided with benches, hung
with many bells, adorned with rare and wonderful jewels, covered with jewel
wreaths and garlands of flowers . . . led by a multitude of servants. . . . The
children climb up on the carts with feelings of astonishment and wonder. . . .

So too, Śāriputra . . . the Tathāgata, endowed with boundless and perfect
Buddha-knowledge . . . is the father of all worlds, who has attained the highest perfection in knowing skillful means, and who is most merciful, patient,
benevolent, and compassionate. He appears in this world, which is like a house
. . . burning with a mass of misery, in order to free from affliction, hatred and
delusion, all beings who are subject to birth, old age, disease, death . . . and
the dark and enveloping mist of ignorance. He does so to rouse them to
supreme, perfect Awakening . . . to bestow on them the immense and inconceivable joy of Buddha-knowledge. . . .

Thus, Śāriputra . . . in order to save all living beings from this world which
is like a burning house . . . [the Buddha] shows them by his knowledge of skillful means, three vehicles: that of the disciples, the *pratyekabuddhas*, and the bodhisattvas. By means of these three, he attracts all beings forth . . . so that all
beings, who are his children, are led to no other vehicle than the One Buddha-
vehicle. (*Saddharmapuṇḍarīka-Sūtra*, III)

One is reminded here of the Second Sermon of the Buddha in which he
says that the condition of the world of the Five Aggregates is "burning" with
"a whole mass of *duḥkha*"—a burning about which humankind is ordinarily unaware. In the *Lotus Sūtra*, it is being said that a Buddha, who is outside and free from the world, uses skillful means to bring people out of this
condition by offering different ideals, that of the *arhat*, the *pratyekabuddha*,
and the bodhisattva. But in the end all persons escape this condition through
one doorway and find one ideal, that of Buddhahood, which is more wonderful than anyone could imagine.

Land of Bliss Sūtras

A devotional side of Mahāyāna was also enriched by another set of early *sūtras*,
called the *Larger* and *Smaller Land of Bliss Sūtras* (*Sukhāvatī-Vyūha-Sūtras*),
which began to be written in the late second century C.E. The main intent of
the *Larger Land of Bliss Sūtra* is to tell the story about Amitābha Buddha, the
Buddha of Immeasurable Light. In the *sūtra*, Gautama Buddha tells how in
another world eons ago, there was a bodhisattva named Dharmākara, who
knew that Buddhas have the power to create Buddha realms in the heavens
of the cosmos in which they can reside. With the aid of a Buddha who was

BOX 4.1

THE DRAGON KING'S DAUGHTER

The *Lotus Sūtra* has two meanings for me: its surface meaning and its deeper "experienced" meaning. Years ago, I decided to practice Nichiren Buddhism, a Buddhist school founded centuries ago in Japan that focuses on the *Lotus Sūtra*. When I first began reciting the *Lotus Sūtra* and chanting its title, *Nam-myōhō-renge-kyō*, I insisted on learning its literal meaning, though I was encouraged to experience it through sound, too.

Since the ancient Chinese characters are complex, there are many translations of the *sūtra*'s title. The more suggestive one I particularly liked was "fusion with the mystic law of simultaneous cause and effect through vibration." I was assured I could draw infinite energy from such dynamic fusion for alleviating my own suffering and the sufferings of others. I tucked that away in the back of my mind and began to chant. But, I wondered, what about the rest of the *Lotus Sūtra* recited by Nichiren Buddhists?

The short explanation given to me at the time was that the *sūtra* had two parts. The first part makes the point that all human beings have the potential to attain enlightenment. Buddhahood is latent in the depths of their lives. The second part explains in parables and similes what enlightenment is. This rough sketch was a good start, but I still painstakingly wrote the literal meaning in pencil above each ancient character in my liturgy book.

Before long, as I undertook the daily practice and witnessed exciting changes in my life, the pencil jottings receded from my radar screen. Living the *Lotus Sūtra* and experiencing what my Nichiren society, Sōka Gakkai International (SGI), calls "human revolution" took on the greater importance. It is only now after eighteen years that I've returned again to the surface meaning. SGI President Daisaku Ikeda, through a series of recently published dialogues on the *Lotus Sūtra*, led me back to it.

To me, the most moving part of these dialogues concerned the Devadatta Chapter. In that chapter, Devadatta, who tried to kill Śākyamuni Buddha, receives the assurance that he, too, will attain a great enlightenment. This occurs before a huge assemblage of living beings from all directions of the universe. Perhaps more shocking to the assembly is what happens next.

The Dragon King's daughter, an eight-year-old girl with the body of a dragon, is said to have reached enlightenment in an instant upon hearing the teaching of the *Lotus Sūtra*. Yet Śāriputra, a learned disciple of the Buddha, does not accept the authenticity of her attainment, and cites reasons why women cannot gain enlightenment. Through dramatic acts reflecting wisdom and compassion, the dragon girl refutes all these reasons. This incident affirms the absolute spiritual equality of women.

As a little girl, my biggest fear was to be left out of or put down by a social group. When I reached adolescence, this fear intensified and became a major preoccupation. My mother, trying to help, advised me that whenever I felt left out, I should find someone else on the sidelines and go talk with them. Well, this was good as far as it went, but it didn't change the whole group dynamic: The sad and seemingly inevitable tendency of human beings to cluster and, in the process, exclude others. The *Lotus Sūtra* sets forth a totally different group dynamic, and it does so on a cosmic scale. No one is excluded from Buddhahood.

VIRGINIA STRAUS

Executive Director
Boston Research Center for the 21st Century

living at that time, Dharmākara learned about the excellent characteristics of these realms. He then resolved to generate a Buddha realm that would combine these excellent qualities into the purest of Buddha realms. With this possible pure Buddha realm in mind, Dharmākara expressed his bodhisattva resolve for Buddhahood in forty-eight vows. One of the main points of these vows is that Dharmākara promised that he would not become a Buddha until he had gained the powers needed to produce such a pure Buddha realm and to bring all who want to be reborn there to his Land of Bliss. After telling this story in the *sūtra*, Gautama Buddha then commented that this is exactly what happened: Dharmākara Bodhisattva is now Amitābha Buddha living in a Buddha realm called the "Land of Bliss" (*Sukhāvatī*). In the *Smaller Land of Bliss Sūtra*, this "Pure Land" is then described in some detail.

An important part of this story for Buddhist devotional practice and experience has to do with the power of Dharmākara's bodhisattva resolve to bring to this Land of Bliss all those who seek to be born there. There are differing explanations as to how one can be born in the Land of Bliss. But in general it requires faith in Amitābha Buddha and a sincere desire to be born in his Buddha realm. In some verses, it is said that one must generate the thought of becoming a Buddha (*bodhicitta*), cultivate certain virtues, and chant homage to Amitābha Buddha. As we shall see later, the Mahāyāna schools in East Asia that base themselves on these *sūtras* emphasize the saving grace of Amitābha for birth in the Land of Bliss. Once there—given Amitābha's presence and power along with the purity of his Buddha realm— it will be easier to attain Awakening. At any time in the Land of Bliss, one can hear and understand more clearly the Dharma and practice that lead to Awakening. One will not encounter any evil or hindrances to spiritual attainment. Here is how the Buddha realm is described:

> This Land of Bliss, Ānanda, which is the realm of Lord Amitābha, is rich and prosperous, comfortable, fertile, delightful and full of many gods and people. In this realm, Ānanda, there are no hells, no animals, no ghosts or *asuras*—no inauspicious places to be reborn. That realm of the Land of Bliss, Ānanda, produces many fragrant odors, is rich in the variety of flowers and fruits, adorned with jewel trees, which are visited by flocks of different kinds of birds conjured up by the Buddha's miraculous power. . . . On all sides it is surrounded by golden nets, and covered by lotus flowers made of precious things. . . .
>
> And everyone hears the pleasant sound that they wish to hear. If they just wish it, they may hear about the Buddha, the Dharma, the Saṅgha, the Six Perfections, the Ten Stages . . . emptiness . . . calmness, quietude and peace, great loving kindness, great compassion, great sympathetic joy, and great equanimity. . . . This brings about the state of mind that leads to the attainment of Awakening. Also, nowhere in the realm of the Land of Bliss does anyone hear of anything unwholesome, nowhere are there any hindrances or states of punishment. . . . And that, Ānanda, is the reason for this realm called the Land of Bliss. . . . All the beings who have been born, who are born, and who will be born in this Buddha realm are all fixed on the right method of salvation until they have attained Nirvana. . . .

BOX 4.2

STRENGTH FOR LIVING, COURAGE FOR DYING

I first encountered the Name of Amitābha or, in Japanese, Amida Buddha while I was in the army of occupation in Japan after World War II. Through my doctoral study, I became aware of the spiritual richness and meaning of this Name for countless believers in East Asia. I later became a convert to the Amidist teaching of Shinran, the Japanese founder of Shin Buddhism, after meeting many devoted members in Hawaii for whom it was a vital reality within their lives.

A heart attack made Amida's compassion and wisdom real to me in a deeply personal way through the skill of the doctors and the restorative powers of our bodies. Though I faced death, I was at peace in the experience of Amida's embrace of boundless compassion and wisdom.

Amida Buddha, whose Name means "Infinite," is the Buddha of Eternal Life and Infinite Light. In form and concept, he is the symbol of indefinable and inconceivable reality, which embraces all life and being in Oneness. He is the power of ideals, moving us to higher aspiration, though not a substantial entity. In Buddhist terms, he is empty, but manifest in all forms of existence. His mythic Vows highlight the interdependence of all beings and the cosmos. As the spiritual foundation for all value and meaning, Amida inspires our ideals of love, compassion, and wisdom.

Through intoning his Name in Japanese, *Namu Amida Butsu*, with others or voicelessly in our heart and mind, we are grateful to Life. Expressing our oneness with the Buddha, *Namu* ("I take refuge in") refers to our own ordinary or "foolish" being, and *Amida Butsu*, the Infinite. In quiet contemplation we receive strength for living and courage for dying.

ALFRED BLOOM
Professor Emeritus, Department of Religion
University of Hawaii

If any beings, Ānanda, over and over reverently devote themselves to this Buddha, if they plant a large . . . root of goodness, having raised their thoughts to Awakening, if they vow to be born in that realm, then, when the hour of their death approaches, Amitābha Buddha . . . will stand before them, surrounded by hosts of monks. Then having seen that Lord, and having died with serene hearts, they will be born in precisely that realm of the Land of Bliss. (*Sukhāvatī-Vyūha-Sūtra*, 15–16, 18, 24, 27)

Finally, it is important to note that the practice of "remembering the Buddha's name" (*buddhānusmṛti*) was popular in early Mahāyāna Buddhism. In this practice, one begins with saying the word *nāmah*, meaning "hail to," and then adds the name of a Buddha. As we shall see later, when Mahāyāna develops in East Asia, the actual chanting of "Hail to Amitābha Buddha" (Chinese: "*Nan-mo O-mi-t'o fo*"; Japanese: "*Namu Amida Butsu*") becomes quite popular. With a sincere faith in the power of Amitābha's vow, these devotees hope to be born in his Land of Bliss, or what they refer to as the "Pure Land."

THE GREAT JOURNEY OF THE BODHISATTVA

In Mahāyāna, the Great Journey of the bodhisattva begins with hearing the Dharma of the Buddha and taking up the practice of the Six Perfections. These six virtues (giving, morality, patience, vigor, meditation, and wisdom) were first advocated in the *Tripiṭaka,* and Mahāyāna agrees with the earlier tradition that one's motivation is what determines the real quality of one's life of virtue. For Mahāyāna, the true aspiration that should motivate the practice of virtue is "the thought of, or aspiration for, Awakening" (*bodhicitta*). In Mahāyāna, after some time of merit-earning practice and with the aid of a teacher, the person on the Great Course experiences the compassionate aspiration to attain Awakening *for the sake of all living beings.* This aspiration inspired by compassion then becomes the motivation of the entire bodhisattva journey.

The altruistic element of this aspiration for Awakening grows stronger as the bodhisattva realizes the truth of emptiness through growth in wisdom. By this wisdom, he or she experiences the ordinary duality between self and the world as a fiction. That is, one experiences that all things arise dependently so that oneself and the universe are empty of existing as independent entities. With this wisdom, one is also enabled to perform the Six Perfections "perfectly," that is, with selflessness. One is able to give to others, for example, without distinguishing between oneself and the others such that the virtue of the giving is "pure," without any self-centered involvement. Therefore, in Mahāyāna practice of the Six Perfections, the sixth virtue, namely the wisdom (*prajñā-pāramitā*) so extolled in the *Perfection of Wisdom Sūtras,* is necessary to practice the other five to the degree that one can attain Buddhahood. With this wisdom base, the bodhisattva goes ahead on his or her Great Journey, cultivating the qualities of Buddhahood for the good of all living beings. The altruistic disposition of the heart is also given particular concrete expression in the bodhisattva "vows," taken by lay and monastic Mahāyāna Buddhists alike. These vows are experienced as being powerful forces in one's psyche, guiding and impelling one toward a deeper level of compassion and practice of the Bodhisattva Path.

Between 100 and 300 C.E., after the Six Perfections had been practiced for centuries, Mahāyāna Buddhism introduced the doctrine of the Ten Stages (*daśabhūmi*) in order to clarify further the Great Journey of the bodhisattva. Mahāyāna also added four more perfections so that there is one perfection stressed in each of the Ten Stages. These four perfections include skillful means, vows, power, and omniscient knowledge. When one considers the description of Ten Stages, two things become clear about the Bodhisattva Path. First, it is claimed that while the bodhisattva journey takes eons to complete, it enables one to aid many more beings in their pursuit of Awakening than one could by following the path to Arhatship. Second, it is also clearly taught that for a person to journey on this path, he or she requires the aid of celestial Buddhas and bodhisattvas to reach the goal. With this in mind, we will first look at the original Six Perfections, and then at the Ten Stages, where we also introduce the other four perfections.

The Six Perfections

The first perfection is called *giving* (*dāna*). This virtue involves giving of material things, time, the invaluable gift of instruction about the Dharma, even one's own life for the sake of other beings in need. For giving to be a "perfection," it should be practiced with a selfless attitude based on insight into the nonduality of oneself and others. That is, when one has transcended the perceived separation between oneself and another person, then one's giving to that person becomes an action where oneself and the other are united in the pure act of giving and receiving. One should also "transform" merit gained by this generous action into fuel for one's own eventual Buddhahood and "transfer" merit for the Buddhahood of others. This dedication of merit is also done in the practice of the other perfections. It helps the person overcome attachments to any immediate material or spiritual gratification.

The second perfection is *morality* (*śīla*), which is the first of the three aspects of the Theravāda Path of Purification discussed in Chapter 3. In fact, the other two aspects of that Way of the Elders (concentration and wisdom) are included under the fifth and sixth perfections. With these inclusions, the Great Journey of the bodhisattva is seen in Mahāyāna as a expansion, rather than a rejection, of the path of the *arhat*. In terms of morality, while some Mahāyāna monastics observe all the *Vinaya* rules, Mahāyāna teaches both lay and monastic Buddhists to practice the Ten Good Actions. These moral actions include (1) not to kill, (2) not to steal, (3) not to engage in illicit sexual behavior, (4) not to lie, (5) not to use harsh words, (6) not to use words that cause enmity between people, (7) not to engage in idle talk, (8) not to be greedy, (9) not to be angry, and (10) not to hold wrong views. It is believed that the Ten Good Actions can begin the necessary moral purification of unwholesome thoughts and dispositions, as well as the actions that arise from such afflictive thoughts and mental attitudes. The result of this perfection of morality is freedom from troubling passions and, thereby, a greater inner balance, mental calm, and equanimity which are highly valued in all forms of Buddhist spirituality. This freedom and balance provide the basis for deeper spiritual advancement in meditation and wisdom.

The third perfection is *patience* (*kṣānti*). This perfection entails the patient endurance of hardships and the forgiveness of those who harm the bodhisattva in those hardships. With wisdom, one can see that the person who harms one is just caught up in negative attitudes and ways of living based on previous causes and conditions. While the perfection of giving helps one overcome greed, patience aids in the conquest of hate, another of the Three Root Evils. Patience also means to be patient with difficult Buddhist doctrines—such at those about emptiness—that can be confusing to persons with little experience on the bodhisattva journey.

The fourth perfection is *vigor* (*vīrya*), which refers to the effort, zeal, and energy needed to overcome unwholesome thoughts and attitudes, to cultivate positive virtues, to study the Dharma, and to do good actions. Vigor corresponds to Right Effort in the Eightfold Path taught by the Buddha, and includes the four types of Right Effort we discussed when we introduced the Eightfold Path. However, as a perfection in Mahāyāna, it also implies the heroic compassionate effort one should exert to benefit all living beings. Finally, vigor refers to the sustained fervor that is necessary to maintain enthusiasm on the spiritual journey—which at times can seem long and arduous. This vigorous determination is inspired by the deep compassion that arises from seeing others in need of help and realizing that as a Buddha, one can be of most help to all living beings.

The fifth perfection is *meditation* (*dhyāna*), corresponding to concentration (*samādhi*), which is the second of the three aspects of the Theravāda Path of Purification. In Mahāyāna, the layperson as well as the monastic is welcome to study and practice meditation. In advancing in meditation practice, the bodhisattva perfects certain forms found in earlier traditions, such as the Four Meditations, the Four Formless Meditations, the Four Divine Abodes, and the practice of tranquillity and insight meditation. However, the Bodhisattva does not accept rebirth into the heavenly realms to which some of these meditations lead. Instead, he or she seeks to be reborn only in the Buddha realms where he or she can progress in the Bodhisattva Path to Buddhahood.

It is said that the bodhisattva perfects innumerable other forms of meditation and *samādhi* states, thus opening the Mahāyāna tradition to an acceptance of new types of meditative practices. Also, Mahāyāna stresses three types of meditation from the earlier tradition because they can be used so well to cultivate their experience of emptiness. First is meditation on "emptiness" itself, which is used to realize the lack of independent selfhood of the things one ordinarily perceives. The second form of meditation is on "signlessness." Here, the ordinary cognition of things is transcended so that one does not see their "signs," or perceptible characteristics. This implies the meditative transcendence of the "signs," or characteristics, that distinguish between one's mind and the objects of experience, between subject and object. Thus, one strengthens a "signless" experience of emptiness. The third meditation is on "wishlessness." Here, based on meditations on emptiness and signlessness, one eliminates attachments to, or "wishes" for, the things of the world. The bodhisattva is also free from any wish for liberation from the world as long as there are beings in the world who need his or her help.

The sixth perfection is *wisdom* (*prajñā*), corresponding to the third of the three aspects of the Theravāda Path of Purification. In the above description of three forms of Mahāyāna meditation, we can see that the fifth perfection aids in the attainment of wisdom. The experience of wisdom penetrates the empty, signless, and wishless nature of reality with such power that one finds greater freedom and peace. Therefore, this wisdom is the door to Awakening and Buddhahood. Because of this generative function, Mahāyāna often personifies wisdom as a goddess and refers to her as "the mother of all Buddhas." That is, wisdom—like a mother—"gives birth to" all the qualities of the enlightened character. For example, as we have said, it is by experiencing the emptiness of any independent selfhood with the eye of wisdom that one is able to practice the other five virtues with perfect selflessness.

In Mahāyāna, wisdom penetrates the various factors and processes of life and understands how some of these lead to happiness and others to suffering. It penetrates the dependently arisen nature of life and understands the causes and conditions that make some relations satisfying and others not. In these ways, Mahāyāna wisdom is similar to that of Theravāda. However, the ultimate realization of the bodhisattva's insight is emptiness, the true suchness of life. With this perfection of wisdom, the bodhisattva finds that in living the Dharma, he or she is free from the afflictive thoughts and emotions and the unwholesome words and actions that produce a life of suffering for oneself and others. According to Mahāyāna, this insight into emptiness is such a powerful antidote to *duḥkha* that it overturns ignorance and the attitudes that lead to these negative thoughts, feelings, words, and behaviors. In their place, compassion arises as the spontaneous expression of emptiness and deepens the altruistic attitude (*bodhicitta*) of the bodhisattva toward all living beings.

The Ten Stages

After practicing the Six Perfections for centuries, the Mahāyāna tradition began to teach that there are certain discernible stages (*bhūmi*) of spiritual growth on the bodhisattva's Great Journey. Eventually, Ten Stages became the accepted steps in this spiritual itinerary. In this traditional view, the Six Perfections were related to the first six stages, and four more perfections were added to fit with the final four stages. As we shall see, in the final four stages, bodhisattvas evolve beyond what is possible for human beings. They are born in Buddha realms—such as the Land of Bliss of Amitābha Buddha—in order to pursue the last four stages. We will introduce these Ten Stages with passages from the *Daśabhūmika Sūtra*, as it is preserved in the Twenty-Sixth Book of the *Flower Garland Sūtra* (*Avataṃsaka Sūtra*).

The first of the Ten Stages is called *joyous*. Here the bodhisattva produces, based on previous good deeds, the "aspiration for Awakening" (*bodhicitta*). Thereby, he or she enters the family of the Buddhas and becomes "joyous." At this stage, the bodhisattva works especially on the first perfection of giving, or generosity. By experiencing with wisdom the emptiness of all things, he or she can give selflessly to benefit others without regret, worry, or desire for praise. Also, by seeing the "nonseparateness" between self and other, the bodhisattva can give to others with the proper attitude of empathy and compassion. Here is how this stage is described in the *sūtra*:

> So, in beings who have developed the roots of goodness . . . who have developed pure intentions . . . who have developed pity and compassion . . . the as-

piration for Awakening [bodhicitta] is aroused, the quest for enlightened knowledge . . . for the salvation of all beings.

With this arousing, the bodhisattva . . . is born into the family of the Buddhas . . . is established in the lineage of the Buddhas . . . and is certain to attain perfect Awakening. Thereby established in this condition, the bodhisattva attains the first stage of the Bodhisattva Path, that of great joy. . . . One becomes joyful thinking of the Buddhas and the Dharma, of bodhisattvas and their practices, of the purification of the Perfections . . . and of the ability they will have to benefit all beings. . . .

Seeing the mass of duḥkha suffered by beings . . . the bodhisattva develops great compassion, and seeks to free them from their sufferings . . . to bring them to the everlasting bliss of Nirvana. Thus . . . by sympathy and loving kindness, and by great effort, the bodhisattva relinquishes all things with equanimity . . . for the sake of the salvation of all beings. . . . Of the Ten Perfections, the perfection of giving is foremost . . . so the roots of goodness become more pure and useful.

The second stage is called *purity*. This purity is the result of practicing the second perfection, morality. Here the bodhisattva develops the Ten Good Actions and overcomes impure inclinations to engage in unwholesome actions. With wisdom, the bodhisattva's selflessness from stage one is expressed in all the wholesome actions of moral living. With purity of mind, speech, and action, there grows an inner equanimity in the person that is the basis for more profound meditation practice, and a deeper attainment of wisdom. In the words of the *sūtra*,

Bodhisattvas in the stage of purity naturally develop the Ten Good Actions. . . . By means of these good ways of acting . . . effort is made to achieve the complete purification of all aspects of action. . . . Thus many Buddhas come to be perceived by the bodhisattvas who live in accord with the power of morality. . . . They attend those Buddhas, and they learn the Ten Good Actions from them with great respect . . . thereby they purify generosity and morality.

The third stage is called *luminosity*. Here, the bodhisattva's luminous wisdom is like the light of the sun as it penetrates the suchness of all things. This same luminous wisdom is like a fire in that its insight into the emptiness of life burns away attachments. It also burns away any perception of duality between oneself and the world during the practice of meditation. This luminous state is strengthened by the third perfection of patience. It is here too that the bodhisattva—with a luminous, patient, and gentle mind—practices with greater success the Four Meditations, Four Formless Meditations, and Four Divine Abodes. The practice of patience helps the bodhisattva overcome anger, hatred, and even annoyance over any harmful acts or words. In luminous wisdom, everything is viewed with patient endurance and compassion. Finally, it is here that the bodhisattva develops the five supernormal abilities (*siddhis*) that are also recognized in earlier Buddhism. Here again are passages from the *sūtra*:

The bodhisattva in the third stage examines the impermanent nature of all conditioned existence and sees it in its suchness. . . . Seeing all conditioned existence in this way, the bodhisattva's mind is more and more free from attachment to all these conditioned things, and is directed toward gaining enlightened knowledge.

Bodhisattvas at this stage of luminosity leave behind desires, evil, and unwholesomeness for the realization and practice of the Dharma. . . . With pure mindfulness, they achieve and are established in the fourth stage of meditation . . . the realm of neither perception nor non-perception . . . not for enjoyment, but for the realization and practice of the Dharma. . . . In the same way, their minds are full of loving kindness . . . compassion, joy, and equanimity . . . and experience the five supernormal abilities. . . . Furthermore, the [bodhisattva's] patience and gentleness are purified along with friendliness, freedom from anger . . . and pride. . . . For among the Ten Perfections, the perfection of patience is foremost.

The fourth stage is called *radiance*. At this stage, the bodhisattva cultivates the fourth perfection of vigor, by which he or she is able to eliminate mental and emotional afflictions. Here, mindfulness and the four types of Right Effort taught by the Buddha are practiced more deeply. With the removal of these afflictive obstructions to the spiritual life, the bodhisattva's wisdom becomes even more "radiant." With this new vigor in the Great Journey, the bodhisattva pursues the traditional Eightfold Path with even greater effort. Thereby, doubts are cut off and the person's disposition becomes more relaxed, kindly, gentle, and peaceful. As the *sūtra* says,

The bodhisattvas in this radiant stage examine . . . internal and external phenomena with awareness and mindfulness . . . overcoming worldly desire and aversion. . . . The bodhisattvas use vigorous effort to keep unwholesome states of mind from arising . . . to destroy unwholesome states that have arisen . . . to give rise to wholesome states that have not arisen . . . to cultivate wholesome states that have already arisen. . . .

Based on detachment . . . they develop Right Understanding . . . Right Thought . . . Right Speech . . . Right Action . . . Right Livelihood . . . Right Effort . . . Right Mindfulness . . . Right Concentration . . . As the bodhisattvas develop the aspects of the [Eightfold] Path with skillful means and wisdom . . . they attain patience, self-control and peace. Being patient, self-controlled and peaceful, they contemplate the aspects of the [Eightfold Path] in order to purify the higher stages with constant vigor . . . and they produce great roots of goodness, they destroy worldly defilements . . . all doubts are cut off, and they attain joy and inner peace.

The fifth stage is called *difficult to conquer*. With great purity and equanimity, the bodhisattva's wisdom is now able more deeply to penetrate the Four Noble Truths about existence. With this indestructible wisdom, the bodhisattva is "hard to conquer" by persons caught in ignorance and evil, but wants to free them from their suffering condition. On this level, the bodhisattva cultivates the fifth perfection of meditation so that he or she is also "hard to conquer" by any inner tendencies toward distractions, as well as temptations or trials. Also at this level, out of compassion for others, the bodhisattva learns about culture, the arts, science, and medicine in order to help other sentient beings. The *sūtra* says,

> [They] attain concentration that cannot be conquered, and by so doing, they know correctly the truth of *duḥkha*, the truth of the cause of *duḥkha*, the truth of the cessation of *duḥkha*, and the truth of the [path to cessation's] attainment. . . . They know how the mass of *duḥkha* has been caused by ignorance and craving. . . . And it occurs to them, "How strange and sad that these ignorant beings . . . increase the fetters of *duḥkha* . . . do not pull out the arrows of pride and wrong views . . . do not extinguish the flames of hate, greed and delusion, and do not destroy the darkness of ignorance."
>
> Whatever good the bodhisattvas undertake . . . they do so to lead all beings to freedom, to the ultimate Nirvana. . . . The bodhisattvas, thus engaged in helping living beings, practice whatever might benefit these beings, such as writing and teaching, mathematics, the various sciences including medical science . . . song and dance, drama and music . . . these things the bodhisattva undertakes to learn out of compassion. . . . For bodhisattvas in this stage, the perfection of meditation is most important . . . and having attained concentration, they affect a trillion worlds.

The sixth stage is called *face-to-face*. Here, the bodhisattva reaps the fruit of the meditative attainments of the fifth stage and realizes the sixth perfection, wisdom. Thereby, the bodhisattva is brought "face-to-face" with reality itself. What he or she sees with wisdom insight is the empty, signless, and wishless nature of things. One comes to this realization by observing the dependent arising of existence. In a way that is similar to how Buddhaghosa described the person on the Four Paths contemplating over and over the dependently arisen factors of existence, the bodhisattva is said to contemplate the dependent arising and dependent cessation of all factors of existence from ten different perspectives. The bodhisattva does so in such a way that he or she overcomes any attachment not only to the world but also to Nirvana. Having practiced all the aspects of the Theravāda Path of Purification that leads to being an *arhat*, the bodhisattva could now enter Final Nirvana after death if he or she wishes. But because of his or her detachment to Nirvana and compassionate aspiration to attain Awakening for the benefit of all living beings, the bodhisattva decides to continue being reborn into the world. As long as there are beings in need, he or she will continue the Great Journey to full Buddhahood in order better to help others. Here are the *sūtra's* words:

> Based on a meditative understanding of the true nature of all things, the bodhisattva . . . guided by great compassion . . . observes the arising and cessation of the world. . . . Bodhisattvas contemplate dependent arising in ten patterns, and because of contemplating it in terms of . . . its inherent emptiness . . . the door of emptiness and salvation is realized by them. Because of the

emptiness of own-being . . . the signlessness of all things is realized by them. For those who have entered into emptiness and signlessness . . . the door of wishlessness and salvation is realized by them. Entering these three doors of salvation, they leave behind the views of self and object . . . of being and non-being. Filled with even more compassion, they go ahead in working for the Awakening yet to be achieved. . . . Among the Ten Perfections, the perfection of wisdom is most important to these bodhisattvas, but they also practice the others.

The seventh stage is called *going far*. Skillful means as a seventh perfection is added to the original six, and is especially practiced at this level of spiritual life. Remaining in the world and perfecting skillful means in order to help others gain enlightenment, the bodhisattva is "going far" beyond the *arhat's* attainment. By skillful means, the bodhisattva is able to adapt his or her teaching the Dharma to the needs of different persons. By developing an ability to know the minds and hearts of others, he or she can practice skillfully all the perfections in each moment for the benefit of others. For the bodhisattva to cultivate all the wisdom and skillful means he or she needs at this point in the Great Journey, it eventually becomes necessary that he or she no longer be born as a human being. Therefore, the bodhisattva must be born as a "celestial bodhisattva" in a Buddha realm in order to develop certain abilities. As *sūtra* says,

> They achieve access to the seventh stage by . . . skillful means, the perfection of wisdom and knowledge. . . . They train their mind well in realizing emptiness, signlessness and wishlessness, but they also collect a great supply of virtue and knowledge. They obtain selflessness . . . but they continue to live loving kindness, compassion, sympathetic joy and equanimity. . . . They become calm and peaceful by removing the fires of afflictions, but they continue to extinguish the fires of afflictive greed, hatred and delusion in all beings.
>
> While the bodhisattvas at this seventh stage have transcended most of the mass of afflictions . . . they cannot be said to be defiled by afflictions, or to be free from afflictions. Why? Because their afflictions do not affect their behavior, they cannot be said to be defiled by their afflictions. Because they are still seeking full Buddha-knowledge . . . they cannot be said to be free from afflictions. . . . [But] by attaining certain concentrations in which skillful means and wisdom are purified, and with the power of great compassion, bodhisattvas go beyond the stages of the disciples [of Theravāda] and the *pratyekabuddhas*. . . . [In this] seventh stage called "going far," most of the bodhisattvas become celestial beings . . . skilled at leading all beings to certainty.

The eighth stage is called *immovable*. The bodhisattva has now gone beyond any false or inadequate conceptualization of the world and is completely established in the Dharma—a position from which he or she is "immovable." It is as though the bodhisattva awakens from a dream and sees the Truth in a new and fresh way. His or her practice now becomes effortless. In this new experience, the bodhisattva's commitment to the Great Journey is also said to be "irreversible." This irreversibility is similar to that of the Streamwinner of the earlier tradition who will never turn back. The difference is that the bodhisattva's Great Journey, Mahāyāna claims, leads beyond the *arhat*'s attainment to full Buddhahood. In this new freedom, the bodhisattvas focus on the eighth perfection of "vows," which are the concrete expressions of the aspiration to attain Buddhahood for the benefit of all living beings. Also at this stage, the bodhisattvas gain more advanced forms of skillful means associated with Buddhahood. For example, they obtain the ability to manifest in various emanation bodies throughout the universe in order to instruct the Dharma to all forms of life. Here we can see why the bodhisattva must be a celestial being rather than a human being—no human could gain such an ability. As the *sūtra* puts it,

> When they attain the eighth stage, called the immovable, bodhisattvas become free from all effort having attained the condition of effortlessness that is freed from mental, physical and verbal striving. . . . It is like a boat . . . that is dragged with great effort to the ocean; but once in the ocean, sails effortlessly by the wind.
>
>   They know the ways in which the realm of desire . . . the realm of form . . . and the formless realm [are] constituted. . . . They know the varieties of beings . . . and they apply their knowledge to producing emanations . . . in whatever forms in which beings are born . . . for the purpose of aiding these beings to mature . . . to perfect Awakening. . . . With this knowledge at this stage, not moving from their Buddha-realm, they can appear in . . . untold Buddha realms, taking on the different characteristics of beings . . . according to their attitudes and dispositions . . . with endless forms of emanation bodies for the development and teaching of all beings.
>
>   This eighth stage is named "immovable" because the bodhisattvas abiding there cannot be turned back from their journey; thus it is called the stage of irreversibility. . . . These bodhisattvas primarily practice, among the Ten Perfections, the perfection of vows . . . and with the power of these vows, they produce . . . countless emanations of bodies.

The ninth stage is called *good insight*. At this advanced stage, the bodhisattva perfects even more skillful means for bringing others to Awakening and uses them in all the realms throughout the entire cosmos. Here again, we can see why this stage can only be fully practiced by a celestial bodhisattva. At this level, the bodhisattva's understanding of all the "paths" of Buddhism is perfected into "good insight." He or she has clear insight into how people are "entangled," as Buddhaghosa also puts it, in *duḥkha*. Based on this good insight, he or she is enabled to teach the Dharma skillfully, and with a skill and eloquence that even surpasses the abilities of the gods. In order to do so, the bodhisattva practices the ninth perfection of "power." For example, with one such power, he or she understands and uses all the languages and means of communication of all living things in all parts of the cosmos. Here again are the *sūtra's* words:

> Bodhisattvas at the stage of good insight have penetrating insight into good, evil and neutral conduct . . . the conduct of disciples [of Theravāda], the con-

duct of *pratyekabuddhas*, the conduct of bodhisattvas, and the conduct pertaining to Buddhahood. . . . With this awareness, bodhisattvas know how all beings get entangled mentally, entangled with afflictions . . . they know the aspects of the mind . . . of the afflictions . . . of weakness and strength. . . . Thus, bodhisattvas know the differences between all living beings' conduct, and undertake to liberate them according to their condition.

Knowing all this, the bodhisattvas give the Dharma to all beings . . . according to their mental dispositions and attitudes . . . their entanglements and afflictions . . . their actions and habits. They apply whatever skillful means may bring liberation by appearing in numerous forms in all worlds . . . knowing the language of all beings . . . with the necessary knowledge to explain the Dharma. . . . Thus, having attained mental power . . . they infuse a billion worlds and teach the Dharma to all beings according to their differences in mentality. . . . Most of the bodhisattvas at this stage become [celestial beings] with great powers, lords of millions of worlds.

The tenth and final stage is called *Dharma cloud*. Here, the bodhisattva practices the tenth perfection of "omniscient knowledge." He or she masters all forms of concentration (*samādhi*) and resides in the *samādhi* of the "knowledge of the omniscient." In this concentration, the rays of wisdom from all Buddhas rest on the bodhisattva's head, sharing their wisdom and consecrating him or her with the qualities of Buddhahood. The bodhisattva is then able to keep in mind this "Dharma cloud," showered on him or her by the Buddhas, from which he or she rains the Dharma throughout the cosmos. However, he or she must be born one more time in order to undertake the full life of a Buddha and create his or her own Buddha realm. Meanwhile in this tenth stage, the bodhisattva produces limitless emanation bodies throughout the cosmos, raining down the Dharma for the benefit of all beings. As a tenth-stage bodhisattva, obstructions to omniscience are removed, and skillful means, confidence, and power reach their utmost in preparation for birth as a Buddha:

Those bodhisattvas . . . are said to have attained the stage of consecration with the knowledge of the omniscient in all of its aspects. . . . They realize innumerable millions of concentrations. . . . At the end of innumerable millions of concentrations, he or she realizes a bodhisattva concentration called "receiving consecration by the special knowledge of the omniscient."

Upon the attainment of this concentration . . . the bodhisattva appears seated on a great jewel lotus . . . then as many bodhisattvas as there are other jewel lotuses encircle that bodhisattva on those other jewel lotuses, entering a million concentrations, gazing upon the bodhisattva in the middle of the circle. . . . Then from between the eyebrows . . . of all the Buddhas there come rays of light possessing the knowledge of the omniscient . . . illuminating all worlds . . . causing Buddha realms to quake . . . reaching throughout space, until they return to the encircling assembly, where they disappear into the top of the head of the bodhisattva being consecrated. . . . When the rays of light enter that bodhisattva's head, he or she is said to be consecrated in the realm of the perfectly Awakened Ones. . . . Thus, he or she enters the ranks of the perfect Buddhas.

Thus consecrated, the bodhisattva, mature in virtue and knowledge, is established in the tenth stage, called "Dharma cloud." Bodhisattvas at this stage have complete knowledge of the totality of the cosmos. . . . Since the vast knowledge of the Buddhas is immeasurable, the penetrating knowledge of the bodhisattva at this stage is also considered omniscient. . . . [And] in the arising of just a moment of thought, the bodhisattva can now go throughout the universe . . . manifesting infinite embodiments all at the same time. . . . They can also cause the wonderful qualities of the Buddha realms to appear in their own bodies. . . . [Thus] they illumine numerous worlds and cause numerous beings to mature.

CELESTIAL BODHISATTVAS AND BUDDHAS

We can see from this introduction of the Ten Stages that the Mahāyāna journey proceeds through eons of time and eventually takes the bodhisattva beyond the human to the celestial world—to birth in a Buddha realm. From there, one eventually evolves to become a celestial Buddha. This achievement and the powers gained by such bodhisattvas and Buddhas mean to Mahāyāna that there are many celestial sources of help for Buddhists on the Great Journey.

Celestial Bodhisattvas

Mahāyāna eventually produced a pantheon of bodhisattvas who could be venerated and worshiped. Three of the most important of these bodhisattvas are Maitreya, Mañjuśrī, and Avalokiteśvara. Maitreya, or "Kindly One," is mentioned in the early Pali texts as the bodhisattva who in the distant future will become a Buddha in this world. At the present time, Maitreya is living in the Tuṣita Heaven waiting to be born as the next Buddha after Gautama. In the meantime, he uses his powers and skillful means to respond to the needs of all living beings, especially to those expressed in prayers by worshipers. In tenth-century China, there was a Ch'an (Zen) monk named Pu-tai. Pu-tai was a happy and rather portly monk who gave presents to children from a bag he carried with him. After his death, a legend developed in China that he was, in reality, an emanation body of Maitreya. In the West, his image is sometimes called "the Laughing Buddha."

Mañjuśrī, or "Sweet Glory," is a celestial bodhisattva who resides in many worlds and is so revered for his great wisdom that he is called the "prince of the Dharma." He often appears in dreams and visions and protects Buddhists in times of need with his great powers. Mañjuśrī is known especially for using his great wisdom to destroy ignorance and awaken knowledge.

Avalokiteśvara resides in the Buddha realm of Amitābha Buddha. His name means "the Lord Who Looks Down," indicating that Avalokiteśvara looks down from Amitābha's realm with love and compassion, ready to respond to the needs of living beings. So, while he possesses all virtues, he is especially known for his love and compassion, which he expresses in his limitless forms of skillful means. He often takes on an emanation body in

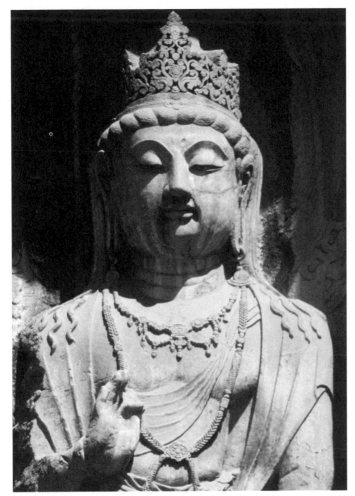

Figure 4.2. Mahāyāna Buddhism's spread to China: Kuan-yin (Guanyin); Chu Sian (Ju Xian) Temple, T'ang (Tang) Dynasty (618–907 C.E.), Lung-men (Longmen), China.

order to appear compassionately in this world. In Tibet, His Holiness the Dalai Lama is believed to be an emanation of Avalokiteśvara. Later Buddhist art portrays Avalokiteśvara as having many heads and arms, representing his ability to notice and respond to the needs of many beings at the same time. In East Asia, Avalokiteśvara is represented as a female bodhisattva who is widely worshiped. In China she is known as Kuan-yin, and in Japan as Kannon.

The Three Bodies of the Buddha

Turning now from bodhisattvas to Buddhas, early Buddhism distinguished between the Dharma-body (*Dharmakāya*) and a form-body (*rūpakāya*) of a

Buddha. The Dharma-body entails all the enlightened qualities shared by the Buddhas, while the form-body is the human form of each Buddha. The Yogācāra School of Mahāyāna, which we introduce in the next chapter, is credited with a more developed theory about the Buddha based on Mahāyāna experience. It is known as the "Three Bodies" (*trikāya*) of the Buddha, which became a standard doctrine in much of later Mahāyāna. First is the "manifestation body" (*nirmāṇakāya*) of a Buddha. This refers to the emanating physical form of a celestial Buddha that manifests in this or other worlds using skillful means to teach the Dharma.

The celestial Buddha that produces manifestation bodies is the "enjoyment body" (*saṃbhogakāya*) of a Buddha. The subtle celestial Buddha form is itself produced by the merit and powers obtained during the bodhisattva journey. This celestial form is for the enjoyment, blessing, and teaching of bodhisattvas. It appears to earthly bodhisattvas in visionary experiences or to celestial bodhisattvas by its direct presence. Celestial Buddhas create and preside over their Buddha realms, wherein bodhisattvas can be born.

Perhaps the first celestial Buddha to be mentioned in the early Mahāyāna *sūtras* is Akṣobhya, or "Immovable," Buddha. In one of the early *Perfection of Wisdom Sūtras*, Gautama Buddha is said to have enabled his hearers to see Akṣobhya Buddha. In the *Vimalakīrti Sūtra*, it said that Vimalakīrti showed Akṣobhya's Buddha realm, named Abhirati, to his hearers. A combination of good actions and the grace of Akṣobhya can bring one to birth in Abhirati. One of the most famous of the celestial Buddhas is Amitābha, or "Unlimited Light," Buddha discussed in the *Land of Bliss Sūtras*. In East Asia, he is the most worshiped of the celestial Buddhas, and being born in what is called the "Pure Land" of Amitābha is the hope of many East Asian Buddhists. Finally, Vairocana, or "Shining Out," Buddha is believed to be like a sun at the center of the cosmos, radiating the Dharma in all directions. Since ignorance is like darkness, Vairocana's light dispels the obstructions to Awakening with its luminous rays, often represented in Buddhist art.

The third body of a Buddha is called the "Dharma-body" (*Dharmakāya*). This is the essential nature of the Buddha (*Buddhatā*) that is also the "suchness" of all existence. This inner nature shared by all Buddhas is one of perfect luminosity with all the shining qualities of Buddhahood. In the *Flower Garland Sūtra*, Vairocana Buddha is presented as a personification of the Dharma-body shining in all beings, indeed, in all elements of the cosmos. This means, at least according to this text, that the luminous qualities of Buddhahood can be found not only in human and celestial Buddhas, but also in all things, even in a grain of sand.

This doctrine of Buddhahood presents the goal of the Great Journey in ways that inspire Mahāyāna Buddhists to travel the bodhisattva course to full Buddhahood. It also encourages Buddhists who are on that way of spiritual transformation to seek the help of those who are more advanced on the Bodhisattva Path and those who have already achieved the goal. This and the other teachings of Mahāyāna present the world with the religious experiences of Mahāyāna Buddhism. Another task of Mahāyāna has been to explain the philosophical implications of these experiences in systematic ways. This led to the founding of certain Mahāyāna schools of thought in India that, together with their Abhidharma counterparts, contributed to the intellectual Indian Buddhist culture that we introduce in the next chapter. As we shall see in later chapters, these Indian Mahāyāna schools would eventually be brought to other parts of Asia where they inspired more recent forms of Mahāyāna Buddhism.

SUGGESTIONS FOR FURTHER READING

Cleary, Thomas, trans. *The Flower Ornament Scripture: A Translation of the* Avataṃsaka Sūtra [With translation of the *Daśabhūmika Sūtra*]. Boston: Shambhala Publications, 1984.

Conze, Edward, trans. *Buddhist Wisdom Books*. London: George Allen & Unwin, 1958.

———, trans. *The Large Sūtra on Perfect Wisdom*. Berkeley, CA: University of California Press, 1975.

Gómez, Luis O., trans. *The Land of Bliss, The Paradise of the Buddha of Measureless Light*. Honolulu: University of Hawaii Press, 1996.

Griffiths, Paul J. *On Being Buddha: The Classical Doctrine of Buddhahood*. Albany, NY: SUNY Press, 1994.

Kato, Bunno, Yoshiro Tamura, and Kojiro Miyasaka, trans. *The Three Fold Lotus Sūtra*. Tokyo: Kōsei Publishing Co., 1975.

King, Sallie B. *Buddha Nature*. Albany, NY: SUNY Press, 1991.

Kiyota, Minoru, and Elvin W. Jones, eds. *Mahāyāna Buddhist Meditation: Theory and Practice*. Honolulu: University of Hawaii Press, 1978.

Lopez, Donald S., Jr. *Elaborations on Emptiness: Uses of the* Heart Sūtra. Princeton, NJ: Princeton University Press, 1998.

Paul, Diana. *Women in Buddhism: Images of the Feminine in the Mahāyāna Tradition*. Berkeley, CA: University of California Press, 1985.

Ray, Reginald. *Buddhist Saints in India: A Study in Buddhist Values and Orientations*. New York: Oxford University Press, 1994.

Sponberg, Alan and Helen Hardacre, eds. *Maitreya: The Future Buddha*. Cambridge: Cambridge University Press, 1988.

Suzuki, D. T., trans. *The Laṅkāvatāra Sūtra: A Mahāyāna Text*. London: Kegan Paul International, 1987.

Watson, Burton, trans. *The Vimalakirti Sutra*. New York: Columbia University Press, 2000.

Williams, Paul. *Mahāyāna Buddhism: The Doctrinal Foundations*. London: Routledge & Kegan Paul, 1989.

FIVE

THE INDIAN EXPERIENCE
OF BUDDHISM

The experience of Buddhism in India began, of course, with Gautama Buddha. So we have already been introducing the Indian experience of Buddhism in the four previous chapters of our story. We have seen how this experience took shape in Gautama's life and was presented to the world in his teachings. We have also seen how the experience of Buddhism in India has produced two different major expressions in Theravāda and Mahāyāna. In this chapter, we introduce some of the important schools of Indian Buddhist thought. These schools have attempted to present the varieties of Buddhist experience in more systematic and critical philosophies. As we shall see, this means that while this part of our introduction to Buddhism is more philosophically stimulating, it is also more intellectually challenging. However, it is a fundamental part of the story because the Buddhist ideas forged in the Indian context have played crucial roles in the later development of Buddhism throughout the world.

THE ABHIDHARMA SCHOOLS

In Chapter 3, we saw how different schisms in the early Buddhist community produced such schools as Mahāsaṅghika, Pudgalavāda, Sarvāstivāda, and Theravāda. These eventually were numbered among what are called the eighteen Abhidharma schools because they attempted to explicate philosophically the kinds of ideas presented in the *Abhidharma Piṭaka*. One common feature of these schools was their utilization of the types of analyses that are characteristic of the *Abhidharma* texts themselves. As we have seen, those texts claimed that existence could be analyzed into a number of fundamental elements called *dharmas*. These *dharmas* were either physical or mental in nature and were the basic constituents of ordinary mental life and of physical objects in the world. The physical elements of existence were further analyzed in terms of an atomic theory that was popular in India at the time. In this theory, all matter is produced by the same four types of atoms

126

one finds in early Greek philosophy: earth, air, fire, and water. The mental elements of existence were divided into two categories: the mind (*citta*) itself, which is one element, and its various mental states (*caitasika*), such as perceptions, desires, decisions, and afflictions. A further examination of these mental states was important for mental cultivation because it identified the positive states of mind, such as patience and loving kindness, that should be cultivated in the spiritual life, as well as the negative ones, like hatred and greed, that should be eliminated.

Most Abhidharma philosophers considered these elementary factors of existence, the *dharmas*, to be like psychic and somatic "events" that exist only for a few moments in the processes of life. There were disagreements as to how many moments a dharmic event lasts. Sarvāstivāda taught that there are four moments: arising, stasis, decaying, and passing away. Theravāda identified only three moments: arising, stasis, and passing away. In any case, what one finds generally in the Abhidharma traditions is that a doctrine of "momentaryness" was developed out of the Buddha's doctrine of impermanence. As we shall soon see, this led to a number of philosophical problems. The different Abhidharma schools came up with various solutions to these problems, and these positions philosophically divided them even further.

In the doctrine of momentaryness, it is claimed by most Abhidharma schools that even though the elements of existence are momentary events, they are each essentially self-existing. That is, they are said to have *svabhāva*, or "own being," that enables them each to exist on their own. This attribute was important to the Abhidharma philosophers because it meant that they did not need a creator God to account for the existence of these distinct elements. Also, each element has its own characteristic (*svalakṣaṇa*) that accounts for its unique identity. Thus, the popular Abhidharma view of existence was one of radical pluralistic realism. In other words, the world is constituted by many mental and physical elements or events that are real, self-existing, momentary, unique, and distinct from one another.

There are a number of philosophical problems with this Abhidharma view of life. One major problem has to do with causality. If, for example, you imagine a sequence of momentary mental events, how can one momentary event be causally connected with another in that sequence? If there is some causal factor that connects them, as Sarvāstivāda suggested, then you still have the problem of explaining the relation between that causal factor and the two elements it connects. In other words, if all that exists are elements, and if you imagine two elements side-by-side in a sequence and then insert a third causal element between then, how can one explain the actual connection between the causal element and the elements on either side of it? One is here led to an infinite regress.

Another problem with the doctrine of momentaryness has to do with perception. Most Abhidharma Buddhists believed that perception is only possible if an object is present to the senses. They also believed that perception entails a process of momentary mental events that takes some time to complete. But if this is so, how can one perceive an object that exists only for a moment? The object one knows at the end of the process of perception would be different from the object as it was at the beginning of the process. Then there is the problem of explaining memory. If one's knowledge now must have an object, and if the object one remembers is no longer existing, how can one explain the fact that one remembers something that no longer exists?

One of the most influential Indian Abhidharma schools to address these kinds of problems was the Sarvāstivāda School. As we saw in Chapter 3, members of this school attempted to solve the philosophical problems of Abhidharma thought by positing that all periods of time (the past, present, and future) exist simultaneously. This unusual view of time is why the school was called *Sarvāstivāda*, which means "All-Exists School." While there are variations of this theory in Sarvāstivāda, in general what was taught is that the past, future, and present are like realms where the elements exist. The elements of existence have substantial "own-being" that enables them to always exist in one of these time realms. An element first exists in the future, then appears in the present, and finally resides in the past. Since these three time periods always exist, right now there are elements existing in the future that will eventually exist in the present, and there are also elements existing in the past that had once existed in the present. This being the case, any past element, for example, can continue to be known and can causally affect other elements in the present. This also means, of course, that future elements can affect the present, and could be known in the present by supernormal abilities.

A second Abhidharma school tried to avoid this theory concerning time by remaining more faithful to the *Sūtra Piṭaka*; hence the school's name, *Sautrāntika*, or "Adherents to the *Sūtras*." They also accepted the notion of momentaryness, but understood it more in terms of the Buddha's teaching of impermanence. That is, while life is a series of momentary events, its elements do not have any own-being. So the fundamental elements of existence are not separate and self-subsisting, but are interconnected parts of the impermanent flow of existence. One can distinguish the elements, but since they are not really separate from each other, one does not have such a problem with explaining causal relations.

Thus the Sautrāntikins believed that the Sarvāstivāda theory that all times exist simultaneously is nonsense. Things only exist momentarily in the present, not in the future, and they do not remain existing in the past. This being so, Sautrāntika accepted that in the process of perception, what one knows at the end of this process is not the object as it was constituted at the beginning of this process. They went on to propose a representational theory of perception. In this theory, what one knows in his or her mind is an "impression" or a "representation" of a perceived object. In other words, one does not know objects directly, but only mental representations of them. Finally, as for memory, Sautrāntika introduced a "seed" theory. A momentary event in one's life process can leave a "seed," or potentiality, in the flow of "subtle consciousness" that can manifest as a memory when the mind wills to remember it. As we shall see, something similar to this seed theory would later be advanced by the Yogācāra School of Mahāyāna philosophy.

The Theravāda School approached these philosophical problems from another direction. Instead of trying to find a causal factor that connects the elements of life, they proposed that causality really involves the cooperation of a multiplicity of "conditions." That is, when a number of elements are present, their very presence functions as a set of conditions that entails the arising of an effect, of a new element. This notion goes back to the Buddha's doctrine of dependent arising. When certain conditions are present, there is an arising of something new dependent on those conditions. The Theravādins compiled a list of twenty-four kinds of conditions that influence the process of existence. They were especially interested in the kinds of conditions that account for the arising of *duḥkha* and the types of conditions that contribute to Nirvana.

In dealing with conscious life, Theravāda proposed the existence of a "life-continuum" (Pali: *bhavaṅga*) at the subliminal level of consciousness. This life-continuum supplies the continuing consciousness over a period of time. It is also at this level of subconscious activity that "vibrations" from conscious experience continue to remain within oneself. So, when conditions are right, one can remember past events by recalling to mind their traces in the unconscious. It is also at that subconscious level that one's karma matures and affects one's life, even when one is unaware of its presence. Again, this idea of a subliminal level of continuing consciousness, along with the Sautrāntika notion of seeds, will later appear in Yogācāra philosophy.

One other school was rather unique in that it turned its attention from the elements of existence to the person who is seeking Nirvana. This is the Pudgalavāda School. *Pudgala* means "person," and this Personalist School was concerned that in the analyses of life into impersonal physical and mental elements of existence, Buddhist philosophers were forgetting the person who is seeking Nirvana. For the Pudgalavādins, the sense of themselves as "persons," their humanity as persons, is not fully accounted for by impersonal physical and mental elements. Yet the person is not entirely different from the elements either. Personhood is not some entity separate from one's mental and physical life. Also, since it is the person who attains Nirvana, the condition of Nirvana is not different from the elements that constitute his or her life. Based on this view of personhood, Pudgalavāda claimed that it is the person who continues to perceive momentary objects, remember things from the past, and attain Nirvana. What is behind this philosophical position seems to be Pudgalavāda's intuition of a personal identity that is distinct but not separate from people's physical-mental life and a Nirvana that can permeate this personal identity in all of its mental and physical states.

The major Abhidharma schools flourished in India for centuries, even after the rise of Mahāyāna Buddhism. They founded their own universities and were present in Mahāyāna universities. Chinese pilgrims wrote that members of the Abhidharma schools outnumbered those of the Mahāyāna schools in the seventh century, and Tibetan sources claim that this was true until the thirteenth century, when Buddhism ceased to exist as a viable religion in India. During the early centuries C.E., a Sarvāstivādin work entitled the *Mahāvibhāṣā*, or *Great Option*, was written. This work was highly influential, and in the early fifth century it inspired a person named Vasubandhu to write one of the greatest works of Indian Buddhism. This is the voluminous *Abhidharmakośa*, which is an encyclopedia of Abhidharma thought. Vasubandhu's work has two parts: verses that present the Sarvāstivāda teaching and commentaries that give the Sautrāntika interpretation of those teachings. This work became central to the study of Buddhism in India and East Asia during subsequent centuries. The author is considered by Mahāyāna to be the Vasubandhu who converted to the Yogācāra tradition of Mahāyāna, but modern scholars question this claim. Finally, as we saw in Chapter 3, the Theravāda School spread to Sri Lanka and Southeast Asia, thus being the one Abhidharma school to survive until today.

The Mahāyāna Schools

The Abhidharma schools were concerned with two major philosophical issues: (1) the nature of the things and processes of the world and (2) the nature of consciousness and its knowledge of the world. One Abhidharma school, the Mahāsaṅghika School, presented a view concerning these issues that is similar to those found in Mahāyāna. As we said in the previous chapter, this may actually be due to Mahāyāna influence. In any case, in the Mahāsaṅghika positions, we can find certain ideas that are developed in the two major schools of Mahāyāna philosophy. For example, the Mahāsaṅghika philosophers taught that the elements (*dharmas*) of the world are "empty" of any "own-being" (*svabhāva*). Instead, they only exist functionally in the dependent arising of existence. Therefore, the true and "empty" nature of the *dharmas* can only be understood in the relational nexus of dependent arising. As we shall see, this kind of relational view of life plays a central role in the Mādhyamika School of Mahāyāna philosophy.

As for the nature and functioning of consciousness, the Mahāsaṅghika School taught that there is a "base" (*mūla*) consciousness, which, like the Theravāda life-continuum, provides a basis for continuing conscious life at the subliminal level. Also, Mahāsaṅghika taught that consciousness contains "seeds" (*bījas*), good and bad, that condition one's experience of life. Ideas like these about the nature of the mind are also found in the second major school of Mahāyāna philosophy, Yogācāra. As we shall see, both Mahāyāna schools developed their philosophies in response to the philosophical issues being addressed by the Abhidharma schools. With this in mind, we can now introduce the Mahāyāna schools in India. We will spend more time discussing these traditions than we did the Abhidharma ones because of their influence on Buddhism in Tibet and East Asia, which we explore in the next four chapters.

The Mādhyamika School

The Mādhyamika, or "Middle Way," School of Mahāyāna was founded by Nāgārjuna, who lived sometime during 150–250 C.E. Nāgārjuna used the forms of argumentation and principles of logic that were widely accepted in India during his day in his major work, the *Stanzas on the Middle Path* (*Mūlamadhyamaka-kārikā*). There, Nāgārjuna articulates the concept of emptiness. Since in that work Nāgārjuna does not mention any Mahāyāna *sūtras*, nor does he even use the word Mahāyāna, some scholars have doubted that he was a Mahāyānist. However, his views are so close to those expressed in the Perfection of Wisdom Literature that most consider him part of the Mahāyāna movement.

Nāgārjuna taught that people are caught in *duḥkha* and the *saṃsāric* chain of rebirth because of the power of karma that arises from unwholesome thoughts, words, and deeds that are motivated by negative mental dispositions. Here, he agrees with Abhidharma Buddhhism. But the key question for Nāgārjuna was: From where do these mental defilements come? The answer for Nāgārjuna is that this negative condition is produced by the way people "conceive of" the world in which they live. People misconceive the world, and their "wrong views" lead them to misbehave in ways that bind them to a life of *duḥkha*. One's misconception of the world happens in what Nāgārjuna calls *prapañca*. *Prapañca* means something like "the meaningful conceptualization of the world by the use of language." In other words, it refers to how people use concepts and language in order to understand the world.

With his concern about *prapañca's* negative affect on people's experience of the world, Nāgārjuna set out to show how the way people use concepts in language produces a "false view" of life. He proposed that when one conceives such entities as an agent of action or a dharmic element, one ordinarily assumes that these entities exist as discrete and independent. Or if one conceives of a process like motion or perception, one again assumes that there are entities that first exist as independent beings and then move or perceive other independent beings. Words like "perceiver" and "perceived object," "mover" and "movement," "agent" and "action," "substance" and "qualities" all imply that the world in constituted by independent entities that engage in relationships with one another.

This assumption of the substantial independence of phenomena is always at work in the human mind, determining how people experience life. By a person's ordinary linguistic use of concepts that imply the existence of independent substantial entities, one actually experiences things as existing independently. This view of life as made up of independent things is, for Nāgārjuna, a "wrong view" that keeps one from seeing the true nature of things. That is, *prapañca* keeps one from seeing that all things are really dependently arisen, they have no "own-being," or substantial independent nature. With this incorrect view of life, Nāgārjuna says, one becomes attached to things in ways that produce the negative dispositions and mental defilements that, in turn, produce *duhkha*.

What Nāgārjuna did in his writings was to use a very sophisticated logical analysis of concepts such as causality, perception, motion, agency, selfhood, and elements of existence in order to show that any assumption of there being independent entities involved in these phenomena leads to absurd conclusions. Using this logical method of *reductio ad absurdum* (*prasaṅga*), Nāgārjuna deconstructed the ordinary way of conceiving of reality. In so doing, he proposes that the Buddha teaches the correct view of life, namely, that things are what they are because of the relatedness of life, their dependent arising. If things, including the *dharmas*, arise dependently, then they cannot be independent entities. Since they exist in function of dependent relatedness, they are "empty" of own-being; they are nothing by themselves. This does not mean that things do not exist or that processes like motion and perception do not take place. It just means that this movement, action, or perception does not imply the interaction of any substantially independent entities. Instead, existence, movement, action, and perception take place because of a relational matrix of dependent arising.

An example of Nāgārjuna's thinking can be seen in his analysis of *duhkha*, the dissatisfactoriness of life. In the few verses of Chapter 12 of his *Mūlamadhyamaka-kārikā*, he says that ordinarily *duhkha* is assumed to be either self-caused, caused by another, both caused by self and another, or not caused at all. Nāgārjuna goes on to show that since each of these views assumes a substantial causal agent (either oneself or another) behind the arising of *duhkha*, they each lead to problems:

> Some people assume that *duhkha* is either self-caused, caused by another, caused by both self and another, or does not have a cause. Assuming *duhkha* is such an effect is not justifiable.
>
> If *duhkha* is self-caused, then it will not have arisen dependently. Indeed, it is dependent on these aggregates that others arise.
>
> If from these [aggregates], others arise, or if from those [aggregates], these arise, then *duhkha* would be caused by another, for these would be caused by those.
>
> If *duhkha* is caused by one's own person, then that person can exist apart from the *duhkha*. What is this [independent] personhood that self-causes its *duhkha*?
>
> If *duhkha* is caused by another person, who is that other [independent] person that is without *duhkha*, but causes it and gives it to another?
>
> Since the self-cause [of *duhkha*] cannot be established, how can *duhkha* be caused by another? For indeed, if *duhkha* were caused by another person, then in relation to that other person, the *duhkha* would be self-caused.
>
> In fact, there can be no self-caused *duhkha*, it cannot be caused by oneself. And if another cannot bring about his or her own *duhkha*, how can *duhkha* be caused by another?

If *duḥkha* could be caused by both oneself and another, it would have to be caused by each person individually. And where can there be any *duḥkha* without a cause, either by oneself or another?

These four views of *duḥkha* are impossible; it is also not possible to apply these four views to any other elements of existence.

So, if the arising of *duḥkha*, or any other element of existence, cannot be explained by the use of concepts that assume a substantial causal agent, how can it arise according to Nāgārjuna? In Chapter 26 of his *Mūlamadhyamaka-kārikā*, Nāgārjuna analyzes the dependent arising of the "mass of *duḥkha*." In other words, for Nāgārjuna *duḥkha*, like all factors and processes of life, arises dependently. Being dependently arisen, all phenomena are "empty of own-being." This is what Nāgārjuna means when he says, "We declare that whatever is dependent arising is emptiness" (*Mūlamadhyamaka-kārikā*, XXIV, 18). Wisdom, for Nāgārjuna, sees this truth of "emptiness" (*śūnyatā*), that all phenomena are dependently arisen. With this insight into emptiness, one escapes *duḥkha*: "The ignorant person creates mental formations which are the source of *saṃsāra*. While the ignorant person does so, the wise person does not because of his or her seeing the truth" (*Mūlamadhyamaka-kārikā*, XXVI, 10).

Wisdom seeing emptiness reveals that all *dharmas*, all elements and processes of life, are empty of the substantial independence people assume them to have in their use of linguistic conceptualizations about them. To be more precise: Wisdom reveals that the many mental and physical elements (*dharmas*) discussed in detail by the Abhidharma philosophers are "empty" of substantial independence. Nāgārjuna uses the term "emptiness" to refer to the lack of any independence to things due to their dependent arising.

What is this condition of "emptiness," this nexus of dependent arising, that is the ultimate truth about existence? Emptiness is not, for example, an Absolute that is separate from the world of ordinary experience. In fact, emptiness does not refer to a thing; it refers to the way all things actually are, namely, empty of the independent way they ordinarily seem to exist. To make emptiness into an entity about which one can have a view is to make the fundamental mistake Nāgārjuna is trying to expose, namely, seeing anything as having a substantial identity. As Nāgārjuna says, "Those who adhere to a view of emptiness are incorrigible" (*Mūlamadhyamaka-kārikā*, XIII, 8).

On the other hand, the proper realization of emptiness, for Nāgārjuna, brings *prapañca* and its wrong views to an end. One sees things as they are in truth. In Nāgārjuna's words, "Beyond conditional [realization], quiescent, without conceptualizations by *prapañca*, not discriminating a variety of meanings, these are the characteristics [of one who has attained] the truth" (*Mūlamadhyamaka-kārikā*, XVIII, 9). With this wisdom insight into emptiness, one's attachment to things and the negative mental formations that result in unwholesome thoughts, words, and actions are also brought to an end. This freedom results in the cessation of *duḥkha* and the attainment of Nirvana.

BOX 5.1

THE FLAVOR OF EMPTINESS

From the very first time I encountered the word in English, "emptiness," I liked the sound of it. Others may find it chillingly abstract, even scary; for me it was a fresh breath of freedom. I chanted the *Heart Sutra* ("form is emptiness, emptiness is form . . . ") every day for years before I ever studied what it meant. I remember once, at the beginning of my practice, walking up and down in a blizzard, snow piled two feet high and drifting, chanting that wonderful text over and over again. Only much later did I plunge into the vast philosophical edifice of Mahāyāna Buddhism, from the *Diamond Sūtra* and Nāgārjuna on, that adumbrates this saving and elusive teaching.

The logic of emptiness is air-tight: Since we know that we are, we know that things affect one another: Unless they do there is no world appearing, but if they do they must touch one another; if so they must have parts: If not they can't touch (they'd melt into one another), and if so there's an infinite proliferation of parts, smaller and smaller, clouds of them. So, if you look closely enough at anything it disappears into a cloud, and the cloud disappears into a cloud, and so on: All is void. The only thing real is connection: void touching void.

I have delighted in this simple but profound teaching, but it is the taste of emptiness in the body, spirit, and emotions that has meant the most to me. Knowing that what happens is just what happens. My body, my thoughts, my emotions, my desires, and hopes—this is the stuff that makes up my life. But it can't ever be desperate because I know it as a cloud. That cloud is all I am: It is my freedom to soar, my connection to all. I can float in it, and watch it form and reform in the endless sky.

This doesn't mean I am disconnected from life: Quite the contrary, I know there is no way not to be connected, no person or place that is beyond my concern.

When I practice meditation I rest in emptiness: My breath goes in and out, a breath I share with all who have lived and will live, the great rhythm that began this world of physical reality, and that will never cease, even when the earth is gone. It's nice, in the predawn hours, to sit sharing that widely, knowing that this zero point underlies all my walking and talking and eating and thinking all the day through: Is it.

They say that wisdom (the faculty that cognizes emptiness) and compassion are like the wings of a great bird. Holding both in balance against the wafting winds allows you to float, enjoying the day. Really though the two wings are one wing. Where you can appreciate the flavor of emptiness on the tongue you know immediately (without mediation) that love is the only way, and that everything is love and nothing but love. What a pleasant thing to hold in mind! All problems, all joys, all living and all dying—it's love.

ZOKETSU NORMAN FISCHER

Co-Abbot
San Francisco Zen Center

In Nāgārjuna's understanding of this Nirvana, we find another important aspect of his philosophy. That is, with wisdom, one sees that the ordinary conditioned world of *saṃsāric* bondage is not apart from unconditioned nirvanic freedom. Nāgārjuna says, "Nothing distinguishes *saṃsāra* from Nirvana; and nothing distinguishes Nirvana from *saṃsāra*. Between even the extremities of *saṃsāra* and Nirvana, one cannot find even a subtle difference" (*Mūlamadhyamaka-kārikā*, XXV, 19–20). In short, there are not two realities, *saṃsāra* and Nirvana. There is only the "field" of emptiness that is experienced through ignorance and unwholesome mental formations as *saṃsāra* or through wisdom as Nirvana. When one's experience of the world is conditioned by *prapañca*, it is known as *saṃsāra*, full of *duḥkha*. But when by wisdom one experiences the ultimate truth that this same world is empty of own-being, then one finds Nirvana and freedom. In that freedom, one is attached neither to the worldly things nor to the state of Nirvana, which is itself arising in the field of emptiness. With wisdom's penetration into the ultimate truth of emptiness, one is detached from both the world and Nirvana, so that one can freely turn with compassion to address the needs of all living beings.

This nondualism between the freedom of Nirvana on the one hand and the ordinary world of *saṃsāra* on the other brings us to the Mādhyamika doctrine of the Two Truths. Nāgārjuna says, "The teaching of the Dharma by the Buddhas is based on two truths: the conventional truth and the ultimate truth. Those who do not understand the distinction between these two truths do not understand the profound nature of the Buddha's teaching" (*Mūlamadhyamaka-kārikā*, XXIV, 8–9). The "conventional truth" (*saṃvṛti-satya*) is about the world as experienced by ordinary perception and the conceptualization process of *prapañca*. Through this experience, one knows a number of conventional truths about the world, such as the fact that fire is hot, that something is moving, or that a certain person is President of the United States. The "ultimate truth" (*paramārtha-satya*) about existence is that all things are empty of own-being, or are dependently arisen. This ultimate truth is realized in the attainment of wisdom which produces nonattachment and the freedom of Nirvana. The goal of Mādhyamika is to convince people that the conventional truths about things do not give one the ultimate truth about existence.

This ultimate truth does not deny conventional truths; it simply reveals the true nature of what one knows at the conventional level of truth. Nāgārjuna says, "Without relying on convention, the ultimate truth cannot be expressed. Without understanding the ultimate truth, Nirvana cannot be attained" (*Mūlamadhyamaka-kārikā*, XXIV, 10). In other words, first one understands the things and processes of the ordinary world in the conventional way. Then one gains wisdom and sees the emptiness of these things and processes, that they are what they are because of dependent arising. Only in this way can one gain freedom within the dynamic of existence, Nirvana in *saṃsāra*. However, one still experiences conventional truths about the world such as fire being hot, things moving, and a person being President of the United States. By the light of the ultimate truth of emptiness, one reenvisions the ordinary world so that one is no longer attached to things in ways that generate *duḥkha* for oneself or others.

Here, we see why Nāgārjuna's school is called *Mādhyamika,* or the "Middle Way." It does not reject the mundane world for Nirvana. Nāgārjuna takes a middle position where one reenvisions the mundane world from the standpoint of the ultimate truth. In this Middle Way, one enjoys the freedom of Nirvana on the one hand, while dealing compassionately with the conditions of *saṃsāra* on the other. Realizing the emptiness of both *saṃsāra* and Nirvana, one is detached from both *saṃsāric* conditions and the unconditioned status of Nirvana. Thus, one's Great Journey courses in the Middle Way, where one is transformed by the power of the enlightened vision of emptiness, nonattached and free, full of compassion, living for the benefit of all beings.

After Nāgārjuna died, his disciple Āryadeva (ca. third century C.E.) carried on his work. These two philosophers were the founders of the "early period" of Mādhyamika philosophy. The "middle period" of the school is marked by a disagreement between two philosophers. The first philosopher of this middle period was Buddhapālita (fifth century C.E.). While Buddhapālita employed the logical method of *reductio ad absurdum* to disprove the views of his opponents, he never attempted to formulate a position of his own. He believed that the ultimate truth cannot be formulated by words, which are always tied to conventional viewpoints. His school of Mādhyamika is called *Prāsaṅgika* after his *prasaṅga* method of logic. The second philosopher of this middle period was Bhavaviveka (ca. 500–570 C.E.). He had a more optimistic view of language's ability to bridge the gap between the conventional and ultimate truths. Influenced by the Buddhist logician Dignāga, whom we will introduce later, Bhavaviveka used logic to present positive expositions of emptiness. His school of Mādhyamika is called *Svātantrika* because it provided a positive position concerning emptiness by "autonomous" (*svatantra*) logical means.

The "later period" of Mādhyamika was initiated by Candrakīrti (ca. seventh century C.E.), who wrote commentaries on Nāgārjuna's and Āryadeva's works that supported the Prāsaṅgika School of Buddhapālita. It was also during this later period of Mādhyamika that attempts were made to synthesize Mādhyamika philosophy with the philosophy of the second great school of Mahāyāna thought, Yogācāra. In Candrakīrti's *Clear Words* (*Prasannapadā*), considered the fullest exposition of Mādhyamika, he clarifies not only Mādhyamika writings but also their spiritual purpose. He shows how the use of concepts and logic cannot reach the ultimate truth, and therefore concludes that only the practice of the Six Perfections in the bodhisattva journey can provide access to ultimate truth and freedom. Here is the way that Candrakīrti explains Nāgārjuna's statement that "Hate, greed and delusion are said to arise from thought-construction" in *Mūlamadhyamaka-kārikā,* XXIII, 1:

All discursive ideas [which are thought-constructions] without exception are stopped in emptiness, where one sees the emptiness of the own-being of all phenomena. . . . Those who see emptiness do not apprehend the Five Aggregates, the elements and sense-fields, as if they existed as independent entities. Consequently, they do not construct discursive ideas, thought-constructions, about these phenomena with the notions of "oneself" and "objects to be possessed by oneself." Therefore, they do not give rise to a host of defilements, which have the false view of independent individuality as their source. Thus, they do not produce karma, and do not experience *saṃsāra* with [its mass of *duḥkha*]. . . . Hence, one calls emptiness Nirvana, since it stops all discursive ideas [that produce samsaric *duḥkha*]. (*Prasannapadā*, 18)

A famous follower of Prāsaṅgika was Śāntideva (eighth century C.E.). Śāntideva was a Buddhist poet and philosopher who wrote two major works. One of them, entitled *Undertaking the Way to Awakening* (*Bodhicaryāvatāra*), became a classic of religious literature. In it, Śāntideva describes the Bodhisattva Path from the arising of the thought of Awakening for the benefit of all living beings (*bodhicitta*) to wisdom's realization of emptiness and full Awakening. Practicing the Six Perfections obtains the mind of Awakening penetrating emptiness, which produces the kind of freedom for which humankind longs. Śāntideva is perhaps most treasured by Buddhists for the following kinds of poetic descriptions of the compassionate heart of the bodhisattva inspired by *bodhicitta*:

When the thought of Awakening [*bodhicitta*] has arisen in a wretched one bound in existence, he or she is instantly proclaimed to be a child of the Buddhas, worthy of being praised in the realms of gods and humans.

[Adopting the thought of Awakening,] I am medicine for the sick. May I be their doctor and their nurse until sickness does not occur.

Showering down food and drink, may I avert the suffering of hunger and thirst . . . may I become food and drink.

Without any regrets, may I give my bodies, pleasures and goodness . . . in order to achieve the welfare of all beings.

Those who falsely accuse me, harm me, or mock me, may all of these persons share in Awakening.

May as many beings as there are who are suffering pain in body or mind find, through my merits, oceans of happiness and joy.

As long as there is *saṃsāra*, may beings never lose their happiness. May the whole world always receive happiness from bodhisattvas.

May all suffering from the cold be warmed; may all suffering from heat be cooled by oceans of rain from the bodhisattva clouds.

May blind people see forms; may deaf people always hear; and may pregnant women give birth without pain, like the mother of the Buddha.

BOX 5.2

THE WEB OF RELATIONS

From the day it is born, an animal enters the world of interdependence quite naturally. Food, water, shelter, contact with others—all are central concerns. Almost immediately it becomes obvious that existence depends on others. At minimum, the successful animal learns quickly which beings it must eat or pursue, and which it must avoid in order to survive.

My first insights into the nature of interdependence came from observing the natural world as an ecologist. The science of ecology studies the biological realm of plants and animals to understand relationships within ecosystems. Who eats whom? Which animals or plants are harmful to which others? Why do certain animals prefer only specific host plants? Exploring the ten thousand beings this way, the truth of interdependence is unmistakable, the manifestations endless. The entire life community is nothing but mutually dependent existence continually arising.

When I began to study Buddhism in earnest, I spent a lot of time sitting by the side of a stream, considering the nature of humane existence. Trees, too, provided good companionship in this endeavor. Climbing mountains, walking long beaches, I wondered if Buddhism was another way to understand the natural world. But how to explain the wide range of human behaviors and attitudes toward nature? I found it deeply troubling that some of these behaviors were extremely destructive to plants and animals.

Buddhist practice, in contrast to ecology, emphasizes the study of the conditioned mind as a locus for understanding interdependence. When we observe mental processes, we discover the existential truth of the Buddhist teaching concerning dependent arising. We see that each thought reveals connections to others, each patterned response is a demonstration of relational existence. Fear of predators, exploitation of resources, environmental pollution, all can be linked to patterns of thinking which themselves have historical, causal origins. This central Buddhist teaching permeates not just ecological relations, but all human mental and emotional processes as well.

Human thoughts create and justify human actions, and these have profound impacts on the natural world. In my practice field as a professor of environmental studies, I work with this teaching in all my courses. It provides a grounding point of stability from which to thoughtfully engage the most difficult concerns arising from human impact on the Earth.

STEPHANIE KAZA

Associate Professor of Environmental Studies
University of Vermont

May the fearful be without fear, and those who are oppressed with sorrow find joy, and those who are anxious be free from anxiety and at peace.

As long as there is space, and as long as there is the world, for that long may I live tending to the sufferings of the world. (*Bodhicaryāvatāra*, I, 9; III, 7–8, 10, 16; X, 2–3, 5, 19, 21, 55)

The Tathāgata-garbha *Literature*

During the period of time between the founding of the Mādhyamika School and the Yogācāra School, a number of Mahāyāna texts were written about the *Tathāgata-garbha*, the "womb" or "embryo" of the Buddha. The earliest of these texts is the *Tathāgata-garbha Sūtra*, composed between 200 and 250 C.E. Most important is the *Sūtra on the Lion's Roar of Queen Śrīmālā (Śrīmālā-devī Siṃhanāda Sūtra)*, composed between 250 and 350 C.E. Soon after this *sūtra*, the *Analysis of the Jewels and Lineages (Ratnagotra-vibhāga)* was written as a summary of *Tathāgata-garbha* thought. These writings did not present a system of philosophy and did not result in a separate philosophical school like Mādhyamika or Yogācāra. However, while their ideas did not have a great influence on Buddhism in India, they did strongly influence Mahāyāna thinking about the nature of consciousness, Awakening, and Buddhahood in East Asia.

This Mahāyāna literature proclaims that all living beings possess the *Tathāgata-garbha*. This inner reality is like a "womb" in that it contains the potential to become a Buddha, along with the many qualities of Buddhahood. It is also like an "embryo" since it can itself develop into full Buddhahood. It is said to consist of pure and luminous consciousness shining brightly like a jewel. Ultimately the *Tathāgata-garbha* is said to be identical with the Dharma-body (*Dharmakāya*) of the Buddha, the very essence of Buddhahood. Therefore, its condition is always nirvanic, and it responds to the teaching of the Dharma by generating from itself the thought or aspiration to attain Awakening for the benefit of others (*bodhicitta*). It was taught that all living beings already possess this innate essence of Buddhahood; they just do not ordinarily realize that fact. This last claim, about the universality of *Tathāgata-garbha*, was made in response to a debate in India in which some claimed that certain persons, who are "cursed ones" (*iccantika*), have no potential for Buddhahood. This debate would also appear in China, with all versions of East Asian Buddhism accepting the universalist position.

The reason people are unaware of the *Tathāgata-garbha* within them is because it is concealed by defilements like ignorance, hatred, greed, and delusion. These unwholesome mental formations cover over the *Tathāgata-garbha* "like a rag covering a Buddha statue." Once one is free from these defilements, the inner essence of Buddhahood shines forth with its luminous nirvanic nature and pure qualities. In other words, it is not possible for human thought or willfulness to attain Nirvana and Buddhahood any more that a rag can produce the Buddha statue that is wrapped within. Since the *Tathāgata-garbha* is the Dharma-body of the Buddha, it alone is the source of the attainment of Nirvana and Buddhahood. This line of thinking about the generation of Buddhahood is seen by the *Tathāgata-garbha sūtras* to be a positive addition to the Mādhyamika notion of emptiness. That is, when one attains the purification of mental formations and gains wisdom realizing emptiness, one can see this inner Buddha potential shining in all beings, including oneself. One's vision, clarified by the ultimate truth of emptiness, can realize the inner Dharma-body resplendent with Nirvana and the pure qualities of Buddhahood, like a Buddha statue breaking through a rag that had previously covered it. As we shall see, in China this innate and universal potential for Buddhahood came to be called "Buddha-nature" and played an important role in East Asian Buddhism.

The following verses from the *Ratnagotra-vibhāga* express these ideas:

> Because Buddha knowledge is contained in all beings, because it is pure and non-dual in nature, because those who belong to the lineage of the Buddha advance towards it as their goal, therefore all living beings have the *Tathāgata-garbha* within them.

> The body of perfect Buddhahood irradiates everything, its suchness is not differentiated. The path to Buddhahood is open to all, so at all times do all living beings have the *Tathāgata-garbha* within them.

> If it did not exist in all beings, there would be no disgust with *duḥkha*, no wish for Nirvana, no striving for Buddhahood, no resolve to gain it for the benefit of all beings [*bodhicitta*].

> Like a Buddha in a faded lotus flower, like honey covered by bees, like a fruit in its husk, like gold within its impurities, like a treasure hidden in the dirt . . . like a valuable statue covered with dust, so is this [*Tathāgata-garbha*] within all beings.

> Nothing can be taken from it, nothing can be added to it. So, it must be seen in its suchness, and seeing the truth, one is liberated. (*Ratnagotra-vibhāga*, I, 27, 28, 40, 96, 97, 154)

The Yogācāra School

The writers of the *Tathāgata-garbha* literature were aware of the *Perfection of Wisdom Sūtras* and knew of Mādhyamika philosophy. Today, scholars argue that these writers, like many other Buddhists at that time, were concerned with the negative impression conveyed by the notion of "emptiness." They felt that the notion of emptiness focused just on the *lack* of independent selfhood and did not do justice to the positive and *full* nature of enlightened experience. So, their *sūtras* stressed the Awakening to one's Buddha potential that exists within as a luminous treasure waiting to be discovered. The followers of the second Mahāyāna school, Yogācāra, also shared this concern about Mādhyamika. They may well have been influenced by the *Tathāgata-garbha* texts. However, the exact relationship between Yogācāra and these texts is the subject of debate between Buddhist scholars today. In any case, the Yogācāra philosophers were less interested in emptiness and more interested in how the mind generates the experience of the dependently arisen world in which things are empty of own-being.

The Yogācāra School draws its inspiration from certain *sūtras* that began to appear in the third century C.E. Among these are the *Resolving the Underlying Meaning Sūtra* (*Saṃdhinirmocana Sūtra*), the *Mahāyāna-abhidharma Sūtra*, and the

Figure 5.1. Gandhāran Maitreya; dark grey schist; second–third century C.E., India. The Royal Ontario Museum, Toronto, Canada.

Laṅkāvatāra Sūtra, which we introduced in Chapter 4. The actual founder of the school was Asaṅga, who lived in the fifth century C.E. Asaṅga's mentor was said to have been the semilegendary Maitreya, who was thought to be an emanation of Maitreya Bodhisattva. Asaṅga converted his half-brother, Vasubandhu, to his school. Both brothers gave a systematic foundation to the Yogācāra School in their writings. Asaṅga wrote, among other things, the *Compendium of Mahāyāna*, the *Abhidharma Collection*, and a commentary on the *Saṃdhinirmocana Sūtra* and, it is said, was inspired by Maitreya to write a number of texts, the most important being the *Discrimination between the Middle and the Extremes.* The important works of Vasubandhu include the *Twenty-Verse Treatise,* the *Thirty-Verse Treatise,* and the *Exposition on the Three Natures.*

The term *yogācāra* means "practice of yoga." In Buddhism, yoga is understood to be the practice of the Bodhisattva Path, especially the practice of meditation. Since the focus of the school is on the nature and functioning of the mind, Yogācāra was later referred to as *Vijñānavāda,* meaning "School of Mind." As we have seen, the philosophers of the Abhidharma schools taught that consciousness arises when the senses are in contact with objects. Yogācāra turns this commonsense Abhidharma position upside down. What Yogācāra claims is that consciousness actually produces the experience of sensations and their objects. It is not that a subject and an object come together to produce conscious experience, as in the Abhidharma model. Rather, for Yogācāra, there is a fundamental process of consciousness that produces one's experience of subjective selfhood on the one hand and the objective world on the other. One's experience of both oneself and the world arise dependently from a more fundamental process of consciousness.

Traditionally, scholars of Buddhism have accepted this view as a form of Idealism, the theory that the world is a product of the mind. Today, this interpretation is being debated. Another interpretation claims that the world *as we know it* is produced by the mind; what the world is in itself, we have no way of knowing. Related to this view is an interpretation that approaches the matter from a nondualistic point of view, where the subject and the objects of experience arise together. In any case, for Yogācāra, one's *experience* of self and world is certainly generated by the mind. Given this position, the philosophical task for Yogācāra was to explain how consciousness can be the basis for both the subjective and objective aspects of experience.

To begin with, they claim that all the mental and physical elements (*dharmas*) in experience are arising dependently within a more fundamental process of consciousness. While Mādhyamika emphasized the emptiness of this dependent arising, Yogācāra goes a step further and claims that consciousness is the causal force behind such dependent arising. Consciousness forms itself into the six senses (including the mental faculty that "senses" thought objects) and the objects of these senses. As the *Laṅkāvatāra Sūtra* says, consciousness is like water forming itself into waves. These six senses and their objects arise dependently from consciousness, accounting for the mental and physical elements of one's experience through a process that Yogācāra calls "ideation only" (*vijñaptimātra*).

Behind this ideation process of the six sense-consciousnesses is, according to Yogācāra, a seventh form of consciousness that they call "mind" (*manas*). They claim that this more unitary faculty of consciousness is the basis of both inner reflection and self-awareness. Self-awareness arises in the mind as it reflects on, or "follows," the dependent arising of the six senses and their objects. Because of this self-awareness, the mind concludes that it exists as an independent self apart from the objects it experiences. But in fact, both one's self and the world are two dependently arisen aspects of an experiential process that is being produced by consciousness—by ideation only.

Yogācārins also claim that behind the mind of self-awareness and reflection is the ultimate source of this whole ideation process. They call this eighth and final level of consciousness the "storehouse consciousness" (*ālaya-vijñāna*). In the storehouse consciousness is the fundamental unity of consciousness that is prior to all its forms. In its use of the above water and waves metaphor, the *Laṅkāvatāra Sūtra* also says that storehouse consciousness generates from itself all forms of experience like the ocean whose water takes form as waves. In other words, out of its "storehouse," consciousness constructs the subjective experience of one's mind and senses, as well as the objective world of their experience. While one's self and the world seem to be so distinct from each other in experience, they are really just dependently arisen formations from the storehouse consciousness.

Yogācāra claims that the storehouse consciousness contains the karmic "seeds" deposited in it from the process of conscious experience. These seeds influence the storehouse's ongoing construction of experience and account for its continuity. The seeds are influenced or "perfumed" (*vāsanā*) by one's positive and negative attitudes. For example, one's negative dispositions, such as the Three Root Evils (hatred, greed, and delusion), condition the seeds of future experience within the storehouse consciousness in ways that often lead to unwholesome thoughts, words, and actions. These unhealthy thoughts, words, and actions then produce new negative karmic seeds in the storehouse consciousness that, in turn, will affect one's future experience. Therefore, the storehouse consciousness accounts not only for one's experience of oneself and the world but also for the moral and spiritual qualities of that experience. This being the case, Yogācāra taught that one must change the karmic condition of the storehouse consciousness by the practice of the Six Perfections. These perfections cultivate "pure seeds" within the depths of the storehouse consciousness itself.

On the bodhisattva's Great Journey, mental defilements and afflictions are gradually eliminated, pure qualities are cultivated, and the mind is stilled by meditation. Then, when the inner conditions are right, at the very foundation of consciousness there is a sudden "conversion of the basis" (*āśraya-parāvṛtti*). One's ordinary processes of consciousness stop, and one gains an intuitive insight into the storehouse consciousness at its basis. Thereby, one attains freedom from all conditioned states of consciousness, Awakening, and Nirvana.

Yogācāra's presentation of this radical and sudden turning over of the basis of consciousness greatly influenced East Asian Buddhism. Some East Asian Buddhist writers read Yogācāra as agreeing with the *Tathāgata-garbha* Literature. These writers believed that both traditions taught that the purity of spiritual life comes from the inherent luminous Buddha-qualities found within one's deepest center. The sudden turning over of the basis of consciousness was thought to reveal a nondual nirvanic nature of luminous and pure consciousness, the unlimited Dharma-body, which is the essence of Awakening and Nirvana. As we shall see, others Buddhist writers disagreed with this interpretation of Yogācāra, and this issue became important to the development of East Asian Buddhism.

Returning now to early Indian Yogācāra, besides its theory of consciousness, the school also presented what are called the Three Natures (*trisvabhāva*) of experience. First is the "imagined" (*parikalpita*) nature of experience. That is, in one's ordinary experience, oneself and the objects of that experience seem to be independent entities, when, in fact, this independent status is an "imagined" fabrication. For Mādhyamika, this fabrication of the "imagined" independent nature of things in one's experience is made by *prapañca*. For Yogācāra, the imagined nature of experience is generated by the karmic seeds in the storehouse consciousness, along with the ego-awareness of the mind.

Second is the "interdependent" (*paratantra*) nature of experience. Here, we find the Mādhyamika "ultimate truth" that all entities are arising dependently or interdependently and are therefore empty of "own-being." Yogācāra points out that this interdependent nature of the self and entities of experience is produced by consciousness. That is, while people "imagine" that themselves and the objects of their experience are independent, in fact, they arise in experience interdependently from the processes of consciousness. However, since ignorance leads people to imagine that oneself and the objects of the world are independent, one develops attachments, defilements, and *duḥkha*. Thereby, unwholesome seeds are planted in the storehouse consciousness, which, in turn, play a part in this dependent arising of experience. Therefore, the "interdependent" nature of experience is both pure and impure, good and evil.

Because of attachment to the imagined independent things of ordinary experience and the resulting impurity of the interdependent nature of experience, Yogācāra posits a third nature. It does so to stress the need to purify oneself from the ignorance that is superimposing the imagined fabrication of independence onto the interdependent nature of things. By this purification, one can cease making this superimposition, see the truth about the dependent arising of experience, and become free from attachment and the defiling of experience. One does so by following the Bodhisattva Path. The result of this purification is the third nature, which is called the "perfected" (*pariniṣpanna*) nature of experience. This perfected nature of experience is ultimately attained by the realization of Awakening, wherein one sees that all ordinary experience is a product of "ideation only" (*vijñaptimātra*). With enlightened wisdom, one realizes Nirvana.

With these ideas in mind, let us now look at some verses from a text by Vasubandhu:

> Since our ideation gives rise to false ideas concerning the self and the [mental and physical] *dharmas* . . . this ideation, which depends on the mind, goes through three different transformations.
>
> First is the storehouse consciousness, which brings to fruition all of its seeds. . . . It is not affected by the darkness of ignorance or by the memory. . . . It always flows like a torrent. . . .
>
> Second is the mind (*manas*), which depends on the storehouse consciousness, while, in turn, conditioning it. Its nature and characteristic is reflection.

It is always accompanied . . . by ignorance of the self, views of the self, self-pride and self-love. It follows the objects of the mind in their dependent arising.

Third consists of the six senses of discrimination . . . that discriminate objects. Their mental functions include [all the *dharmas*]. . . . Based on the mind, these sense consciousnesses arise dependently with their objects . . . just like waves dependent on water.

Therefore, all the consciousnesses are transformations . . . and for this reason everything is mind-only. As the result of ideation, which renders seeds [in the storehouse], different transformations take place. The influence of these ideation seeds gives rise to different discriminations.

Because of false discriminations, various objects are falsely discriminated. But the objects that are grasped in these false discriminations are empty of own-being. The ultimate truth of all *dharmas* is nothing more than suchness . . . which is the true nature of mind-only.

The state of mind-only is realized when the six senses and their objects are not present. Without grasping and beyond discriminations is perfect wisdom. Because of the abandonment of energies of the karmic seeds, and the six senses and their objects, the conversion from relative knowledge to perfect wisdom is realized. This is the realm of purity . . . where one finds freedom, peace and joy. (*Triṃśika-kārikā*, 1, 2, 4–9, 15, 17–18, 20, 25, 28–30)

LOGIC, TANTRA, AND THE EXTINCTION OF BUDDHISM IN INDIA

As Abhidharma and Mahāyāna Buddhism developed in India, there arose the need to train monastics in the many philosophical systems of thought as well as the practices associated with them. Hence, some monasteries evolved into universities. One of the earliest centers of learning, dating back to the second century C.E., was Nālandā in northeastern India. Nāgārjuna and Asaṅga were said to have taught at Nālandā. Another monastic university was Valabhī in western India. Over time, Buddhist universities like these built vast complexes of libraries and lecture halls, instituted stringent admission standards, and developed curricula that included everything from grammar and linguistics to music, architecture, and science. They became centers of Buddhist culture throughout India. From these universities, missionaries were sent to other parts of Asia, and Buddhist scholars from throughout Asia came to them for advanced education and training.

In this Buddhist university setting, monastic scholars became more and more interested in questions of logic and dialectics. These more critical concerns led to an intellectual Buddhist movement that focused its attention on theories of knowledge. Dignāga (ca. fifth century C.E.), said to be a student of Vasubandhu, was the founder of this movement, called Buddhist logic. Dignāga's work presents and defends what he considered the various forms of valid cognition. He defined what the objects are of such cognition and discussed its relation to language and meaning. He argued that Buddhism provides a means of obtaining a correct cognition of reality, which, in turn, produces true meaning.

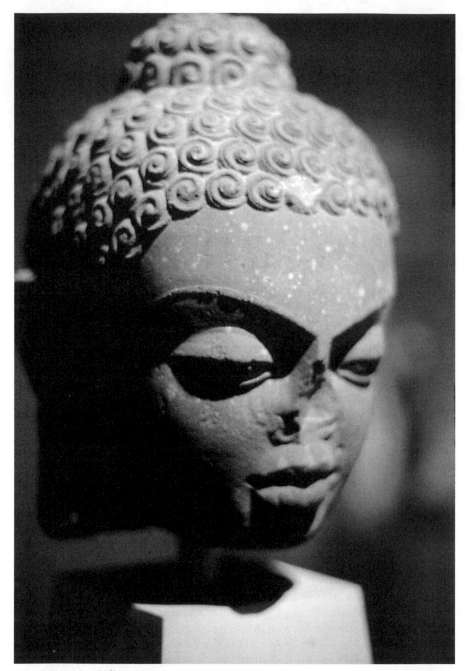

Figure 5.2. Head of Buddha from Mathurā; Gupta Period (320–647 C.E.), India. Cleveland Museum of Art.

Dharmakīrti (ca. seventh century C.E.) developed Dignāga's ideas about cognition and meaning into a systematic presentation of Buddhist theory and practice. That is, Dharmakīrti argued that the valid cognition of the true nature of existence obtained by practice and enlightened insight can give one's very life a whole new meaning. Therefore, the logic of valid cognition needs to be understood, so that such cognition can be pursued in Buddhist practice. Also, logical arguments can give one a cognitive certainty about the truths of Buddhism. This certainty can strengthen one's faith in the Dharma and inspire one to follow the path to Awakening with more vigor and hope.

Buddhist logic later became an important part of the Tibetan Buddhist tradition and still contributes to Tibetan culture today. In Tibet, Buddhist logic is part of both the secular branch of learning and religious training. However, in India this movement eventually lost its creative life and withered away to the production of dry summaries and logic handbooks. It never really spoke to the needs of the general Buddhist population in India, nor did it gain influence in Southeast Asian or East Asian Buddhism.

As the monastic scholars in the Buddhist universities became more and more consumed in abstract academic pursuits, the lay Buddhist community began to look for inspiration elsewhere. This opened the doors of the Indian Buddhist world to a religious phenomenon called Tantra. Tantra is named after texts, called *Tantras*, that present its esoteric teachings and practices. Its roots may go back to even before 2500 B.C.E., to the time of the magic and fertility cults of pre-Āryan India. In the most general terms, this early Tantric tradition in India emphasized the power of ritual, meditative visualization, and esoteric practices to unite male and female energies in a way that is spiritually liberating. At the time Tantra began to influence the Buddhist community in India, perhaps sometime just prior to the sixth century C.E., it was well established in certain Śaivite sects of Hinduism. In that Śaivite setting, Tantra included physical postures of body and hands called *mudras*, the use of magical phrases called *mantras*, the invoking and visualization of deities, breathing exercises, the movement of subtle forms of energy through psychic channels in the body, and the cultivation of sensual bliss through sexual rituals.

While many of these esoteric practices would have seemed quite foreign to Buddhists, some did not. For example, Gautama Buddha himself allowed for the use of *mantras* in certain cases—for example, in protecting oneself from snakes or sickness. After the reign of King Aśoka in the third century B.C.E., early Buddhism adopted some of the magical practices of ritual Hinduism, especially in the frontier areas. When the Mahāyāna *sūtras* were written, some included *mantras*. Also in Mahāyāna, the belief emerged that celestial bodhisattvas and Buddhas could manifest themselves in this world in order to benefit people in certain ways. Particular *mantras* and meditative visualizations were used in Mahāyāna rituals to invoke these bodhisattvas and Buddhas in order to gain their aid for some particular purpose. During the early centuries C.E., powerful *mantra* verses called *dhāraṇī*, hand gestures showing prayerful homage, and offerings of incense, flowers, and candle-light were used in these ritual practices. It is important to note that in these cases, the ritual practices were never seen to be a way of obtaining Awakening and Nirvana from these celestial beings.

As lay Buddhist communities were introduced to Hindu Tantric practice, they absorbed some of their practices and adapted them into a new Buddhist spirituality. In this Tantric Buddhist spirituality, the esoteric practices (*sādhana*) were used not only to acquire supernatural aid for mundane needs, but also to aid in the pursuit of Awakening, Nirvana, and Buddhahood. Both laymen and laywomen would use Tantric practices to heal psychophysical "blocks" to their spiritual energies and to attain states of communion with celestial beings, who would thereby share their spiritual knowledge and qualities of Buddhahood. This esoteric attainment was said also to produce certain supernatural powers, which lay Buddhists would use in serving others. Such an "accomplished person," called a *siddha*, would become a teacher of Tantra, often outside the monastic communities. *Siddhas* would gain their reputation by helping others identify their own psychophysical blocks, overcome them, and progress toward Awakening and Buddhahood.

By the sixth century C.E., some of these Buddhist practitioners composed Buddhist Tantras that attempted to systematize their esoteric ideas and practices. These Tantras taught that one needs a guru, or teacher, to initiate one into the Tantric rituals and practices. The instructions and demands of one's guru must, it was taught, be followed with strict obedience. The ritual practices involved *maṇḍalas*, or sacred diagrammatic circles, as well as *mantras* and *mudras*. *Maṇḍalas* affect one's mind, *mantras* one's speech, and *mudras* one's body. Thus, one's whole being was to be transformed by the Tantric ritual. The *maṇḍalas* painted on the floor also provided spiritual "sites" for ritual transformation. Some initial rituals help one pacify ills, attain prosperity and merit, and destroy danger. Other Tantric practices were designed to invoke union with Buddhas and bodhisattvas in order to be empowered by them in ways that give one access to their wisdom and to pure qualities of Buddhahood. Thereby, one progresses more quickly toward Awakening. More advanced practices unblock the flow of subtle energies in psychophysical channels in ways that generate wisdom's blissful realization of luminous emptiness. This latter practice also facilitates, it was believed, the development of a celestial body for the next life.

A particular aspect of Tantric practice that was at first not deemed acceptable by the monastic Buddhist communities was the ritualized violation of certain social values and religious precepts. Besides the breaking of sanitary and dietary precepts, such as the ban on consuming alcohol, of special concern were Tantric sexual rituals. These practices were intended to break down certain psychological and emotional blockages of repressed energies that could then be used in spiritual attainments. Buddhist monastics following the earlier non-Mahāyāna traditions rejected any ritualized precept-breaking as unskillful, not conducive to the Path of Purification. However, Mahāyāna monastic scholars were more open to the possibility of Tantra functioning as a form of skillful means. By the tenth century, some Mahāyāna scholars at Buddhist universities had accepted certain forms of Tantra into their curriculum, but with an important qualification, namely, the ritual performances that unblock and arouse certain energies by the breaking of precepts, such as sexual acts, were to be done only in the imagination. From that time on, there has been a controversy over whether such purely mental practice is sufficient for Tantric attainment.

Tantra assimilated into Buddhism is referred to as *Vajrayāna*, the "Diamond/Thunderbolt Vehicle." It is also called *Mantrayāna*, because of the importance attributed to the Tantric *mantras*. Vajrayāna produced various schools that focus on different Tantras and have their own systems of practice. Given the serious nature of Tantric practice, and its inherent dangers and possible abuses, the Buddhist universities sought to ensure proper teaching and guidance in Vajrayāna. The missionary travels of scholars from Buddhist universities, especially Nālandā, where Vajrayāna was accepted and taught, led to its spread to other parts of Asia. As we shall see in the next four chapters, Tantra spread from India to China, Korea, and Japan. It also spread south into Sri Lanka, Southeast Asia, and down to Indonesia, where it flourished for some time. In all of these countries, scholarly Tantra has not enjoyed great popularity. The only vital school of Tantra in East Asia today is the Shingon School in Japan. On the other hand, Tantra was also brought to Tibet, where it remains an integral and lasting part of orthodox Tibetan Buddhism today. Tantra has also remained a part of Buddhism in regions of Asia, such as Mongolia and Siberia, that were influenced by Tibetan Buddhism. We introduce some of the Tantric texts and particular practices of Buddhist Tantra in the next chapter.

As Buddhist logic and Tantra were taking their places within Buddhism, a number of events happening in India would contribute to the eventual disappearance of Buddhism in the country of its birth. By the seventh century, Buddhism was gradually being replaced in the south of India by forms of devotional Hinduism. Since the monasteries depended on popular support, many of them became deserted in that region of India. In the northwest, invasions by the Ephthalite Huns in the sixth century had devastated hundreds of monasteries. In the eighth century were invasions by the Muslim Turks in northwestern and western India. As these invaders moved south, they pillaged Buddhist monasteries, burned Buddhist *sūtras*, and butchered Buddhist monastics. The famous Buddhist monastic university of Valabhī was destroyed. Buddhist refugees fled to the east, where they found refuge in the Ganges Plain. However, the Pala Empire that ruled that area was overthrown in 1162, and by the end of that century, the Muslim Turks conquered that region as well. Nālandā was destroyed in 1198. Without the leadership of the monastic Saṅgha and their great universities, the Buddhist communities could not survive. They were assimilated into devotional Hinduism; by the next century, Buddhism in India virtually disappeared. However, as Buddhism disappeared in its homeland, it took on new and vital forms in other parts of Asia, which we introduce in the next four chapters.

SUGGESTIONS FOR FURTHER READING

Akira, Hirakawa. *A History of Indian Buddhism: From Śākyamuni to Early Mahāyāna*. Honolulu: University of Hawaii Press, 1990.

Conze, Edward. *Buddhist Thought in India: Three Phases of Buddhist Philosophy*. London: George Allen & Unwin, 1962.

de Bary, Wm. Theodore, Ainslie Embree, and Stephen N. Hay, eds. Revised in 1988 by Stephen N. Hay. *Sources of Indian Tradition*. 2 vols. New York: Columbia University Press, 1988.

Frauwallner, Erich. *Studies in Abhidharma Literature and the Origins of Buddhist Philosophical Systems*. Edited by Ernst Steinkellner; translated by Sophie Francis Kidd. Albany, NY: SUNY Press, 1996.

Garfield, Jay L., *The Fundamental Wisdom of the Middle Way: Nāgārjuna's Mūlamādhyamakakārikā*. New York: Oxford University Press, 1995.

Goudriaan, Teun, ed. *Ritual and Speculation in Early Tantrism* Albany, NY: SUNY Press, 1992.

Huntington, C. W. *The Emptiness of Emptiness: An Introduction to Early Indian Mādhyamika*. Honolulu: University of Hawaii Press, 1989.

Jayatilleke, K. N. *Early Buddhist Theory of Knowledge*. London: George Allen & Unwin, 1963.

Kalupahana, David. *Causality: The Central Philosophy of Buddhism*. Honolulu: University of Hawaii Press, 1975.

———. *Nāgārjuna: The Philosophy of the Middle Way*. Albany, NY: SUNY Press, 1986.

Kinnard, Jocob N. *Imaging Wisdom: Seeing and Knowing in the Art of Indian Buddhism*. Richmond, UK: Curzon Press, 1999.

Nagao, Gadjin. *Mādhyamika and Yogācāra: A Study of Mahāyāna Philosophies*. Albany, NY: SUNY Press, 1991.

Śāntideva, *The Bodhicaryāvatāra*. Translated by Kate Crosby and Andrew Skilton. Oxford: Oxford University Press, 1995.

Schopen, Gregory. *Bones, Stones, and Buddhist Monks: Collected Papers on the Archaeology, Epigraphy, and Texts of Monastic Buddhism in India*. Honolulu: University of Hawaii Press, 1996.

Snellgrove, David L., trans. *The Hevajra Tantra*. London: Oxford University Press, 1959.

———. *Indo-Tibetan Buddhism: Indian Buddhists and Their Tibetan Successors*. Vol. 1. Boston: Shambhala Publications, 1987.

SIX

THE TIBETAN EXPERIENCE OF BUDDHISM

By the sixth century C.E., Tibet was becoming a more unified country with a strong military presence in the region. Finding itself surrounded by nations heavily influenced by Buddhism, Tibet's reaction was at first not at all positive. The Tibetans practiced a shamanistic and animistic religion with elaborate sacrificial rituals, a court priesthood, magicians, and worship of local, regional, and national deities. Uninterested in Buddhism, the Tibetan armies destroyed the Buddhist monastic institutions they encountered while carrying out their military incursions. However, under the reign of King Songtsen Gampo (ca. 617–649) this resistance to Buddhism changed.

THE FIRST DISSEMINATION OF BUDDHISM IN TIBET

Having inherited a unified Tibet, Songtsen Gampo strengthened and expanded the Tibetan Empire. Eventually, Tibet became the most powerful kingdom in Central Asia. Songtsen Gampo moved his capital to the city of Lhasa and built his palace on the hilltop where the Potala was later constructed as the residence of the Dalai Lamas. In two of his political marriages, one to the daughter of the king of Nepal and the other to the daughter of the emperor of China, his wives were Buddhists. These two women had some influence on the king and, through him, softened the Tibetan attitude toward the Buddhist religion. The king also built the first Buddhist temple in Tibet, had the Tibetan alphabet and grammar developed using Sanskrit as a model so as to better translate Buddhist texts, and founded law codes based on certain Buddhist principles. In pursuing these tasks, Songtsen Gampo sent scholars to India; eventually Buddhist monks from surrounding areas also traveled to Tibet. Many Tibetans involved in these early contacts were especially interested in Tantra, which fit well with their shamanistic sensitivities.

The openness and efforts of Songtsen Gampo set the stage for Tibet's first Buddhist king. King Trisong Detsen (ca. 742–798) was a devout Buddhist who wished to propagate the Buddhist religion throughout Tibet. He sent for the great Indian Buddhist scholar at Nālandā University, Śāntarakṣita (ca. 705–788), asking him to journey to Tibet to teach the Dharma. He also wanted Śāntarakṣita to preside over the building of the first Buddhist monastery in Tibet. This was the Samyé Monastery, built near Lhasa from 763 to 775. Unfortunately, when Śāntarakṣita arrived in Tibet, a number of natural disasters were interpreted by the priests as signs of displeasure from local demonic forces. Śāntarakṣita was forced to leave Tibet. But before doing so, he advised the king to bring to Tibet a great Tantric practitioner named Padmasambhava, whom Śāntarakṣita thought had the power to defeat the demonic forces. Tibetan tradition teaches that Padmasambhava did indeed defeat these forces, and Śāntarakṣita was able to return to Tibet to continue his work. Padmasambhava also conquered the minds and hearts of many members of the Tibetan aristocracy, warlords, and common people throughout the Tibetan region. In 775, the Samyé Monastery in Tibet was consecrated, with Trisong Detsen, Śāntarakṣita, and Padmasambhava in attendance. Seven members of Tibet's aristocracy, called the "Seven Elect," were ordained, thus founding the first Tibetan Saṅgha. Their monastic discipline was based on the Mūlasarvāstivādin *Vinaya*.

Building on this monastic foundation, King Trisong Detsen invited Buddhist scholars from India and China to translate Buddhist scriptures into the Tibetan language. This work was overseen by a council approved by the king. One command that he gave this council was that they were not to translate any Tantric texts. The Indian and Chinese scholars involved in this project introduced not only translations of Buddhist texts into Tibet, but also the philosophical ideas and meditative practices of their own respective traditions. This, in turn, led to an important controversy that later helped to define the unique character of Tibetan Buddhism. The Chinese masters preferred the teachings and practice of Ch'an (Zen) Buddhism, which we introduce in the next chapter. They taught that what is necessary in the monastic life is the attainment of sudden Awakening through the practice of meditation. This direct insight into one's "Buddha-nature" enables that inner nature to express itself in enlightened living. It is the realization of one's Buddha-nature, they claimed, that purifies one of all mental afflictions and defilements. So, the need for gradual moral cultivation is not the principle directive of monastic life.

The Indian masters, on the other hand, did not believe that any particular religious experience can eliminate all the mental defilements and afflictions that have been engrained into one for countless lifetimes. Rather, they taught that purification for Buddhahood has to be gradually perfected in the Ten Stages of the Bodhisattva Path. One must familiarize oneself with the roots of one's unhealthy thoughts, words, and actions, as well as with the enlightened thoughts, words, and actions of the Buddhas and bodhisattvas. Ridding oneself of the former, and cultivating the latter, involves a long process of growth in wisdom and compassion that no sudden insight can accomplish.

The Tibetan tradition teaches that a debate was held in Lhasa around

790–792 in order to settle the matter and that the Indian position prevailed over the Chinese one. On the other hand, the Chinese record claims that the Chinese masters won the debate. Some modern scholars doubt if any such official debate ever occurred. But in any case, in the Tibetan record, it was a historically significant event, and by the end of the eighth century, the Indian teachings concerning the need for moral and meditative cultivation for the removal of defilements, and for gradual insight into the Dharma, had gained favor in Tibet.

King Trisong Detsen's reign helped define the character of Tibetan Buddhism. The new religion spread widely in the country, especially among the educated class. Soon, the written language was further refined to render more accurately the Sanskrit Buddhist texts into Tibetan. Indian and Tibetan scholars worked together on translation committees, where Indians made sure the doctrines were correctly transmitted and Tibetans checked the grammar. This "First Dissemination" of Buddhism into Tibet was also supported by Trisong Detsen's son and grandson.

However, the growing power of the Saṅgha made it unpopular with some of the aristocracy. Given this concern of the ruling class, King Lang Darma (ruled 838–842) began to persecute Buddhism. In the end, he closed monasteries, forced monks and nuns to return to the laity, and cut cultural and religious contacts with India. The religion was driven underground, and eventually the king was assassinated. The upheaval caused by his assassination led to a period of political chaos in Tibet. Given the lack of any central authority, the Tibetan armies retreated within Tibet's natural borders, thus ending its empire in Central Asia. Within Tibet, the collapse of the dynasty led to regional fragmentation under which Buddhism continued to be suppressed. Behind this continued suppression was the view that Buddhism weakens the military resolve of the nation. However, even under this suppression, Buddhism continued to be practiced by the laity through the guidance of lay teachers. Meanwhile, Buddhist monastic masters retreated to remote regions of the country and to neighboring countries, where they preserved their traditions for over a century.

THE SECOND DISSEMINATION OF BUDDHISM IN TIBET

At the end of the tenth century, a measure of political stability developed in some regions of Tibet. A few of the new rulers in those regions took an interest in Buddhism. The rulers of Western Tibet, where this interest was high, began to send monks to India for study so that they could revitalize Buddhism in Tibet. The return of two Tibetan monastics with some Indian scholars in 978 marked the beginning of what is called the "Second Dissemination" of Buddhism in Tibet. The eventual success of this renewal effort was, in many ways, because of the efforts of the great Indian scholar Atīśa (982–1054), who arrived in Tibet in 1042. Atīśa, who had been the dean of Nālandā University, brought with him a mature synthesis of Indian Buddhism. This synthesis integrated Abhidharma, Mahāyāna, and Tantric forms of Buddhism.

One of Atīśa's works, *A Lamp for the Path to Awakening*, gives a survey of this synthesis of the Buddhist path. In brief, Atīśa taught that the monastic life must be guided by the *Vinaya* rules. He believed that the discipline and practice of the early forms of Buddhism like Theravāda provide penetrating insight into the Dharma, which, in turn, gives one an authentic taste of Nirvana. The Buddhist path, Atīśa taught, also needs Mahāyāna's arising of *bodhicitta*, and its gradual bodhisattva way to Buddhahood. Mahāyāna provides the proper understanding of reality in its *sūtras*, and in its fully developed philosophies. Atīśa personally supported the Prāsaṅgika School of Mādhyamika, which became the major school of Tibetan Buddhist philosophy. Finally, Atīśa taught that the bodhisattva journey to Buddhahood could be facilitated and shortened by the practice of Tantric techniques. Tantra was seen by Atīśa as the most powerful means for transforming a common person into a Buddha. As a student of the famous Indian Tantric master Nāropa (1016–1100), Atīśa is also credited with introducing certain Tantric lineages of initiations into Tibet.

Atīśa emphasized the ideal relationship between master and disciple as the most important means for the proper transmission of the Dharma. For Atīśa, personal Dharma transmission was more important than all the *sūtras* and their commentaries. This is because while the *sūtras* provide proper teachings, the enlightened master has the ability to know which teaching is needed by his or her disciple and has the power to apply that teaching to the disciple's life in a transformative way. Atīśa said that the disciple is like a patient, the Dharma is like medicine, and the master is like the doctor who diagnoses the patient's illness and prescribes the correct medicine for his or her therapy. This emphasis on the role of the teacher, or guru, became a central element in Tibetan Buddhism. The following verses from Atīśa's *A Lamp for the Path to Awakening* outline his synthesis:

> With great faith in the Three Refuges, bend your knee to the ground, fold your hands, and first take the Three Refuges three times. . . . Then with compassionate thoughts for all creatures, look out at the suffering of the world. . . . At the sight of those who suffer, one suffers; and if one wants to free the world from the cause of suffering, he or she must give rise to the thought of Awakening [*bodhicitta*], and vow never to go back.

> Right resolve cannot be furthered without vows. . . . Only those who take the lasting vows given in the *Vinaya* rules are fit to take the bodhisattva vow. . . . The Buddha said that of all the ranks of persons taking vows, the vowed life of the monastic is the highest.

> According to the ritual given in the chapter on conduct in the *Daśabhūmika Sūtra*, one takes the bodhisattva vow from a good guru. . . . When one strives in the vows that make up the pure and perfect bodhisattva vow, one will bring to perfection the merit [from virtue] and wisdom [from penetrating insight] needed for perfect Awakening.

> When tranquillity meditation [*śamatha*] is achieved, so too are the [five] supernatural abilities. But hindrances to Awakening are not extinguished with-

out the perfection of wisdom. So, to remove these hindrances that produce afflictions and obscure knowledge, one must cultivate the perfection of wisdom and skillful means.

Wisdom is fully explained as knowing the emptiness of own-being in the non-arising of the Five Aggregates, the sense fields and elements of existence. . . . *Saṃsāra* arises from conceptual thought. . . . [T]he complete removal of that conceptual thought is the highest Nirvana.

Through the rituals . . . effected by the power of *mantras* . . . the merit and wisdom needed for Awakening are perfected with ease. If one wants to practice *mantras* as taught in the Tantras, action, performance and the others, then one must gain initiations from a holy guru. (*Bodhipathapradīpa*, 9–11, 19–22, 33, 41–42, 47, 55, 60–62)

Atīśa's efforts to stimulate and formulate Buddhism in Tibet led to the founding of the Kadam ("Bound to Commands [of the Buddha]") School of Tibetan Buddhism by his disciple Dromdön (1008–1064). This foundation was supported by certain aristocratic families, thus providing a model for other developing schools. For example, Gönchok Gyelpo (1034–1102), a member of the famous Khön family, founded the Sakya Monastery in 1073. Gönchok Gyelpo was a disciple of Drokmi (992–1074), who had obtained Tantric initiations in India. Gönchok Gyelpo's son, Günga Nyingpo (1092–1158), systematized the teachings of this new Tibetan lineage and adopted the Kadam *Vinaya* discipline. Thus, he founded the Sakya School of Tibetan Buddhism. The Sakya Monastery became a center for Buddhist study, eventually evolving into a monastic university.

A third important Buddhist school that was founded around this time was the Kagyü ("Teaching Lineage") School. One of its founders, Marpa (1012–1096), traveled to India for monastic training. He, like Atīśa, studied under Nāropa, who had once been the head scholar of Nālandā University. Marpa returned home, married, and inspired his disciples with his wisdom and example. Also like Atīśa, Marpa supported a reform of Buddhism that would synthesize *Vinaya* discipline, the Bodhisattva Path, and Tantric practice.

Marpa's most famous disciple was Milarepa (1040–1123). Milarepa had emerged from a troubled family as a great sorcerer, who even used black magic for reasons of revenge, exacting the deaths of his uncle and others. Eventually overcome with guilt for being a murderer, Milarepa turned to Marpa for guidance in the purifying Dharma. Given Milarepa's defiled state of mind, his purification was a long and arduous process. But in the end, Marpa introduced Milarepa to higher Tantric practices; after twelve years of long retreats, Milarepa attained full Awakening. After his enlightenment, Milarepa spent most of his life as a hermit, living in caves and practicing meditation. Thus, he provided a Tibetan Buddhist model for the renunciate life and for the miraculous transformative power of the Dharma.

Although a renunciate, Milarepa did gain a certain following, and he helped people with his special powers. As he traveled around Tibet, he presented his teachings in folk songs, which are still beloved by all Tibetans.

Milarepa's successor was Gampopa (1079–1153), who was responsible for the actual founding of the Kagyü School on the basis of Kadam's monastic practice and educational system, along with the particular Tantric practices developed by Nāropa, Marpa, and Milarepa. Gampopa's disciples split Kagyü into five sects, the major one being Karma Kagyü. The following are verses from two songs attributed to Milarepa:

> Homage to the feet of Marpa of Lhobrak!
> May this hermit be successful in holding fast to solitude.
> The principle that sustains life sprouts from the earth;
> Ambrosia showers from the blue dome of heaven.
> These join together to confer blessings on all living beings;
> And in religious life, this happens in the best way.
>
> The transient body is nourished by one's parents;
> The sacred Dharma is given by one's holy guru.
> These join together to confer the religious life;
> And in perseverance lies true success.
>
> The rocky cave provides solitude;
> Devotion is zealous and sincere.
> These join together and bring success;
> Of spiritual wisdom does this consist.
>
> Patience fortifies Milarepa's meditation;
> Faith comes from all living beings.
> These join together in skillful means;
> Of which compassion is the essence.
>
> The hermit meditates in rocky caves;
> the layperson provides sustenance.
> These join together in gaining Buddhahood;
> These merits are offered for the Awakening of all living beings. . . .
>
> Within the temple of the hill of Awakening, my body,
> Within my breast where an altar lies,
> Within the highest chamber of my heart,
> There is the horse of my mind.
>
> What lasso can catch this horse?
> What post can it be tied to when it is caught?
> What food is it to be given when it is hungry?
> What drink is it to be given when it is thirsty?
> What enclosure can it be kept when it is cold?
>
> To catch the horse, use the lasso of equanimity.
> When caught, it must be tied to the post of meditation.

When hungry, it must be fed the guru's teachings.
When thirsty, it must be given the purity of consciousness.
When cold, it must be kept in the enclosure of emptiness.
(*Jetsün-Kahbum*, II, 10)

As the great reforms of the Second Dissemination were taking shape, many of the older Buddhist communities in Tibet resisted the changes. One such group had mixed Buddhist teachings with the indigenous shamanistic traditions, thus creating its own Bön lineage that declared itself to be a separate religion. Another group stayed within the Buddhist fold and created the Nyingma ("Ancient School") lineage, based on the older Tantric texts and practices. Therefore, by the end of the Second Dissemination, the Tibetan religious landscape consisted of four major Buddhist schools—Kadam, Sakya, Kagyü, and Nyingma—as well as one adamantly indigenous tradition, which called itself Bön.

One of the greatest feats of Tibetan Buddhism coming from the Second Dissemination was the compilation of the Tibetan Buddhist canon. This voluminous work contains two major sections. The first, called the *Kanjur* ("Translations of Teachings"), contains teachings attributed to the Buddhas. The *Kanjur* has four parts: the Mūlasarvāstivādin *Vinaya*, the Perfection of Wisdom Literature, other Mahāyāna *sūtras*, and Tantras. The second section, called the *Tanjur* ("Translations of Treatises"), contains all the commentaries that had come from India, as well as those written in Tibet. When this canon was completed, its hundreds of volumes were carved in mirror images on wooden blocks, which could be inked and pressed onto paper for printing.

In 1247, the Mongolian ruler Godan Khan commanded a Tibetan representative to his court. The leader of the Sakya School, Günga Gyeltsen (1181–1251), known by his Sanskrit name, Sakya Pandita, assented to take this post. The khan was so impressed with Sakya Pandita that he converted to Buddhism and promised to protect Tibet against all foreign threats. For its part, the Sakya School would provide spiritual teachers for the khan. This arrangement became known as the "patron-priest" relationship, and it continued for several generations. Sakya Pandita also talked the khan into naming him and his successors in the Sakya School regents of Tibet. This started the Tibetan custom of Buddhist monastic leaders taking responsibility for the social and political welfare of the Tibetan people in addition to pursuing their purely religious activities. On the practical level, however, the country was divided into thirteen regions ruled by aristocratic families, each with ties to monastic centers of one of the Buddhist schools.

Sakya Pandita was known not only for his knowledge of such things as Buddhist logic and theory of knowledge, but also for his practical wisdom concerning the art of living. The following are verses from his famous literary work, *A Jewel Treasury of Good Advice*:

The wise person who develops a treasury of good qualities becomes a treasury of good advice. . . . A wise person who has fully developed all the good qualities gives light to the earth.

Wisdom is what brings happiness in this and future lives. . . . If one is wise, one can understand other people from their demeanor, even if they do not say anything. . . . These wise persons are more respected in other lands than in their own home country. . . . One is wise when one can live in harmony with other living beings. . . . Wise persons accept fully the good advice of even children.

When noble people become poor, they still behave honorably. . . . The characteristics of a noble person is not to be happy with praise, and not to be sad with criticism, but in all things maintain one's good qualities.

Bad people often attribute their faults to others. . . . Among fools, a man with a monkey on a leash is more respected than a wise person. . . . People devoid of good qualities are especially hostile to persons who have those qualities.

Practicing meditation without studying may bring temporary results, but they quickly vanish. . . . In meditation, one pacifies faults and their causes by the use of penetrating insight. . . . Therefore, by understanding well the nature of all phenomena, by attaining meditative stabilization, all faults and their causal dispositions are extinguished, and one becomes a fully realized Buddha. (*Subhāṣitaratnanidhi*, 1, 9, 22, 23, 26, 30, 36, 54, 63, 75, 76, 443, 444, 446)

THE GELUK SCHOOL AND THE DALAI LAMA

About one century after Sakya Pandita, there lived another great religious figure in Tibetan history, Tsong Khapa (1357–1419). He is revered, along with Padmasambhava and Atīśa, for his spiritual attainment and contributions to Tibetan Buddhism and culture. Tsong Khapa, a member of the Kadam School, trained in Atīśa's system of monastic formation. He is believed to have attained full Awakening in 1398 after a six-year retreat. His Awakening included a vision through which he understood how all the systems of Buddhist teaching mutually reinforce each other. Of particular interest, he saw how the doctrine of emptiness supports the ethical rules of the *Vinaya* and also provides the proper foundation for Tantric attainment. His ideas are most fully expressed in his major work, *The Great Exposition of the Stages of the Path*. We will look more closely at his ideas when we introduce his writings later in this chapter. There, it will be evident how Tsong Khapa relied on the earlier synthesis of Atīśa.

Tsong Khapa went on to found the Ganden Monastery near Lhasa in 1409, and called his order "New Kadam." His disciples also founded two other universities, one at Drebung in 1416, the other at Sera in 1419. Tsong Khapa's reform of Kadam included a curriculum with works by such Indian scholars as Asaṅga, Candrakīrti, Vasubandhu, and Dharmakīrti. His course of study also included Tantra and a strict adherence to the *Vinaya* discipline. This program was so popular that the New Kadam order became known as the Geluk ("Order of Virtue"), which eventually replaced the Kadam School. The Geluk School became famous for its high standards of discipline, scholarship, and practice. Tsong Khapa's life and work contributed to a spiritual renaissance in Tibet in which numerous monasteries were constructed throughout the country. In Lhasa alone, there were three major monasteries with over twenty thousand monastics.

Gendün Druba (1391–1474), a disciple of Tsong Khapa, attained his own insights into the Dharma and founded a monastic university in southern Tibet. It is said that he reincarnated as Gendün Gyatso (1475–1542), who was himself a famous teacher and founder of monastic institutions. Gendün Gyatso is said to have reincarnated as Sönam Gyatso (1543–1588), who was invited to the court of Altan Khan. Altan Khan was so impressed with the famed lama (Tibetan for *guru*), that he gave him the title of *Dalai Lama*. *Dalai*, meaning "ocean" in Mongolian, indicates that the lama's attainment of wisdom was as deep as the ocean. Since Sönam Gyatso was considered to be the reincarnation of his two predecessors, he became known as the Third Dalai Lama. He and every succeeding Dalai Lama have been recognized as the spiritual leader of the Geluk School. Sönam Gyatso also recognized Altan Khan with the title "King of the Dharma," thus establishing the "patron-priest" relationship between the Mongolian khans and the Geluk School of Tibetan Buddhism. This patron-priest relationship replaced that of the Sakya School, which had ended in 1354.

By the end of the sixteenth century, new conflicts arose between the aristocracy and all the Buddhist schools. Many of the warlords felt, as they had centuries before, that the Buddhist monastic lifestyle was weakening the martial spirit of the people, and thus the country. The warlords persecuted the monasteries and tried to turn the different Buddhist schools against each other. Eventually, the Fifth Dalai Lama, Ngawang Losang Gyatso (1617–1682), called for help from the Mongolians, who destroyed the coalition of warlords. With the support of the Mongolians, political power was consolidated in the hands of the Fifth Dalai Lama, who became the first Dalai Lama to rule a newly unified Tibet. The Fifth Dalai Lama built the Potala Palace in Lhasa. It consisted of three buildings: a monastery for the head of the Geluk School, a fortress for the king of Tibet, and a monument to Avalokiteśvara Bodhisattva, the bodhisattva of compassion dearly beloved in Tibet. For Tibetans, Avalokiteśvara is not a bodhisattva, but a Buddha who attained Buddhahood in a previous world era and vowed to appear in the eras of future Buddhas to help bring the Dharma to the people. The Dalai Lamas are believed to be emanation-bodies of this Buddha, who, it is said, leads the Tibetan people both spiritually and politically.

In 1644, China was conquered by the Manchus, a people from north of Korea. They also defeated the Mongolians and founded the Ch'ing Dynasty in China, which lasted until 1911. Given the Dalai Lama's influence over the Mongolians, he was seen to be a formidable ally by the Manchus. So in 1653, an alliance was made between the Fifth Dalai Lama and the Manchu emperor. The Manchus recognized the Dalai Lama's spiritual and political authority in Tibet, and the Dalai Lama recognized the Manchus' political rule over Manchuria and China, as well as their protectorship over Tibet and Mongolia. This agreement allowed for a certain stability in Tibet up until the twentieth century.

Figure 6.1. The Potala, residence of the Dalai Lamas; founded seventeenth century C.E., Lhasa, Tibet.

THE TANTRIC EXPERIENCE

By the time of the Fifth Dalai Lama, there were four major schools of Tibetan Buddhism. Three were from the Second Dissemination—the Geluk, Sakya, and Kagyü schools. The fourth was the Nyingma School, which continued to follow the teachings and practices said to be developed by Padmasambhava during the First Dissemination. These four schools remain the major schools of Tibetan Buddhism today. All of these schools have integrated elements of Tantra that were created in India. It is this Tantric dimension of spirituality that has helped to define the unique religious experience and culture of Tibetan Buddhism. While the different Tibetan schools broadly agree on the basic vision of Tantric spirituality, each focuses on particular Tantric texts; has its own lineages of Tantric masters, scholars, and writers; and teaches its own distinctive systems of Tantric practices. These Tantric lineage traditions present what they believe are powerful and practical esoteric methods for spiritual advancement on the journey to Buddhahood.

As we have seen, the name Tantra is derived from the esoteric texts written in India about one thousand years after the historical Buddha. The word *tantra* itself comes from the verb meaning "to weave" and the noun meaning "thread." What is implied here is that Tantra gives one the esoteric material needed to weave a spiritually visualized realm of Buddhas and bodhisattvas. The experience of this realm brings to one's consciousness the essence and qualities of Buddhahood embodied in what one is visualizing. In Tantric practice, one eventually comes to discover this essence of Buddhahood and its qualities as innate within oneself. According to Tibetan Buddhism, this method provides the shortest and most effective path to full

Buddhahood. What in Mahāyāna is a ten-stage bodhisattva journey that takes many eons of time to complete can be traversed with the help of Tantra in as little as a single lifetime.

Tantra, as it was created in India, accepts the Mādhyamika teaching that identifies a fundamental unity between *saṃsāra* and Nirvana. For Tantra, this means that all the elements of *saṃsāra* are "in reality" nirvanic in nature. Because of ignorance, people do not see this nirvanic essence of existence; what is really Nirvana "appears" to be *saṃsāra*. This means that all living beings are already Buddhas but do not know it. According to the *Hevajra Tantra*, "All beings are Buddhas, however this fact is obscured by defilements. When these are removed, all beings are doubtlessly at once Buddhas" (*Hevajra Tantra*, II, 4.69). In good Mādhyamika fashion, the *Hevajra Tantra* characterizes this nirvanic "reality" in negative terms: "In reality, there is no form nor seer, no sound nor hearer, no smell nor one who smells, no taste nor taster, no touch nor one who touches, no thought nor thinker" (I, 5.1)

The goal of Tantra is to remove ignorance and defilements in order to realize this innate ultimate reality and attain Buddhahood. In the context of describing this Tantric experience, the texts portray nirvanic reality in more positive terms. In this way, Tantra follows in the footsteps of the *Tathāgatagarbha* texts, especially as they influenced later Yogācāra in India, in that these traditions were concerned that the negative language of Mādhyamika does not capture the wondrous experience of innate reality. Tantric texts use such terms as "Innate" (*sahaja*) to refer to this inner nirvanic essence of Buddhahood common to all phenomena. The following passages from two Tantric texts give us an idea of the positive nature of this innate nirvanic essence of Awakening:

This . . . is free from distinction between self and other, is like the sky that is pure and empty. It is itself the supreme essence of non-existence and existence, a union of wisdom and skillful means. . . . It is the life of living beings . . . all-pervading, innate in all embodied things. It is the very stuff of which the world is made. . . . It is the essential nature of all phenomena. . . . First is joy, second is joy supreme, third is the joy of cessation, and fourth is the Joy Innate. The first three joys are of this world, but the Innate does not exist in these three. . . . Because of its freedom from the other three, the Innate is called perfect Awakening. . . . The Innate is calm and undifferentiated . . . the single unity of all phenomena. . . . So, the whole world just is the Innate, for the Innate is its very essence. When the mind is in a purified state, it sees that this essence is also Nirvana. (*Hevajra Tantra*, I, 10.8–13, 15, 17, 34, 41; II, 2.44)

By means of that essence [of the Innate], one is born, lives and dies; by means of that essence, one gains the highest joy. . . . Here, there is . . . neither *saṃsāra* nor Nirvana. In this highest joy, there is neither self nor other. . . . When the mind is calm and the body is free from bondage, then the single flavor of the Innate pours forth, and there is neither Brahmin nor outcaste. . . . Abandon conceptual thinking and be like a child, devote yourself to the teachings of your guru, and the Innate will become manifest to you. . . . It is this highest joy that pours forth unceasingly as existence. . . . In it, all forms are the same, like space, and the mind has this sameness as its nature too. When the mind ceases to be separate from this sameness, the true essence of the Innate shines forth. . . . It is profound and vast, neither self nor other. Know this experience of the Innate in the highest joy. Just as the moon produces light in the darkness, so in one moment the highest joy removes all defilements. . . . Gain purification in this highest joy, for here one finds final perfection. (*Saraha Dohākośa*, 21, 27, 46, 57, 77, 96–97, 99)

In Tantra practice, one uses elements of *saṃsāra*, such as word and sounds, images and diagrams, and bodies and substances, in order to produce mental visualizations of a transformed spiritual universe that reflects the essence of Nirvana and qualities of Buddhahood. In this way, one comes to discover this reality as innate within all existence, and therefore as one's own essential nature. This discovery is furthered by Tantric techniques that help one experience the union of wisdom and skillful means (compassion), of *saṃsāra* and Nirvana, of self and other. From this experiential union of opposites results a "seed" of *bodhicitta*, which is understood to be the highest joy of the Innate. The energy of *bodhicitta* is also related to the union of feminine and masculine energies within the body that correspond to wisdom and skillful means. The result of this union is said to pass through a central energy channel in the body of the Tantric practitioner in a way that infuses his or her being with its compassionate clarity. The resulting joy of the Innate brings a "final purification" as the notion of independent selfhood is overcome. The person discovers, thereby, Awakening, Nirvana, and Buddhahood.

In Tantra's use of different elements of *saṃsāra* to produce states of mind that reflect the innate essence of Awakening into one's experience, there are practices that cultivate mental states of joy or bliss. These joyful states of consciousness are joined with wisdom's realizing emptiness in order to deepen one's understanding of the blissful unity of the Innate. To generate these states of joy in some advanced forms of Tantra, practitioners may visualize sexual union, or actually perform sexual acts with a partner. In these acts, one is to have no sexual desire in the common sense, but one uses the energy from the joy of union to cultivate a blissful consciousness of wisdom realizing emptiness with compassion. The union of self and other represents the union of *saṃsāra* and Nirvana and of wisdom and compassionate skillful means. In this greater experience of union, sensual desire is actually overcome. As one Tantra states: "Those things that bind people of evil conduct, others use as a skillful means to gain freedom from the bonds of *saṃsāra*. The world is bound by passion, but by passion too it can be freed" (*Hevajra Tantra*, II, 2.50–51)

Preliminary Practices

Tantra practice begins with certain preliminary practices. Sometimes these practices are divided into two types. First are the "external" preliminaries, which utilize the basic teachings of Buddhism to help one turn away from attachment to *saṃsāra* and seek Buddhahood. One is to consider that human existence offers one the freedom and opportunity to seek Buddhahood. One is then to consider the impermanence of existence and the defects and sufferings associated with it. With these in mind, one goes on to consider how karma, the principle of cause and effect, applies to all action, so that one commits oneself more fully to avoid negative actions and adopt positive ones. Then one is to consider the means to attain, and the benefits of, liberation from *saṃsāra*. Finally, one considers the importance of following and emulating a guru in order to attain this goal.

The "internal" preliminary practices are more specifically related to Tantra. The first such practice involves taking refuge in the Buddha, Dharma, and Saṅgha and affirming the precepts associated with this "refuge-taking." This is a practice shared with all Buddhist traditions. In Vajrayāna, it is believed that refuge-taking holds a power in itself that plants the seeds of spirituality within the ordinary mind and heart. For the practitioner of Tantra, this taking refuge includes "refuge-empowerment" by a guru and may also involve seeking refuge with celestial beings. These beings, who are thought to have empowering roles in Tantra practice, include a number of celestial Buddhas and bodhisattvas that Tantra refers to as "deities." Along with the refuge-taking is an act of faith in the Three Refuges, the guru, and the practice lineage as essential aids to spiritual growth.

A second internal preliminary practice is the arousing of *bodhicitta*, the intention to gain Buddhahood for the good of all living beings. In this regard, one is to develop *bodhicitta* by different means, and one may express this altruistic aspiration in vows before one's guru or visualized Buddhas and bodhisattvas. One can also train in *bodhicitta*, for example, by extending through meditation good intentions to others, by developing the willingness to exchange oneself for others in need, or by realizing more deeply that just like oneself, all persons seek happiness and freedom from suffering. One can also develop *bodhicitta* by training in the perfections of the Bodhisattva Path. Here, we see clearly the rootedness of Buddhist Tantra in the Mahāyāna tradition.

A third preparation is the practice of prostration and confession. Prostration may take place before an image, symbol, or altar and must be done with the proper attitude of humble recognition of one's personal need for spiritual aid. In doing prostrations, one recognizes this need and acknowledges the superior wisdom and compassion of the Buddhas and bodhisattvas. One imagines these spiritual beings, along with one's lineage and personal guru, before oneself. One often chants a prayer of confession to them for one's sins against the Three Refuges, vowing not to act, speak, or think in those afflictive ways in the future.

A fourth common preparatory practice is Vajrasattva purification. Vajrasattva is a Buddha associated with the purification of the mind. Different schools have their own ritual methods. But in general, one confesses and reflects on one's past negative actions, vows not to do them again, and seeks purification from Vajrasattva. This latter part of the practice may involve visualization of Vajrasattva displacing one's negative emotions, mental afflictions, and other defiling states that resulted from past misdeeds. This experience of healing most likely will not be complete in just one practice. It may need to be repeated over and over, like removing a stubborn spot on a piece of cloth.

A fifth popular preliminary practice is the *maṇḍala* offering. Physical *maṇḍala* offering may involve the use of a round plate and some grains or small grainlike substances. The practitioner pours grains on the plate and moves them in a manner that symbolizes wiping away the Three Root Evils of hate, greed, and delusion or the development of enlightened mind, speech, and body. Eventually, the practitioner uses the grain to form a *maṇḍala* that symbolizes the whole universe. This *maṇḍala* is then offered to the Buddhas, and then the grain is poured into one's own lap. This symbolizes offering everything to the Buddhas and receiving back the blessings of the Buddhas. There is also an "inner" *maṇḍala* offering where one visualizes one's own body as a *maṇḍala* that is pure and can be offered to the Buddhas for the benefit of all sentient beings. Finally, in the "secret" *maṇḍala* offering, one's own mind becomes the *maṇḍala* to be offered for transformation into the mind of enlightenment. It is also common in preliminary practices to offer the merits of one's action for the good of all living beings.

Finally, there is guru yoga. Tibetan Buddhism stresses the need for a qualified guru, or lama, in order to learn and perform Tantric practices properly. This is because Tantra cannot be transmitted by Tantric texts, which are often not even understandable without the aid of a guru. Rather, proper transmission comes from a spiritual lineage, and an authentic teacher embodies the transmission power of his or her lineage. He or she is able to apply properly and effectively the Tantric teachings and practices to the life of the disciple. To do so, the guru bestows initiations on the disciple in order for the practitioner to enter and progress in the path of Tantra. These initiations link the student through the guru/lineage to the deities who will empower the practitioner to discover his or her potential for Awakening and Buddhahood. Initiations in Tantra involve rituals, visualizations, prayers, and offerings. They can be taken more than once, since each time they are believed to confer deeper empowerment and blessings.

Guru yoga involves visualizing one's teacher as an embodiment of the clear wisdom and pure compassion of Buddhahood. This provides the disciple with a concrete experience of the goal he or she is trying to attain. In this experience of yoga, one receives the teachings and initiations united with their source and their goal. One is led by guru yoga eventually to find this source/goal within the heart of one's own being. That is, one discovers that the guru is an embodiment of one's own innate essence of Buddhahood. Because of the unquestioning faith and devotion associated with guru yoga, the power of the guru can be abused. So, one is advised to choose one's guru with great care.

Maṇḍalas, Mantras, *and* Mudras

Tantric practice uses *maṇḍalas*, *mantras*, and *mudras*. A *maṇḍala* is a circular diagram that contains images of a deity in his or her celestial realm, along

Figure 6.2. Kālacakra sand *maṇḍala;* created August 1999 at the Tibetan Cultural Center, Bloomington, Indiana.

with symbols and images that depict enlightened virtues associated with the deity and that indicate core Buddhist ideas and ideals. Thus, the *maṇḍala* uses *saṃsāric* elements in order to bring the practitioner into familiarity with the nirvanic joy and beauty of Buddhahood and its enlightened qualities. This familiarity with something so spiritually attractive helps the practitioner let go of obstructions to, and defilements of, this ideal in his or her life. The *maṇḍala* also represents one's own awakened potential that can be realized by overcoming these obstructions and defilements. By visualizing the *maṇḍala,* one invokes within oneself the enlightened attitudes, understandings, and virtues that are symbolized by the deity and his or her realm. The *maṇḍala* is, in short, a symbolic diagram of a Buddha realm, a realm that can display in visualization spiritual forms of the essence of innate Awakening to the practitioner, thereby helping him or her to realize this essence innate within himself or herself.

Mantras are powerful invocations addressed to the deities. The practitioner repeats these *mantras* to deepen his or her spiritual connection to a deity and to actualize the positive qualities the *mantras* symbolize. One might use, for example, a *mantra* associated with Avalokiteśvara Bodhisattva to find a deeper unity with that deity and to cultivate a more compassionate mode of living. *Mudras* are body movements, especially hand movements, that have symbolic significance and bring the body more directly into Tantric practice.

In Tantric ritual, one blends these three practices so that one's mind med-
itates on a *maṇḍala*, one's speech repeats a *mantra*, and one's body performs
a *mudra*. In this way, one's whole self (body, speech, and mind) enters Tantric
practice, giving its symbolism a broader transformative effect on one's life.
In many Tantric practices, one holds a *vajra*, a small scepter associated with
kingship in India, usually made of metal with five prongs at one end. The
vajra symbolizes the active power of method combined with wisdom that
leads to the attainment of the sovereignty of Buddhahood. The *vajra* here is
the symbol of the Buddha's authorization to reign. Sometimes the *vajra* is
held in one hand, and a bell in the other. In this case, the *vajra* represents
method, and the bell represents wisdom.

Deity Yoga

Deity yoga in Tantra refers to the experience of meditative visualization of
the Buddhas and bodhisattvas represented, for example, in the *maṇḍalas*.
These deities personify one's own Buddha potential and give the practitioner
a heightened awareness of the essence of this potential as well as its qualities. In this sense, Tantra is sometimes referred to as "training in the effect"
that one is trying to achieve. That is, the effect of one's practice, namely the
realization of Buddhahood, is visualized in the form of a deity. One then
"trains" in that effect in the meditative visualization. The theory here is that
as one familiarizes oneself with the beauty and joy of the innate essence of
Awakening and the qualities of Buddhahood visualized in the meditation,
one is enabled to let go of afflictive emotions and delusion. Thereby, one is
purified and better able to manifest, like the deities, the joy and wisdom of
innate Awakening in thought, word, and action.

This process of deity yoga is not just a leap into enlightened living, as the
visualizations also expose one's lack of realizing Awakening. That is, deity
yoga forces the practitioner to face one's defilements, limitations, negative
attitudes, unwholesome thoughts, and afflictive emotions that need to be
addressed in order to attain the freedom of Awakening. This encourages the
practitioner to follow more seriously the precepts handed down from the
Vinaya tradition, to meditate on emptiness in accordance with the teachings
of Mahāyāna thought, and to commit oneself more fully to the compassionate bodhisattva ideal. Here, Tantra supports the traditional goals of
Mahāyāna Buddhism: to escape the *saṃsāric* way of living, to compassionately attain Awakening for the benefit of all sentient beings (*bodhicitta*), and
to achieve the correct vision of the Dharma through the perfection of wisdom realizing emptiness.

Deity yoga can aid in this process because most people are so affected by
their *saṃsāric* condition that they are not familiar with the freedom, joy, and
beauty of the enlightened life. If in visualizations they can become familiar
with these qualities of Buddhahood, they can develop a deep attraction to
them. Then, they will be led more quickly in the right direction. Behind this
practice is the view that within *saṃsāra* is a nirvanic reality, innate in all

things, that is the highest joy. This means that all mental-emotional defile-ments and afflictions are adventitious; they are like stains on metal that can be removed. What one sees in deity yoga is the inherent beauty of what this removal produces, namely, pure forms of nirvanic reality experienced in a blissful union of wisdom and compassion.

Four Types of Tantric Practice

Tantric texts are classified into four categories depending on the types of practice they emphasize: (1) action Tantras, (2) performance Tantras, (3) yoga Tantras, and (4) highest yoga Tantras. Action Tantras teach practitioners to see themselves as servants of the meditational deities and to use external objects, images, rituals, and activities to aid inner purification. The deity is visualized as a person who is externally present to the practitioner. The de-ity is also seen as helping the practitioner understand the essence and qual-ities of the deity's enlightened nature and as giving the practitioner certain blessings. These blessings could include destroying danger or illness or gen-erating success and prosperity.

Performance Tantras teach practitioners to see the deities as equal to one-self, like a friend. The goal is to break down the gap between the enlight-ened qualities seen in the deity and one's own potential for such enlight-ened states of consciousness. One visualizes not only the deity, but also oneself as an enlightened being. One can also use a "signless" form of med-itation, wherein the practitioner does not actually visualize the form and qual-ities of the deity. Rather, he or she meditates on the essential nature of the deity, which is the nature of oneself and all beings, namely, emptiness. This fosters a deeper wisdom realizing the emptiness of oneself and the deity.

Yoga Tantras take this realization of emptiness a step further by actually merging oneself with the visualized deity. This brings one an even more profound experience of the nirvanic essence and enlightened qualities rep-resented by the deity. Since these are the very essence and qualities of one's true nature, this yoga experience brings that fact to even more clarity for the practitioner. There is also a "signless" form of this practice wherein one med-itates on the "suchness" (*tathatā*) of the deity. Since all beings have the same suchness or essence of Awakening as their true nature, this signless medi-tation enables one to discern more clearly the suchness of all existence.

Highest yoga Tantras teach the practitioner to work with the luminous power of consciousness realizing emptiness in ways that cultivate a deeper realization of the innate essence and qualities of Buddhahood. Highest yoga Tantra gives the practitioner access to subtle forms of consciousness and in-ner energies that can be used to progress more quickly toward Buddhahood. Because of the mental and emotional dangers of these practices, long prepa-ration in the monastic life, careful initiation by an authentic guru, as well as the taking of certain vows are necessary before pursuing this powerful es-oteric practice. While there are different systems of this advanced yoga, in general the practice includes methods of manipulating inner psychophysical energies that open one to very subtle levels of consciousness. These purer levels of consciousness can be used to discern more deeply the reality of emptiness in a way that generates a more profound, transforming, and blissful experience of Awakening.

At the "stage of completion" in highest yoga Tantra, the practitioner reemerges, as it were, with his or her self transformed. In other words, in the earlier "stage of generation" all seems to dissolve into the innate blissful essence of Buddhahood. Then in the stage of completion, the practitioner reemerges with a subtle and compassionate wisdom consciousness that mirrors this blissful essence reflected in the visualized deities. With this blissful clarity of insight, even the most rarefied forms of attachments and afflictive desires are eliminated, and a more profound compassion for all sentient beings is attained. Thereby, one advances more fully toward the ideal of Buddhahood.

SCHOOLS OF TIBETAN BUDDHISM: DISTINCTIVE PRACTICES

The Major schools of Tibetan Buddhism—Nyingma, Sakya, Kagyü, and Geluk—all share many of the aspects of Tantra introduced above. The various differences between the schools have to do with the application of Indian Buddhist philosophy, especially the Mādhyamika and Yogācāra traditions, as well as with what particular Tantras and Tantric practice lineages they utilize. In this section, we introduce only a few distinctive practices of these schools.

The Nyingma School

Nyingma classifies the teachings of Buddhism into three categories. First are the teachings of the Abhidharma and Mahāyāna traditions. Second are the teachings having to do with "outer Tantra," namely, action, performance, and yoga Tantra. The last category is the "inner Tantra" teachings that involve highest yoga Tantra as well as *dzogchen* ("Great Perfection"), a spiritual practice unique to Nyingma. Nyingma considers *dzogchen* practice to be more profound than even highest yoga Tantra. In Tantra, one uses visualizations, in part, to realize that all phenomena are empty of own-being. In *dzogchen*, one more directly examines what Nyingma considers the source of phenomenal experience, namely, consciousness in its fundamental nature. While Tantric visualizations create mental phenomena that are in accord with liberation, *dzogchen* trains the practitioner to experience the essential nature of mind itself, which it claims is originally pure and free from all defilements. To discover the essence of consciousness suddenly in a flash of enlightened insight through *dzogchen* practice enables one to realize this original innate purity and freedom.

Actual *dzogchen* practice must be guided by a guru who has already achieved Awakening. The teacher guides the student in calming the mind and in an abiding awareness of the rising and falling of mental-emotional states as empty of own-being. One is then guided into a state of pure aware-ness that is precisely the very nature of the mind itself. Pure awareness here is understood as being of the nature of innate luminosity and emptiness. While this sounds like the sudden path of Zen Buddhism, the theory and practice of *dzogchen* are said to be more in line with the Indian *Tathāgata-garbha* tradition as it influenced Tantra and later Yogācāra thought. In this interpretation, ordinary experience is believed to be like "waves" on the "ocean mind" of wisdom and purity. In *dzogchen,* one does not produce more mind-waves through visualization, but trains in the pure awareness of the innate calm and blissful wisdom-mind. This original clear reality of mind is seen to be the innate essence of Awakening, which is always pure and un-affected by the thought-waves on the surface of the ocean mind. As the prac-titioner of *dzogchen* realizes the depth of wisdom and mental purity, Bud-dhahood spontaneously manifests itself and is realized in a pure, wise, and compassionate mode of living.

Within the Nyingma tradition are also certain objects called *terma. Terma* are texts, instructions, figures, or other objects and insights that are said to have been hidden throughout Tibet by early masters such as Padmasamb-hava. These articles are found by certain gifted persons, called *tertöns* ("treas-ure finders"), at times when their message is important to the Nyingma community. This *terma* system of transmission has proven to be quite effec-tive in bringing renewal into the Nyingma School at crucial times in history, while always keeping the tradition rooted in its origins.

The Sakya School

Sakya has a system called "path and fruit" (*lamdre*) based on the *Hevajra Tantra*. The Sakya system teaches that these two, the path to Nirvana and Nirvana itself, cannot ultimately be distinguished. This idea is derived from the identity of *saṃsāra* and Nirvana. Following the path in *saṃsāra* is to al-ready have the fruit of Nirvana, but one just does not know it. In the words of the *Hevajra Tantra*, "Then the essence, being pure and full of knowledge, is where there is no difference between *saṃsāra* and Nirvana. Nothing is pro-duced mentally in the highest bliss, and there is no one producing it" (*Heva-jra Tantra*, I, 10.32–33). In other words, when one attains the fruit of Nirvana by walking the path in *saṃsāra*, one has not produced anything that was not there all along the journey. The innate fundamental mind is in essence empty of own-being, and its characteristic (*lakṣaṇa*) is luminosity, whether one is on the path or enjoying its fruit. What is found in Awakening is the pure knowledge that had been covered from view by the defilements of *saṃsāra*.

To uncover on the path what is already innate to the mind, Sakya em-phasizes the need for an experienced guru who can give one necessary in-structions for the attainment of this realization. This teacher can also give one Tantric initiations, as well as the proper interpretations of the experi-ences these initiations produce. While the initiations generate connections with the Tantric deities, the interpretations orient one properly on the path.

In the generation stage of Tantra, one visualizes deities who embody in bliss-ful forms the qualities of Buddhahood. In the completion stage, one is trans-formed by the essence of Awakening as it pours forth and clears the defile-ments that hide its inner presence. In this way, the path reveals its innate basis that is also the fruit of Buddhahood.

The Kagyü School

An important teaching in all Kagyü sects is *mahāmudrā*, meaning "great seal" or "great symbol." *Mahāmudrā* teaching has both theoretical and practice as-pects. Theoretically, *mahāmudrā* refers to the essential nature of reality that is a unity of luminosity and emptiness, of bliss and wisdom. In terms of prac-tice, *mahāmudrā* entails the Tantric techniques used to realize this ultimate re-ality. As in *dzogchen* practice, the realization of *mahāmudrā* involves a direct and sudden insight into the innate luminosity and emptiness of existence in a manner that brings liberation from ignorance and afflictive emotions.

To be successful in this practice, one needs an enlightened guru and a deep and strong *bodhicitta* for the good of all who are suffering in *saṃsāra*. In the practice of *mahāmudrā*, one quiets and stabilizes the mind. Thereby, one finds a basis in the path to overcome the negative mental-emotional ha-bitual tendencies that, in turn, condition unwholesome thoughts, words, and actions. As these obstructions to realization are removed by certain medita-tive antidotes, one experiences the essential clear and blissful state of the mind that was covered from view by the afflictions and defilements.

Experiencing phenomena with this clear mind, one finds that all things are empty of own-being. All phenomena are seen to be of the "one taste" of emptiness. This insight, when applied to one's mind, brings further freedom because one sees that all mental states are not parts of one's real nature. So, when hatred may arise, for example, it is understood for what it really is. It is not an aspect of the essential luminous mind, but is empty of any sub-stantiality. Thus, it loses power over oneself and produces no afflictions. In this freedom, the positive and wholesome states of consciousness are more easily cultivated. Since *mahāmudrā* is the luminous mind with its innate wis-dom and its compassion for all sentient beings, it is also the essential body (*Dharmakāya*) of the Buddha. Thus, it is the essential basis for realization of the bliss and virtues of Buddhahood.

The Geluk School

The typical Geluk presentation of the path to Awakening is called "stages of the path" (*lamrim*). This approach to Buddhist spirituality emphasizes what is common to both the Mahāyāna *sūtra* tradition and the Vajrayāna Tantra tradition. This common basis is seen to be essential to the attainment of Buddhahood for both traditions. One of the best explications of this ap-proach was given by Tsong Khapa in his *Great Exposition of the Stages of the Path*. The inspiration for this work was presented in a much shorter "root text" entitled *The Three Principal Facets of the Path*. In that shorter piece, from which we quote some verses below, the following three stages are introduced.

First, one develops "renunciation" based on an aspiration to gain liberation from *saṃsāra*. One does so by recognizing that in the impermanence of *saṃsāra*, it is rare to be born as a human. It is even rarer to be a human who has access to the Dharma, as well as to written texts and teachers who can aid one in the attainment of Awakening. One should therefore resolve to take advantage of this fortunate situation. One should also contemplate the *duḥkha* associated with *saṃsāra* in order to gain an aversion to being reborn in *saṃsāra* and a deeper aspiration to gain liberation.

Second, one realizes that one's renunciation at the first stage of the path is still self-centered. One is seeking liberation in order to free oneself from *duḥkha*. So, one needs to develop *bodhicitta*, the altruistic aspiration to gain Awakening for the good of others. In fact, Tsong Khapa points out, one cannot gain liberation if one's desire for it is selfish because liberation is freedom from such self-centeredness. One can develop *bodhicitta* by contemplating two facts. The first fact is that all beings are undergoing suffering in *saṃsāra* even though they want happiness and freedom from suffering. The second fact is that given that all beings have been reborn numberless times, in the past each of these beings has been one's own mother. With these two facts in mind, one should consider how all living beings who are now suffering had, in the past, treated one with the utmost loving kindness. This insight will generate the compassionate desire to make all beings happy and free them from suffering. This compassion will, in turn, nourish the development of *bodhicitta*.

Third, even with renunciation and *bodhicitta*, one cannot gain Awakening without "right view": penetrating insight into emptiness. Wisdom must be added to renunciation and compassion because one's mind contains afflictive states and defilements that hide its innate essence, which Geluk calls "clear light." It is the "mind of clear light" that is the essential and ultimately nirvanic status of consciousness. Wisdom realizing emptiness destroys the afflictive and defiling states of mind, and gradually the innate mind of clear light is realized as "of one taste" with emptiness. It is this realization that results in Buddhahood. For Tsong Khapa and the Geluk School, this spiritual realization is common to both the Mahāyāna and Vajrayāna paths.

The following verses about these three stages are taken from Tsong Khapa's *The Three Principal Facets of the Path*:

Listen with clear minds, you fortunate people,
Who aspire to the path that is pleasing to the Buddhas.
Strive to use well your freedom and opportunity,
Not attached the pleasures of *saṃsāra*.

All those with bodies are bound by the craving for existence.
Attraction to the pleasures of *saṃsāra*
Is only stilled by pure renunciation.
So, first of all seek renunciation.

BOX 6.1

TRAPPED IN A SUFFOCATING SCREAM

Recently, I recalled a bothersome incident with my mother.

I had come home during my first year at college and was enthusiastically explaining to her about the fascinating courses I was taking in psychology/anthropology and English and American literature. She bitterly resented the fact that she had not attended college and also had an antipathy to intellectual enthusiasm even though she was intellectually active herself.

Much like my grade-school experiences when I would come home and tell her what was happening and she would start criticizing me bitterly to the point that I shut up, she launched into her invective. We ended up with her in the kitchen on one side of the house and me on the other in the living room in a bright, light-blue rocking chair that she had painted and stenciled. We were literally screaming at each other. I so deeply wanted to get back on the bus and return to college and my studies, but I didn't, remaining in a suffocating scream.

I have often thought, "What would have happened in my life, had I just walked out and gotten on the bus down the road?" And I thought it again the other day when this scene reappeared in my mind.

Then, suddenly it occurred to me that following my Tibetan Buddhist practice, I should reflect within the body of the person screaming from the living room, "Just as I want happiness and don't want suffering, so Mother (that's what we called her) wants happiness and doesn't want suffering." Wow! What a revolution! No need to leave; within that same body, I calmed down within a poignant sense of how she caused so much misery for herself—she'd get so angry on the telephone with her best woman-friend that she would literally hold the phone from her face and scream into it!

I cannot put into words the sense of commiseration. Also, I had found a road out of that scream from the living room without taking the bus back to college. What a relief!

JEFFREY HOPKINS

Professor of Religious Studies
University of Virginia

Freedom and opportunity are difficult to get, so there is no time to waste.
Reflect on this fact, and you will overcome your attraction to this life.
Reflect repeatedly on the sufferings of this world,
and you will overcome attraction to future lives.

Renunciation without *bodhicitta*
Does not produce the supreme bliss
Of unsurpassed Awakening.
Therefore, bodhisattvas generate the excellence of *bodhicitta*.

Born over and over in boundless *saṃsāra*,
Ceaselessly tormented by the three forms of *duḥkha*,
All beings, having been your mothers, are in this condition.
Think of them and generate *bodhicitta*.

Though you cultivate renunciation and *bodhicitta*,
Without wisdom realizing emptiness,
You cannot cut the root of *saṃsāra*.
Therefore, strive to realize dependent arising.

One who sees the unfailing causality
Of all phenomena, *saṃsāra* and Nirvana,
And destroys all perception [of own-being],
Has entered the path that is pleasing to the Buddhas.
    (*Lam gtso rnam gsum*, 2–4, 6, 8–10)

RECENT EVENTS IN TIBET

As the Tibetan Buddhist schools grew and developed after the seventeenth century, for the most part, Tibet enjoyed its autonomy, isolated from its neighbors. There were only two exceptions during the eighteenth century. The Manchus were involved in helping the Tibetans settle some political issues for about fifteen years at the beginning of the eighteenth century. For a short time during those years, they kept a garrison of troops in Lhasa. Then at the end of the eighteenth century, the Manchus sent troops to Tibet to drive out a Nepalese army that had invaded the country in the south. In the nineteenth century, the Manchu's Ch'ing Dynasty was weakened in China; they lost any interest in Tibetan affairs, and Tibet's isolation became even more pronounced.

At the beginning of the twentieth century, the Thirteenth Dalai Lama, Tupden Gyatso (1874–1933), sought to modernize his country and bring it into closer relations with the international community. He believed that by so doing, Tibet would be more protected from the British in India, the Russians, and the Chinese, all of whom, many thought, had designs on Tibet given its strategic location in Central Asia. In fact, in 1903, a British expeditionary force marched into Lhasa and demanded the country open trade relations with British India. After the Tibetan government agreed, the British withdrew.

Then in 1910, a Chinese general, Chao Erh-feng, decided to annex Tibet and also entered Lhasa. At that time, the Manchu Chinese government was weak, and some generals in different regions of China were pursuing conquests to bolster their personal power. The Dalai Lama fled from Tibet to India to avoid having to negotiate with Chao. Chao vented his wrath by destroying Buddhist monasteries and killing Tibetans. However, in 1911, Sun Yat-sen's Nationalists overthrew the Manchus, and Chao was executed.

--- BOX 6.2 ---

A DAY IN THE LIFE OF THE DALAI LAMA

I must say that I am a very poor practitioner. Usually I get up at 3:30 in the morning. Then I immediately do some recitations and some chanting. Following this until breakfast, I do meditation, analytical meditation mainly. Then after each analytical meditation, I do single-pointed meditation. The object of my meditation is mainly dependent arising. Because of dependent arising, things are empty. This is according to the Mādhyamika philosophy of Nāgārjuna and the interpretation of Chandrakīrti which is called Prāsaṅgika philosophy.

That philosophy is very profound, and, for me, it is really something marvelous. It gives me a kind of conviction about reality, about emptiness, and through that conviction I get the feeling that there is the possibility of eliminating all afflictive emotions. As Nāgārjuna says in his *Treatise on the Middle*, by extinguishing contaminated karma and afflictive emotions through wisdom there is liberation. Therefore liberation is a state of having extinguished contaminated actions and afflictive emotions. So then, from what is contaminated karma or contaminated actions produced? Contaminated actions are produced from afflictive emotions. Then from what are afflictive emotions produced? They are produced from improper mental conceptuality, improper mental application. And then from what is that produced? It is produced from conceptual elaborations. Those conceptual elaborations are the elaborations of the mind conceiving objects to exist truly in their own right. These elaborations are ceased through meditating on emptiness.

So, meditating on this gives me a kind of firm conviction of the possibility of cessation. This is one main object of practice. Another is compassion. These two are my objects of practice. If you ask me about experience in my practice, I think it is better than zero. On that basis, I can assure you that the mind is always changing, so no matter how strong the afflictive emotion, there is always the possibility of change. Transformation is always possible. So therefore, you see, there is always hope. I think that what is really worthwhile is to make an effort.

Then also, in the Tibetan Buddhist tradition, Buddhist Tantrayāna is also involved. So you see, a lot of time is also spent on visualization in deity yoga. This includes visualizing the process of death and rebirth. In fact in my daily prayer or practice, I visualize death eight times and rebirth eight times. This is not necessarily the Dalai Lama's reincarnation, but some reincarnation. These practices I feel are very powerful, and very helpful in familiarizing oneself about the process of death. So when death actually comes, one is prepared. Whether these practices of preparation are really going to benefit me at the time of death, I do not know at this moment. I suppose that even with all this preparation for death, I may still be a complete failure! That is also possible. There is another type of meditation which is like praying. Its purpose is to recollect the various levels and stages of the path by going through something that you have memorized and reflecting on each stage.

So from around 3:30 A.M. until 8:30 A.M., I am fully occupied with meditation and prayer, and things like that. During that time I take a few breaks, including my breakfast, which is usually at 5:00 A.M., and some prostrations. After 8:30 A.M., when my mood is good, I do some physical exercise. One very important thing is that I always listen to the BBC for the news. Then I do office work until noon. And if it is a holiday, I also start reading important texts. Prayer and meditation are usually done without any texts. Then at noon, I have my lunch. Afterward usually I go to the office and do some more work. At 6:00 P.M., I have my evening tea and dinner as a Buddhist monk. Finally, around 8:30 P.M., I go to sleep, my most favorite, peaceful meditation!

HIS HOLINESS TENZIN GYATSO

The Fourteenth Dalai Lama

Upon his return to Tibet, the Dalai Lama resumed his efforts to modernize his country and to develop relations with the international community. But given their long history of isolation, conservative forces in Tibet resisted these changes. Before he died, the Dalai Lama predicted that if Tibet did not modernize and break out of its isolation, it would be conquered, many of its people would be killed or enslaved, and Buddhism in Tibet would be destroyed.

In 1940, Tenzin Gyatso (born 1935) was enthroned as the Fourteenth Dalai Lama. At that time, the communists in China were talking about annexing Tibet. The communists saw themselves as surrounded by enemies of their cause, and Tibet provided a strategic position in relation to India, Russia, Nepal, and Mongolia. Tibet was also thought to have natural resources, which could be used in the communist restructuring of China. In the early months of 1950, Chinese troops began to mass on the Tibetan border. The Dalai Lama appealed to the United Nations, but it refused to consider Tibet's appeal since it was not a member of the UN. With no resistance from the international community, the Chinese army entered Lhasa in 1951.

In 1954, the Dalai Lama met with Mao Tse-tung in Beijing. However, by that time the Chinese had begun a violent process of communist collectivization in Tibet. They were also using execution, torture, and public humiliation to destroy Tibetan Buddhist institutions. Given the resistance of the Tibetan people to these oppressive tactics, the Chinese government turned to drastic measures. In 1959, it initiated a plan to capture the Dalai Lama himself. After the Chinese began to fire on people who were trying to protect the Dalai Lama, the Dalai Lama and his party escaped the Chinese troops at night and fled into India. Today, the Dalai Lama lives in exile in Dharamsala in the north of India. For his work toward a peaceful resolution of the situation in Tibet with the Chinese communist government, the Dalai Lama was awarded the Nobel Peace Prize in 1989. In Chapter 10, we discuss the ways that Buddhism has guided the Dalai Lama's socially engaged work for peace. In Dharamsala and in southern India, some of the great monasteries of Tibet have re-created their institutions for the training of their monastics in exile.

A few concluding words on the Chinese communist occupation of Tibet are in order. The communist government of China has hailed this occupation as the "liberation" of Tibet and has claimed that it is supported by the

Tibetan people. In reality, during the first ten years of occupation, it is estimated that 1.2 million Tibetans, one sixth of the population, died by torture, starvation, or killings. Of the 6254 monasteries, thirteen remained after this period. Tibet was also divided into three areas, with only one named "Tibet" and the other two merging into nearby Chinese provinces. This allows the Chinese communist government to claim that there are only 1.8 Tibetans, while actually over five million Tibetans live in these other regions.

Much of this destruction in Tibet was carried out during the Cultural Revolution under which the Chinese people themselves also suffered. When Mao died, his successor, Teng Hsiao-p'ing, admitted that "mistakes were made" in Tibet. There is now a limited amount of religious expression allowed, but any demonstration for religious freedom or human rights is met with a severe use of force. Perhaps the most troubling ongoing Chinese communist policy for the future of Tibet is the massive repopulation of the country by the transferring of Chinese citizens into Tibet. Today, these settlers actually outnumber Tibetans by several million. Since the Tibetan leaders and educated citizens have been either killed or exiled and since only Chinese settlers are given positions of influence, Tibetans have become an impoverished and oppressed minority in their own country.

Suggestions for Further Reading

Beckwith, Christopher. *Silver on Lapis: Tibetan Literary Culture and History.* Bloomington, IN: Indiana University Press, 1987.

Cabezón, José I. *Buddhism and Language: A Study of Indo-Tibetan Scholasticism.* Albany, NY: SUNY Press, 1994.

Davanport, John T. *Ordinary Wisdom: Sakya Pandita's Treasury of Good Advice.* Boston: Wisdom Publications, 2000.

Goldstein, Melvyn C., and Matthew T. Kapstein. *Buddhism in Contemporary Tibet: Religious Revival and Cultural Identity.* Berkeley, CA: University of California Press, 1998.

Gyatso, Tenzin, The Fourteenth Dalai Lama. *The World of Tibetan Buddhism: An Overview of Its Philosophy and Practice.* Boston: Wisdom Publications, 1995.

Hopkins, Jeffrey. *Emptiness in the Mind Only School of Buddhism.* Berkeley, CA: University of California Press, 1999.

———. *Meditation on Emptiness.* London: Wisdom Publications, 1983.

Kapstein, Matthew T. *The Tibetan Assimilation of Buddhism: Conversion, Contestation, and Memory.* New York: Oxford University Press, 2000.

Klein, Anne C. *Meeting the Great Bliss Queen: Buddhists, Feminists, and the Art of the Self.* Boston: Beacon Press, 1995.

Lopez, Donald S, Jr., ed. *Religions of Tibet in Practice.* Princeton, NJ: Princeton University Press, 1997.

Napper, Elizabeth. *Dependent Arising and Emptiness*. Boston: Wisdom Publications, 1989.

Powers, John. *Introduction to Tibetan Buddhism*. Ithaca, NY: Snow Lion Publications, 1995.

Rhie, Marylin M., and Robert A. F. Thurman. *Wisdom and Compassion: The Sacred Art of Tibet*. New York: Harry H. Abrams, 1991.

Sherburne, R. F. *A Lamp for the Path and Commentary by Atīśa*. London: Allen & Unwin, 1983.

Snellgrove, David L. *Indo-Tibetan Buddhism: Indian Buddhists and Their Tibetan Successors*. Vol. 2. Boston: Shambhala Publications, 1987.

Thurman, Robert A. E. *The Central Philosophy of Tibet: A Study and Translation of Jey Tsong Khapa's* Essence of True Eloquence. Princeton, NJ: Princeton University Press, 1991.

———. *Essential Tibetan Buddhism*. San Francisco: HarperSanFrancisco, 1995.

———, trans. *The Tibetan Book of the Dead*. New York: Bantam Doubleday Dell Publishers, 1994.

Thurman, Robert A. E., and Denise P. Leidy. *Mandala: The Archetype of Enlightenment*. New York: Tibet House, 2000.

Wayman, Alex. *Ethics of Tibet*. Albany, NY: SUNY Press, 1991.

White, David Gordon, ed. *Tantra in Practice*. Princeton, NJ: Princeton University Press, 2000.

Willis, Janice D. *Feminine Ground: Essays on Women in Tibet*. Ithaca, NY: Snow Lion Publications, 1989.

SEVEN

THE CHINESE EXPERIENCE
OF BUDDHISM

It is said that King Aśoka sent Buddhist missionaries to Central Asia, and in fact, Aśokan inscriptions have been found in Afghanistan. Traditional sources also say that Aśoka's son, Kustana, founded the kingdom of Khotan to the northwest of Tibet in 240 B.C.E., some thirty years after the first Buddhist monastery was constructed in Khotan. In the first century C.E., the Kuṣāṇa Dynasty was founded. The Kuṣāṇa Empire ruled much of Central Asia, including Afghanistan and parts of northern India, and lasted until the middle of the third century. Members of this dynasty converted to, and supported, Buddhism throughout their empire. This included the Silk Road, which was the major east-west trade route that linked Persia (Iran) to China. It was by way of the Silk Road that Central Asians began to actively export Buddhism into China around the first century C.E. Chinese records indicate that Central Asian Buddhism included both Sarvāstivāda and Mahāyāna sects.

The Silk Road had northern and southern routes, which converged in the city of Tun-huang, China. Tun-huang was a cosmopolitan city, which eventually became a center for translating Buddhist texts into Chinese and for the development of Buddhist art. As Buddhism became more known in China, Tun-huang also became the starting place for Chinese Buddhist pilgrims and scholars to travel on the Silk Road to India in order to gain more knowledge about their new religion. Much later, in the eleventh century, the Chinese sealed Buddhist texts in the caves at Tun-huang to preserve them from Mongol invaders. In 1907, these caves were found and twenty thousand Buddhist texts and drawings dating from the fifth to the eleventh centuries were discovered. This material has given modern scholars a better understanding of the history of Buddhism in both China and Tibet.

Chinese imperial records first refer to Buddhism during the reign of Ming Ti (ruled 58–75 C.E.). The Buddhist tradition in China claims that Emperor Ming Ti actually brought Buddhism to China. However, historical records indicate that Buddhism was brought into the country by merchants from

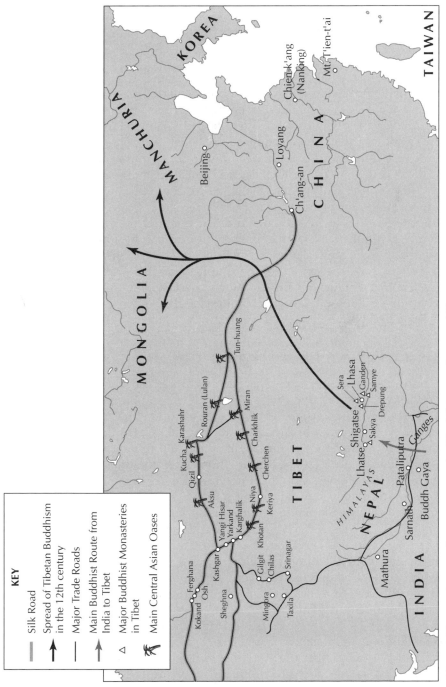

Map 3. The northern and eastern spread of Buddhism: c. first–twelfth century C.E.

Central Asia. In any case, the Chinese were intrigued by Buddhist monks and images of the Buddha, whom they took to be a great god from India. By the middle of the first century C.E., Buddhist monks were present in the Chinese capital, and the Buddha was worshiped at the imperial court as a god alongside Lao-tzu, the founder of Taoism, and another popular god named the Yellow Emperor.

Buddhism's introduction into China met resistance from what was already a vigorous intellectual and cultural tradition based on Confucian classics and Taoist religion. Confucianists were not impressed with Buddhist monasticism, which they felt abandoned family and society, going against the responsibilities of filial piety. The Buddhist belief in rebirth was also incompatible with the veneration of ancestors. Taoists were disappointed that the Buddhists could not provide elixirs and practices that lead to the immortality they sought. On the other hand, as we shall see, early on, Buddhists used Taoist terms and concepts to convey their ideas. We will also see that in the process of its inculturation, Buddhism adapted to Chinese culture. For example, given the Taoist value of harmony and nature, Chinese Buddhism emphasized the experience of the interdependence of phenomena and the living out of that experience through simplicity and naturalness in daily life. Also given the Confucian values of human perfectability, sagehood, and social harmony, Chinese Buddhism emphasized the Bodhisattva Path, the universal ideal of Buddhahood, and contributing to the social good.

TRANSLATION AND INCULTURATION

The transmission of the actual teachings of Buddhism into China necessitated the translation of Buddhist texts. These translations began to be made in earnest during the second century C.E. Some of the first translations were made by An Shih-kao, who arrived in the capital of Loyang in 148 C.E. Since at that time Taoism stressed inner cultivation and refining of the spirit, the most popular of An Shih-kao's translations were the ones about Buddhist meditation, mindfulness, and breathing practice. A Mahāyāna monk named Lokakṣema also arrived in Loyang in 168 C.E., where he translated the *Small Perfection of Wisdom Sūtra* and a *Land of Bliss Sūtra*. It was around this time, the middle of the second century C.E., that the first Buddhist monastery in China was constructed and the first Chinese monks were accepted into the Saṅgha. However, full monastic ordination was not possible until the *Vinaya* was brought to China, translated, and implemented in the fifth century.

This early work of translating texts and preaching the Dharma continued into the third century. Thus, the ground was prepared for the great Dharmarakṣa (born 230), a native of Tun-huang, who established intellectual respectability for Buddhism in north China from 266 to 308. Dharmarakṣa translated a large number of *sūtras*, including the *Lotus Sūtra* and the *Large Perfection of Wisdom Sūtra*, and founded a vigorous Saṅgha by building monasteries, ordaining monks, and expounding the Dharma. Through the efforts of Dharmarakṣa and his disciples, Buddhist monastics gained respect for their wisdom, simplicity, purity of heart, and fellowship with people from all classes of Chinese society. When barbarians sacked the northern Chinese capitals, Loyang in 311 and Ch'ang-an in 316, these monks were pillars of strength, compassion, and virtue in a world torn apart by destruction and chaos.

With the loss of north China to the barbarians, many Buddhists from that region traveled to other parts of China, thus spreading Dharmarakṣa's intellectual and disciplined style of Buddhism. In south China, Buddhism developed in peace among the ruling class, and monastics gradually gained influence at the imperial court. With the support of the ruling class, the center of Buddhism in south China was established in the capital city of Chien-k'ang. There, monks produced new translations of Indian texts, lived comfortably, and devoted much of their time to more philosophical pursuits and literary activity. Large monastic estates, supported by the rulers, provided their monastics with both religious education and spiritual formation. There were also smaller monasteries in villages where the less educated monastics provided the populace with devotional services. Finally, forest monasteries were founded for monastics who wanted to devote all of their time to the practice of meditation.

Meanwhile in north China, things were much more difficult. Most Buddhist intellectuals had fled to the south, so the Buddhist community in the north focused more on practice than on theory. Individual monks gained prominence among the barbarian rulers as "holy men" and "wonder workers." For example, around 310, Fo-t'u-teng arrived in China, where he witnessed massacres when the capitals fell. By performing what are referred to as "feats of magic," Fo-t'u-teng sought to gain the barbarian rulers' admiration in order to exert a civilizing influence on them. In this way, he hoped to help those innocent people who were suffering under the cruel oppressors. The example of Fo-t'u-teng and others like him gave witness to the spiritual power and the moral values of Buddhism. Some modern scholars argue that the real "magic" of Fo-t'u'teng was the conversion of the barbarians.

Fo-t'u-teng did not pretend to be a scholar like Dharmarakṣa, but stressed the practice of meditation and devotion. His major achievements included his disciplined method of training monks and the foundation of the Chinese Buddhist order of nuns. In 317, Chu Ching-chien (c. 292–361) became the first Chinese woman to take novice ordination. She was soon joined by other women and founded a monastery in Ch'ang-an. However, full women's ordination would not be available in China until 434, when Sri Lankan *bhikṣuṇīs* came for the purpose of establishing such a lineage.

NEW TRANSLATIONS AND SCHOLARSHIP

During the fourth century, some of the more intellectual Buddhist monastics in the south of China were using Taoist and Neo-Taoist terms and concepts to aid in the translation of Buddhist texts and in the understanding of

Buddhist ideas. For example, some Neo-Taoists held, based on original Taoist texts, that the world of phenomena is the "functioning" of the Tao, which is itself Ultimate Reality. All phenomena are the self-determinations of the Tao, formed by the Tao's dynamic functioning. This means that the "essence" of all things is the Tao itself. The Neo-Taoists referred to the phenomena of the world as "being" and the ultimate and formless Tao that is the essence of all phenomena as "non-being." Buddhist scholars used these distinctions in discussing the Mahāyāna notion of emptiness. Emptiness was understood to be, like the Tao, the causal source and formless essence of all phenomena. As essence, emptiness is non-being; but in its functioning of dependent arising, it takes form as being.

In time, some Buddhist scholars came to realize that looking at Buddhism through a Taoist lens could be distorting the meaning of Buddhist texts. One such person was Tao-an (312–385), a disciple of Fo-t'u-teng who was forced to migrate south due to civil war. In 379, Tao-an returned to Ch'ang-an in the north and began a new translation center. Indian monks were brought to Ch'ang-an to work with Chinese scribes. The most famous monk to come to Ch'ang-an shortly after Tao-an was the great Kumārajīva (344–413). When he arrived in 402, he was already well known in China and was therefore able to gain the ruler's patronage. Kumārajīva, along with a large number of Chinese disciples, undertook a massive translation project. A number of popular *sūtras* were retranslated, and new translations were completed. Kumārajīva's translation of Mādhyamika texts, the Perfection of Wisdom literature, the *Lotus Sūtra*, and the *Vimalakīrti Sūtra* sowed the seeds of a deeper understanding of Buddhism in China. This clearer understanding would later flower in a number of highly creative schools of Chinese Buddhist thought. In this way, the inculturation of Buddhism in China took a giant step forward.

One of Kumārajīva's disciples, Seng-chao (374–414), helped to clarify the central Mahāyāna notion of emptiness. Before Seng-chao, Chinese Buddhists based their understanding of the meaning of emptiness on the previously translated *Perfection of Wisdom Sūtras* in which emptiness is identified with the forms of the world. As we have seen, the Chinese Buddhist understanding of this identity of emptiness and the world had been colored by Taoism. In that Buddhist/Taoist interpretation, emptiness was thought to be a causal force that creates the universe and remains in things as their essence. With the new translation of Mādhyamika texts, Seng-chao was able to explain emptiness in a more orthodox fashion. He used the texts of Nāgārjuna and Āryadeva to show that all phenomena are "empty" of the self-existence we attribute to them through our conceptual understanding of things. The work of Seng-chao contributed to the establishment of the Chinese Mādhyamika School of Buddhism in the sixth century.

Another notion that was of great interest to Chinese Buddhists at the time of Kumārajīva was *Tathāgata-garbha*, a term the Chinese rendered as "Buddha-nature." The *Lotus Sūtra*, and later the *Nirvana Sūtra*, introduced to China the notion that there is within us an innate Awakening that can develop through religious practice into the full Buddhahood. The early Chinese understanding of Buddha-nature was also influenced by Taoism. The Taoists believed that people have an inner spirit of light that manifests the power of the Tao, the creative source of the universe. Tao-sheng (fl. 397–432), another student of Kumārajīva, argued that Buddha-nature should not be understood as a particular spiritual power, but should be understood as one universal reality that is the same in all beings. He also taught that Buddha-nature cannot be grasped gradually, but only all at once, in a single stroke of sudden Awakening. Tao-sheng's teaching about "sudden" Awakening in which one "recognizes one's innate Buddha-nature" contributed to a line of Buddhist thought that was influential throughout all of East Asia.

PERSECUTION AND REFORM

As Buddhism spread in north China during the fourth century, it enjoyed the support of the emperor. Eventually, a monastic "Saṅgha-director" was appointed to establish the government's support and control of the monasteries. While Buddhism flourished under this new system, its prosperity also led to corruption. Much of this corruption was due to the Saṅgha's extensive property holdings. Because of corruption in the Saṅgha, and in response to pressure from Taoist and Confucianist leaders who were afraid that Buddhism was gaining too much temporal power, there was a severe persecution of Buddhism in the north beginning in 446. Many temples and scriptures were destroyed, some of the monks were executed, and others fled to the south. However, with a new emperor in the north, the persecution ended in 452, and Buddhism again enjoyed royal patronage.

While the more philosophically minded monastics like Seng-chao and Tao-sheng emphasized emptiness and the inner essence of Buddhahood, many Chinese lay Buddhists were more interested in worshiping the Buddha according to Mahāyāna's devotional tradition. During the Buddhist revival that began after the persecution in the north ended in 452, Chinese artists glorified the Buddha in a manner that became popular with the masses, and lay worship of the Buddha was reinforced by the architecture of the Buddha-temples. In the temples, the central Buddha statue was the focus of devotion; from this time on, Buddhist art and liturgy offered a strong emotional appeal to the Chinese people. Besides the worship of the Buddhas, by the fifth century there were many popular forms of piety directed to bodhisattvas. One of the most lasting of these has been the devotion to Avalokiteśvara, known in China as Kuan-yin. Kuan-yin is worshiped as a female deity in China. Over the centuries, she has remained the most popular deity in all of China, often portrayed as a graceful woman holding a lotus flower. She is considered to be compassionately concerned for the plight of humanity, rushing to the aid of beings in need with her boundless skillful means. In Buddhist temples, a statue of Kuan-yin has always been a popular site for both lay and monastic devotion.

Another aspect of the Buddhist revival was an early type of social reform in China. Around 470, a Saṅgha leader named T'an-yao devised a plan to aid the poor and needy in rural areas. A peasant family could become part of a "Saṅgha household" by donating an amount of grain to the local Saṅgha. The member family could then receive a share of the Saṅgha's grain in times of need. Within this extended Saṅgha family of monks, nuns, and laypeople, the members saw themselves as brothers and sisters supporting each other in the spirit of Buddhist compassion. Another example of social reform was found in the urban areas where the city temples encouraged new types of lay-oriented Buddhist piety. In this system, the monks set aside the monastic contemplative life in order to be Dharma teachers, supporting and guiding the laity in living their religion in daily urban life. Buddhist householders were taught that the bodhisattva precepts meant that one should generously care for the needy in the community.

In time, a belief developed among Chinese Buddhists in both rural and urban areas that a "Buddha-kingdom" was being built on earth. However, this social vision of a Buddha-centered society disintegrated as the Wei Dynasty fell into civil war and the capital city was sacked and abandoned. Buddhists took both sides in the conflict: high priests supporting the state and lower clerics supporting the peasant uprisings. The disillusionment that rose from this disunity was reinforced when from 574 to 578, the Chou emperor in the north supported Confucianism and suppressed Taoism and Buddhism. Again monastics from the north fled for refuge to the south.

Some say that the fruit of the persecutions of 446 and 574 was that the monastic migrations south led to a blending of northern Buddhist practice with southern Buddhist scholarship. This blending of theory and practice is said to have influenced the founding of more fully inculturated schools of Chinese Buddhism during the sixth century. The founding of these schools was also influenced by an idea that was strengthened by the disillusionment stemming from the persecution of 574. The persecution that had attacked the sophisticated forms of Buddhist social, intellectual, spiritual, and devotional life meant for many Chinese Buddhists that they were witnessing the degeneration of the Buddha's Dharma. In Indian Buddhist literature, there was a prediction that the teaching and practice of the Dharma would weaken over time. It would be strong and true at first, but then weaken to the point that it would finally fall into a state of degeneration. It was said that this process would take place during three ages: the "age of the True Dharma," the "age of the Semblance Dharma," and the "age of the Degenerate Dharma." Given the situation of Buddhism in China and calculations that were made at that time, it was believed by many that the age of the Degenerate Dharma had arrived. What this meant to many Chinese Buddhists was that Buddhism had to produce stronger forms of practice, since, in the degenerate age, Awakening would be very difficult to attain using only traditional methods that had proven successful during the previous two ages.

THE CHINESE SCHOOLS I: LAYING THE FOUNDATION OF THE CHINESE EXPERIENCE

The Sui Dynasty, founded in 581, reunited China through its conquest of the south in 589. The first ruler of this dynasty was Wen-ti (ruled 581–604), a devout Buddhist. The capital of Ch'ang-an became the center of Chinese Buddhism as eminent monastics taught in the city with imperial patronage. In this atmosphere of religious freedom and spiritual renewal, various schools of Buddhism emerged. The Chinese have traditionally identified ten principle schools. Of these ten, six were primarily Indian schools in China. They exerted more or less influence on the Chinese experience of Buddhism, but did not last very long as independent schools. The other four, which we introduce in the following section, were more fully inculturated forms of Chinese Buddhism, and defined the lasting spirit and worldview of the Chinese Buddhist experience.

The Chü-shê School

After the *Abhidharma-kośa* of Vasubandhu was translated into Chinese by Paramārtha (499–569) from 563 to 567, the Chü-shê (*kośa*) School was founded. Based on Vasubandhu's work and the Sarvāstivāda School that it represented, the Chü-shê School held a realistic view of the world. It taught that the elements of existence, the *dharmas*, are real. It categorized the mental and physical elements of life, and it defined the causal forces that structure life and experience. This school's teachings concerning Abhidharma philosophy became a basic part of Buddhist studies in China. However, Chü-shê never became popular in the larger Buddhist community. It is said to have been brought to Japan in the seventh century, where it was known as the Kusha School.

The Ch'eng-shih School

Kumārajīva translated the *Satyasiddhi* ("Establishment of Truth") *Treatise*, which was written in India by Harivarman (c. 250–350 C.E.), and is associated with the Indian Sautrāntika School. The Ch'eng-shih (*Satyasiddhi*) School used this text to refute the independent reality of the *dharmas*, thus opposing the Chü-shê School. The *Satyasiddhi Treatise* was quite popular during the fifth and sixth centuries, but eventually the text and its school of thought were absorbed into the Chinese Mādhyamika tradition. This assimilation into Mādhyamika was facilitated by the fact that Ch'eng-shih taught that while the *dharmas* and their causal relations can be assumed by our commonsense experience of the world, they are all seen to be empty from the supreme experience of Awakening. The goal of Buddhist practice is, therefore, to achieve this wisdom into the emptiness of existence. These ideas parallel the Mādhyamika teaching of the Two Truths. The Ch'eng-shih

School was transmitted to Korea, and from there to Japan in the seventh century. In Japan it was known as the Jōjitsu School, but it was never recognized as separate from Mādhyamika.

The Lu School

While the Chü-shê and Ch'eng-shih schools taught doctrines from the Indian Abhidharma traditions, another school from that tradition did not transmit any formal doctrinal teachings. Instead, it preached the monastic discipline of the *Vinaya*. Without the *Vinaya*, there was no way to establish ordination procedures or ensure the authenticity of the lineages. This Lu (*Vinaya*) School was successful in China, and enjoyed significant influence in the formation of the Saṅghas in Korea and Japan. Founded by Tao-hsüan (596–667), the purpose of this sect was to develop a stricter observance of the *Vinaya*'s monastic rules. The school was concerned that Mahāyāna placed more emphasis on the spirit of the rules than on the letter. So, Lu emphasized a stricter observance of the two forms of Buddhist ordination—novice and full. In the seventh century, it was transmitted to Korea, where it contributed to the vitalization of Korean monasticism. In the eighth century, the sect was brought to Japan, where it had the same vitalizing effect and was known as the Ritzu (*Vinaya*) School.

The Chên-yen School

The fourth school is the Tantric Chên-yen ("True Word") School, which developed during this time period but was more formally established later by Amoghavajra (705–774). As a Tantric tradition, the school's name indicates the importance the use of *mantras* have in its practices. We have already looked at Tantra in India and Tibet. In the Chinese context, this school developed from the early Chinese fascination with Tantric masters, who were said to be able to use magic powers and rites for blessings, for averting catastrophes, and for influencing the fate of people after death. Fo-t'u-teng was famous for his magical powers and knowledge of Tantric ritual formulas.

As more systematized Tantric texts were introduced into China, the focus of Tantra shifted to meditation involving visualization of Buddhas and bodhisattvas used to aid practitioners in the realization of Buddhahood. Eventually, the Indian monk Śubhākarasiṃha (637–735), and his Chinese disciple I-hsing (683–727), translated the *Mahāvairocana Sūtra*, which became quite popular in Tantric traditions in China and Japan. Then the Indian monk Vajrabodhi (671–741) came to China in 719. His disciple from Central Asia, Amoghavajra, is said to be the founder of the Chên-yen School. Amoghavajra was also one of the greatest translators of Buddhist texts in Chinese history. One of his disciples, Hui-kuo (746–805), taught the Japanese monk Kūkai (774–835), who, in turn, founded the Shingon School of Tantric Buddhism in Japan. While the Chên-yen School did not survive in China, elements of its ritual practice, such as *mantras*, texts, and prayers, were used by other Chinese schools. Some scholars claim that the Chinese Confucian culture could not accept the sexual imagery in the practice of Tantra. Chên-yen did exercise some influence in Korea, and the Shingon School continues to be an important Buddhist sect in Japan.

The San-lun School

The fifth school was the San-lun School founded by Chi-tsang (549–623). This school, devoted to Indian Mādhyamika philosophy, is based on the work of Kumārajīva and his disciple Seng-chao. *San-lun*, meaning "Three Treatises," refers to two texts by Nāgārjuna and one by his disciple, Āryadeva. Chi-tsang argued that the Mādhyamika doctrine of emptiness does not imply a dualism between emptiness on the one hand and the ordinary reality of human experience on the other. There is but one reality, namely, this world grasped either by a person's discriminating mind or by the wisdom-mind. By the former, one experiences the ordinary world of things; by the latter, one finds the truth of emptiness. That is, one discovers that the "suchness" (*tathatā*) of the objective world is emptiness; things in their suchness are empty of the independence that the discriminating mind attributes to them. Things are in fact empty because, as Mādhyamika logic explains, they exist in the nexus of dependent arising. With wisdom insight, one's mind is like a "bright mirror" that beholds the true nature or suchness of things, how they truly are apart from one's misconception of them. This view is, for Chi-tsang, the essence of the "Middle Truth" that embraces both the conventional truth that things are real and the ultimate truth that they are also empty.

The following passages from Chi-tsang present the Buddhist goal of nirvanic freedom achieved by experiencing the "principle" of the Middle Truth:

> As one understands this correct principle, correct views arise. When correct views arise, useless discussions cease. When useless discussions cease, the wheel of *duḥkha* will be destroyed. . . . [A]s the *Ching-ming* (*Famous for Purity*) says: "Buddha, unattached to the mundane world, is like the lotus flower. He skillfully enters the paths of emptiness and silence. He penetrates the . . . *dharmas* free from impediment or obstruction. Bow your head to the Buddha who, like space, leans on nothing." (*San-lun hsüan-i*, I)

Chi-tsang's Chinese audience liked the idea that emptiness is identified with the true nature of the things of the world. This Mādhyamika identity of *saṃsāra* and Nirvana affirmed the Chinese traditional religious ideal of beholding what is ultimate in the things of nature. However, Chi-tsang was often criticized for his use of logic in order to destroy the "erroneous" views of others without ever presenting a positive depiction of the nature of ultimate reality itself. Of course, here he is simply following the example of Nāgārjuna and Āryadeva. However, this reticence to characterize ultimate reality in more positive terms, and thus reclaim the value of conditional reality, meant that San-lun did not flourish in China. San-lun was brought to Korea by the Korean monk Hyegwan, who studied under Chi-tsang. Hyegwan also traveled to Japan in 625, where he transmitted the doctrine and helped found the Japanese Sanron School.

The Fa-hsiang School

The sixth school, derived from the Indian Yogācāra tradition, took form in three stages. The first tradition of Yogācāra in China was called the Ti-lun School, founded in the early sixth century. This school struggled with the question of whether the functioning mind, including what Indian Yogācāra calls the storehouse consciousness, is pure or defiled. If it is defiled, Ti-lun taught, then it is in need of purification through the realization of an even higher innate Pure Mind. This school was replaced by the Shê-lun School, named after a Yogācāra treatise by Asaṅga. Shê-lun is based on the later writings of the Indian monastic scholar Paramārtha, who arrived in China in 546.

Paramārtha's intellectual work was foundational not only to Yogācāra in China, but also to the development of all of Chinese Buddhism. This is because of his role in promoting the *Tathāgata-garbha* tradition. This notion, rendered *Buddha-nature* in China, provided a positive way of depicting ultimate reality. For Paramārtha, Buddha-nature is another name for what he taught was an innate Pure Mind (*amala-vijñāna*) that remains unchanged and undefiled behind the transformations and defilements of the functioning mind. This Pure Mind, he taught, is a ninth consciousness beyond the eight consciousnesses (including the storehouse consciousness) that constitute ordinary mental life. With the realization of the higher Pure Mind, or one's Buddha-nature, all defilements of the ordinary mind are eliminated by its inherent purity, and one lives in the pure freedom of nirvanic Buddhahood.

For Paramārtha, again following the Indian *Tathāgata-garbha* texts, Buddha-nature is not just the essence of consciousness. Given Yogācāra's teaching about the nonduality of mind and phenomena, Buddha-nature is also seen to be the essence of all things. The suchness (*tathatā*) of all existence is Buddha-nature; everything has the Buddha-nature. Since this Buddha-nature is the nirvanic essence of Buddhahood (*Dharmakāya*), then all existence (*saṃsāra*) is the manifestation of the Dharma-body of the Buddha (Nirvana). To see the world with wisdom, which itself is the functioning of Buddha-nature, is to discover the inner Buddha-nature shining with luminosity in all phenomena. Awakening is the "uncovering" of the Pure Mind of Buddha-nature so as to find Nirvana in *saṃsāra*, Buddhahood in all things. It was this positive notion of ultimate reality that the Chinese found to be lacking in San-lun Buddhism. This notion paralleled the Taoist understanding of the inner "unborn nature." It impressed the Chinese intellectual world and influenced the evolution of Chinese Buddhism. As we shall see, it contributed directly to the more fully inculturated T'ien-t'ai, Hua-yen, and Ch'an Buddhist schools.

It is not a coincidence, then, that at around the time of Paramārtha, a text teaching the Buddha-nature doctrine, and claiming to be an Indian Buddhist *sūtra*, was composed in China. This is the famous *Treatise on the Awakening of Faith in the Mahāyāna*, or simply, *The Awakening of Faith*. Written in the mid-sixth century, *The Awakening of Faith* became a seminal text in East Asian Buddhism, influencing such major schools as Hua-yen and Ch'an, which we introduce in the next section. This important text taught that Buddha-nature is the "One Mind" which is the source of all the universe. Drawing on Yogācāra, *The Awakening of Faith* states that the One Mind has two aspects. First, it is the always pure nirvanic suchness of existence, the very *Dharmakāya*. Second, it is the basis for the storehouse consciousness to generate the *saṃsāric* world of experience. Thus, it is in the One Mind that one finds an identity of *saṃsāra* and Nirvana, of purity and defilement. The image used by the text to depict this identity is the Yogācāra one of water (Nirvana) within waves (*saṃsāra*).

The third stage in the evolution of Yogācāra in China was achieved by Hsüan-tsang (596–664). Hsüan-tsang was unsure of the Shê-lun teachings about the nature of the mind, so he traveled to Central Asia and on to India to resolve the question. The teachings of Hsüan-tsang and his disciple K'uei-chi (632–682) became the basis of the Fa-hsiang ("The Characteristics of the *Dharmas*") School. Hsüan-tsang taught that the experience of one's mind and of objects, of self and world, arise dependently as two sides of an interdependent pattern of consciousness. He says that "both the self and the *dharmas* of the world are constructions based on false ideas, and have no independent reality. . . . How are the self and these *dharmas* produced? They are all constructions based on the . . . transformation of consciousness itself" (*Ch'eng-wei-shih lun*, 2a). The transformations of the first six forms of consciousness construct one's experience of the world, while the transformations of the sev enth form construct the experience of self. Hsüan-tsang says that given that "self-delusion, self-view, self-conceit, and self-love" are associated with these transformations, the eighth consciousness, the storehouse consciousness, "is defiled" (*Ibid.*, 7).

This means that the strorehouse consciousness contains both pure and impure (moral and immoral) states that then affect one's experience of self and world. One's defiled consciousness can be purified by spiritual practice so that a person can mature in the purity of Awakening and attain Buddhahood. For Hsüan-tsang, there is no innate Pure Mind as a kind of ninth consciousness behind the transformations of the eight consciousnesses. While Hsüan-tsang's view on this matter was accepted as the Indian Yogācāra position, it was Paramārtha's *Tathāgata-garbha* notion of a Pure Mind behind the defiled ordinary consciousness that spoke more strongly to the Chinese religious way of thinking. Perhaps it was because the Fa-hsiang School did not accept Paramārtha's more popular position that it eventually lost its following in China. Fa-hsiang was also transmitted to Korea in the seventh century; one of Hsüan-tsang's own students, a Japanese priest named Dōshō

(628–700), took its teachings back to Japan, where he founded the Hossō School of Yogācāra.

THE CHINESE SCHOOLS II: DEFINING THE CHINESE EXPERIENCE

While the six schools described in the previous section played foundational roles in the development of Chinese Buddhism, they were essentially schools of Indian Buddhism in China. The four schools described in this section are significantly distinct and creative forms of inculturated Chinese Buddhism. Since these four schools will help us understand more clearly the particular Chinese Buddhist experience, we spend more time introducing them.

The T'ien-t'ai School

The T'ien-t'ai ("Heavenly Terrace") School is named after the mountain in southeast China where it originated. Tradition states that T'ien-t'ai was founded by Hui-wen (c. 550), who is considered its First Patriarch. Hui-wen's disciple was Hui-ssu (514–577), who crafted many of the teachings of the school. However, it was Hui-ssu's disciple who was the real architect of T'ien-t'ai. This was the famous Chih-i (538–597). At the time of Chih-i, Chinese Buddhists were struggling with how to deal with the diversity of Buddhist texts coming from India. Stressing the Chinese spiritual preference for harmony, Chih-i sought to reconcile and synthesize different Buddhist teachings by emphasizing the *Lotus Sūtra*'s notion of *ekayana*, the "One Vehicle." In so doing, Chih-i defined one important task of T'ien-t'ai as being the reestablishment of the unity of Buddhism.

Chih-i taught that the differences between the varieties of texts and teachings of Buddhism were due to the Buddha's having accommodated his teaching to his listeners at different times in his life. At the beginning of what Chih-i called the "Five Periods" of the Buddha's ministry, the Buddha taught the *Avataṃsaka Sūtra*, with the message of sudden Awakening to the Buddha-nature in all things. This message not being understood, the Buddha then taught the *Sūtra Piṭaka*, followed by the early Mahāyāna *sūtras*, and then the Perfection of Wisdom Literature and its doctrine of emptiness. Finally, he taught the *Lotus Sūtra* and the *Mahāparinirvāṇa Sūtra*, both of which again emphasized the sudden realization of Buddha-nature.

Chih-i also taught that the essential message of Buddhism, the notion of the universal Buddha-nature, is most clearly expressed in the *Lotus Sūtra*, the central text of the T'ien-t'ai School. However, he also taught that this message is present in all the Buddha's teachings preserved in the variety of Buddhist texts coming from India. Thus, Chih-i rejected the idea that the teachings of the different texts and schools contradict each other. Instead, they present different perspectives of the One Vehicle; they complement each other and blend into a harmony of different perspectives on the one Buddha Dharma. He also taught that because of the clarity of its presentation of this Dharma, the *Lotus Sūtra* most fully realizes the purpose of the Buddha's

Figure 7.1. *Lotus Sūtra*; gold on indigo; Sung (Song) Dynasty (960–1279 C.E.), China. Cleveland Museum of Art.

advent on earth, namely, to save all living beings. Thereby, Chih-i recognized the relative validity of the teachings and scriptures of all forms of Buddhism, while at the same time proclaiming T'ien-t'ai, given its reliance on the *Lotus Sūtra*, to be the highest form of Buddhism. Other forms of East Asian Buddhism may not have accepted T'ien-t'ai's claim to superiority, but many were influenced by the general idea that there is an internal unity in Buddhism and that its highest teaching affirms the universal presence of Buddha-nature in all forms of existence. Here we see the influence of Paramārtha's work, with which Chih-i and his teachers were familiar.

In terms of its teachings, T'ien-t'ai presents the oneness of the Three Levels of Truth. The first level is the truth of emptiness, that all things (*dharmas*) are empty of own-being because they are all dependently arisen. The second level is the truth that all things possess a temporary existence due to dependent arising. The third level is that the nature of things is both empty and temporarily existing. This third truth is called the Middle Truth; to behold it, according to Chih-i, is to see all three truths as one.

To behold this identity between emptiness and phenomena is to see the suchness (*tathatā*) of things. This suchness is the true nature of things which T'ien-t'ai calls Buddha-nature. Therefore, Buddha-nature is not something that one can see in itself, apart from phenomena. Given emptiness, Buddha-nature is not an independent thing, but is the essence of Buddhahood seen in the phenomena of the world. The metaphor that is used to express this presence of Buddha-nature in phenomena is water in waves. One cannot see water in itself apart from the forms it takes. So too, the suchness of existence, Buddha-nature, is found when one sees the identity of emptiness and the temporary forms of life.

This identity means that all living beings are embraced by the Buddha-nature, and so can attain Buddhahood. To further emphasize this doctrine of universal salvation, T'ien-t'ai points to its understanding of the world and the mind. The cosmos is said to be made up of three thousand worlds. This is not just an enumeration, but indicates the interpenetration and unity of all worlds. In T'ien-t'ai philosophy, it is said that there are ten worlds from the Buddha realms down to the hellish realms. These ten worlds arise dependently, and thus interpenetrate each other, resulting in one hundred worlds. Each of these worlds possess the ten characteristics of suchness, resulting in one thousand worlds. Finally, each of these 1000 worlds consist of three distinct worldly conditions, resulting in three thousand worlds.

Given the interpenetration of these three thousand worlds, each element (*dharma*) of any world contains the elements of all other worlds. Chih-i says that this means that the three thousand worlds are present in one moment of thought:

> Now, one mind contains ten *dharma*-realms, but each of these *dharma*-realms contains ten *dharma*-realms, resulting in 100 *dharma*-realms. One realm contains 30 kinds of worlds, hence 100 *dharma*-realms contain 3,000 worlds. These 3,000 worlds are contained in a fleeting moment of thought. . . . All one can say is that the mind is all *dharmas*, and that all *dharmas* are the mind. . . . It is obscure, but also subtle and extremely profound. Knowledge cannot understand it, and words can not express it. Therefore, it is called "the realm of the inconceivable." (*Mo-ho chih-kuan*, V)

One implication of this notion of the interpenetration of worlds is that all living beings from the realms of hell to those of the Buddhas are found within the mind. This means that the innate suchness of all beings, Buddha-nature, and all the qualities of the Buddha realms are present in the mind. Therefore, Buddha-nature can be experienced in a moment of thought, a sensation of fragrance, or a perception of color. Each moment of one's experience is united with the dependent arising of all forms of life in the cosmos expressing the suchness of existence, the Buddha-nature in all things. Here again we see the reason why all living beings possess Buddha-nature, and are thereby capable of salvation.

Hui-ssu, the Second Patriarch of T'ien-t'ai, described the mind's relation to its inherent Buddha-nature:

> The mind is the same as the mind of pure self-nature, true suchness, Buddha-nature, and the *Dharmakāya*. . . . Although the mind has always been obscured by *dharmas* based on ignorance, its nature has always been pure; thus it is called pure . . . and is originally enlightened. . . . The Buddhas past, present and future, as well as all living beings have this pure mind as their essence. . . . It is therefore called suchness. . . . This pure mind is called Buddha-nature because "Buddha" means Awakening, and "nature" means the mind. . . . The mind is called *Dharmakāya* because the meaning of *Dharma* consists in functioning, and the meaning of *kāya* [body] consists in establishing. . . . The functioning [of the

Dharma] is established on the basis of this one mind. . . . Therefore, the mind is called the *Dharmakāya*. (*Ta-ch'eng chih-kuan fa-men*, I–II)

The spiritual goal of T'ien-t'ai is to awaken to this identity between the suchness of existence, the interpenetrating unity of life, the inner Buddha-nature, and the innate purity of mind. Therefore, Chih-i was not only a philosopher, but also a practitioner and teacher of meditation. In fact, it was while reading a passage in the *Lotus Sūtra* that he gained the highest *samādhi* in which he realized Awakening. In order to guide others to this attainment, Chih-i established an ordination lineage and taught forms of meditation practice that would have great influence on the spiritual practice and experience of all East Asian Buddhism.

The spiritual journey of T'ien-t'ai is intended to lead from the unenlightened life, conditioned by blind attachment to the world, to an enlightened vision of the world that brings inner freedom and outer harmony with the universe. To further this ideal, Chih-i taught meditation methods that fostered both sudden and gradual attainment, tailoring them to the needs of his disciples. For example, he guided his monks in nondual forms of sitting meditation where one moves beyond the distinction between the meditator and the object of meditation to a more sudden experience of Buddha-nature. He also taught forms of quiet walking meditation with focus on one's body and breathing for gradual deepening of concentration. And he taught his disciples how to use the ordinary events of daily life as objects of meditative reflection. All three of these kinds of meditation have enjoyed wide popularity in the Buddhist world of East Asia.

Chih-i also taught a rather unique type of meditation. He believed that since the suchness of the three thousand worlds is found in all moments of thought, then even blind attachments express suchness. Given the fact that these negative states of mind are common to the unenlightened human condition, they were Chih-i's favorite objects of meditation. When one realizes the deeper interrelated unity of reality, one sees that the unwholesome states of mind are arising dependently, that they are empty of any substance, and then one finds freedom from any bondage to these negative factors of existence. However, this does not mean that the liberated person is purified of all negative mental factors. Given the interpenetration of all realms, even the hellish ones, these factors can always be found in the mind. While the liberated person is not himself or herself moved or defiled by any negative mental factors, he or she uses them to stay united with all beings in their struggle for liberation and to work as a bodhisattva for their salvation. This meditative use of the negative factors of mental life in order to penetrate the mystery of their suchness appealed to Chinese Buddhists who believed they were living in the age of the Degenerate Dharma.

Chih-i also showed how traditional Buddhist tranquillity meditation is harmonious and complementary to traditional Buddhist insight meditation. As when the water is still one can see the bottom of the pond, so too when the mind is still one can see one's innate Buddha-nature reflected in the clear mirror of the mind. Finally, following the teachings of the *Lotus Sūtra*, Chih-i taught that Gautama Buddha was a manifestation of an ever-present Buddha, thus affirming the value of devotional practice such as the repetition of the Buddha's name. In the end, T'ien-t'ai Buddhism emphasized the need in one's spiritual journey to balance study of the Dharma with both appropriate meditation practices and devotionalism. For centuries, this T'ien-t'ai balance in religious living influenced the development of the Chinese Buddhist experience.

Chih-i was regarded as a person of great wisdom, learning, and moral character. He organized Buddhist doctrines, produced an impressive system of philosophy, and trained his disciples in ways that have been respected throughout the ages. His teachings spoke to the minds and hearts of the Chinese Buddhist world, and T'ien-t'ai became the first really Chinese form of Buddhism. A Korean monk named Hyŏn'gwang (fl. 539–575), studied under Hui-ssu and later returned to Korea, where he became famous as a teacher of T'ien-t'ai. However, it was much later that Ŭich'ŏn (1055–1101) actually founded an independent school of T'ien-t'ai in Korea, where it is known as Ch'ŏnt'ae. The Japanese monk Saichō (767–822) studied under a disciple of the Sixth T'ien-t'ai Patriarch, from whom he received T'ien-t'ai doctrine and bodhisattva ordination. Saichō returned to Japan and founded the Tendai School on Mt. Hiei near Kyōto, which remains active to this day.

The Hua-yen School

The next great school that helped define the Chinese Buddhist experience is the Hua-yen ("Wreath") School, founded by Tu-shun (557–640). Tu-shun was a practitioner of meditation and a student of the *Avataṃsaka (Hua-yen) Sūtra*. While Tu-shun was the First Patriarch of Hua-yen Buddhism, it was really the Third Patriarch, Fa-tsang (643–712), who was the real architect of the school. Fa-tsang served as preceptor to four emperors and wrote the systematic philosophy of Hua-yen Buddhism. This philosophy is considered to be one of the most complex and difficult to understand in the Buddhist world. However, it gives us a glimpse into one of the profound dimensions of the Chinese Buddhist experience.

The T'ien-t'ai notion that dependent arising implies the interdependence, or interpenetration, of all phenomena was greatly appreciated by the Chinese people, for whom the harmony of nature and society were so important. Hua-yen thought also reflects the experience of the dependent arising as interrelatedness. Specifically, Hua-yen was interested in the interrelatedness of what is called the *Dharmadhātu*, the "realm of all *dharmas*," or the totality of the cosmos. In its devotional writings based on the *Avataṃsaka Sūtra*, Hua-yen taught that the great *Dharmadhātu* is itself the very body of Vairocana Buddha. Therefore, to realize the true nature or suchness of the cosmos is to discover the Buddha-nature of all existence. In its philosophical writings, again based on the *Avataṃsaka Sūtra*, Hua-yen taught that the totality of the *Dharmadhātu* arises in an interdependence that is wondrous and

---

BOX 7.1

FREE AND AT EASE

The strength of Chinese Mahāyāna Buddhism lies in its all-encompassing character and flexibility, enabling it to adapt to all situations and to the needs of those of all capacities and backgrounds. Thus Chinese Buddhism makes one feel pure, vigorous, and free and at ease under any circumstances.

Take myself for example. I left home to become a monk as a child, and later joined the army. I was ordained once again after ten years and since then have remained a monk. Based on my own Chinese Buddhist experience, all people I have met during these decades I consider friends, never enemies.

For example, when I meet people with different religious beliefs, I always respect them as people appearing in this world with different statuses, assuming different responsibilities, and fulfilling different missions. Although they might not agree with me and become Buddhists, as far as I am concerned, they help me in a variety of ways. To me, they are all bodhisattvas and benefactors. By seeing and treating others in this way, they also become my friends, and do not regard me as an enemy.

This is the beauty of Chinese Mahāyāna Buddhism in my experience.

DHARMA MASTER SHENG YEN

Dharma Drum Mountain, Taiwan

---

harmonious. When one sees this marvelous harmony, one generates a deeper commitment to living the Bodhisattva Path in a way that embodies that harmony in daily life. Hua-yen sought to explain its experience of this wondrous vision of the cosmos in order to help Buddhists attain a liberating insight into the harmonious nature of the *Dharmadhātu*.

Hua-yen teaches that there are four ways of experiencing the *Dharmadhātu*. First is the ordinary experience of existence that reveals the "realm of phenomena" (Chinese: *shih*), or the myriad *dharmas*. According to Hua-yen, this is the vision of the cosmos with which the early Buddhist tradition, such as Theravāda, works in order to gain Nirvana by the purification of the negative phenomena in one's consciousness. Second is the experience of existence that reveals the emptiness of all phenomena, the true suchness of all things. This is the "realm of principle" (Chinese: *li*), with which Mahāyāna works in order to attain Buddhahood. Through this second vision, one realizes that the real and inherent "principle," or nature of things, is always pure. While phenomena may be either pure or impure, in essence they are empty of the independent nature one conceives them to have. Realizing this emptiness, the dependent arising of existence, reveals the inherent purity as the Buddha-nature of all phenomena. This inherent purity as the principle of existence is likened to a clear mirror. While the mirror may reflect pure and impure images, its essential clarity is never lost. Here again we see the influence of Paramārtha.

Now we come to the third experience of the cosmos, namely, seeing "the realm of the non-obstruction between principle (*li*) and phenomena (*shih*)." This non-obstruction refers to the fundamental Mahāyāna identity of emptiness with phenomena, or Nirvana with *saṃsāra*. For Hua-yen, these two aspects of reality "interpenetrate" such that the essential purity of suchness is not lost, and the diversity of dependently arisen phenomena is maintained. The two sides of reality do not "obstruct" each other: The essence of things is always pure, while the free expression of phenomena is preserved. This non-obstruction is, as in T'ien-t'ai, likened to water and waves. The water (representing the one suchness of phenomena) is always "still," while the waves (representing the diverse phenomena) are always "in motion." The inherent still nature of the water does not obstruct the movement of the waves, and the movement of the waves does not obstruct the still nature of the water. For Hua-yen, this third vision of reality is at the heart of the T'ien-t'ai experience of Buddha-nature in all phenomena.

Finally we arrive at the fourth experience of the cosmos in which one sees "the realm of the non-obstruction between phenomena (*shih* and *shih*)." Here, we are not looking at the relationship between emptiness and phenomena, but at the relationship between the phenomena themselves. For Hua-yen, the vision of this non-obstruction reveals that the dependent arising of all phenomena exists as a totality of dynamic interrelatedness. It also reveals that the phenomena making up this totality are related to one another by what Hua-yen calls "mutual identification" and "mutual penetration." To try to understand something about this fourth vision of reality, let us look at these two characteristics one at a time.

The *mutual* identification of all things does not imply a kind of *static* identification by which one might say, for example, that fire is the same as ice. Rather, in the Hua-yen vision, all phenomena in the cosmos are dependently arising together simultaneously. Each phenomenon provides a condition for the arising of the whole cosmos, and the particular totality of the cosmos is dependent on the conditions provided by all of its parts. If one part, one thing, was different or not present, the totality would itself be different. In dependent arising, each phenomenon plays an identical role in the mutual forming of the universe. While there may be many differences between phenomena, as between fire and ice, in terms of their mutually conditioning roles, they are identical. Mutual identification refers to the identical way that all phenomena share in the conditioning mutuality of interrelatedness. They are mutually one with each other in providing the conditions for the dependent arising of the totality of the cosmos.

One implication of this idea of mutual identification is that each thing in the world is what it is because of the conditioning effect of all other things in the universe. Therefore, each being one experiences exists due to oneself, due to one's conditioning presence in the universe. For the same reason, one's self exists due to that being. So, despite the many differences between oneself and the beings one encounters, there is a fundamental unity or oneness in which each being finds a mutual identification with all other beings.

In realizing this mutual identification, a person discovers that he or she owes his or her existence to countless beings throughout the universe. This discovery gives one a deeper sense of gratitude and respect for other beings. One also feels a deeper sense of responsibility for how one uses his or her existence, given its effect on the universe. This discovery will also give one a greater aspiration to benefit all living beings (*bodhicitta*).

The idea of mutual penetration takes this notion of mutual identification a step further. In the Hua-yen teaching about the mutual penetration of phenomena, we find the high point of Hua-yen experience that has been so important to defining East Asian Buddhism. Once, Fa-tsang presented this notion of mutual penetration in a lecture to Empress Wu. In her palace, he used a golden statue of a lion to illustrate his ideas. Later, he used this lecture to compose his famous *Treatise on the Golden Lion*. In what follows, we use passages from that treatise to help explain the Hua-yen notion of mutual penetration.

At the beginning of his treatise, Fa-tsang clarifies the idea of the mutual arising of the cosmos using the gold of the statue to represent emptiness ("principle": *li*), the lion to represent the totality of the cosmos, and the parts of the lion to represent the phenomena (*shih*) of existence:

> The gold has no self-nature. . . . The arising [of the lion] is due only to dependence, so it is called dependent arising. . . . The lion is empty [not self-sustaining]; there is only the gold. . . . Also, emptiness, having no self-nature, manifests itself through form. . . . This means that since the gold takes in the totality of the lion, apart from the gold there is no lion to be found. . . . This means that when we see the lion coming into existence, we are seeing only the gold coming into existence as form. There is nothing apart from the gold. (*Chin-shih-tzu chang*, 1, 2, 4, 5)

Fa-tsang goes on to present the Ten Mysterious Gates as a way of explaining the mutual penetration of this dependent arising of the cosmos. In the first gate, it is said that the gold (emptiness) and the lion (the totality of phenomena or forms) come into being simultaneously. In the second gate, it is said that the oneness of this dependent arising in which all things condition each other does not obstruct the unique identities of each thing in the cosmos:

> [1] The gold and the lion arise simultaneously, perfectly complete. . . . [2] The gold and the lion arise compatible with each other, the one and the many not obstructing each other. In this situation, emptiness [*li*] and forms [*shih*] are distinct. Whether one considers the one [emptiness] or the many [forms], each entity maintains it own position. (*Ibid.*, 7)

In the third and fourth gates, Fa-tsang says that even though the forms of life are distinct, they also interpenetrate so that they "contain" each other. By this he means that in dependent arising, the very presence of each phenomenon influences or conditions the other phenomena of the cosmos. The

conditioning influence of one phenomenon "enters" into all other phenomena, Fa-tsang says, like reflections of objects enter a mirror. Note here that
Fa-tsang does not say that the phenomena physically enter each other. Once,
in order to demonstrate this interpenetration to Empress Wu, Fa-tsang
placed a statue of the Buddha with a lamp in the middle of a room with
mirrors all around it. He then showed the empress how the image of the
Buddha-statue (representing emptiness), while physically remaining at the
center of the room, was reflected in each mirror (representing phenomena).
He also showed her that each mirror, while physically remaining where it
is, was reflected in all other mirrors, and that their mutual reflection (representing mutual penetration) was repeated infinitely. In a similar way, each
phenomenon in the cosmos contains the presence of all other phenomena in
the cosmos, while at the same time retaining its uniqueness:

> [3] If the eye of the lion takes in the whole lion, then the whole lion is purely
> the eye. . . . [4] Since the various organs, and even each hair of the lion, takes
> in completely the whole lion in so far as they are all gold, then each [element
> of the lion] penetrates the whole [of the lion]. The eye of the lion is its ear, its
> ear is its nose, its nose is its tongue, and its tongue is its body. Yet, they all ex-
> ist freely and easily, not hindering or obstructing each other. (*Ibid.*)

In the fifth and sixth gates, it is said that when one looks at the cosmos
(the lion), emptiness (the gold) is hidden; and when one looks at emptiness,
the cosmos is hidden. But whether they are hidden or manifest, emptiness
and the phenomena of the world "mutually shine," revealing to the enlightened that they are "completely compatible":

> [5] If one contemplates the lion, there is only the lion, and the gold is not seen.
> The gold is hidden and the lion is manifest. If one contemplates the gold, there
> is only the gold, and the lion is not seen. The lion is hidden and the gold is
> manifest. . . . [6] The gold and the lion may be hidden or manifest. . . . The
> principle [emptiness] and the jointly arisen [phenomena] mutually shine. Prin-
> ciple and phenomena appear together as completely compatible. (*Ibid.*)

The seventh gate presents the metaphor of Indra's net. In the *Avataṃsaka
Sūtra*, it is said that the Hindu god Indra has a net made with jewels at its
knots. Each of these jewels reflects the image of every other jewel, and does
so on to infinity. Like the mirror example, Indra's net represents the awakened vision of the mutual penetration of the cosmos:

> [7] In each eye, ear, limb, joint and hair of the lion is [reflected] a golden lion.
> All these golden lions in all the hairs simultaneously enter into a single hair.
> Thus in each hair, there are an infinite number of lions. In addition, all single
> hairs, together with their infinite number of lions, enter into a single hair. In
> a similar way, there is an endless progression [of realms interpenetrating
> realms] just like the jewels of Indra's net. (*Ibid.*)

The last three gates relate this vision of mutual penetration to ignorance and insight into suchness, to how all time frames also interpenetrate in the totality of the cosmos, and to how both emptiness and the world of phenomena depend on the transformations of the mind. Note that this final gate presents the Yogācāra position:

> [8] The lion is spoken of in order to demonstrate the result of ignorance, while its golden essence is spoken of in order to make clear its true nature. . . . [9] This lion is a created *dharma*, arising and passing away in every moment. . . . Yet, since the different periods of time are formed dependent on one another, they are merging harmoniously and mutually penetrating together without obstruction in each moment of time. . . . [10] The gold and the lion may be hidden or manifest . . . but neither has any own-being. They are constantly being evolved through the transformations of the mind. (*Ibid.*)

The treatise ends with the following comments about the attainment of wisdom and Nirvana:

> Wisdom . . . means that when we see the lion, we realize right away that all *dharmas* are produced by causes, and are from the very beginning quiescent and empty. By being free from attachments to the world and from renunciation of the world, one flows along this way into the sea of perfect knowledge . . . [and the] afflictions that result from desires will no longer be produced. Whether one sees beauty of ugliness, the mind is calm like the sea. Wrong views cease, and there are no negative mental formations. One escapes bondage, is free from hindrances, and forever cuts the roots of *duḥkha*. This is called the entry into Nirvana. (*Ibid.*, 9, 10)

In Hua-yen practice, tranquillity meditation is used to enable a person to find emptiness as the quiescent nature of all things. This leads to detachment and inner calm in the midst of the world. Then through insight meditation, one sees this emptiness functioning as the forms of the world. This functioning is experienced as an interpenetrating, fascinating, and wonderful matrix of dependent arising. This insight, in turn, leads to a rejection of world renunciation and a compassion for all living beings who fail to see this hidden harmony and are caught in afflictive mental formations. Thereby, one dwells spiritually neither in *saṃsāra* nor Nirvana but courses freely as a bodhisattva in the matrix of the cosmos seeking the benefit of others. Hua-yen's vision of this matrix of mutual identification and penetration, where all things are interwoven in perfect balance and harmony, was very appealing to the Chinese world, which had always appreciated both harmony and nature.

From China, Hua-yen spread to other parts of East Asia. The Korean monk Ŭisang (625–702) studied Hua-yen Buddhism along with Fa-tsang under the guidance of Hua-yen's Second Patriarch, Chih-yen (602–668). Ŭisang, a close friend of Fa-tsang, later brought Hua-yen Buddhism to Korea. In the eighth century, Hua-yen was brought to Japan by Korean and Chinese monks, and the Japanese emperor built the Eastern Great Monastery (*Tōdai-ji*) as a sanctuary for the preaching of the Hua-yen doctrine. *Tōdai-ji,* with its gigantic bronze stature of Vairocana Buddha, still stands near Nara. Hua-yen thought is studied today in Buddhist centers of learning throughout East Asia.

The Ch'an School

The original Chinese word for meditation is *ch'an-na*, a rendering of the Sanskrit word for meditation, *dhyāna*. Later, Ch'an-na was shortened to Ch'an. During the sixth century, meditation was just one of many religious activities practiced by the various sects of Chinese Buddhism. In fact, most practitioners of Buddhism would attend lectures, study *sūtras*, participate in devotional rituals, and practice various pious works—often leaving little time for meditation. For those Buddhists who wanted more intense training in the practice of meditation, numerous monastic centers were dedicated to such practice. These monasteries were often located in mountainous areas in central and southwestern China and were led by meditation (Ch'an) masters. These masters taught powerful meditative practices in ways that were accessible to anyone. Ch'an techniques were said to be so powerful that they could bring a person to Awakening in the age of the Degenerate Dharma, when this feat was thought to be so difficult.

The manuscripts discovered at Tun-huang have given modern scholars a better understanding of the history of the Ch'an School that emerged from these early meditation lineages and traditions. These manuscripts indicate that many of the legends concerning the founding of Ch'an Buddhism are most likely myths. Historically, we know that one of the first Ch'an masters to gain a wide following in China was Hung-jen (601–674), master of the East Mountain School. According to the legends about this school, Hung-jen was the Fifth Patriarch of Ch'an; the First Patriarch being Bodhidharma. As time went on, this legendary line of transmission was accepted as the founding lineage of Ch'an School of Buddhism.

Bodhidharma was a monk from India who arrived in south China about 470 and who was famous for his meditative prowess. According to legend, it is said that the emperor asked Bodhidharma how much merit his building of Buddhist temples, donating to the Saṅgha, and worship offerings had brought him. Bodhidharma is said to have answered that all these acts of piety had brought the emperor no merit at all. The point of this story is that according to Ch'an, only the direct experience of one's Buddha-nature is truly meritorious. Thus, the whole purpose of Ch'an is to enable a person to discover his or her Buddha-nature through the practice of meditation. Eventually, the legend goes, Bodhidharma settled in a mountain retreat in north China near Loyang, where he gathered disciples, guided them in silent meditation, and taught them the *Laṅkāvatāra Sūtra*. It was in this place that Bodhidharma is said to have spent nine years in meditation in front of a wall. This "wall-gazing" meditation demonstrated the power of one-pointed concentration for achieving the goal of Ch'an.

Legend associates Bodhidharma with the *Laṅkāvatāra Sūtra* as a way of explaining the Ch'an experience of Awakening. As we have seen, the *Laṅkāvatāra* states that the foundation of the mind is the storehouse consciousness that contains the *Tathāgata-garbha*, the Buddha-nature. When one attains a meditative state in which there are no thoughts, there can be a sudden "reversion of the foundation of consciousness" whereby the wisdom light of the pure Buddha-nature reveals itself. Ch'an teaches that to reach this sudden turning over of consciousness that reveals Buddha-nature, one must negate all ordinary distinctions and conceptualizations through meditative stillness of mind. Ch'an meditation is said to be able to still the mind's functioning in a one-pointed concentration that reaches the ground of consciousness. It is there that the pure wisdom nature of the mind's essence is revealed in a direct and sudden intuition of Awakening.

This goal of Ch'an practice was stated clearly in a stanza composed around the eleventh century and attributed to Bodhidharma:

A special tradition outside the scriptures;
With no dependence upon words and letters.
A direct pointing into the mind;
Seeing there one's own nature, and attaining Buddhahood.

The first two lines of this stanza imply that Ch'an does not emphasize the study of *sūtras* or attempt to harmonize the Buddhist scriptures as did T'ien-t'ai. Nor does Ch'an use words to compose high mystical tracts as did Hua-yen. Rather, as the last two lines imply, Ch'an guides, or "points," disciples through the inner levels of consciousness in order to discover their Buddha-nature and attain, thereby, Buddhahood.

In the fully developed legend, the Ch'an lineage was traced back from Bodhidharma to the historical Buddha himself. In this extended line of transmission, Bodhidharma was said to be the Twenty-Eighth Patriarch in India, and the First Patriarch in China. The legend also states that once when asked about the ultimate truth, Gautama Buddha held up a flower. Among his disciples, only the Mahākāśyapa understood this gesture and received "from mind to mind" the "seal of the Buddha-mind." Mahākāśyapa is said to have personally passed this seal of sudden Awakening on in what became an Indian lineage that centuries later was brought to China by Bodhidharma.

Moving now from legend to history, we come again to Hung-jen, the Ch'an master designated in legend to have been the Fifth Patriarch. Hung-jen was invited by Empress Wu to teach the Dharma at the imperial palace. This gave his East Mountain School some national prominence. It was the disciples of Hung-jen who claimed that he was the Fifth Patriarch in a lineage dating back to Bodhidharma. These disciples also claimed that one of Hung-jen's students, Shen-hsiu (c. 606–706), was the Sixth Patriarch. While the East Mountain School enjoyed some popularity in the capital, in 732 a monk named Shen-hui (684–758) attacked the teachings of Shen-hsiu. Shen-hui had been a student of Shen-hsiu, but when Shen-hsiu was called to the imperial court, Shen-hui went to the south of China to study with another disciple of Hung-jen named Hui-neng (638–713).

In his attack on Shen-hsiu's school, Shen-hui claimed that Shen-hsiu taught gradual Awakening rather then sudden Awakening. In fact, Shen-hsiu taught that a gradual clearing of afflictions and defilements from the "pure mirror mind" was helpful in the attainment of sudden Awakening. Shen-hui also claimed that Shen-hsiu's school was the "Northern School" of Ch'an and that Hui-neng had founded the "Southern School" of Ch'an, which taught sudden Awakening. Shen-hui went so far as to claim that Hui-neng was the true Sixth Patriarch of Ch'an Buddhism and that Hui-neng had Bodhidharma's robe, the symbol of Ch'an transmission. The result of Shen-hui's attack on the East Mountain School led to a period of sectarianism among the Ch'an schools. About a century later, the emperor called a council to settle the controversy, and Hui-neng was proclaimed the true Sixth Patriarch. The so-called Northern School of Ch'an continued only until the tenth century, while the Southern School gave life to a number of important Ch'an schools, two of which continue today.

Before introducing these schools, let us look at some verses from a Chinese text, the *Platform Sūtra of the Sixth Patriarch*. This text purports to convey the teachings of Hui-neng and provides a famous legend about how Hui-neng became the Sixth Patriarch. Indeed, partly because of this *sūtra*, Hui-neng is venerated as one of the greatest Ch'an figures in Chinese history.

> While I [Hui-neng] was a child, my father died and my elderly mother and I, her only child, moved to Nan-hai. We suffered extreme poverty, and I sold firewood in the market place. By chance, a man bought some firewood. . . . Having received my money . . . I happened to hear another man reciting the *Diamond Sūtra*. Upon hearing it, my mind became clear and I attained Awakening.
>
> I asked the man, "Where do you come from with this *sūtra*?" He answered, "I pay reverence to the Fifth Patriarch, Hung-jen, at the East Mountain." . . . Hearing what he said, I realized that I was meant to hear him. I took leave of my mother [making arrangements for her] and went to East Mountain.
>
> Hung-jen asked me, "Where are you from, and why did you come to this mountain to pay reverence to me? What do you want from me?" I answered, "I am from Ling-nan [southern China]. . . . I have come a long distance to pay reverence to you. I ask for nothing but the Buddha's Dharma." The master reproved me saying, "If you are from Ling-nan, then you are a barbarian. How can you become a Buddha?" I answered, "While people may be distinguished as northerners and southerners, there is neither north nor south in the Buddha-nature. The bodies of a barbarian and a monk are different; but what difference is there in Buddha-nature?". . . . Then a lay attendant ordered me to the rice-pounding area to pound rice. This I did for more than eight months.
>
> One day the Fifth Patriarch suddenly called his disciples to come to him. When they were assembled, he said, "Let me say this to you. Life and death are serious matters. You disciples are engaged all day in making offerings . . . and you make no effort to achieve freedom from this bitter sea of life and death. If you are still deluded about your true nature, how can these blessings save you? All of you return to your rooms . . . write a verse and present it to me.

After I see the verses, I will give the robe [of the Patriarch] and the Dharma to the person who understands the true meaning [of the Dharma], and will appoint him to be the Sixth Patriarch."

At midnight, the head monk, Shen-hsiu, holding a candle wrote a verse on the wall of the south corridor, without anyone knowing about it. The verse said:

> The body is the *Bodhi* Tree,
> The mind is like a bright mirror standing.
> Take care to wipe it diligently,
> Keep it free from all dust.

The Fifth Patriarch said [to Shen-hsiu], "The verse you wrote shows that you still have not reached true understanding. You have merely arrived at the front gate, but you have not yet entered it. . . . You must enter the gate and see your own nature."

One day, a young novice passed by the rice-pounding area reciting this verse. I knew as soon as I heard it that the person who had written it did not yet know his own nature. . . . I said to the novice, "I beg you to take me to the south corridor, so I can see this verse. . . . " [There], I made a verse and, since I could not write, I asked someone to write it on the wall of the west corridor, so that I might offer my own original mind. If you do not know the original mind, studying the Dharma is to no avail. If you know the mind and realize its true nature, then you will awaken to the true meaning [of the Dharma]. My verse read:

> *Bodhi* originally has no tree,
> The bright mirror is nowhere standing.
> Buddha-nature is forever clear and pure,
> Where can there be any dust?

The Fifth Patriarch suddenly realized that I had understood the true meaning. . . . At midnight, the Fifth Patriarch called me into the hall, and expounded the *Diamond Sūtra* to me. As soon as I heard this, I was immediately awakened. That night the Dharma was imparted to me without anyone else knowing about it. Thus the Dharma of sudden Awakening and the robe were transmitted to me. The Fifth Patriarch said, "You are now the Sixth Patriarch. This robe is proof of transmission from generation to generation. But the Dharma must be transmitted from mind to mind. You must help people awaken to themselves. . . . But if you stay here, there are people who will harm you. So, you must leave at once." I set out at midnight with the robe and the Dharma. . . . After taking my leave, I set out for the south. (*Liu-tsu t'an-ching*, 2–4, 6–10)

In his verses, Shen-hsiu says that Awakening can be found within one's own body by gradually purifying the mirror mind by meditation so that no mental "dust" is present. Hui-neng, on the other hand, says in his verses that Awakening is not something that arises from a mind that is purified, but suddenly from the Buddha-nature, which is inherently pure beyond the duality of mind and body. The *sūtra* points out that Shen-hsiu's experience of meditative purifying of the mind has brought him to the gate of Awakening. But Hui-neng's experience of the purity of Buddha-nature is Awakening itself. Elsewhere in the *Platform Sūtra*, Hui-neng speaks more about Buddha-nature being the source of Awakening:

> The nature of humankind is originally pure. It is because of false thoughts that true suchness is obscured. If you are free from delusions, the original nature reveals itself. . . . As the *Vimalakīrti Sūtra* says, "At once, we gain clarity and recover the original mind." Good friends, when I was at Priest Hung-jen's place, as soon as I heard him [recite the *Diamond Sūtra*], I immediately gained great Awakening as I realized that true suchness was my original nature. (*Liu-tsu t'an-ching*, 18, 30–31)

By saying that Buddha-nature must reveal itself, Hui-neng is not rejecting meditation. He is simply stating that Awakening is possible in any situation since it is not a product of mental purification. Rather, Awakening comes from our original Buddha-nature that can reveal itself anytime and anywhere. Here, Hui-neng shares his own experience of Awakening to Buddha-nature when he heard the recitation of the *Diamond Sūtra*. This story also indicates that Ch'an recognizes levels of Awakening and that the private interview with a Ch'an master is a central element to the process of Dharma transmission from "mind-to-mind."

To clarify the relationship between meditation (*samādhi*) and wisdom (*prajñā*) in light of his notion of Buddha-nature, Hui-neng uses the distinction between essence and function. That is, meditation is not one thing that precedes and causes another thing called wisdom. Rather, since true meditation is for Hui-neng the realizing of one's Buddha-nature, meditation is the very essence of wisdom, and wisdom is the functioning of meditation. This means that meditation and wisdom are not two different things, but a unity of the essence and functioning of Buddha-nature:

> Never mistakenly say that meditation and wisdom are different; they are a unity, and are not two different things. Meditation is itself the very substance of wisdom; and wisdom is itself the function of meditation. . . . Be careful not to say that meditation produces wisdom. . . . How then are meditation and wisdom alike? They are like a lamp and its light. If there is a lamp, there is light. . . . The lamp is the essence of light; and the light is the function of the lamp. (*Liu-tsu t'an-ching*, 13, 15)

The eighth century saw the collapsing of the T'ang Dynasty, and the more intellectual forms of Ch'an in the capital cities began to lose their status. Other schools tracing themselves to Hui-neng began to rise up in rural areas, where a number of innovative Ch'an masters developed radical techniques to help their disciples awaken to their Buddha-nature. Among the most original of these Ch'an masters was Ma-tsu (709–788). Ma-tsu was said to have had a "remarkable appearance": He walked "like a bull" and glared "like a tiger." He was the first Ch'an master to use shouting and hitting mixed with paradoxical dialogue to trigger Awakening in his disciples. While he did not reject meditation, he helped Ch'an acquire a more practical approach focused on everyday life. In the context of daily living ("drawing water and chopping wood"), it was believed that one could find Awakening with the help of a master. This approach to Ch'an would later give rise to popular collections of biographies, sayings, conversations, and questions and answers of famous Ch'an masters. One of the most famous collections was the *Record of the Transmission of the Lamp* (1004).

In terms of Ma-tsu's own Awakening, it is said that one day when he was sitting in meditation, his master asked him what he was doing. Ma-tsu responded, "I wish to become a Buddha." The master then picked up a tile and began to grind it with a stone. Ma-tsu asked his master what he was doing; to which the master responded, "I am polishing this tile to make a mirror." Ma-tsu replied, "No amount of polishing will ever make a mirror out of a tile." The master then said, "And no amount of cross-legged sitting will ever make a Buddha out of you." In other words, while meditation is valuable for producing a spiritual environment wherein Awakening can take place, this Awakening is the revealment of the Buddha-nature itself. In short, you cannot make yourself *become* a Buddha because you already *are* a Buddha.

As various techniques developed in Ch'an, the Southern School split into different subschools called the Five Houses. Of these five, two are of special historical importance and continue to be influential today. First is the Ts'ao-tung School named for its two founders, Tung-shan (807–869) and Ts'ao-shan (840–901). Instead of practicing unusual techniques, this school emphasizes silent meditation as the best means of fostering enlightenment. This silence is itself understood to be a living expression of the primal stillness of the Buddha-nature. Therefore, sitting in silent meditation is the living manifestation of one's original Awakening. Living one's Buddha-nature in silent meditation allows this original Awakening to gradually show itself in one's complete life. This approach is based on Hui-neng's own view that wisdom and meditation are really one reality. It is not that meditation leads to wisdom, but that meditation is itself the essence of wisdom. The Japanese Zen master Dōgen (1200–1253) introduced this form of Ch'an into Japan, where it is known as Sōtō Zen.

The second of the Five Houses that has had continued popularity is the Lin-chi School, named after its founder Lin-chi (died 867). This school aims at a more sudden attainment of Awakening by using various innovations pioneered by people like Ma-tsu. They stress the use of paradoxical sayings called *kung-ans* (Japanese: *kōans*). The term *kung-an* means "public legal case," implying that the sayings used in Lin-chi practice are authoritative "cases" for Ch'an practice. The *kung-an* stories contain a mysterious question (e.g., "What is the sound of one hand clapping?"), a paradoxical answer to a question, or a irrational phrase that can be used by the practitioner to set aside rational dualistic thought. By moving beyond conventional reason, and with guidance from a master, the person can become one with the quandary of the *kung-an* itself. Then, in a state of spiritual questing intensified by the *kung-an* practice, the sudden answer to the *kung-an* arises "like the sun from behind a cloud." Since one's very existence is identified with the *kung-an*, in this sudden insight one glimpses one's Buddha-nature as it reveals itself at the depth of one's questing mind. Collections of *kung-ans* became popular in China and the rest of East Asia. A Lin-chi master named Yüan-wu K'o-chin (1063–1135) wrote the famous *Blue Cliff Records* that records one hundred *kung-ans* with his commentary. Later, forty-eight selected *kung-ans* were compiled with commentary by Wu-men Hui-k'ai (1183–1260) into *The Gateless Gate*, which is held in high regard in Japan.

The Lin-chi sect and its *kung-an* practice had a formative influence on Korean Buddhism. Early on, the Korean monk Pŏmnang (fl. 632–646), studied Ch'an with Tao-hsin (580–651), considered in legend to be the Fourth Patriarch. Pŏmnang brought Ch'an to Korea, where it is known as Sŏn Buddhism. However, it did not really develop in Korea until the Lin-chi sect was later introduced in the ninth century. Since that time, the Lin-chi style has defined all forms of Korean Sŏn Buddhism. The Lin-chi sect was also brought to Japan by Eisai (1141–1215), where it is known as Rinzai Zen.

The Ching-t'u School

The last of the great Chinese schools of Buddhism is the Ching-t'u ("Pure Land") School. Pure Land Buddhism, more than any other Chinese school, formed the devotional experience of Buddhism in China and throughout all East Asia. It is considered along with Ch'an to be a "practical school" because it sets aside more theoretical issues in order to stress practice. Pure Land Buddhism bases its teachings and practices on the *Land of Bliss Sūtras* composed in India. As we saw in Chapter 4, in those *sūtras* it is said that Dharmākara Bodhisattva traversed the Ten Stages of the bodhisattva's Great Journey to become Amitābha Buddha (Chinese: O-mi-t'o Fo; Japanese: Amida). In doing so, Amitābha fulfilled certain vows and gained the power necessary to create a Buddha realm referred to in China as the Pure Land. Through the realization of his vows, Amitābha also gained the power to enable people to be born in his Pure Land, where they can gain Awakening much more easily than in the human realm. Pure Land Buddhism stresses faith in this power of Amitābha to save humankind from rebirth into the realms of ignorance and suffering by bringing those who call on him to his Pure Land.

Pure Land Buddhism in China traces its roots back to when one of the *Land of Bliss Sūtras* was translated into Chinese in the second century C.E. Many scholars believe that the Pure Land tradition in China most likely developed from many sources of devotional practice. However, the tradition itself points, in what may be a more stylistic account, to three patriarchs as the primary founders of Pure Land Buddhism in China. The first acknowledged patriarch was T'an-luan (476–542). T'an-luan was once convalescing from an illness and had a vision of a heavenly gate opening to him. Inspired by this dream, he began to seek eternal life through the practice of Taoism. However, one day he met the Indian Buddhist monk, Bodhiruci, who had arrived in Loyang in 508. Bodhiruci introduced T'an-luan to teachings about

Figure 7.2. Central Buddha; Chu Sian (Ju Xian) Temple, T'ang (Tang) Dynasty (618–907 C.E.), Lung-men (Longmen), China.

Amitābha Buddha and Pure Land piety. T'an-luan converted, pursued Pure Land practice, and eventually wrote a book that unified the teachings of the *Land of Bliss Sūtras* with a sophisticated explanation of how to visualize and invoke Amitābha Buddha.

In his writings, T'an-luan introduced some of the themes that would become foundational to Pure Land Buddhism. T'an-luan was inspired by the

Amitābha's eighteenth vow, which stated that "all beings" who think of the Amitābha Buddha for even one thought moment with sincerity and faith when they hear his name will be reborn into the Pure Land. T'an-luan interpreted "all beings" to mean that not just saintly bodhisattvas, but even common persons, including sinners, can be reborn into the Pure Land through the help of Amitābha Buddha. With this possibility in mind, T'an-luan distinguished between the "difficult" and "easy" paths to Awakening. Given that the human condition is affected by ignorance and defilements, practice based just on one's own efforts is the difficult path. This is especially the case in the age of the Degenerate Dharma. On the other hand, practice becomes the easy path if it is based on one's recognition and acceptance of the power of Amitābha Buddha and one's desire to be reborn in the Pure Land. This inspiration opened the doors to popular Pure Land devotionalism in China.

The task for T'an-luan was to define what the "easy" practice should be that depends on the grace of Amitābha Buddha and results in birth in the Pure Land. Studying the Pure Land texts, T'an-luan concluded that all beings, even evil persons, can be released from their defilements by reciting the name of Amitābha Buddha. Now, if this "recitation of the Buddha's name" (nien-fo) depends just on the efforts of the recitor, the results would be minimal. However, T'an-luan believed that the effectiveness of the recitation was dependent on Amithāba Buddha himself. Tao-luan claimed that the name of Amitābha Buddha itself embodies the Buddha reality for which it stands. To invoke Amitābha's name is to make present in one's life the Buddha reality it represents. To explain how this name could have the power to purify one's life, T'an-luan likened it to a "Maṇi gem." Tradition teaches that if you throw such a gem into muddy water, the jewel cleanses the water of impurities. T'an-luan taught that since the name Amitābha means "infinite light," and since the name embodies the reality it represents, then to recite this name brings its infinite light into one's life. Its brilliance, like with a Maṇi gem, penetrates the mind of the recitor, bringing it immeasurable wisdom-light that purifies it of ignorance and defilements.

Finally, T'an-luan drew a distinction between "self power" and "Other power," which became fundamental for Pure Land thought. Self power refers to relying on one's own efforts in taking up a discipline and engaging in religious practice. This self-power attitude, T'an-luan taught, manifests a certain pride and can actually reinforce the self-centeredness one is trying to overcome. On the other hand, by relying on Other power in one's practice, that is, on the action of Amitābha Buddha, one is humbly allowing oneself to be transformed. T'an-luan identified five practices, called the Five Recollection Gates, that he considered helpful to this Pure Land practice: (1) prostration to Amitābha, (2) reciting his name, (3) resolving to be born in the Pure Land, (4) visualizing the Pure Land, and (5) sharing the benefits of the Pure Land. This latter practice means to share one's merit in this world and to be born again in this world in order to help others after gaining Awakening in the Pure Land.

The next great patriarch of Pure Land Buddhism was Tao-ch'o (562–645). He, like T'an-luan, had a deep concern for the plight of the common person. In fact, Tao-ch'o converted to Pure Land Buddhism after visiting a monument praising Tan-luan's devotion to spreading the Pure Land faith to the common people. Looking at the sheer numbers of persons who had not gained Awakening, the question that most bothered Tao-ch'o was the following. If all persons have the Buddha-nature, and if they have certainly met a Buddha during their numberless past lives, then why do they continue to be reborn in this world of *duḥkha*? Referring to the image in the *Lotus Sūtra* of children caught in a burning house, Tao-ch'o asked, why have so many people not found a way to escape?

In answering this question, Tao-ch'o makes a distinction between the Holy Path and the Pure Land Gate. The Holy Path refers to the Buddhist discipline of practicing morality and meditation in order to still the mind and purify oneself of defilements, and rooting out ignorance by gaining wisdom insight. This path to Awakening and Buddhahood makes for a long and arduous journey, especially in the age of the Degenerate Dharma. On the other hand, the Pure Land Gate can be entered even by a person who is still lost in ignorance and full of afflictions and defilements. Once in the Pure Land, the person can make the journey to Awakening and Buddhahood without any hindrances.

Tao-ch'o concluded that the Pure Land Gate is the only viable way for people to gain liberation. Using the terms "self power" and "Other power," he felt that in the age of the Degenerate Dharma, the Holy Path of self power is not only difficult, but is actually useless. The Other power of Amitābha Buddha leading through the Pure Land Gate was the exclusive way to liberation. Of Tan-luan's Five Recollection Gates, Tao-ch'o stressed the second, reciting the name of Amitābha Buddha. He is also credited with introducing prayer beads, later used in Pure Land piety throughout East Asia. Besides being known for his own ideas, Tao-ch'o is also honored for being the teacher of the next patriarch of Pure Land Buddhism, Shan-tao (613–681). Shan-tao's teachings brought Chinese Pure Land thought to its peak.

When Shan-tao was twenty-nine, he met Tao-ch'o and was impressed by his lectures. Converting to the Pure Land School, Shan-tao became its leading exponent in the capital of Ch'ang-an. The foundation of Shan-tao's thought was his empathy with the sufferings of the common people and his awareness that this suffering is a function of the human condition. This condition, shared by all persons, is marked by defilements, afflictions, and erroneous views that are themselves the result of numerous past lifetimes in which evil actions were committed. Everyone has, during his or her many births, repeatedly killed or injured living beings, stolen from people, treated others unjustly, and spoken to or about others unkindly. Everyone has had evil thoughts, spoken evil words, and done evil actions, breaking all the Buddhist precepts.

Shan-tao taught that if a person is aware of his or her evil tendencies and actions in this life, even the most insignificant, and repents of these evils, he or she will begin to gain an insight into the shared human condition that is so flawed by the mistakes of past lives. Then, one can better turn with authentic repentance, true humility, and self-knowledge to Amitābha Buddha for his help. This turning to Other power is a matter of faith entrustment. Drawing on Pure Land texts, Shan-tao defined this faith, or faithful turning to Amitābha, as having three expressions of sincerity: a sincere or honest attitude, a deep mind of sincere faithfulness, and the sincere aspiration to be born in the Pure Land. This faith is nurtured by Pure Land practice. Shan-tao, following the teachings of Tao-ch'o, stressed the recitation of the name of Amitābha Buddha as the primary practice of Pure Land piety. All other practices were to be seen as auxiliary.

The following passages are taken from a work by Shan-tao. It presents his *Parable of the White Path* that illustrates Pure Land spirituality. Shan-tao first gives the parable, and then his explanation of its meaning:

[Wishing to be reborn in the Pure Land] is like a man who desires to travel 100,000 *li* to the west. Suddenly . . . he sees two rivers. On the south is a river of fire; and on the north is a river of water. . . . Between the fire and water is a white path barely four or five inches wide, and 100 steps long. . . . The man is in the middle of a wasteland . . . and a horde of vicious ruffians and wild beasts seeing him there alone, vie with each other in their rush to kill him.

[Facing death all around], he is seized with inexpressible terror. . . . Then he hears someone from the east bank call out encouraging him, "Friend, just resolutely follow this path and there will be no danger of death. . . . " And on the west bank, someone calls out, "Come straight on, single-minded and with a fixed purpose. I can protect you, so never fear falling into the fire or water."

Hardly had he gone a step or two, and the horde of vicious ruffians calls to him, "Friend, come back! The way is too perilous, and you will never get across. Doubtlessly you will die. None of us mean you any harm." Though he hears their calling to him, the man does not look back, but straight-away proceeds single-minded on the path. In no time, he is on the west bank, forever far from all troubles. He is greeted by his good friend, and there is endless joy.

The east bank is likened to this world. . . . The west bank is likened to the precious Land of Bliss. The ruffians and wild beasts, which seem to be friends, are likened to the six sense organs, six consciousnesses, six defilements, five aggregates, and four elements. The lonely wasteland is likened to the following of bad companions and not finding good and wise ones. The two rivers of fire and water are likened to attachment, like water, and aversion or hatred, like fire. The white path . . . is likened to the aspiration to be born in the Pure Land, which arises in the very midst of the passions of attachment and aversion. . . .

The man on the path is likened to one who directs all his or her actions and practices towards the west [Pure Land]. Hearing the voices from the east . . . is like hearing Śākyamuni Buddha, who has disappeared from sight, but whose Dharma is still pursued, and therefore likened to "voices." The calling of the ruffians . . . is likened to teachings, practices and evil views that . . . lead people astray. . . . Someone calling from the west bank is likened to the vow of Amitābha. Reaching the west bank, being greeted by a good friend and rejoicing is likened to . . . attaining the Pure Land after death, where one is met by the Buddha, and knows unending bliss. (*Kuan-ching su*)

As a footnote to this parable, it should said that in Pure Land piety, reciting "Namo O-mi-t'o Fo" ("Praise to Amitābha Buddha") with the sincerity of a deep faith, attention, and seriousness brings the "infinite light" of Amitābha Buddha into the mind and heart of the practitioner in this world. Therefore, the spiritual journey of Pure Land Buddhism does not just lead through the Pure Land Gate after death. Rather, the Other power of Amitābha Buddha experienced within gives one a taste of the Pure Land even in this life. This experience can also translate into a more compassionate life of humility, gentleness, and kindness toward other beings. By the ninth century, even Ch'an recognized the positive fruits of Pure Land piety, and began to accept the practice of *nien-fo*. Today, recitation of the name of Amitābha Buddha is practiced in Buddhist communities of all types in China. Pure Land practice also spread to Korea and Japan in the seventh century. In Japan, it was instituted into the Tendai (Chinese: T'ien-t'ai) School, and later became independent as two major Japanese Pure Land schools through the efforts of Hōnen (1133–1212) and his disciple Shinran (1173–1262).

PERSECUTION AND DECLINE

While the various schools of Buddhism flourished in China during much of the T'ang Dynasty (618–907), the Buddhist Saṅgha became quite wealthy. It used national resources to construct huge Buddha statues, and its monastic institutions were exempt from taxation. As the national economy was more and more affected by Buddhist institutions, there was pressure to "purify" the Saṅgha. When the Empress Wu (c. 625–706), who had patronized Buddhism, was driven from the throne, the new emperor, Hsuan-tsung (ruled 712–756), moved against the Buddhist Saṅgha. He laicized about one-fourth of the monastics who were on the imperial rosters. However, the most severe persecution took place a century later under Emperor Wu-tsung (ruled 840–846). Influenced by Taoism, he attempted actually to destroy Buddhism in China. From 842 to 845, he ordered the destruction of a vast number of Buddhist temples, the confiscation of much of the Saṅgha's property and holy objects, and the laicization of most monks and nuns.

While this great persecution ended when the emperor died in 846, some schools of Buddhism disappeared and others were greatly weakened. Of the scholarly schools that depended on monastic libraries only Hua-yen and T'ien-t'ai survived, although severely damaged. Ch'an was not so badly affected because it did not depend on libraries and was centered in more remote regions of China where the emperor's decrees were less effective. Pure Land also survived with little damage because it was not monastic centered, but depended on support of laypeople. After the earlier persecutions, Buddhism had always made a remarkable recovery. But after the persecution of 845, no such recovery was achieved. In fact, even with government support, Buddhism entered a process of decline.

The Sung Dynasty (970–1279) began with renewed support for Buddhism. The first Sung emperor undertook the Buddhist layperson's vows and encouraged the religion in many ways. He ordered the first printing of the Chinese Tripiṭaka, which was written on 130,000 wooden printing-blocks; the task took eleven years. Succeeding Sung emperors were also helpful to Buddhism. By the thirteenth century, there were almost a half million monks and nuns and around forty thousand temples. Sung rulers created monastic estates, which they divided for three purposes. A few were *Vinaya* monasteries for training in the precepts and ordination. A larger number were teaching monasteries dedicated to the formal study of doctrines and texts. The majority of monasteries were for meditation, headed by Ch'an monastics. This system gave raise to the Three Traditions, whereby a monastic was identified by ordination lineage, lineage of meditation training, and doctrinal lineage.

With government support, two Buddhist schools managed to remain active during the Sung Dynasty. Pure Land Buddhism increased in numbers as Pure Land Societies sprang up all over China. Ch'an temples increased in numbers and became involved in the social and political life of the nation. There arose what is known as Literary Ch'an with its many written collections of *kung-ans*. In this way, Pure Land and Ch'an contributed to Chinese culture, inspiring Chinese art and literature. There were also efforts to develop a closer relation among the existing Buddhist schools. Here, too, Ch'an played an active role in finding a common ground that would harmonize meditation, devotion, and study. Ch'an masters began studying the totalistic ideas of Hua-yen and the unifying teachings of T'ien-t'ai. Ch'an practitioners also saw affinities between mental concentration in meditation and in the invocation of Amitābha Buddha.

Even with government support and these notable accomplishments, Buddhism entered a time of decline in China during the Sung Dynasty. Scholars identify two major causes, one internal and the other external. Within the Saṅgha, there was a certain moral and spiritual degeneration caused in part by the government's sale of ordination certificates. The Sung Dynasty was threatened by invasions along its northern frontiers. This threat resulted in huge military expenses, as well as annual payments to the northern barbarians. The government had also greatly increased its costly bureaucracy. To meet these expenses, the government decided to sell ordination certificates, which up until that time had been issued to monastics when they were officially ordained and had passed an examination. These certificates exempted the holder from taxation and labor service required of citizens. Under the new policy, even a layperson could purchase such a certificate in order to avoid taxation or labor service. Others who were criminals or just lazy could use the certificate to seek refuge in monasteries where they would be safe and cared for without any expense or labor service. This policy brought many undesirable persons with no interest in Buddhism into the Saṅgha, contributing to the moral and spiritual decay of the community, which lost respect in the eyes of the Chinese society.

The external cause of the decay of Buddhism in China at this time was the rise of Neo-Confucianism as the unifying force behind Sung culture and society. This new form of Confucianism criticized Buddhism for its doctrines as well as its lack of social responsibility. Neo-Confucianism inspired the important thinkers of the age to reclaim China's classical heritage, thus restoring Confucianism to prominence in Chinese culture. Instead of discussing such notions as emptiness and Buddha-nature, Neo-Confucianism focused on reason, the formative forces of nature, the moral potential of the human mind, and the ethical nature of humanness. Since Confucianists eventually controlled the educational system as well as the social service examination system, Buddhism seemed much less attractive to the educated classes in China, and very few entered the Saṅgha.

LATER DEVELOPMENTS

The Yüan Dynasty (1280–1368) of the Mongols, who ruled China from the new capital in Beijing, favored the Tibetan form of Buddhism. The Mongols understood that they needed the cooperation of the masses of China in order to have a stable government. But they could not embrace either Confucianism or Taoism given the views of those religions concerning Chinese superiority and barbarian inferiority. Buddhism, on the other hand, considered all people as equals, and Tibetan Buddhism had a cultural connection with the Mongolian nation. During this dynasty, Buddhist culture did not advance in China. In fact, secret Buddhist-related societies, such as the Maitreya Society and the White Lotus Society, became quite active. These groups were actually political entities that fomented political rebellions.

One uprising led by Chu Yüan-chang was successful in overthrowing the Mongols in 1368. Chu, who had formerly been a Buddhist monk, then founded the Ming ("Enlightened") Dynasty (1368–1644). He encouraged Buddhist ordination, and the Saṅgha grew due to this support. Following the pattern of the Three Traditions, the monasteries during the Ming Dynasty were divided into three types: the Ch'an or meditation training centers, the monasteries dedicated to study of the *sūtras*, and the "instruction" monasteries. This last category, an extension of the *Vinaya* institutions, included rituals, prayers, and Tantric ceremonies for the welfare of the common people.

One of the leaders of Ming Buddhism was Chu-hung (1535–1615). Chu-hung, who practiced Pure Land Buddhism and was trained under Hua-yen, T'ien-t'ai, and Ch'an masters, played an important role in a movement to harmonize the different schools of Chinese Buddhism. This movement was one of the significant features of Ming Buddhism. Chu-hung taught that the two major schools of practice, Pure Land and Ch'an, both focus the mind in meditation or recitation on ultimate reality, which he called "Absolute Mind." This Absolute Mind is ever pure of all passions and defilements, free from all illusions and ignorance, and is the essence of Awakening itself. Chu-hung taught that both Hua-yen and T'ien-t'ai teach about this nature of mind that embraces all phenomena. In this attempt to bring a greater unity between the schools, the common ground included the state of mind that is conducive to advancement in the spiritual life, as well as the foundation of that advancement, namely, the Absolute Mind. In the broader movement toward harmonization, it was not uncommon for Ch'an practitioners to recite the name of Amitābha Buddha, for Pure Land practitioners to practice meditation, and for both to study the *sūtras*.

Another activity of Chu-hung that contributed to a second feature of Ming Buddhism was his work for the laity. Given its degeneration during the Sung and Yüan Dynasties, many people did not wish to join the Saṅgha, but wanted to practice Buddhism as laypersons. This interest led during the Ming Dynasty to the growth of Pure Land piety as well as new forms of lay activities and the printing and distribution of its Buddhist texts. Pure Land devotional experience expressed in the fine arts also made lasting contributions to Chinese culture, especially in literature and poetry. Chu-hung himself supported the formation of lay Buddhists according to Buddhist principles and practices adapted to their daily life.

Under the Manchu emperors of the Ch'ing Dynasty (1644–1912), Buddhism was also supported, especially the Lin-chi branch of Ch'an and Tibetan Buddhism. Support of the latter won allegiance from the Mongols and Tibetans. The importance given to Tibetan Buddhism can be seen in the fact that the Beijing Edition of the Tibetan *Tripiṭaka* was completed in 1724, and only later was the Dragon Edition of the Chinese *Tripiṭaka* completed under imperial auspice in 1738, with a Manchu translation completed in 1790.

Activity among the Buddhist laity also continued during the Manchu Dynasty. This was especially true after the T'ai-p'ing rebellion (1851–1865), during which the rebels destroyed Buddhist images, texts, and temples wherever they went. In response, Buddhist laypersons played crucial roles in reviving the tradition through publishing and disseminating Buddhist literature. Yang Jen-shan (1837–1911) brought Buddhist texts from Japan and founded the Chinling Sūtra Publishing Center to print and disseminate Buddhist material throughout China. This kind of publication work was complemented by other Buddhist lay organizations dedicated to social and cultural renewal.

With the fall of the Manchu Dynasty in 1911 and the establishment of the Republic of China, many intellectual leaders saw Buddhism as a part of the premodern Chinese culture that must be set aside to facilitate the modern development of the nation. This opinion was reinforced some ten years later by the introduction of Marxism. To counter this attack on Buddhism, T'ai Hsü (1890–1947) inspired a reform movement that had wide-ranging consequences. T'ai Hsü promoted an educational program that founded schools where modern secular subjects were taught along with traditional Buddhist scholarship in Western-style classes. He also founded a number of new institutes to educate Buddhist monastic and lay leaders. T'ai Hsü's reforms stressed the regeneration of the monastic life and the dedication of monastic structures to aid the needy in society. He developed new contacts with Buddhists in other countries and supported the notion of a closer fellowship of Buddhists around the world. Finally, he supported the study of Buddhist texts and doctrines and the publication of Buddhist books and periodicals.

BOX 7.2

A NUN'S STORY

When I joined the Buddhist order at the age of twenty, I was still a student in law school. My sudden renunciation was beyond my parents' comprehension; therefore, they opposed my decision.

I recall that my father, whose thinking is strongly influenced by Confucianism, challenged me by asking a question: "Being a nun living in a monastery, how are you going to repay your debt of gratitude to family, school, and society, all of which have raised you and have provided for your education?"

I replied to him that by joining the order without a future family of my own, I could devote myself completely to helping society. My father did not say a word, but I knew that he was wondering how I could be of help to society living as a nun.

Afterwards, I did not give up my study of the law; instead, my order supported me in finishing law school and then going to the United States for further education. When I received my doctoral degree from Yale University, my parents, as well as my eldest brother and sister, who both represented my other siblings, flew to the East Coast to attend my graduation. On this occasion, my father told me that he was very proud of me. Due to my accomplishment, my parents received the Father and Mother of the Year Awards in my hometown.

Being a Buddhist nun in Taiwan, especially as a member of Fo Guang Shan, I was fully ordained, received both a clerical and a secular education, and have the opportunity to teach at universities outside the monastery. Through participating in the educational process in Taiwan, I can make a positive contribution to society.

My teacher, the Venerable Master Hsing Yün, advocates "Humanistic Buddhism," a teaching that brings Buddhism into society. Spiritual cultivation is not the sole prerogative of monks and nuns in a monastery, but is considered a necessary element for humanizing our society. Society should not be seen as just a source of temptation, and thus as an obstacle to spiritual cultivation. On the contrary, society should serve as the soil for nourishing spirituality. From the viewpoint of Humanistic Buddhism, witnessing suffering in society generates compassion. Facing and overcoming temptation in society means not to shy away from desire, but to encounter it without being tainted by it. Training oneself to attain equanimity does not require a solitary place to hide, but rather a peaceful and unmovable mind in the midst of the social turmoil of the world.

Humanistic Buddhism, from which I myself have benefited deeply, provides a philosophy that encourages me to walk into society, keeping social commitment and spiritual cultivation in balance.

VEN. DR. YIFA

Fo Gaung Shan Monastery
Hsi Lai University
Hacienda Heights, California

This kind of Buddhist renewal in mainland China was cut short when communism took control in 1949. In the 1950s, Saṅgha land holdings were confiscated, most monasteries and temples were closed, younger monks and nuns were laicized, older monastics were forced to work, and a governmental Chinese Buddhist Association was established to control the remaining Buddhist communities. During the Cultural Revolution (1966–1976), many Buddhist buildings and works of art were destroyed. However, the government has safeguarded some of the more famous Buddhist temples and works of art, and more recently has rebuilt other Buddhist sites. While these events were taking place on the mainland, Chinese Buddhism began to flourish in Taiwan. As we shall see in the chapter on modern Buddhism in Asia, the internal renewal and social engagement begun by people like T'ai Hsü have born fruit in contemporary Taiwanese Buddhism.

SUGGESTIONS FOR FURTHER READING

Chappell, David. *T'ien-t'ai Buddhism: An Outline of the Fourfold Teachings.* Tokyo: Daiichi Shobo, 1983.

Ch'en, Kenneth. *Buddhism in China: A Historical Survey.* Princeton, NJ: Princeton University Press, 1964.

———. *The Chinese Transformation of Buddhism.* Princeton: Princeton University Press, 1973.

Cleary, Thomas, trans. *Entry into the Inconceivable: An Introduction to Hwayen Buddhism.* Honolulu: University of Hawaii Press, 1983.

de Bary, Wm. Theodore, Irene Bloom, and Richard Lufrano, eds. *Sources of Chinese Tradition.* 2 vols. 2nd ed. New York: Columbia University Press, 2000, 2001.

Dumoulin, Heinrich. *Zen Buddhism: A History.* Vol. 1, *India and China.* New York: Macmillan, 1988.

Ebrey, Particia Buckley, and Peter Gregory, eds. *Religion and Society in T'ang and Sung China.* Honolulu: University of Hawaii Press, 1993.

Faure, Bernard. *The Rhetoric of Immediacy: A Cultural Critique of Chan/Zen Buddhism.* Princeton: Princeton University Press, 1995.

Gregory, Peter N., ed. *Sudden and Gradual: Approaches to Enlightenment in Chinese Thought.* Honolulu: University of Hawaii Press, 1987.

Hakeda, Yoshito S., trans. *The Awakening of Faith.* New York: Columbia University Press, 1967.

Jones, Charles Brewer. *Buddhism in Taiwan: Religion and the State, 1660–1990.* Honolulu: University of Hawaii Press, 1999.

Kieschnick, John. *The Eminent Monk: Buddhist Ideals in Medieval Chinese Hagiography.* Honolulu: University of Hawaii Press, 1997.

McRae, John R. *The Northern School and the Formation of Early Ch'an Buddhism.* Honolulu: University of Hawaii Press, 1986.

Nattier, Jan. *Once upon a Future Time: Studies in a Buddhism Prophecy of Decline*. Berkeley, CT: Asian Humanities Press, 1991.

Robinson, Richard H. *Early Mādhyamika in India and China*. Madison, WI: University of Wisconsin Press, 1967.

Tsai, Kathryn Ann. *Lives of Nuns: Biographies of Chinese Buddhist Nuns from the Fourth to Sixth Centuries*. Honolulu: University of Hawaii Press, 1994.

Yampolsky, Philip. *The Platform Sūtra of the Sixth Patriarch*. New York: Columbia University Press, 1967.

Yü, Chün-fang. *Kuan-yin: The Chinese Transformation of Avalokiteśvara*. New York: Columbia University Press, 2000.

Zürcher, Erik. *The Buddhist Conquest of China: The Spread and Adaptation of Buddhism in Early Medieval China*. 2 vols. Leiden, Netherlands: E. J. Brill, 1972.

EIGHT

THE KOREAN EXPERIENCE OF BUDDHISM

Starting in the first century B.C.E., clans vied with one another to gain control of different parts of the Korean peninsula. During the first centuries of the common era, the Koguryŏ clan conquered its neighbors and formed the first of what were to become the Three Kingdoms of the peninsula. The Kingdom of Koguryŏ ruled the northern part of the peninsula and the south central part of Manchuria. By the middle of the third century, the Kingdom of Paekche was consolidated in the southwestern part of the peninsula. And by the middle of the fourth century, the Kingdom of Silla was established in southeastern Korea. With the emergence of the Three Kingdoms of ancient Korea, diplomatic and cultural contacts with China increased through which Buddhism found its way into the peninsula.

THE ADVENT OF BUDDHISM DURING THE THREE KINGDOMS PERIOD

In the fourth century, Koguryŏ became allied with north China against the northern barbarian tribes threatening both of their borders. In 372, the emperor of north China sent the Buddhist monk Shun-tao with some companions to the Koguryŏ court of King Sosurim (ruled 371–384). It is said that Shun-tao brought with him a number of Buddhist scriptures and statues. While tradition teaches that Shun-tao's mission was the first introduction of Buddhism into Korea, there is evidence that the Saṅgha was already present in Koguryŏ when Shun-tao arrived. In any case, the idea behind this mission was to have these Buddhist monks use their prayers and rites to help protect Koguryŏ from its enemies. The king constructed a temple for Shun-tao's use, and Buddhism was officially welcomed into the kingdom. Soon, the aristocratic leaders of Koguryŏ saw Buddhism not only as offering supernatural protection for the nation, but also as a force for internal unification and moral guidance. As the common people adopted the religion, they integrated it with the country's indigenous shamanism.

Meanwhile, Paekche had developed an alliance with south China. Legend has it that in 384, the Indian monk Mālānanda, who had been traveling in south China, came to Paekche by ship, where he was also welcomed and supported in propagating Buddhism. As in Koguryŏ, the Buddhism introduced into Paekche was Mahāyāna. Soon after the introduction of Buddhism into Koguryŏ and Paekche, Korean monastics from both of these kingdoms were traveling to China to study with great Chinese masters like Kumārajīva. When these monks returned to Korea, they brought with them some of the teachings of the Chinese schools of Buddhism. There is evidence that at this time in Korea, the study of Sarvāstivāda, Sautrāntika, the *Nirvana Sūtra*, and other Chinese schools such as San-lun and T'ien-t'ai was taking place. Despite this activity in Koguryŏ and Paekche, the introduction of Buddhism into the Kingdom of Silla was protracted compared to the other kingdoms. Silla was the less developed and most isolated of the Three Kingdoms, and the first Buddhist missionaries to Silla were said to have been martyred. It was not until 527 that Buddhism was finally accepted as Silla's state religion under King Pŏphŭng (514–540).

During the sixth century, Buddhism in Koguryŏ and Paekche developed their own traditions. At the same time, the two kingdoms also sent missionaries to Japan. The Paekche king, Sŏng-myŏng, sent a Buddhist statue, ritual implements, and scriptures to the Japanese emperor in 552, with the result that Buddhist doctrine began to spread among the Japanese aristocracy. Eventually, Korean teachers of the Buddhist scriptural traditions, masters of Sŏn (Zen) practice, as well as temple artisans and architects reached Japan from Korea. Indeed, Korean Buddhists were actively involved in the propagation and development of Buddhism in Japan for over 150 years. This mission included not only the training of monks and nuns in doctrinal study and meditative practice, but also the transmission of sophisticated Buddhist art and architecture. During this time, not only were Korean Buddhists traveling to Japan, but Japanese Buddhists were also going to Korea for further study.

The Silla monk Chajang (flourished 636–645) journeyed to China for study in 636. Returning to the Silla Kingdom, he worked to import Chinese culture and Buddhism, and also helped spread Buddhism from the aristocratic community to the general population. Chajang reorganized Buddhism in Silla by issuing four rules of monastic discipline: (1) study of the *sūtras*, (2) seminars on doctrine with examinations, (3) a central temple for ordination, and (4) a government department to maintain temples and other Buddhist property. Chajang helped to establish a solid monastic structure in Korea based on his view that monastic discipline plays a central role in the attainment of Awakening. This strong monastic foundation became a key element in the Korean Buddhist experience, contributed to the eventual success of the Saṅgha, and has been an important reason for the vitality of Korean Buddhism over the centuries. The following passages record some of Chajang's contributions to the monastic discipline of the Korean Saṅgha:

> The [Silla] court discussed, "Although the eastern journey of Buddhism has been continuing for hundreds . . . of years, there is a lack of rules concerning

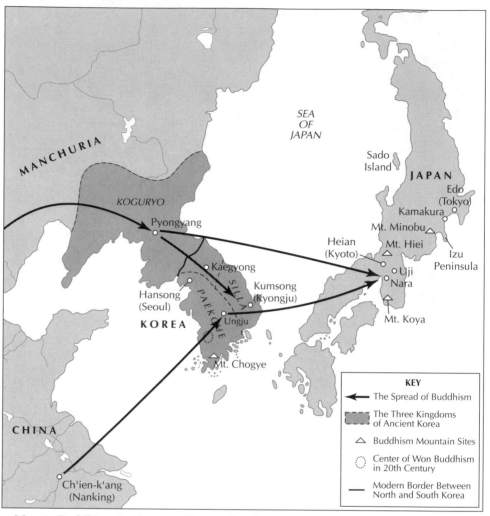

Map 4. Buddhism in Korea and Japan: fourth–seventeenth century C.E.

its monastic structure. Without them, how can the Saṅgha be kept respectable and pure?" So, by royal decree, Chajang was made the Great National Over-seer. . . .

Chajang . . . encouraged each division of the Saṅgha to enhance its training through the following: recite the precepts every two weeks, hold winter and summer examinations, establish an office to make sure the monastics follow the precepts, and send investigators to outlying monasteries to admonish monastics for their faults, and to ensure they carefully and regularly maintain their scriptures and statues. . . . Later, Chajang founded T'ongdo Monastery, where he constructed a Precepts Platform used to ordain those coming from the four directions. (*Samguk yusa*, 4: 192–193)

BUDDHISM DURING THE UNIFIED SILLA DYNASTY: INNOVATION AND SCHOLARSHIP

Silla conquered Paekche in 663 and Koguryŏ in 668, thus unifying the Korean peninsula for the first time and bringing the Three Kingdoms Period to an end. This unification ushered in the Silla Dynasty, which lasted until 918. During this period, Buddhist scholarship flourished, and major doctrinal developments of Korean Buddhism were made that still define the Korean Buddhist experience today. On the devotional level, the worship of Amitābha Buddha, Avalokiteśvara Bodhisattva, and especially Maitreya Bodhisattva was popular. In regard to Maitreya, the Silla kings claimed to be his emanations in order to justify their rule, and the common people sought to be reborn with him in the Tuṣita heaven. Within this creative environment, two major figures emerged who made major contributions to the developing uniqueness of Korean Buddhism: Ŭisang (625–702) and Wŏnhyo (617–686).

Ŭisang

Ŭisang traveled to China to study with Chih-yen (602–668), the Second Patriarch of Hua-yen Buddhism. He also became the lifelong friend of Fa-tsang (643–712), Hua yen's famous Third Patriarch and systematizer of the school's doctrines. Fa-tsang greatly respected Ŭisang's understanding of Hua-yen thought, and corresponded with him after Ŭisang's return to Korea. Ŭisang taught the doctrines of Hua-yen in Korea, thus inspiring the intellectual development of Korean Buddhism. He founded the Hwaŏm (Hua-yen) School, which under his guidance became the basis for much of Korean Buddhist doctrinal scholarship. Over the centuries, Hwaŏm has continued to have the greatest influence of the scholastic schools in Korea. Besides this scholarly work, Ŭisang stressed practice and monastic discipline, and also founded many of the most famous Buddhist temples in Korea. His seminal work, *Chart of the* Dharmadhātu, is one of the most important works in Korean Buddhist literature. The following are passages from this early work:

> The Dharma nature is perfectly interpenetrating; it has no duality.
> All *dharmas* are unmoving; they by nature are quiescent, without [the] names or characteristics [we attribute to them]. . . .
> Only by the realization of wisdom is it known, not by any other means.
> True nature is profound and subtle; with no own-being, arising
> dependently. . . .
> The one is the many, and the many are the one.
> The ten directions are contained in a mote of dust. . . .
> The first arising of *bodhicitta* is the same as true Awakening.
> *Saṃsāra* and Nirvana are always harmonious. . . .
> Śākyamuni Buddha, from his ocean-seal *samādhi* manifesting super-normal

powers, rains down jewels benefiting all living beings, filling all space. All living beings benefit according to their capacity.

Therefore, the one who practices good conduct must also return to the original source, which one cannot attain without ceasing false conceptions.

By unconditional skillful means, one attains complete liberation, returns home, and receives food according to one's capacity. . . .

Finally, one is seated on the throne of the ultimate truth of the Middle Way, from which one has never moved. Thus, one's name is Buddha. (*Ilsŭng pŏpkye to*)

Wŏnhyo

The second famous figure of the Silla era was Wŏnhyo. Wŏnhyo, a friend of Ŭisang, is considered one of the great early Korean Buddhist scholars. He was a prolific writer, author of 240 works, and was considered one of the foremost Buddhist scholars in East Asia during his own lifetime. One of his major contributions to Buddhist studies was his attempt to show how the many Buddhist texts and schools reflect in different ways the One Mind that is their true source of inspiration. In this way, he hoped to unite the Buddhist schools in Korea into a new and more comprehensive form of Buddhism. Wŏnhyo was especially concerned about the sectarian friction between the Buddhist schools that were being imported from China. He wanted to produce a new Korean Buddhist ecumenical harmony that reflects the ontological harmony, or mutual penetration, preached by the Hwaŏm School. His work in this regard inspired later and more successful efforts to unify Korean Buddhism. Scholars also see this desire for religious unification as expressing the same spirit that was behind the political unification of Korea in the unified Silla state.

An example of Wŏnhyo's method of "harmonization of all disputes" (*hwa-jaeng*) can be seen in his use of the essence-function distinction from Hwaŏm Buddhism. In his commentary on *The Awakening of Faith*, Wŏnhyo says that the many doctrines of Buddhism are manifold forms of "unfolding" or "opening" of the Dharma. When these doctrines are traced back to their source, they are "sealed" in the unifying principle of One Mind, the Buddha-nature that is their ultimate basis. In this way, the many forms of Buddhism are the functioning of the essence of the Dharma, namely, the One Mind. Opening the Dharma in its many expressions does not exhaust the essence, and sealing the Dharma in its one essence of Awakening does not diminish its expressions. Wŏnhyo extends this kind of analysis in his discussion of the Three Refuges. There, he defines the Buddha, Dharma, and Saṅgha in terms of the Three Greatnesses (essence, attribute, and function). The Buddha is the very essence of the One Mind, the Dharma is its attribute, and the Saṅgha is its function in the world.

The following are some of Wŏnhyo's comments about unfolding and sealing the Dharma from his commentary on *The Awakening of Faith*:

The essence of Mahāyāna is described as completely empty and very subtle. But no matter how subtle, how can it be anywhere but in the world of the myr-

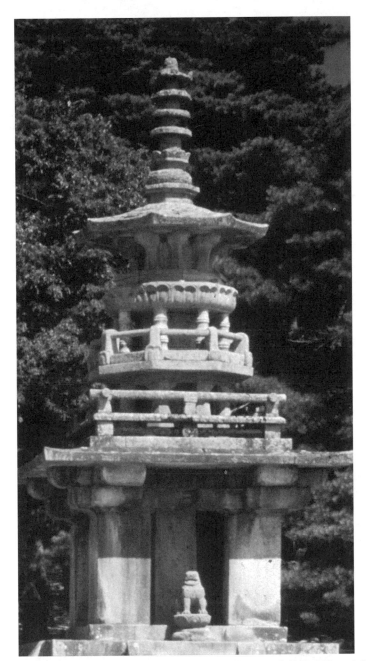

Figure 8.1. Pagoda at Pulguk-sa Temple; Unified Silla Period (668–935 C.E.), Kyŏngju, Korea.

iad phenomena? . . . Although it is nowhere but in phenomena, no eye can see
its form. . . . One can call it great, but it enters the interior where nothing remains. One can call it small, but it envelopes the exterior without exhausting
itself. One might say it is a thing, but everything is empty because of it. One
might say it is not a thing, but the myriad phenomena arise because of it. Not
knowing how to describe it, I call it the Mahāyāna. . . .

   Although what is discussed [in *The Awakening of Faith*] is vast, it can be summarized in the following words: By revealing [the suchness and causality] of
the One Mind, it comprehends the [many] jewels of Mahāyāna doctrines. . . .
When the treatise is unfolded, there are innumerable meanings found in its
doctrines. When it is sealed, the principle . . . of the One Mind is found as its
essence. . . . Therefore, it freely unfolds and seals without obstruction. . . . (*Kisil-
lon so*, 1, 3–4)

Toward the end of his life, Wŏnhyo traveled around the countryside practicing meditation in the mountains and living close to the common people
preaching hope in Pure Land devotion. Thereby, Wŏnhyo was instrumental in Buddhism spreading to the general Korean population and the popularity of Pure Land piety in Korea. Wŏnhyo also felt that meditation practice and Pure Land devotion were complementary in Buddhist experience.
This view, that both meditation and chanting can contribute to the Buddhist
journey to Awakening, became the general opinion in Korean Buddhism.
Besides influencing Hwaŏm doctrine and defining the place of Pure Land
devotion in Korean Buddhist practice, Wŏnhyo is also considered the
founder of the Haedong sect of the Hwaŏm School.

   While Wŏnhyo spread Buddhism among the general Korean population,
Ŭisang established its centers of scholarship and culture. In many ways, these
two Silla monks gave the Korean Buddhist experience its special character
of intellectual study, meditative practice, monastic discipline, and personal
devotion. Although, as we shall see, there has been tension between these
aspects of Buddhism in Korea, they have all played crucial roles in forming
the Korean experience of the Buddha Dharma. Also in the writings of
Wŏnhyo, we can see the beginnings of the Korean desire to fashion a har-
monized form of Buddhism that could unite the Buddhist Saṅgha, as well
as contribute to a more united Korean society.

The Five Buddhist Schools

During the Silla period, the Five Buddhist Schools emerged in Korea. These
schools became the orthodox scholastic Buddhist tradition in Korea from the
Silla period onward. Of these Five Schools, three were derived from Chinese schools of Buddhism, and two were unique to the Korean scene. The
first variation of a Chinese school was the Kyeyul (*Vinaya*) School. Kyeyul
was the Korean version of the Chinese Lu School that propagated the *Vinaya*
teachings. As in China, Kyeyul taught that Buddhism is not just a set of doctrines or meditative practices, but must entail a Saṅgha that adheres to
monastic precepts. Kyeyul helped in the formalization of monastic educa-

tion, ordination, and organization throughout Korea. Following the inspiration of Chajang, this school's emphasis on building a well-disciplined monasticism contributed to the vital and enduring Korean monastic Saṅgha that has lasted until the present day.

The second school was the Hwaŏm School, founded by Ŭisang. This rich vein of Chinese Hua-yen Buddhist thought generated another school in Korea that did not have any counterpart in China. This third school of Korean Buddhism was the Haedong School, based on the tecahings of Wŏnhyo. Since Wŏnhyo wanted to produce a unified form of Buddhism in Korea, while this school taught the importance of the *Avataṃsaka Sūtra*, it did not insist on the exclusive use of this *sūtra*. Wŏnhyo, with his desire for unity between the schools, taught that while the *Avataṃsaka Sūtra* was the greatest of all Buddhist *sūtras*, others could also be used to lead a person to Awakening. Both of these early schools show the importance of Ŭisang's and Wŏnhyo's groundbreaking work.

The fourth school was the Pŏpsang ("Characteristics of the *Dharmas*") School. A pioneer of this school was Wŏnch'ŭk (613–696), a Korean monastic scholar who studied and lectured on Yogācāra in Chang-an, the capital of China. While Wŏnch'ŭk espoused Paramārtha's views concurring Yogācāra, he also respected Hsüan-tsang's interpretations. Wŏnch'ŭk's disciples returned to Korea, where they inspired Yogācāra scholarship. From this doctrinal study, the Pŏpsang School was born. This school taught that all phenomena are formed by the mind. Thus, the world *as we experience it* is not the way the world really is. The true nature of all things is found in transcending the duality between mind and phenomena. The Pŏpsang School developed a Buddhist psychology and a theory of knowledge for Korean Buddhism. It also contributed to the Korean Buddhist method of mental purification.

The last of the Five Schools was the Yŏlban (Nirvana) School, based on the *Nirvana Sūtra*. There was no counterpart to this school in China, and it emerged from the popular study of the *Nirvana Sūtra*. The major teaching of this *sūtra* that impressed the Koreans was the *Tathāgata-garbha* doctrine that all beings have Buddha-nature. This doctrine as presented in the *Nirvana Sūtra* strengthened Korean Buddhist faith that all persons can, in fact, experience the happiness of the Buddha through the practice of Buddhist spirituality.

While these Five Schools were being founded, Chinese T'ien-t'ai Buddhism also existed in Korea, but not as an independent school. Known as Ch'ŏnt'ae, its first appearance was during the sixth century when Hyŏn'g-wang (flourished 539–575) brought it back to Korea after studying with Hui-ssu, the Second Patriarch of T'ien-t'ai in China. However, this school did not become fully autonomous until, as we shall see, Ŭich'ŏn (1055–1101) who was considered the real founder of the Ch'ŏnt'ae School.

Tantric Buddhism was also practiced during the Silla period, especially by the ruling family. A number of Tantric masters in Korea were known for their esoteric powers. Tantra in Korea emphasized ecstatic states of union with celestial bodhisattvas and the use of powerful *mantras* for protection, this-worldly benefits, and healing of diseases. This tradition, based on the Chinese Chên-yen School, never became a formal school in Korea and died out with the fall of the Silla Dynasty. Pure Land Buddhism, known in Korea as Chŏng-t'o, was quite popular with the common people, especially due to Wŏnhyo's influence. Pure Land chanting and piety influenced all the schools of Korean Buddhism and was often expressed in Korean art and literature.

Sŏn (Ch'an/Zen) Buddhism had appeared just prior to the Silla Dynasty through a Korean monk named Pŏmnang (flourished 632–646). Pŏmnang studied Ch'an in China under Tao-hsin (580–651), the person designated as the Fourth Ch'an Patriarch. Pŏmnang returned to Korea and taught the Ch'an doctrines and practices as they existed in China prior to the split between the Northern and Southern schools. However, this first phase of Sŏn in Korea did not leave any strong and lasting school. Then in the ninth century, other Sŏn lineages arrived in Korea. By the tenth century, these lineages had organized themselves, and the Nine Mountains Sŏn School of Buddhism was established. Each of these nine schools took its name from the mountain where its central temple was located. All but two of the nine Sŏn sects were founded by disciples of the successors of the great Chinese patriarch, Ma-tzu.

By the end of the Silla Period, there was a social and economic decline in Korea, and the more intellectual schools of Buddhism were no longer so attractive to the general population. People were looking for a spirituality that helped them deal with hard times. Therefore, both Pure Land and Sŏn Buddhism increased in their appeal. Sŏn Buddhism emphasized that one must remove himself or herself from society to pursue quiet meditation for the attainment of Awakening. Given the social decay at the end of the Silla period, this message was attractive to many Koreans. However, this approach to Buddhist practice was not appreciated by the more scholastic schools of Korean Buddhism. At odds with these schools, Sŏn attacked its opponents. The following is a dialogue between a Hwaŏm master and a Sŏn master that characterizes this division:

> The [Hwaŏm master] asked National [Sŏn] Master Toŭi, "What other *Dharmadhātu* is there besides the four *Dharmadhātus* taught by the Hwaŏm School?" . . . Toŭi responded, "When the four *Dharmadhātus* you . . . have mentioned are suddenly brought up in the [Sŏn] School of the Patriarchs, their essential principle [Buddha-nature] is experienced directly, just like ice melting [on a hot stove]. When this essential principle of all things is brought up, you cannot find the characteristics of those four *Dharmadhātus*. In the Patriarch's mind of Sŏn, in the original wisdom that cannot be cultivated, no characteristics of those four *Dharmadhātus* can be found." (*Sŏnmun pojang nok*, 2)

In the previous chapter, we saw that the four *Dharmadhātus* are the four ways of experiencing existence according to the Hua-yen (Hwaŏm) School. They not only provide this school with a way of analyzing experience and

BOX 8.1

THE BODY AND GESTURE OF LIFE

The core of Korean *Sŏn* Buddhism is the *mom-momjit* paradigm. *Mom* means "body" in Korean, and *momjit* means "gesture," or more broadly, uses of body. The *mom-momjit* paradigm is complex, but in its simplest form, *mom* is a metaphor for the ultimate and concrete reality, often called "suchness" in Buddhist literature, while *momjit* is the world of karma consisted of thought, language, culture, and history. Our present world is the terrain of *momjit* culture. We live our lives in the world preconceived through language and given rules and values, and we often overlook the "body" that precedes and underlies all words and gestures. The preoccupation with performing and imitating socially accepted *momjit* stifles our awareness of *mom*. Our efforts and worries are mainly geared toward acquiring or bettering certain *momjit*.

Over the course of my life, I experienced the importance of regaining the sense of *mom* in this predominantly *momjit-oriented* culture. For me, breaking this tight reign of *momjit*, recovering the sense of *mom*, and embodying its Life is the heart of Sŏn Buddhist teaching. Here is how I first learned this lesson.

In 1975, I lived through a period of personal crisis. I was a doctoral student at Berkeley and was under a great deal of pressure to finish my dissertation. I had difficult times with my professors since I had different views on certain theoretical matters. At the same time, my wife, who was our sole support at that time, fell ill and couldn't continue working. We had two teenage daughters, and suddenly there was no money coming in.

My emotions were in such turmoil that I made little progress with my thesis, and I became genuinely afraid that I would never finish. Would six years of hard work at Berkeley go down the drain, and would I have to return to Korea a failure?

I had spent years studying Buddhist theory, but nothing I had learned in books helped calm my mind. Without realizing what I was doing, I started to pray, and then an experience I had almost a decade earlier when I was an acolyte living in a Buddhist monastery in Korea suddenly came to life again. In 1966, while a monk at Haeinsa, I spent a year living under a vow of silence. Neither speaking nor communicating by writing, I focused all my energy on meditation, concentrating on the *kongan* (*kōan* in Japanese) given to me by my teacher. I definitely had a strong feeling during that year that I was drawing closer to a sense of *mom*, the source of Life itself that underlies all life forms.

Experiencing once again the feeling I had at Haeinsa restored me to a larger, more complete sense of myself, and my panic started to subside. I experienced that we are *mom* and the integrity of *mom* is untouched whether we are rich or poor, whether we get our Ph.D. or not, whether we are a success or failure. This is not to say that the world of *momjit* is unimportant. However, when we live our lives in reverence to the workings of *mom*, rather than trying to impose certain "gestures" onto it, the demands we place onto ourselves to fit into certain standards of "gestures" lose their weight.

As my mind cleared, I was able to study again, finish my Ph.D. work, and get a teaching position. I have spent the past thirty years as a professor, teaching and writing about Buddhism. The core of Buddhist practice for me has always been to live from the sense of *mom*, as I experienced during that year of silence in the monastery.

SUNG BAE PARK

Professor of East Asian Philosophy and Religions
SUNY at Stony Brook

existence, but also define a gradual growth toward the enlightened vision of the mutual identification and mutual penetration of all phenomena. Here, Master Toŭi is claiming that the original wisdom of the Buddha-nature cannot be cultivated in any such gradual way, but actually melts the distinctions so important to Hwaŏm textual study. So, as the Silla Dynasty came to an end, Korean Buddhism was split between the scholastic schools that emphasized textual study and gradual spiritual growth and the Sŏn tradition that stressed meditation and sudden Awakening. Addressing this division would become the primary theme of the next chapter of the story of Buddhism in Korea.

BUDDHISM DURING THE KORYŎ DYNASTY: SEARCHING FOR UNITY

The Silla period ended with the founding of the Koryŏ Dynasty, which reigned from 918 to 1392. From the beginning of the Koryŏ period, the kings supported a strong connection between the government and the Saṅgha, maintaining Buddhism as the state religion. The rulers were confident that by so doing, they could ensure the security and prosperity of the nation. The government also instituted a set of examinations for the Buddhist priests, thus ensuring that there was always a well-educated Buddhist leadership in Korea. The king could make two important appointments to leading members of the Saṅgha: "the teacher to the nation" and "the teacher to the king."

Under this royal patronage, Koryŏ Buddhism grew in influence and wealth. Some monasteries became huge landowners with many serfs. Others started commercial enterprises such as noodle making or tea production. As happened in China, the government became concerned about this worldly power and its corrupting influence on the Saṅgha. However, the Korean reaction was more moderate than the Chinese. In the tenth century, the government set restrictions on the Saṅgha's involvement in worldly affairs. In the twelfth century, it ruled that any monastic who broke their precepts be laicized.

Ŭich'ŏn

By the eleventh century, there was a clear and pressing need to restore high standards to the Korean Saṅgha. Given the continuing strident controversy between the Sŏn and scholastic (Kyo) schools, there was also the need to restore the spirit of unity within the Saṅgha. This dual task was undertaken by Ŭich'ŏn, another of Korea's great Buddhist scholars. Ŭich'ŏn, a son of King Munjŏng (1046–1083), entered a Hwaŏm monastery at the age of eleven. In 1085 at the age of thirty, he traveled to China, where he studied under renowned teachers of Hua-yen, T'ien-t'ai, Pure Land, Ch'an, and *Vinaya*. Ŭich'ŏn continued to be influenced by Hua-yen, but saw in T'ien-t'ai a balance between meditation and study that would be ideal for the Korean situation. Upon his return to Korea, Ŭich'ŏn attempted to bring unity to the

Saṅgha by merging Sŏn meditation with the doctrinal study of the scholastic schools in a new and expanded Ch'ŏnt'ae (T'ien-t'ai) School. As mentioned earlier, he is considered the real founder of the Korean Ch'ŏnt'ae School.

In addressing the sectarianism of the Korean Saṅgha, Ŭich'ŏn criticized both the Sŏn and the scholastic schools for their reluctance to understand the importance of each other's positions:

> While the Dharma is devoid of words and appearances, it is not separate from words and appearances. If you reject words, you can fall into wrong views and defilements. If you are attached to words, you will not find the truth. . . . Students of the *sūtras* often neglect their inner cultivation and become attached to external pursuits. Sŏn practitioners just ignore helping the world and simply look within themselves. Both positions are biases at two extremes. (*Kang Wŏn'-gak kyŏng palsa*, in *Taegak kuksa munjip*, 3, 4–5)

Ŭich'ŏn opposed these biases by teaching the need for *sūtra* study in order to understand the goal and path of Buddhism and for meditation practice in order to follow the path and realize the goal. He taught, following Wŏnhyo, that there is an essential unity behind the diversity of Buddhist teachings that is adapted to the capacities and temperaments of disciples. This unity is variously called Buddha-nature, the One Mind, or the *Dharmadhātu*. Sectarian conflict, Ŭich'ŏn concluded, was caused by those who had not realized this essential unity. It would be, he taught, through a combination of study and practice that one could realize this unity and build a more united Saṅgha. Being more influenced by the tradition of study, which he preferred because of his own study of Hwaŏm and Ch'ŏnt'ae, Ŭich'ŏn sought to achieve this unity by incorporating Sŏn into the scholarly side of the Saṅgha. His efforts to merge the various schools of Korean Buddhism in this way were supported by the ruling family and were respected by Saṅgha leaders of all persuasions. Soon, his new school was gaining disciples from all schools of Korean Buddhism. However, his early death brought an end to this experiment with Buddhist ecumenism and added one more school to the Korean Saṅgha.

Chinul

Perhaps the greatest reformer and unifier of Korean Buddhism lived during the twelfth century: Chinul (1158–1210). When Chinul was a child, he had a serious illness and his father vowed to the Buddha that if his son lived, Chinul would become a monk. The child did live, went on to enter a monastery at the age of seven, and received the Buddhist novice precepts at the age of fifteen. Chinul's preceptor was a Sŏn master. But since Chinul did not have a close relationship with him, he did not have a permanent teacher. Lacking personal instruction, Chinul studied the *sūtras* and practiced meditation himself, combining the two sides of the division between

Sŏn and Kyo in his own experience. In 1182, he traveled to the capital city to take the Sŏn Saṅgha examinations. He passed the exams, but was disillusioned by the worldly state of the Saṅgha. He decided not to pursue a career in the city hierarchy, but instead to return to the country to follow the monastic life. In discussing this choice with some fellow students, they decided to form a retreat society in the mountains dedicated to the cultivation of concentration (samādhi) and wisdom (prajñā).

In attempting to create such a society, Chinul and his friends faced difficulties in finding a site, and Chinul's fellow students went to different monasteries. Chinul decided to travel down the peninsula, and eventually settled in a monastery in the far southwest region. While there, Chinul had the first of three Awakenings, each of which would affect his teachings about Buddhist practice. Reading the Platform Sūtra of the Sixth Patriarch while in the study hall one day, he found a passage that said, "The self-nature of suchness gives rise to thoughts. But . . . it is not tainted by the many images. The true nature is always free and self-reliant." Chinul's reading of this passage brought him to Awakening, and "his heart was satisfied."

After this experience, Chinul continued to study and reflect on the Platform Sūtra as well as writings of other Sŏn masters. He became convinced that while he had attained an "initial Awakening" into Buddha-nature, he needed to continue to cultivate both concentration and wisdom in order to attain "full Awakening." This insight led to his teaching of "sudden Awakening and gradual cultivation," which he adopted from the Chinese Ch'an patriarch Tsung-mi (779–840). Chinul taught that in sudden Awakening, one discovers Buddha-nature, one's innate potential for full Buddhahood. This sudden Awakening, Chinul says, it not just a static insight but a realization of a dynamic reality: the Tathāgata-garbha, or "embryo" (garbha), of full Buddhahood (Tathāgata). Growth of this initial realization into the fullness of Buddhahood entails a gradual process of cultivation because of continuing habitual patterns of unwholesome thoughts, words, and actions. In his Secrets on Cultivating the Mind, Chinul explains the need for this ongoing cultivation process:

> If in one thought moment a person can trace back the luminosity [of his or her mind] and see his or her original nature, that person will discover that the ground of this nature is innately free of any defilements. . . . It is originally endowed with a . . . wisdom that is not a hair's breadth different from the wisdom of all the Buddhas. Therefore, this is called sudden Awakening.
>
> Even if a person is enlightened to the fact that his or her original nature is not different from that of the Buddhas, beginningless habit patterns are hard to remove suddenly. So, while one relies on this Awakening, one must continue cultivation. Through the gradual permeation of one's whole being by this Awakening, one's cultivation reaches completion. After one constantly nourishes the holy "embryo" [garbha] for a long time, one becomes a saint.
>
> While a person must practice cultivation, he or she has already suddenly awakened to the fact that deluded thoughts are originally empty and that the nature of the mind is originally pure. Therefore, one eliminates what is un-

wholesome without eliminating anything; and one cultivates what is wholesome without cultivating anything either. This is true cultivation and true elimination. (*Susim kyŏl*, Q/A 3, 7)

Chinul defined this cultivation after initial Awakening as the simultaneous development of concentration and wisdom. Concentration in the absolute sense, according to Chinul, is the very essence of one's true nature, the Buddha-nature realized in Awakening. Wisdom in the absolute sense is the very functioning of that essence. When one realizes Buddha-nature in initial Awakening, one finds that these aspects of innate suchness are not separate. In the context of cultivation subsequent to initial Awakening, through the gradual permeation of one's whole being by the essence and functioning of Buddha-nature, ignorance and craving are more and more rooted out and the embryo of Buddhahood develops into the full life of Buddhahood. Since this subsequent practice is based on one's prior Awakening, one does not fall into the practice of the gradual school that cultivates concentration and wisdom in order to gradually attain Awakening. Here again are Chinul's words from his *Secrets on Cultivating the Mind*:

> [F]rom the [absolute] standpoint of the self-nature, [concentration and wisdom] are called essence and function. . . . Concentration is the essence, and wisdom is the function. . . . Since wisdom is in concentration, concentration is calm yet always aware. Since concentration is in wisdom, wisdom is aware yet always calm.
>
> On the other hand, even if a person may have initial sudden Awakening, if he or she is affected by defilements, and negative habit patterns are deeply engrained . . . then he or she should use relative concentration and wisdom . . . as countermeasures. . . .
>
> Even if one borrows these countermeasures to bring the negative habit patterns under control, he or she has had sudden Awakening to the fact that the true nature of the mind is fundamentally pure, and that all defilements are empty. Therefore, one will not fall into the degraded practice of . . . the gradual school. . . . In the case of an enlightened person, although one uses these expedients, in every moment he or she is free from any doubts and does not become polluted . . . because one never leaves the true self-nature. (*Ibid.*, Q/A 8–9)

In 1185, Chinul traveled to another monastery, this time on a mountain in the southeastern part of Korea. At that time, it seems that he was especially concerned about the division within the Saṅgha between those monastics dedicated to the practice of meditation (Sŏn) and those dedicated to the study of doctrine (Kyo). Although committed to Sŏn, Chinul was convinced that the experience of Sŏn could also be found in the *sūtras* used by the Kyo schools. So, he retired into the mountains to read the scriptures looking for a passage that would indicate something of the Sŏn experience. One day Chinul found what he was looking for in a Hwaŏm commentary on the *Avataṃsaka Sūtra*. This commentary discussed, among other things, the nature of pure wisdom and the interpenetration of phenomena in Indra's net, which we introduced in the previous chapter. Setting aside the text, Chinul breathed a long sigh and reflected:

> The teachings are what the world-honored One said with his mouth. Sŏn is what the patriarchs have transmitted with their minds. The Buddha's mouth and the patriarch's minds certainly cannot be contradictory. How can [disciples of Sŏn and Kyo] not reach the fundamental source, and instead be complacent in their training and ferment disputes, wasting their time? (*Hwaŏmnon chŏryo*, Preface)

From this second Awakening, Chinul understood that the unity of Sŏn and Kyo resided in their common experience of what the Buddha taught and what the Sŏn masters realized. This conviction of Chinul's became the basis for his work to unify the Sangha in a comprehensive system of Buddhist spirituality. For Chinul, sudden Awakening and gradual cultivation are possible in the Kyo schools. Since the scholastic doctrines of Hwaŏm and the other Kyo schools point the disciple toward Awakening, they can be skillful means to promote enlightened experience. It is just that in the end the doctrines must be set aside in order for Awakening to take place. Although he was a Sŏn master, in his writings Chinul referred to Kyo concepts to explain Sŏn experience. For example, in his *Complete and Sudden Attainment of Buddhahood*, Chinul says that the sudden Awakening of Sŏn entails the realization of what Hwaŏm calls the mutual identification and mutual penetration of the *Dharmadhātu*, or what Wŏnhyo calls *Dharmakāya*:

> We know that the transmission of Sŏn beyond thought is the sudden realization of the *Dharmadhātu*. . . . If . . . sitting quietly in a private room, you can empty your heart and purify your thoughts, then you can trace back the radiance of your mind, returning to its source. You can consider the purity of the sublime mind that appears in that sudden moment of thought to be either original Awakening involved in defilements, or original Awakening of one's pure nature, or the unobstructed *Dharmadhātu*, or the Buddha of complete wisdom, or Vairocana Buddha. . . . [A]ny of these alternatives is acceptable.
>
> The original wisdom of universal brightness [spoken of by the Sixth Patriarch] is the very essence of all living beings and Buddhas. In it, suchness and phenomena . . . are all complete and have faded away. It is likened to the one great *Dharmakāya* taught be Wŏnhyo. . . . [F]rom the standpoint of the meaning of interdependence involved in dependent arising . . . we understand from Awakening that all living beings and Buddhas perfectly interpenetrate in the wisdom of universal brightness. (*Wondon sŏngbullon*, Q/A 3–4)

In 1190, Chinul and some of his fellow monastics who had made the pledge with him to found a Concentration and Wisdom Society finally began their reform experiment. They welcomed all people who were serious about cultivating concentration and wisdom in a secluded environment. By 1197, the community had gained widespread recognition and a large membership. It

Figure 8.2. Songgwang-sa Temple; founded in 1190 by Chinul on Mt. Chogye, Kwangju, Korea.

was said that Chinul's reform was so successful that the number of people who followed him grew so large that his retreat center became "like a city." Needing a larger site for his community, Chinul sent followers to the south-west of the peninsula where a new location was found. Later, the mountain on which this new monastic center was built was renamed *Chogye*, after the mountain on which the Sixth Patriarch lived in south China. Therefore, the order that Chinul's society became was named the Chogye Order.

On his way to this new center in the spring of 1197, Chinul stopped for a time at a monastery for some quiet and solitude. There, he attained his third and final Awakening while reading a passage from the *Records* of the famous Ch'an master Ta-hui (1089–1163). Chinul said,

> [Before this Awakening,] I had not yet let go of passions and views, it was like there was something blocking my chest, or like I was living with an enemy. . . . [After this Awakening,] naturally, my chest was not blocked by anything again, and I never again lived with an enemy. I was always at peace from that moment on. (*Pojo kuksa pimyŏng, Pulgyo t'ongsa*, III, 338.9–12)

Ta-hui was a Chinese Ch'an master in the Lin-chi lineage and a famous popularizer of the *hua-t'ou* (K. *hwadu*) method of practice. Something of this practice must have been behind Chinul's final Awakening, since Chinul became the first Sŏn master to adopt the *hwadu* method. Through his influence, it remains a central practice in Sŏn today. The term *hwadu* literally means "head of speech," and refers to the "critical phrase" in a *kongan* (Chinese: *kung-an*; Japanese: *kōan*). For example, one of the most popular *kongans* in Korea is the following: Once a monk asked Chao-chou, "Does a dog have Buddha-nature, or not?" Chao-chou replied, "No!" In this case, the *kongan* would be the whole exchange between the master and disciple. The *hwadu* would be the single word "no."

From the Sŏn perspective, all living beings, including dogs, are said to have Buddha-nature. So, the question is, why did Chao-chou say "no"? To understand his answer, one has to enter the mind of Chao-chou at the time he made the remark. In practice, the practitioner can penetrate into the mind of Chao-chou through the *hwadu* "no" by concentrating on this single word in all situations: meditating, walking, eating, working, and so forth. The *hwadu* focuses the mind and its paradoxical content bringing the mind's conceptual functioning to a stop. Behind this progression into the depths of the mind is the force of the questioning "doubt" produced by the *kongan* and intensified in the *hwadu*. When one reaches the innate nature of the mind shared by the practitioner and Chao-chou, then there can be a "mind-to-mind transmission" of Awakening.

Chinul drew on his three Awakenings in developing his teachings and system of practice. His life and work have done much to define the Sŏn experience in Korea and to unite the Korean Buddhist Saṅgha. Finally, it is also important to note that Chinul wrote a book entitled *The Essentials of Pure Land Practice*. During the Koryŏ Dynasty, Pure Land Buddhism was gaining general popularity with the laity, and Chinul helped ensure that Pure Land piety would continue to be an important part of Korean Buddhism. It is said that Pure Land devotional experience has added a personal dimension to Korean Buddhism that enriches meditation experience and keeps doctrinal study from becoming dry and impersonal. During the Koryŏ Dynasty, this piety also inspired great works of art and the building of many temples around the country.

The Korean Tripiṭaka

One of the greatest feats of Korean Buddhism took place during the Koryŏ Dynasty. In 983, the Chinese completed a Buddhist *Tripiṭaka* that contained not only the early Pali material but also Mahāyāna *sūtras*, scriptural commentaries, and philosophical texts from both the Abhidharma and Mahāyāna traditions. These texts were sent to Korea in 991. Then in 1010, the Khitans invaded Korea, forcing King Hyŏnjong (ruled 1009–1031) to flee his capital. When he did so, the king vowed to carve the whole Buddhist canon in Korean on wooden printing blocks if the invading forces were driven from Korea. It is said that ten days later, the Khitan army withdrew voluntarily. Hyŏnjong therefore initiated the enormous project in order to ensure continued protection of Korea from foreign invasion. The Korean

Tripiṭaka was completed decades later, and included more than eighty thousand wooden blocks.

Unfortunately, whatever protection was afforded by the *Tripiṭaka* was short-lived. The Mongols invaded Korea in 1231, and the ruling family was again forced to flee the capital. The Mongol invaders burned the wooden blocks of the *Tripiṭaka*. However, in 1236, the carving of a new set of blocks was ordered by royal decree. This second set was completed in 1251, and again contained some 1512 titles carved on over eighty thousand blocks. This second *Tripiṭaka* is still preserved today at the Haein Monastery, where it is rightly considered a national treasure. Both the Chinese and Korean *Tripiṭakas* were "open canons" in that they permitted the inclusion of any materials deemed to be appropriate representations of the "word of the Buddha." This methodology allowed East Asians continually to insert new materials. Given its accuracy and comprehensive nature, the Korean text was adopted by the Japanese for their edition of the *Tripiṭaka*, produced from 1922 to 1934.

REPRESSION DURING THE CHOSŎN DYNASTY

By the end of the Koryŏ Dynasty, Buddhism had achieved immense power throughout Korea. Its network of mountain monasteries and city temples became centers where thousands of monks and nuns pursued spiritual and intellectual life and ministered to the needs of the common people. The monasteries were awarded tracts of land that were worked by serfs, who were also given to the monasteries by the government. Some of the monastics developed commercial businesses. However, this power and affiliation with the government was held against the Buddhist religion when the Koryŏ Dynasty fell and was replaced with the Chosŏn (or Yi) Dynasty (1392–1910).

The Chosŏn government turned its support to Confucianism and severely limited Buddhist organizations. The number of monks and nuns in the Saṅgha was restricted, and at times there was a complete ban on ordination. The number of temples was first reduced to 242, but eventually only thirty-six temples of any importance were allowed to stay open. Monastic lands and serfs were confiscated by the government. The ordination examination system was eliminated, all the city temples were closed, and Buddhist monastics were forbidden to enter urban areas. This meant that the Saṅgha was pushed into the remote countryside, where monastics were isolated from the intellectual and cultural life of the nation. On the other hand, at times conditions did improve for the Saṅgha. During one such period, King Sejong (ruled 1419–1450) united the Sŏn and Ch'ŏnt'e schools into a unified Sŏn School and united the various scholastic schools into one Doctrinal (Kyo) School.

Hyujŏng (1520–1604) was an influential Buddhist monk during the Chosŏn period. Hyujŏng advocated the use of the doctrinal approach to Buddhism taught by the Kyo School in combination with Chinul's practice of sudden

Awakening followed by gradual cultivation as taught by the Sŏn School. In fact, he was appointed director of the Kyo School after taking his monastic examinations, and later was appointed director of the Sŏn School as well. The following are passages from his *Mirror for Meditation Students* that reflect this ecumenical spirit:

> Here, there is only one thing [the One Mind]. From the very beginning it is clear and holy. It was never born, nor has it ever disappeared. It cannot be grasped by either names or forms. . . . The Dharma has different meanings, and people have different capacities. Therefore, it is necessary to present skillful teachings. [In these teachings,] different names are given, such as "mind," "Buddha," and "living beings." But one must not be attached to names and try to correct each other about them. If their essence is [the one thing/One Mind] right here, then that is what is truly correct. If thoughts are stirred up in the mind, then that is a mistake.
>
> The transmission of mind by the Buddha . . . is the reason for Sŏn. What the Buddha said during his life is the way of Kyo. Therefore, it is said that Sŏn is the Buddha's mind, and Kyo is his words. . . . The Gate of Kyo only transmits the Dharma of the One Mind. The Gate of Sŏn only transmits the Dharma of seeing one's true nature. The mind is one's true nature, and one's true nature is the mind.
>
> Therefore, the students of the [Buddhist] path must first discern through the true words of Kyo that the two principles of suchness and causality are the innate nature and the characteristic of one's own mind. Then they must understand that the Two Gates of the beginning and end of their [Sŏn] practice are the gate of sudden Awakening and the gate of gradual cultivation. Only following this can they can set aside the Kyo principles and take hold only of the one thought [*hwadu*] that appears in their mind. Then they can realize what is already right here to be attained. This is called the living path to liberation. (*Sŏnga kugam*, in *Hanguk pulgyo chŏnsŏ*, 7: 619–621)

Hyujŏng also taught that Pure Land recitation and *mantras* from the Tantric tradition could be used in the practice of gradual cultivation. Following Chinul's views about how gradual cultivation can heal negative habit patterns, Hyujŏng especially held Pure Land practice in high regard. He considered it indispensable alongside Sŏn practice. In part as a consequence of the teachings of Hyujŏng and his students, Pure Land practice became quite popular in Korea in the seventeenth and eighteenth centuries, and its practice became the norm in Sŏn monasteries. Another master in the line of Hyujŏng, Sŏngch'ŏng (1631–1700), went so far as to say that in most cases the burden of past karma is so heavy that the vast majority of Sŏn practitioners will end up being reborn into *saṃsāra*. Therefore, Pure Land practice is also important in that it can enable one to be born into Amitābha's Pure Land where there is a greater promise of full liberation.

Toward the end of the Chosŏn Period, Sŏn Buddhism gradually regained it prominence, thanks in part to new Sŏn scholarship and the fact that there was a growing collaboration between Confucian intellectuals and Buddhist monastics. Also, there were individual monastics who worked to modernize the Saṅgha and reach out to the laity. One such Sŏn master who was known for his reform work at this time was Kyŏnghŏ (1849–1912). After his Awakening, he encouraged the growth of Sŏn by rebuilding old training centers; offering retreats for monks, nuns, and the laity; and founding Buddhist societies for all people who wanted to take up Sŏn practice. Another reform-minded monk was Han Yŏgun (1879–1944). Han was very concerned with what he saw as the shortcomings of Korean Buddhism after traveling to Siberia and Japan. He proposed a thorough revising of the religion from the education of the Saṅgha to the particulars of temple management. Han also believed that if Buddhism was to contribute to the modern world, it must balance the search for Awakening with a social consciousness. Monks and nuns should not to be attached to their religious life in the mountains, but should come down to care for the common people and teach them the Dharma. Here, Han appealed to the bodhisattva ideal that teaches a unity between the attainment of wisdom and the compassionate living of *bodhicitta*.

THE JAPANESE OCCUPATION AND RECENT DEVELOPMENTS

The Chosŏn Dynasty fell when the Japanese annexed Korea in 1910. The new government removed restrictions on Buddhism, and monastics were allowed to enter the cities for the first time in three hundred years. At first, this pleased the Buddhist leaders in Korea. However, in the Temple Ordinance of 1911, the Japanese placed control of all Korean Buddhist institutions in the hands of the Japanese governor-general. It soon became clear that the Japanese were planning to place the Korean Saṅgha under the control of the Japanese Sōtō Zen School. Also, the reform proposals of people like Han Yŏgun had included the replacing of the celibate Saṅgha with a married priesthood. The Japanese supported this idea because it would fit the Korean Saṅgha into their own tradition, which accepted married priests. The Japanese leaders in Korea pressured Korean monks to marry and offered Saṅgha leadership positions only to married monks. Gradually, married monks became the majority in the Korean Saṅgha. In 1926, when the Japanese required the Korean monasteries to remove any rules against marriage, there was a serious division in the Korean Saṅgha between its celibate and married members.

In the midst of this crisis and in response to the Japanese threat to control the Korean Saṅgha, the Kyo and Sŏn schools began a series of negotiations in 1928. Seven years later, they reached an agreement and the Korean age-old dream of a united Saṅgha was realized. In 1935, the two schools were united into what was named the Chogye Order. Note that this new order took the name of Chinul's Order that had been founded centuries ago. However, this unity within the Saṅgha was short-lived. When Korea won independence in 1945, the order was split between the minority of monastics who had preserved their celibacy during the Japanese occupation and the majority who had not.

It was not until 1954, after the end of the Korean War, that the South Korean government stepped in to support a celibate order. This led to violent

--- BOX 8.2 ---

WHO AM I?

Won Buddhism has been instrumental in discovering my identity and value as a person, and maintaining centeredness and balance in my life. Won Buddhist practices of sitting meditation, chanting meditation, and meditation in action have helped me to understand myself and the world around me. Through this process, I have learned to cultivate my own wisdom, inner strength, and beauty.

Won Buddhism helps me overcome many challenges and difficulties, such as sexism, racism, and religious discrimination. Through silent meditation, I have gained the self-awareness that I have an unlimited capacity within myself that is far more powerful than those external difficulties.

I was born in a small village in Korea. Korea is traditionally a kinship-oriented society based on the principle of patrilineal descent. I remember vividly the day I first encountered sex discrimination. In Korea, it is customary to maintain a genealogy in a family lineage book. Once every few years, names of new family members are added. One day, the revised genealogy book arrived at my home. I was very excited to see our family page. On this important page, I saw my father's full name, but not my mother's name. My mother was identified only with her father's name. I saw my brothers' names, even my younger brother's name, but not my name nor my sisters' names.

I felt very awkward. What an outrageous custom! "I am nonexistent according to our genealogy book," I thought to myself. "Women simply do not exist." When I asked my father, he told me that the family lineage book does not include any female members unless they are listed subordinate to their husbands. I realized I lived in an unjust and unequal society. I immediately felt rebellious toward patriarchal values.

From that very young age, I have asked simple questions: Who am I? Why am I here and what value does my life have? How and where do I fit in as a female in our patriarchal society?

It has been a long journey to find some of the answers to these questions, and I am still in the process of searching for the rest of the answers. In this journey, I found Won Buddhism, which practices gender equality. In Won Buddhism, women have an active role and are encouraged to cultivate their full potential since both men and women have the same Buddha-nature. Eventually, I joined the Won Buddhist community and received full ordination.

Through much angst and intense deep inner struggle, I have found strong spirituality, the awakening of the Divine within, the Buddha-nature within myself. It is the way of life that I have chosen in order to be in touch with my True Self. Won Buddhism helps me to see meaning in my life, in my place in the world, and in Ultimate Reality.

VEN. CHUNG OK LEE

Representative to the United Nations
Won Buddhism International

confrontations between members of the two factions. Finally in 1962, a South Korean Buddhist Council recognized two distinct orders in the Saṅgha. First is the Chogye Order, which had been originally founded in 1935 and professes celibacy. Second is the new T'aego Order, which accepts married monks. Today, the Chogye Order is flourishing with virtually all the monasteries of South Korea under its control. The T'aego Order is in decline with few members to staff the small number of temples they have maintained. Meanwhile in North Korea, Buddhism has suffered under the communist government, as has been the case in other parts of East Asia. Even today, the real condition of Buddhism and the status of the Saṅgha in the north are not known.

In South Korea, the Chogye Order has attempted to maintain a blending of Buddhist traditions. This can be seen in the fact that at the four head Chogye training monasteries, there are centers for Sŏn meditation, Kyo study, *Vinaya* discipline study, and Pure Land recitation. As in past centuries, the Sŏn tradition is seen to be the heart of Buddhist monastic training. At the beginning, Sŏn is practiced in the meditation hall dedicated to that purpose. Sŏn today uses the traditional *kongan* practice with emphasis on *hwadu* as taught by Chinul. Twice a year, once in the summer and once in the winter, a three-month meditation retreat is held in the meditation hall. After several years of training in at this communal level, the serious student may spend from five to ten years in a hermitage pursuing meditation practice in search of Awakening.

The Chogye Order has also taken steps to reinvigorate Buddhist culture throughout South Korea and to share its experience of Buddhism with the rest of the world. In South Korea, it has developed Sunday schools and private schools for all ages. There are two very active nuns' orders in South Korea, with many of their members active in social work. Numerous lay Buddhist organizations have been founded in South Korea, and Sŏn masters have opened their training centers to lay Buddhists. Lay-oriented Sŏn meditation centers have been opened around the globe with some success. Also, a recently founded Korean reform Buddhist movement, Won Buddhism, has spread to other countries. We introduce this movement in Chapter 10 when we again look at the way Korea is contributing to new forms of modern Buddhism.

SUGGESTIONS FOR FURTHER READING

Buswell, Robert E., Jr. *Tracing Back the Radiance: Chinul's Korean Way of Zen.* Honolulu: University of Hawaii Press, 1991.

———. *The Zen Monastic Experience: Buddhist Practice in Contemporary Korea.* Princeton, NJ: Princeton University Press, 1992.

———. *The Korean Approach to Zen: The Collected Works of Chinul.* Honolulu: University of Hawaii Press, 1983.

Grayson, James Huntley. *Korea: A Religious History*. Oxford: Clarendon Press, 1989.

Kang, Wi Jo. *Religion and Politics in Korea under the Japanese Rule*. Lewiston, NY: Edwin Mellen Press, 1986.

Lancaster, Lewis R., and C. S. Yu, eds. *Assimilation of Buddhism in Korea: Religious Maturity and Innovation in the Silla Dynasty*. Berkeley, CA: Asian Humanities Press, 1991.

————, eds. *Buddhism in the Early Chosŏn: Suppression and Transformation*. Berkeley, CA: University of California Press, 1996.

————, eds. *Introduction to Buddhism in Korea: New Cultural Patterns*. Berkeley, CA: Asian Humanities Press, 1989.

Lancaster, Lewis R., C. S. Yu, and Suh Kikun, eds. *Buddhism in Koryŏ: A Royal Religion*. Berkeley, CA: Institute of East Asian Studies, 1996.

Lee, Peter H., Wm. Theodore de Bary, Yôngho Ch'oe, and Hugh H.W. Kang, eds., *Sources of Korean Tradition*. 2 vols. New York: Columbia University Press, 1996, 2000.

Lee, Peter H., trans. *Lives of Eminent Korean Monks*. Cambridge: Harvard University Press, 1969.

Muller, Charles A. *The Sūtra of Perfect Enlightenment: Korean Buddhism's Guide to Meditation*. Albany, NY: SUNY Press, 1999.

Park, Sung Bae. *Buddhist Faith and Sudden Enlightenment*. Albany, NY: SUNY Press, 1983.

Pihl, Marshall R. *Koryŏ Sŏn Buddhism and Korean Literature*. Honolulu: University of Hawaii Press, 1995.

NINE

THE JAPANESE EXPERIENCE
OF BUDDHISM

Buddhism is traditionally said to have been introduced into Japan in 552 by Sŏng-myŏng, the king of the Korean kingdom of Paekche. However, historians point out that there were colonies of Koreans in Japan prior to that date, and most likely Buddhist priests were among them. In any case, Sŏng-myŏng did present an image of Gautama Buddha, some ritual items, and *sūtras* to Emperor Kinmei (ruled 531–571) in order to foster a political alliance against the neighboring Korean kingdoms of Koguryŏ and Silla. A letter accompanying these gifts said in part:

> This teaching is the very best of all doctrines. However, it is difficult to explain and to understand. Neither the Duke of Chou nor Confucius could comprehend it. This teaching can produce both happiness and rewards of unlimited quantity and boundless measure. It leads to the full appreciation of Awakening. Imagine a person possessing treasures that content his or her heart, and satisfy all wishes as these treasures are used. This is how it is with the treasures of this teaching. Every prayer can be fulfilled, and nothing is left wanting. This teaching has come from distant India to Korea, where all receive it with great reverence as it is preached to them. (*Nihongi*, II, 66)

The emperor consulted his court as to whether he should accept this foreign religion. The Soga clan, descended from Korean immigrants and responsible for foreign affairs, supported the acceptance of Buddhism. However, the Mononobe and Nakatomi clans, responsible for traditional rituals of what would later become known as the Shintō religion, were concerned that the acceptance of Buddhism into Japan would offend the indigenous *kami*, or gods. In the end, the emperor gave the Soga clan permission to adopt Buddhism. The Sogas built a temple to house the Buddha statue and even arranged the ordination of the first Japanese monks and nuns. When a plague broke out, the rival clans charged that the *kami* were in fact angry over this new religion, and they suppressed Buddhism. When this did not affect the plague, Buddhism was again supported.

As the Soga clan eventually dominated the court, Buddhism replaced the indigenous tradition as the state religion within just fifty years. Scholars point out that the acceptance of Buddhism was not so much because of its doctrinal positions or its spiritual practices, but because it was the carrier of an advanced continental civilization. However, most important was the attraction of its rites and ritual formulas, which were perceived to be powerful means for attaining security and prosperity. A major appeal of early Buddhism in Japan was its sacred power expressed in its system of Buddhas, bodhisattvas, temples, rites, and priests that could be called upon in times of need.

PRINCE SHŌTOKU

The first Japanese emperor to actually practice Buddhism was Emperor Yōmei (ruled 585–587), who is said to have believed in the teachings of the Buddha while still respecting the way of the national gods. Emperor Yōmei's son, Prince Shōtoku (574–622), is honored by tradition as the founder of Japanese Buddhism. He supported the building of seven temples in Japan. In 593, he built the Shitennō-ji temple in present-day Osaka, which became the center for social welfare activities in Japan. In 607, he also built the Hōryū-ji temple complex at Nara, which housed many fine pieces of Buddhist art and became the center of Buddhist studies. Since many of the temples were built with the guidance of the Korean missionaries, they were crafted in the Paekche style.

In 594, Shōtoku issued an imperial decree that urged all people to accept the Three Refuges of Buddhism as the highest refuge for all living beings. In 604, he issued the *Constitution in Seventeen Articles*, a set of rules for government officials based on Buddhist, Confucianist, and Shintō teachings. In Article Two, he again emphasized the importance of accepting the Three Refuges, or Three Treasures:

> Give sincere reverence to the Three Treasures. These Three Treasures, the Buddha, Dharma and Monastic Orders, are the final refuge for . . . [all living] beings, and are the highest objects of faith in all countries. Few persons are completely evil; so they can be taught to follow it. But if they do not take up the Three Treasures, how can their crookedness be made straight? (*Nihongi*, II, 128)

Prince Shōtoku also saw a profound moral and spiritual philosophy in Buddhism. He is celebrated as the author of eight volumes of commentary on various *sūtras*. From the *Lotus Sūtra*, Shōtoku emphasized the idea of One Vehicle, or *Ekayāna*, and the idea that the highest teaching of this vehicle presents the view that all living beings have the innately pure Buddha-nature (*Tathāgata-garbha*), which is none other than the *Dharmakāya*, the Body of the Buddha itself. So, Awakening can be attained by laypersons and monastics, men and women alike. On his deathbed, Shōtoku is said to have quoted a passage from the *Dhammapada* that describes the path to this attainment: "Avoid evil, undertake good, and purify the mind. This is the teaching of the Buddha." Since the time of Prince Shōtoku, this conjunction of moral virtue with the purification of the mind in search for the inner luminosity of one's Buddha-nature has been essential to the Japanese experience of Buddhism.

THE NARA PERIOD (710–784): THE SIX SCHOOLS

To learn more about Buddhism, Prince Shōtoku initiated diplomatic relations with China and sent official delegations of monastic scholars to China for study. It was because of this initiative that the Six Schools of Japanese Buddhism were founded based on Chinese models. As the pro-Chinese Fujiwara clan replaced the Soga clan as the dominant force in the imperial court, the new Chinese-based Buddhist schools began to grow into an intellectual and political force in Japan. This influence can be seen in the new capital of Japan established in 710 in the present-day city of Nara. The city was modeled on the Chinese capital of Ch'ang-an, and the plan for Nara included Buddhist temples at several strategic places. Emperor Shōmu (ruled 724–749) ordered the building of the famous temple, Tōdai-ji, that enshrined a huge statue of Vairocana Buddha, fifty-three feet tall and made of 450 tons of bronze gilded with gold. This "Great Eastern Temple," dedicated in 757, was the centerpiece of the Nara system of Buddhist temples. It became the headquarters of the Kegon (Chinese: Hua-yen) School, as well as a place associated with other Buddhist schools. In 741, Emperor Shōmu also ordered the construction of two provincial temples (one for monks and one for nuns) in each province. In this positive environment, the Six Nara Schools flourished.

The Kusha School

The Kusha School, based on the Chinese Chü-shê School, originated from the Indian Sarvāstivāda School. The Japanese Kusha School takes its name from the *Abhidharmakośa* written by Vasubandu. Its teachings and the *Abhidharmakośa* itself were first introduced into Japan in 658 by two Japanese monks who studied in China under Hsüan-tsang. The Japanese Kusha School presents a detailed analysis of the elements (*dharmas*) of existence with the aim of helping people eliminate afflictive emotions and clinging attachments that produce obstructions to the attainment of Awakening. By seeing that oneself and the things of the world are products of these dependently arisen elements, one is able to free oneself from defiled states of consciousness (e.g., hate, greed, and delusion). By the extinction of such defiled mental and emotional elements, one experiences Awakening and reaches the unconditioned freedom of Nirvana. The Kusha School provided the Japanese Buddhist tradition with categories useful for moral, psychological, and philosophical analysis.

Figure 9.1. Tōdai-ji Temple; eighth century C.E., Nara, Japan.

The Jōjitsu School

The Jōjitsu School, based on the Chinese Ch'eng-shih School, originated from the Indian Sautrāntika School. It also has certain affinities with Mahāyāna and is named after the *Satyasiddhi* (*Jōjitsu*) *Śāstra*. Jōjitsu teachings were brought to Japan along with Mādhyamika teachings by the Korean monk Hyegwan (Japanese: Ekwan), who arrived from Koguryŏ and settled at the Hōryū-ji temple in 625. Jōjitsu claims that the Kusha School fails to understand fully the emptiness of the elements it analyzes. Kusha, Jōjitsu says, rightly examines the elements as a way of losing attachment to oneself and the world of things. But one must also discover the emptiness of the elements by experiencing them as impermanent factors in the process of life. However, Jōjitsu also claims that even this experience of emptiness is not enough. One has to transcend the very consciousness of emptiness. Only in this deeper experience of the "completion of truth" (*satyasiddhi*) can the person find the freedom of Nirvana. Also, one is free from both emptiness and things so as to be fully able to live compassionately for others.

The Ritsu School

The third school, the Ritsu School, taught the *Vinaya* (Ritsu) discipline, which would be practiced by other forms of Japanese Buddhism. We saw that in China, there had been a concern that Buddhist monastics were not following true monastic discipline. To counter this tendency, the Lu School was founded to support the *Vinaya* discipline. Emperor Shōmu of Japan also realized that it was essential to have properly ordained and disciplined monks and nuns in order for Japanese Buddhism to prosper. So he sent two Buddhist priests to China to study the *Vinaya* and bring it to Japan. What these monks found was that only those who received the *Vinaya* through a proper ordination program of monastic discipline and were formally accepted at a proper ordination ceremony were considered true Buddhist monks or nuns. So during their ten years of study in China, they first invited the *Vinaya* master Tao-hsüan (702–760) to teach the *Vinaya* in Japan. Later, they also invited the *Vinaya* master Chien-chen (687–763), known in Japan as Ganjin, to formally transmit the *Vinaya* lineage to Japan. After great hardship and five failed attempts, Chien-chen reached Japan and settled at Tōdai-ji. Two months later, in 754, an ordination ceremony was held at Tōdai-ji, and Emperor Shōmu, part of his family, 440 laypeople, and eighty monastics of various schools received the formal *Vinaya* ordination.

The experience of the Ritsu tradition is that the vows taken at the time of ordination constitute a spiritual and moral force that affects one's mind and heart in ways that produce virtuous actions. Also, the mind purified by the *Vinaya* is thought to be more receptive to the teachings of the Dharma and more capable of spiritual progress. The *Vinaya* also creates and maintains a morally formed Saṅgha dedicated to the attainment of Awakening. In such a Saṅgha, the precepts are taught and reinforced in practice, and regularly there is a meeting of the community to confess and repent any infractions. Through the preaching of this kind of *Vinaya* discipline, the Ritsu School sought to provide a solid monastic foundation for the future development of Japanese Buddhism.

The Sanron School

The fourth school, the Sanron School, is based on the Chinese San-lun School, itself a transmission of Mādhyamika from India. The Sanron School was the dominant school of thought in the early Nara period, and it has influenced all of Japanese Buddhism with its teachings concerning emptiness. Its first transmission to Japan came by way of the Korean monk Hyegwan, who also brought the Jōjitsu teachings and was the student of the founder of the Chinese San-lun School. Other transmissions came later, and the Sanron School eventually divided into subsects based on these different transmissions. Given that its teachings concerning emptiness were similar to Jōjitsu's, the latter school was eventually absorbed into Sanron.

Sanron taught that the perceptual and conceptual experience of life gives one only "conventional truths" about the world. The "higher truth" into the real nature of things comes from a spiritual insight that transcends words and concepts. From this higher intuitive viewpoint, one sees that everything in the world is a product of dependent arising or emptiness. Ordinary awareness hides the higher truth of emptiness with its categorizing and conceptualizing mental functioning. Through the meditative cessation of this rational functioning of consciousness, the supreme truth about life can show itself in enlightened experience. To come to this realization, Sanron used the

Mādhyamika dialectical method to refute ordinary conceptual viewpoints and to push the disciple beyond reason to experience the higher truth about life. Then, one could return to the conventional world free from attachments and able to care for each and every being with both wisdom and compassion.

The Hossō School

The Hossō ("Characteristics of the *Dharmas*") School is based on the Chinese Fa-hsiang School, which originates from the Indian Yogācāra tradition with its focus on the nature and functioning of consciousness. Hossō accepted the Sanron position that all things are empty because they are dependently arisen, but sought to understand the way in which things manifest themselves in this matrix to one's consciousness. As with the Sanron tradition, there were a number of transmissions of Hossō to Japan from Korea and China. Perhaps the most important was by Dōshō (628–700), who studied with Hsüan-tsang in China and returned to Japan with Yogācāra teachings.

The chief concern of the Hossō School in Japan was to understand the nature and functioning of consciousness, since it was believed that the mind is the source of both ignorance and liberation. Consciousness is the basis of the lower truth of ordinary experience, as well as the higher truth of Buddha-realization. For the Hossō School, Awakening entails a "reversion" of the deepest level of consciousness so that the mind becomes like a "mirror" and can reflect clearly the truth about oneself and the world. The enlightened mind reflects the true nature of existence, the "suchness" (*tathatā*) of life. This change in one's consciousness transforms the way one thinks and acts. With wisdom, one is able to understand life for what it really is; with compassion, one can live it for the benefit of others. The major contribution of Hossō to the Japanese Buddhist experience was its analyses of human consciousness, the ways in which ignorance hides the truth, and the transformation of mind by which that truth can be found. This contribution helped to make Hossō the predominant school in the late Nara period.

The Kegon School

The last of the Six Schools is the Kegon School, which is based on the Chinese Hua-yen School. Bodhisena, a monk from India, is said to have arrived in Nara around 726, and taught the doctrine of the *Avataṃsaka Sūtra*. Then the Chinese monk Tao-hsüan, who brought the Ritsu School to Japan, also brought Hua-yen texts with him in 736. Korean monks were also influential in introducing Hua-yen ideas. In fact, one such monk was invited by Emperor Shōmu to deliver an imperial lecture on Hua-yen in 740. This lecture inspired great interest and resulted in strong support from the government. The Japanese government saw the Hua-yen teachings concerning the harmonious nonobstructed mutual penetration of all phenomena as a model for a unified Japanese society. The Kegon School, therefore, stressed the Hua-yen Buddhist teachings about the all-embracing interpenetration of the universe and the inherent Buddha-nature in all living beings. These two Kegon teachings are symbolized by the great Vairocana Buddha. Vairocana's radiant body, represented by the sun, symbolizes the luminous unity of all the elements of the universe. Each part of Vairocana's body, containing his Buddhahood, symbolizes the fact that each element of the universe has the Buddha-nature. Emperor Shōmu, inspired by this symbolism, cast the huge Buddha of Tōdai-ji temple in the image of Vairocana and used it to promote the unity of the Japanese nation.

Besides the Six Schools, there were other Buddhist developments during the Nara Period. Tendai (Chinese: T'ien-t'ai) teachings had arrived in Japan with such teachers as Tao-hsüan. Zen (Chinese: Ch'an) teachings arrived with such persons as Dōshō, the founder of the Hossō School. Also, Tantric Buddhism, brought earlier by Korean masters, was being further introduced by people like the Sanron master Dōji (674–744). During the Nara Period, Tantric rituals were encouraged by the Japanese government, which saw the practice of superior abilities as beneficial to the nation. It was also common for practitioners of the Sanron, Kegon, and Hossō schools to study the *Land of Bliss Sūtras* and practice Pure Land piety. On the other hand, Nara Buddhism was mainly a state religion, and most of these developments had little impact on the general population. There were, however, a number of popular charismatic unordained monks who traveled the countryside combining Buddhist teachings with the healing arts and divination. Mountain ascetics also synthesized Buddhism with traditional and esoteric spirituality. This latter development provided a model for mountain retreats that would eventually produce new forms of Buddhism as the Nara schools became affected by the corruption of the court and cities.

THE HEIAN PERIOD (794–1185): THE TENDAI AND SHINGON SCHOOLS

At the end of the Nara Period, the Buddhist schools had gained immense economic, political, and social power in Japan. Wealthy clans could donate land to monasteries and still receive income from that land. So monasteries came to represent the interests of rich landowners. Also, the government granted rice land and tax-exempt privileges to each of the regional temples. Tōdai-ji itself housed four thousand families to cultivate its land and had over one hundred slaves. The acquisition of such wealth and power brought corruption and the need for reform. This situation is a partial reason why the government moved the capital from Nara in 794 and established its new capital in the city of Heian, known later as Kyōto. In this way, it hoped to escape the influence of the powerful monasteries in Nara. With the seat of political power in Heian, two new Buddhist schools began to develop near the capital. These schools are the Tendai and Shingon traditions that produced distinctively Japanese forms of Buddhism, which both drew on and synthesized the ideas and practices of the Nara schools.

The Tendai School

While the Tendai School is the Japanese version of Chinese T'ien-t'ai Buddhism, some major innovations distinguish the Japanese school from its Chinese parent. These innovations are credited to Saichō (767–822), the founder of Tendai. Saichō, born in a village at the foot of Mt. Hiei, left home at the age of fourteen. He received novice ordination at seventeen, and two years later was fully ordained in the city of Nara. After functioning in Nara as a priest, he left the city in 788 to reside in a remote mountain retreat on Mt. Hiei. There, he founded a small monastery and sought to create a more rigorous and purified form of Buddhism. In 794, when the new capital was established in the nearby city of Heian, Saichō met Emperor Kanmu (ruled 781–806). The emperor was impressed with the young monk and his desire to create a new type of Buddhism. Saichō's quest fit with Kanmu's desire for a new form of Buddhism for his new capital. In 798, Saichō presented ten lectures on the *Lotus Sūtra*, which were attended by many scholars from Nara. Given his new fame, Saichō was sent by the emperor to China in 804 to find the best form of Buddhism for the new Japanese capital.

In China, he studied T'ien-t'ai at the headquarters of that school on Mt. T'ien-t'ai. He also studied Ch'an, the *Vinaya*, and Tantric forms of Chinese Buddhism. When Saichō returned to Japan, he developed a synthesis of T'ien-t'ai doctrine and practice, Ch'an meditation, Tantric practice and ritualism, Pure Land recitation, and *Vinaya* discipline. While Saichō stressed the teachings of the T'ien-t'ai tradition, the practices of these other traditions were woven into his new school, called Tendai Buddhism. As we shall see, Tendai also provided a religious foundation for the later development of Zen, Pure Land, and Nichiren Buddhism in Japan. Tendai itself became politically involved in Japan as it sought to protect the nation and make it into a "Buddhaland" during what Tendai considered the age of the Degenerate Dharma (*mappō*).

Saichō's Tendai School stressed the One Vehicle (*Ekayāna*) doctrine of the *Lotus Sūtra* that traditionally had been associated with Prince Shōtoku. Hence, Tendai is referred to as one of the two Heian "One Vehicle Schools," the other being Shingon. Associated with the highest teaching of the One Vehicle is the view that all living beings have the Buddha-nature, and thus partake in the *Dharmakāya*, the Dharma-body or essential enlightened nature of the Buddha. Here is what Saichō says in defense of this emphasis of Tendai in the face of attacks by the older Nara schools:

> I am now establishing the discipline of the One Vehicle for the profit and happiness of all living beings. This essay is being written to initiate this universal discipline. I offer prayers to the everlasting Three Refuges, that they may extend their invisible and visible protection so that this discipline will be transmitted without obstruction or harm, protecting the nation for all time. [By this discipline] may all living beings leading worldly or spiritual lives overcome what is incorrect, bring an end to what is evil, and protect their "seed of Buddhahood" [*Tathāgata-garbha*]. May all beings awaken to the universal [Buddha]-nature of all things, and obtain spiritual bliss in the land of peaceful light. . . .

The emperor is equal to the sun and moon in Awakening, and his virtue is not different from that of heaven and earth. . . . The Buddha-sun is shining brightly again, and the Way to inner realization is flourishing. Now is the time for the Mahāyāna discipline of the perfect Dharma to be preached and promoted. . . . The *Lotus Sūtra* says, "Choose the straight Way, and set aside other means. Teach the perfect Dharma." It also says, "Now we should practice only the Buddha's wisdom." At present however, the six [Nara schools] have so much power that they suppress the Buddha's discipline. . . . How can I remain silent? Instead of speaking, I have used here my brush to express just a few of my thoughts. (*Dengyō Daishi zenchū*, I, 16–17)

To enable people to "awaken to the universal Buddha-nature" and be transformed by it, Saichō taught a comprehensive spiritual journey that synthesized doctrinal and *sūtra* study, meditative discipline, Tantric practice, chanting, and *Vinaya* discipline. On Mt. Hiei, Saichō established two study areas to train his monks for this spiritual journey: One was devoted to study of the *Lotus Sūtra*, and the other was for Tantric studies. Before entering these areas, one had to take the Mahāyāna precepts and make a special vow not to leave Mt. Hiei for twelve years. During those twelve years of seclusion, the discipline of Tendai was rigorous to say the least. The moral, ritual, and *sūtra* training was complemented by a meditation method called *shikan*, meaning "concentration and insight." *Shi* is Japanese for *śamatha*, or tranquillity meditation, and *kan* is Japanese for *vipaśyanā*, or insight meditation. As we have seen, these are the two fundamental forms of Buddhist meditation going back to the original teachings of the historical Buddha.

Four particular types of meditation practice are also used in Tendai to foster the experience of the inner purity of one's Buddha-nature. First is a ninety-day practice during which one does "silent-sitting" meditation in the lotus posture while facing a Buddha image. During that time, one is allowed to chant the name of a single Buddha or bodhisattva to focus the mind. Second is another ninety-day practice that includes "walking" meditation, whereby one circumambulates a statue of Amida Buddha, as Amitābha was called in Japan, and chants repetitions of Amida's name. Third is a thirty-day practice of "half-sitting and half-walking" meditation. At first, one focuses the mind on Tantric images and symbols and chants *mantras* while walking around a Buddha image prior to sitting in meditation. Then one venerates the Buddha, chants passages from the *Lotus Sūtra*, and practices repentance for one's false views about reality. Finally, there is the practice of what is called "non-walking and non-sitting" meditation, which is observed in all of one's daily life. Here, one focuses on *sūtra* chanting and living the *Vinaya* precepts. One reflects on the image of Kannon (Avalokiteśvara) Bodhisattva, the bodhisattva of compassion, as one flavors all daily activities with compassion.

After Saichō's death, Mt. Hiei became the most important monastic center in Japan, with over thirty thousand monks and over three thousand buildings. It also began to emphasize more of the Tantric side of the tradition. Saichō himself did not systematize Tendai's esoteric (*mikkyō*) teachings and

Figure 9.2. Sanzen-in, Tendai garden and temple; Heian Dynasty (897–1185 C.E.), near Kyōto, Japan.

practices before his death. However, some of his disciples later traveled to China, where they deepened their Tantric studies and training, and returned to Japan to systematize Tantra in Tendai Buddhism. Two monks were especially important in this regard. First was Ennin (794–864), who led the Tendai School after the death of Saichō. Second was Enchin (814–891), who founded a center for Tantric study. Enchin became an abbot on Mt. Hiei, thus creating two lineages in Tendai—one from himself and the other from Ennin. In 933, a succession dispute broke out between the two groups. This split became more violent over the years. In these disputes, and to protect the wealth of Mt. Hiei, some monks became armed and formed the "warrior monk" tradition in Japan. These warrior monks sometimes descended Mt. Hiei and attacked the Heian capital when they disagreed with certain government policies and decisions.

The Shingon School

The second One Vehicle School of Heian Buddhism is Shingon, which is based on the Chinese Chên-yen School. The name of this school means "True

Word," and refers to the *mantras* used in its Tantric practices. Shingon, then, is a Japanese form of Tantric or esoteric Buddhism. Indeed, since Tendai also uses Tantric elements, Heian Buddhism is sometimes referred to as the "esotericization" (*mikkyōka*) of Japanese religion. The founder of Shingon was Kūkai (774–835). Kūkai entered a state university at the age of eighteen, and studied the Confucian classics. At the university, he met a Buddhist monk who showed him a scripture with esoteric passages. This inspired Kūkai to leave the university. He took up the life of a wandering ascetic, and during his travels read Buddhist texts. One text was the *Mahāvairocana Sūtra* from the mature Tantric tradition. Kūkai was attracted to its promise of sudden Awakening to the inner essence of Buddhahood, but was not able to understand the esoteric use of *mudras, mantras,* and *mandalas* that the text advocated for this attainment. So, he decided to travel to China to find a teacher who could teach him this esoteric path. In 803, he became ordained as a Buddhist monk and left for China the next year.

In China, Kūkai received his training from the great Tantric master Hui-kuo (746–805). Hui-kuo had received transmission from two Tantric lineages: one based on the *Mahāvairocana Sūtra*, the other based on the *Vajraśekhara Sūtra*. Under Hui-kuo, Kūkai received initiation into the meditative techniques associated with both Tantric lineages, and then received ordination as a Tantric master. In 806, Kūkai returned to Japan with *mandalas,* scriptures, and Tantric ritual materials. In 809, the emperor ordered Kūkai to serve at Takaosan-ji, the temple that was the center of the Heian Buddhist world. There, Kūkai systematized Tantric doctrines, organized Tantric materials and *sūtras,* and vigorously propagated Tantric Buddhism. In 816, the emperor gave Kūkai permission to build a monastery on Mt. Kōya, some distance from the capital. Until his death in 835, Kūkai was also in charge of Tō-ji, a temple in the capital that was to be a center for Tantric art and practice.

Unlike Saichō, Kūkai succeeded in systematizing Tantric doctrine and practice within the Shingon tradition through his many writings. Among his writings is his famous *Ten Stages of Religious Consciousness* (*Jūjū shinron*). These stages present Kūkai's evaluation of different religions and forms of Buddhism. The following is from a condensed version of the *Ten Stages* entitled *The Precious Key to the Secret Treasury:*

1. The animal-like consciousness that is goatish in its desires. The common person in a kind of madness does not see his or her faults. This person thinks only of his or her desires and needs, like a butting goat.
2. The ignorant consciousness that is uncultivated yet abstains from evil. Influenced by various external causes, the consciousness is temperate. The will to be kind grows like a seed in good soil. [Confucianism]
3. The uncultivated consciousness that is without fear. The person hopes for rebirth in a heaven, to reside there for awhile peacefully. This person is like a child, like a calf that follows its mother. [Religious Taoism]
4. The consciousness that recognizes the objects of perception, but not the

self. This person understands that there are only the *dharmas*, and not any permanent selfhood. [Theravāda Buddhism]

5. The consciousness that is freed from the karmic seeds of causation. Mastering the 12-linked chain of causation, the consciousness is freed from the seeds of blindness. When rebirth is ended, the ineffable fruit of Nirvana is obtained. [The *pratyekabuddha*]

6. The Mahāyāna consciousness that seeks the salvation of others. When compassion is aroused from within, then the Great Compassion first appears. It views the distinction between self and other as a fiction, and recognizes only consciousness, denying the reality of the external world. [The Hossō School]

7. The consciousness aware of the negation of causality. By the eightfold negations, foolishness comes to an end. With a single thought of the truth, emptiness becomes apparent. The consciousness now empty and quiet knows undeniable peace and happiness. [The Sanron School]

8. The consciousness which follows the true One Vehicle. The whole universe is essentially pure; in this innate purity, knowledge and all phenomena merge. The person who knows this suchness of reality has the cosmic consciousness. [The Tendai School]

9. The consciousness that completely lacks own-being. Water lacks own-being; when affected by the wind, it becomes waves. The universe has no determined forms; but at the slightest stimulation, it immediately moves forward [into forms]. [The Kegon School]

10. The consciousness filled with the esoteric splendor of the celestial Buddha. With the medicine of the [above] exoteric teachings, the dust and stains of the consciousness are cleared away. Then, the True Words [*mantras*] can open the inner Treasury. When its secret treasures are suddenly displayed, all virtuous qualities [of the Buddha] become apparent in one's consciousness. [The Shingon School] (*Hizō hōyaku*, I, 420)

The teachings of Shingon are intended to guide people to this tenth stage of virtuous Buddha-consciousness. They do so by stressing that the highest Buddha is the *Dharmakāya*, the essential enlightenment nature of Buddhahood. This Dharma-body is a luminous reality of wisdom and compassion that penetrates and embraces all existence such that the *Dharmakāya* is actually one's own innate Buddha-nature. Kūkai identified this ultimate suchness of the universe with Vairocana Buddha, symbolized by the sun, which radiates its light to all beings in the universe. For Shingon, Vairocana, as the Dharma-body of the universe, preaches and acts continuously throughout the cosmos. Vairocana's presence and activity as the mind, speech, and body of the universe provide a "constant teaching." The purpose of this esoteric teaching is twofold: for Vairocana's own enjoyment and for the salvation of all living beings. Shingon seeks to experience this teaching through its esoteric methods in order to realize one's innate Buddha-nature. This direct realization is an esoteric discovery of the very essence of the *Dharmakāya* that Vairocana represents.

Shingon also teaches that the secret and constant teaching of the *Dharmakāya* can actually be communicated to a person through the mysterious words, symbols, and ritual movements of Tantric Buddhism. The *mantras* that one recites bring into awareness Vairocana's speech, the *mudras* that one forms with his or her hands give one a felt sense of Vairocana's body, and the *maṇḍalas* on which one concentrates bring forth Vairocana's states of mind. Thereby, one unlocks the Three Mysteries (*sanmitsu*) of Vairocana: his speech, body, and mind in the universe. With the radiance of the *Dharmakāya* shining through Vairocana's Three Mysteries illuminating the body, speech, and mind of the practitioner, one's innate Buddhahood becomes manifest. Shingon believes that by realizing these mysteries in one's own experience, the long journey to Buddhahood, which in the other traditions may take eons to complete, can be attained in just one lifetime and in one's very mind and body.

In its Tantric empowerment, Shingon emphasizes the power of its *mantras* to open the practitioner to the reality of Buddhahood. Indeed, *mantras* are viewed as "empowerment-bodies" of the Buddha. They embody the power of the Dharma, constantly being taught by the *Dharmakāya*, that brings wisdom to the practitioner, and thereby enables him or her to realize the truth of his or her Buddha-nature. In this *mantra* practice, one focuses on the form, the sound, and the inner meaning of the *mantra* that reveal the form, voice, and mind of the Buddha. In this way, *mantras* are said to embody the very essence of the Three Mysteries. This power of the *mantras* is also "sealed" in the practitioner's body by the *mudras*, so that the practice transforms one's body as well as one's mind. Shingon believes that this dual transformation distinguishes it from the other schools of Buddhism.

In Shingon, two *maṇḍalas* have a special place in bringing the virtuous and enlightened qualities of the Three Mysteries into one's experience. First is the Womb or Matrix (*taizō*) *Maṇḍala*, based on the *Mahāvairocana Sūtra*. This *maṇḍala* represents an enlightened view of the universe from the viewpoint of compassion, and implies that the energy of compassion enfolds, protects, and nurtures one's Buddha-nature like a womb holding a child. The many deities of this *maṇḍala* represent the activities of compassion; in Tantric experience, they foster this same compassion in the practitioner. This first *maṇḍala*, symbolized by the lotus, represents the compassionate gentleness of the universe evolving from unity to diversity.

The second *maṇḍala* is the Diamond (*kongōkai*) *Maṇḍala*, based on the *Vajraśekhara Sūtra*. In this *maṇḍala*, the universe is united in the light of wisdom that merges all beings into one. This wisdom concentrates all the universe into the single light of Vairocana Buddha, who is the luminous source of all the *maṇḍala*'s deities. Penetrating this *maṇḍala* in Tantric experience is said to infuse the practitioner with the light of wisdom, and transforms his or her life into Awakening. This *maṇḍala* balances the gentleness of compassion in the Womb *Maṇḍala* by representing the diamond hardness of wisdom that cuts through illusion and brings diversity into unity.

By using these two *maṇḍalas* with the esoteric practice of *mantras* and *mudras*, the Shingon practitioner seeks to unite his or her human activities (speech, body, and mind) with the Three Mysteries of the universe—the speech, body, and mind of Vairocana Buddha in all things. The experience of this union with the Three Mysteries brings about a "mutual empowerment" in that both the practitioner and the Buddha are affected. While the practitioner attains Awakening and Buddhahood, Vairocana Buddha actualizes Buddha-nature more fully in the phenomenal world, since every act of the enlightened person is an action of the Three Mysteries. In this transformation process, the practitioner is guided by a Tantric master who alone has the ability to transmit these potent teachings and practices.

Shingon and Tendai both stressed the universal Buddha-nature and the need for moral discipline, study, and practice to realize this true nature of all existence. Both traditions weave together different elements of Buddhist thought and practice in order to provide more uniquely Japanese forms of Buddhist experience. However, by the end of the Heian Period, their temples held vast land acquisitions, and the tradition of the "maintenance monks" had given rise to the "warrior monks" mentioned earlier. The problem of corruption within Buddhism, coupled with the political chaos and social decay of the times, led many to despair. They concluded that the age of the Degenerate Dharma had overcome them. This conclusion would have an important role to play in the next stage of Buddhism in Japan.

THE KAMAKURA PERIOD (1185–1333): PURE LAND, ZEN, AND NICHIREN

Toward the close of the Heian period in Japan, the country was divided into estates protected by warriors, and the imperial government was greatly weakened. By 1185, the Minamoto clan defeated its opponents, and its leader, Yoritomo, became the ruling power in Japan. To avoid the corruption found in Kyōto (Heian), Yoritomo established a samurai court in Kamakura far to the east, and ruled as the shōgun. The emperor and his court, remaining in Kyōto, never regained any real power in Japan until the nineteenth century. This began the Kamakura period of Japanese history. It was during this period that three major traditions of Japanese Buddhism were founded: Pure Land, Zen, and Nichiren. All three of the "new" Kamakura forms of Buddhism remain vitally influential today. They were founded by major religious figures who were ordained on Mt. Hiei but found the Tendai tradition to be inadequate. These new schools of Japanese Buddhism appealed to the masses, who wanted more simple, independent, and singular forms of Buddhist practice as they faced living in what they considered the age of the Degenerate Dharma. They did not wish to rely on the overly intellectual learning of the Nara schools or on the complex ritualism and combination of practices of the Heian schools.

Pure Land Buddhism

Mention of the *Larger Land of Bliss Sūtra*, so important in Pure Land Buddhism, was made in writings attributed to Prince Shōtoku. Invoking Amida

Buddha was practiced in Nara Buddhism, and also by Tendai during the Heian period. This invocation chanting practice, called *nembutsu*, was not the exclusive practice for these forms of Buddhism, but was considered only one method of concentration. The Tendai abbot Ennin, upon his return from China, established a center on Mt. Hiei where the perpetual chanting of the name of Amida Buddha could occur. From the tenth to the twelfth century, a number of figures began to emphasize such Pure Land piety.

Genshin (942–1017) left Mt. Hiei to devote himself to the practice of *nembutsu* (chanting *Namu Amida Butsu*), and taught that its simple repetition practice was sufficient for rebirth in the Pure Land. Yōkan (1032–1111) stressed the way in which Amida protects his worshipers, and also proposed a simple repetition of *nembutsu*. Chingai (1091–1152) founded a branch of Shingon that supported *nembutsu* as a means of reaching the Pure Land after death if it is practiced with sincerity and the desire to save all living beings. Finally, Ryōnin (1071–1132) as a Tendai monk was influenced by the Kegon School's vision of a fully interrelated universe. In that interrelated matrix, each person is united to all humankind in such a way that the action of one person can affect all humanity. Given this matrix, Ryonin believed, the *nembutsu* of one person can purify the whole of humankind.

These ideas provided inspiration for the founder of the Pure Land (Jōdo) School of Japanese Buddhism, Hōnen (1133–1212). Hōnen's father, a local samurai, was killed by an estate manager in a night raid. Hōnen, who was only nine years old, fled to a nearby Buddhist temple, where he spent three years. At age thirteen, he entered the Tendai monastic complex on Mt. Hiei and was ordained two years later. He then retired to a quiet retreat area on Mt. Hiei where the Pure Land piety of Genshin was practiced. Here, Hōnen joined a group led by the successor of Ryōnin. Also during this time, Hōnen traveled to nearby Nara, where he studied the philosophy of the Six Schools and practiced *nembutsu* based on the writings of the Chinese Pure Land Patriarch, Shan-tao. In this Shan-tao–inspired practice of *nembutsu*, greater emphasis was placed on the Other-power of Amida, and less on the meditative aspects stressed on Mt. Hiei. Inspired by Shan-tao, Hōnen is said to have eventually attained a spiritual Awakening and inner peace. This attainment led him to leave Mt. Hiei in 1175 and to move to Ōtani on the outskirts of Kyōto. There he began to propagate his Pure Land ideas to people from all walks of life. His new school would become known as a "single-practice" school because *nembutsu* was its exclusive form of practice.

Hōnen believed that *nembutsu* chanting would not only bring one to rebirth in the Pure Land after death, but could purify past sins in this life as well. Therefore, he felt, *nembutsu* should be chanted often. Hōnen was also considered a great ordination master in the Tendai lineage, and even used Tantric rituals. Despite this, his message of single Pure Land practice met opposition from Tendai leaders, who felt that *nembutsu* should only be used in conjunction with other Buddhist practices. In 1206, alleged incidents of improper behavior by some of Hōnen's disciple priests occurred. These priests were beheaded, and Hōnen was exiled for ten months in 1207. He was not allowed to return to Kyōto until 1211, and died the next year. Among Hōnen's followers, Shōkōbō (1162–1238) is generally regarded as a successor. His sect, which stresses *nembutsu*, is called the Chinzei branch of Jōdo Buddhism. Zennebō (1177–1247) founded the Seizan branch of Jōdo, which stresses *nembutsu* and the intimate relationship between the devotee and Amida Buddha. While other branches of Jōdo emerged over the years, these two played historic roles in Japan's religious history and are active in Japan today.

The teachings of Hōnen are simple in comparison to the older Japanese schools. Hōnen emphasized Shen-tao's distinction between the Holy Path (*shōdō*) and the Pure Land (*jōdo*). The journey on the former path requires reliance on one's own effort, or "self power" (*jiriki*). Reaching the Pure Land requires, on the other hand, a reliance on the "Other power" (*tariki*) of Amida Buddha. Hōnen believed that given the condition of humankind in the age of the Degenerate Dharma, the only real hope for humanity is to be born in Amida's Pure Land. This simple and clear message of hope for all people was very attractive to Kamakura Japan. Also attractive was the whole notion of the Pure Land as a place of joy, purity, and peaceful growth in the bodhisattva journey to Buddhahood. Hōnen taught that with further attainments on the bodhisattva path in the Pure Land, one could again be born in this world as a bodhisattva working for the salvation of others.

In his advice concerning *nembutsu* practice, Hōnen emphasized the three states of mind discussed by Shan-tao. Hōnen interpreted these to mean that one should recite *nembutsu* with (1) a *sincere* and devoted mind, (2) a mind of deep *faith*, and (3) a strong *aspiration* to attain the Pure Land. *Nembutsu* strengthens these three mental qualities (sincerity, faith, and aspiration) and directs them toward Amida Buddha. For Hōnen, *nembutsu* turns one's mind from worldly experience, evils, and cares to an undivided attention to Amida Buddha and experience of his light, purity, and grace. *Nembutsu* is practiced daily in a way that frees the mind from doubts, disturbing, evil or idle thoughts, and false ideas. In engenders a growth in virtue and adds a spiritual dimension to one's work, family life, and recreation. In this way, *nembutsu* morally and spiritually enriches the person's ordinary daily experience from the moment it is begun to the moment of death.

One of Hōnen's writings, his *Passages on Selection [of the Original Vow] (Senchakushū)*, is one of the classics of Japanese Buddhism. In it, he argues for selecting the Pure Land over the Holy Path of the other schools of Buddhism. He also expresses his compassion for the many people who sought his solace and healing, urging them to practice *nembutsu* with simple faith in the "Primal Vow" of Other power:

> The way of categorizing the Dharma of the Buddha differs among the various schools and sects. The [Hossō/Yogācāra] School divides . . . it according to existence, emptiness and the Middle Way. The [Sanron/Mādhyamika] School divides the holy Dharma . . . into two scriptures: that of the bodhisattvas and that of the *śrāvakas*. The Kegon School categorizes the five teachings. . . . The

[Tendai] School categorizes the four teachings and the five flavors. . . . The Shingon School categorizes the two teachings . . . the exoteric and esoteric.

Regarding [the categories of] the Pure Land School . . . relying on Master Tao-ch'o, we set up the two gates that encompass the whole [Dharma]: the Gate of the Holy Path and the Gate of the Pure Land. . . . The Gate of the Holy Path is divided into two parts: the Mahāyāna and the Theravāda. The Mahāyāna is sub-divided into the exoteric and esoteric. . . . The Theravāda . . . is a way of realizing the truth by negating delusions and desires. . . . On the other hand, we find the Gate to birth into the Pure Land. . . . Even though persons may have studied the Gate of the Holy Path, if one wills to learn the Gate of the Pure Land, he or she should leave the Holy Path and take refuge in the Pure Land. Examples of persons who did so are T'an-luan . . . and Tao-ch'o. . . . If these wise scholars of the past did so, then why should we fools in the age of the Degenerate Dharma fail to follow their example?

If the Primal Vow required people to build statues of the Buddha and *stūpas*, the poor and destitute would not have any hope of birth [in the Pure Land]. . . . If the Primal Vow required people to attain wisdom and learning, the unintelligent and foolish would not have any hope of birth. . . . If the Primal Vow required people to follow the precepts and monastic rules, those who have broken them or those who have not taken them would not have any hope of birth. . . . For this reason, Amida Buddha, when in the distant past he was Dharmākara . . . moved by compassion for all and wishing to save all universally, did not choose these many practices . . . in his Primal Vow for birth; but instead chose the single practice of reciting *nembutsu*. . . . "They will be like broken tiles and pebbles that are turned into gold."

If you wish to quickly escape *saṃsāra*, between the two superior methods, set aside the Holy Path and choose to enter the Gate of the Pure Land. . . . The practice that correctly fixes one's birth [in the Pure Land] is to recite the name of Amida Buddha. This is so because of Amida's Primal Vow. . . . *Nembutsu* practice is likened to the moon's reflection in the water, freely rising up and down. (*Senchakushū*, 1, 3, 16)

The most famous disciple of Hōnen was Shinran (1173–1263), who founded another school of Pure Land Buddhism named Jōdo Shinshū, the "True Pure Land School," or, more simply, Shin Buddhism. As a result of a change in the political fortunes of his family, Shinran entered the monastery when he was just nine years old. He went to live and study on Mt. Hiei, where he practiced "perpetual *nembutsu*" according to the Tendai tradition until the age of twenty-nine. During those twenty years of practice and discipline, he was not satisfied with his Tendai life and did not attain what he was seeking. Eventually, his concern over the possibility of his Awakening was so intense that Shinran decided to make a rigorous one hundred–day meditation retreat in nearby Kyōto. He hoped to receive inspiration for the future of his spiritual journey. The temple where he carried out his retreat enshrined Kannon Bodhisattva. On the ninety-fifth day of the retreat, Shinran had a dream about Kannon. We do not know the whole content of the dream, but it seemed that Kannon promised to come to him in a feminine form to be his helpmate. Also, the dream led Shinran to leave Mt. Hiei in 1201 and to join Hōnen's Pure Land community in Kyōto.

Expressing the deep awareness of his own inadequacies in the spiritual life, Shinran was consoled when Hōnen personally assured him that he was certainly embraced by the compassion of Amida Buddha; Amida cares for even the most evil of sinners. Shinran became Hōnen's favorite disciple; and Shinran always maintained that he was merely transmitting the real meaning of Hōnen's teachings. However, in 1207 certain indiscretions by some of Hōnen's followers led to the disbanding of his community and the exile from Kyōto of Hōnen and some of his followers. This included Shinran. Both men were sent to different places, and they never saw each other again.

Shinran's exile also entailed his being laicized. It was perhaps during this time that Shinran married Eshin-ni. Many speculate that Eshin-ni was, in fact, the helpmate for Shinran foretold in his dream of Kannon. They had six children, and Shinran's decision to marry became the pattern for Jōdo Shinshū clergy. There are also theories about the names and number of Shinran's wives. In any case, Shinran did not wish by being laicized to pursue the worldly life of the laity. So, he considered himself to be "neither layman nor monk." Shinran was pardoned in 1211, and moved with his wife and children to the town of Ināda. There, he spent twenty years propagating his form of Pure Land Buddhism to the common people far from the cities of power and culture. He ministered to their needs with sympathy and compassion, quietly developing his spiritual thought and his community of followers. In 1224, Shinran completed the *Kyōgyōshinshō* (*Teaching, Practice, Faith, Attainment*), his major religious writing. Around 1234, Shinran returned to Kyōto where he spent the final twenty-eight years of his life.

It seems that one of the most formative events in Shinran's life that shaped his understanding of True Pure Land Buddhism was a religious experience he had shortly after moving to Ināda. He had already embraced the single-practice of *nembutsu* and decided to chant a *sūtra* one thousand times for the benefit of all living beings. After a few days of chanting, Shinran realized that he could not save other beings; that faith in Amida Buddha is itself a gift from Amida. That is, Shinran understood that doing any religious practice on the basis of one's own will, one's "self power," only strengthens one's ego. Relying on self-striving, one has the sense that "*I* am faithful," and "*I* am chanting." Such practice and any results it may bring are poisoned with ego and selfish desire. True Pure Land Buddhism must be based on the realization that all attempts to progress in the spiritual life through one's own efforts are futile. With this realization, one can then experience the gift of true faith as given by Amida Buddha. Thereby, one's *nembutsu* is no longer an assertion of ego in order to gain Amida's grace, but is an expression of thankfulness for Amida's gift of faith.

This view of faith being a matter of grace does not deny the historical Buddha's admonishment to rely on oneself and one's own efforts. The first step in the Buddhist journey is the choice to enter the Buddhist tradition and take up its practice. However, for Shinran, while this step is essential to begin the journey, attaining the goal is quite another matter. As one advances based on one's own choice and efforts, one begins to realize that the ego is hiding behind all of one's spiritual endeavors. This insight leads to a sense of help-lessness, which, according to Shinran, can bring one to surrender to the pure grace of Amida Buddha. This is a very important point: For such a surren-der of faith not to be just another act of the will, it must "arise" also due to Amida's grace. So, Shinran refers to true faith as *shinjin*, which really means the "arising of faith" from the grace of Amida Buddha. Shinran here is turn-ing the tables on traditional Buddhism, where faith is preliminary to prac-tice. In Shinran's view, practice is preliminary to faith in the power of Amida's Primal Vow. Indeed, in these ideas, we can see a mirroring of Shin-ran's own religious life experience.

In this experience of Amida's grace, the True Pure Land devotee realizes what are called the Two Types of Deep Faith. First, one understands the fact that one's human limitations and spiritual defilements entail that one's own "calculated efforts" in the spiritual life are only hopeless attempts. Second, one realizes that the Great Action of Amida Buddha can save one from this condition. In fact, Shinran says that the deeper one's awareness of one's hopelessness and evilness, the greater one's assurance of Amida's compas-sionate action:

> People often say, "If an evil person can attain birth in the Pure Land, it goes without saying that a good person can." While this saying seems right at first, it is counter to the intent of the Primal Vow, or Other power. This is because those who rely on doing good based on self power, do not entrust themselves fully to Other power. . . . But if they overturn this self-power mentality and entrust themselves to Other power, they will attain birth in the true and real land of fulfillment. [They need to understand that] it is impossible for us, who are moved by blind desires, to free ourselves from *samsāra* through any type of practice. [They also need to realize that] Amida, out of pity for us in this condition, made his Vow with the intent of bringing us evil persons to Bud-dhahood. Therefore, the evil persons entrusting themselves to Other power are precisely the ones who truly possess the cause of birth in the Pure Land. So, such a person says, "If a good person can attain birth in the Pure Land, it goes without saying that the evil person can." (*Tannishō*, 3)

Shinran believed that the three states of mind discussed by Shan-tao and Hōnen—sincerity, faith, and aspiration—are the qualities of the mind of Amida Buddha. They are not qualities that people can cultivate by *nembutsu* practice based on their own willpower. Rather, Shinran taught, Amida at-tained these qualities through eons of practice as a bodhisattva, and now transfers them to his devotees. As Amida's mind of "sincerity," or enlight-ened consciousness, "arises" in the minds of the devotees, this sincerity in-forms their own minds and hearts. When this quality of Amida's mind forms one's mind and heart, "faith" is graced by the Other power of Amida. Amida thus is present and active in one's life, and one experiences the "aspiration" to be born in the Pure Land and to save all beings. With these qualities, one's *nembutsu* practice is no longer the product of self power, but the Other power of Amida.

Finally, Shinran expresses his ideas concerning Other power with the terms "action, faith and witness" (gyō-shin-shō). The overturning of the self-power mind and the entrusting faith to Other power are themselves products of Amida's grace. It is the action (gyō) of Amida Buddha that precipitates the arising of faith (shin) in the devotee's mind. Amida enables one to realize the Two Types of Deep Faith: one's pitiful condition and the availability of Other power. Faith then transforms one's life in a way that gives witness (shō) to the presence and action of Amida Buddha. This living witness is one of freedom and humility, virtue and joy that arises spontaneously from Amida's presence in the devotee's life. In other words, it is the very enlightened life of Amida Buddha itself that makes one able to live its enlightened qualities. One is enabled to live in a way that reflects into daily life the wise and compassionate qualities of Amida and his Pure Land.

So for Shinran, Pure Land Buddhism is not just about being born in the Pure Land. It is about being transformed in this life as well. On the other hand, this life may bear fruits here, but it will also need to be completed in the Pure Land. Then one can return from the Pure Land to help others here find their deliverance. For Shinran, it is this bodhisattva life that is the essence of human fulfillment brought about by Amida's grace. The following passages reflect Shinran's views concerning the human condition, the grace of Other power, and of the growth in virtue:

> Although I take refuge in the True Pure Land Way,
> It is difficult to have a true and sincere mind.
> The self is false and insincere,
> I completely lack a pure mind.

> Each of us, in our outward appearance,
> Makes a show of being wise, good, and devout.
> But our greed, anger, perversity and deceit are so great,
> We are full of all types of hatred and cunning.

> It is extremely difficult to destroy our evil nature,
> The mind is like a snake or scorpion.
> So, the good deeds we perform are poisoned,
> They are called false and useless practice.

> Since I lack even a little love or compassion,
> I cannot even hope to help living beings.
> If it were not for the ship of Amida's Vow,
> How could I get across the ocean of this painful existence?
>   (Shōzōmatsu wasan, 94–96, 98)

"Being saved by the inconceivable working of Amida's Vow, I shall certainly be born in the Pure Land!" The very moment that you entrust yourself to the Vow in this way, with the thought of saying nembutsu arising within you, immediately you receive a share in the benefits of being always embraced by Amida. You should know that Amida's Primal Vow does not distinguish be-

---

BOX 9.1

A CHILD'S CARING

One evening as I returned home from work totally exhausted from a demanding day, I slumped down flat on my back on the living room couch. Lying comfortably, almost asleep, I felt a tug on my left sleeve and a murmuring voice calling, "Daddy, Daddy." It was my two-year-old son, Nathan.

I said to myself, "Oh no, it's Nathan. He wants to wrestle with me again. I am in no shape mentally or physically to wrestle with him. Doesn't he see how tired I am? I guess not, and explaining to him won't help." So, I pretended to be asleep.

But my son continued to tug at my sleeve with an undaunted, "Daddy, Daddy!" I became more irritated and began conjuring up all kinds of ill thoughts about my two-year-old, saying to myself, "All he thinks about is himself. Doesn't he understand I'm sleeping? His stubbornness must come from my wife's side!" But he kept tugging, "Daddy, Daddy." Finally, totally frustrated, I opened my eyes ready to scold him.

Lo and behold . . . there he stood holding a blanket in his left hand to cover me. He had dragged it from my bedroom all by himself. And neither his mother nor I had ever taught him to do this. This was completely on his own!

This scene has been deeply etched in my memory. I still recall with shame and embarrassment the selfish thought that I had harbored about my two-year-old son. At the same time, I could not but be amazed by my son's caring act, despite my self-centered thoughts. This event is another concrete, everyday example of the myriad compassionate acts and boundless life forces, seen and mostly unseen, that is symbolized as Amida Buddha in my Shin Buddhist tradition.

In response, I utter quietly or in silence *Namu Amida Butsu* ("Amida Buddha and I are one") in amazement and in gratitude for the realization that I am fine, just as I am, in life and in death!

KENNETH KENSHIN TANAKA

Shin Priest and Professor of Buddhist Studies
Musashino Joshi University, Tokyo

---

tween young and old, good and evil. Only the arising of faith is essential; for it is the Vow to save persons with deep karmic evil and serious blind desires. So, for persons entrusting themselves to this Primal Vow, good acts are not required because no good action surpasses *nembutsu*. And, one should never despair about their evil deeds, for no evil acts can obstruct the work of Amida's Primal Vow.

I myself do not have even one disciple. If I made people recite *nembutsu* by my own efforts, then they would be my disciples. But it is wrong to call anyone "my disciple" because they receive *nembutsu* by the working of Amida. . . . *Nembutsu* is not a practice or a good act by its practitioners. Since it is not recited from one's own intentions, it is not a practice. Since it is not something performed from one's own calculations, it is not a good act. For the practitioner, it is not a practice or a good act because it wholly arises from Other power, free from any self power. (*Tannishō*, 1, 6, 8)

The universal Vow, so difficult to understand, is a great ship that carries us across the ocean that is hard to cross. The unobstructed light is the sun of wisdom that disperses the darkness of our ignorance. . . . We know that the auspicious Name that embodies . . . supreme virtues is the real wisdom which transforms our evil into virtue, and that the difficult to accept and diamond-like arising of faith is true reality; it sweeps away doubts and brings one to the attainment of Awakening. . . . The great practice is saying the Name of the Buddha of Unobstructed Light. This practice . . . that possesses the roots of all virtues is the perfect and quick way of bringing them to fullness. It is the Treasure Ocean of Virtues that is suchness, true reality. This is the reason it is called the great practice. (*Kyōgyōshinshō*, I, Preface; II, 1)

Shinran did not designate a successor, and his disciples led sizable communities of followers. His daughter, Kakushin-ni, established a mausoleum shrine where all followers could come to pay respects and where the caretaker of the shrine was to be a member of Shinran's family. This led to a hereditary line of successors. Her grandson, Kakunyo, eventually came to believe that many of the more powerful communities of Shinran's tradition would evolve into independent sects. So he sought to unify them all under the leadership of the shrine, which came to be referred to as *Hongan-ji*, meaning "Temple of the Original Vow." While different branches did emerge due to the powerful military rulers, the Hongan-ji became the unifying center for propagating Jōdo Shinshū.

Zen Buddhism

Zen Buddhism was most likely present in Japan as early as the time of Prince Shōtoku in the seventh century. During that century, Dōshō, the founder of the Hossō School of Yogācāra in Japan, also brought Zen practice from China. He built the first meditation hall in a temple in Nara. Saichō, the founder of Tendai in Japan, also met with a Ch'an master when in China, and made meditation an important element of Tendai practice. However, none of these early initatives produced a single-practice school of Zen in Japan as existed in China and Korea. It was not until the Kamakura Period that an independent Zen School took root in Japanese soil.

The person whom tradition recognizes as founder of Zen Buddhism in Japan is Eisai (1141–1215). At the age of eleven, Eisai entered a temple to study Buddhism under a priest who followed the Tantric tradition. Two years later, Eisai went to Mt. Hiei and was ordained in 1154. At Mt. Hiei, he studied Tendai teachings, including esoteric doctrines, and focused on the Tendai practice of meditation. At the age of twenty-eight, Eisai traveled to China for six months, where he observed the popularity of Ch'an. Upon his return to Mt. Hiei, he decided to do Zen practice as taught by Tendai. He pursued this path, along with Tantric practice, for the next twenty years.

On a second visit to China that began in 1187, Eisai practiced in the Lin-chi School of Ch'an Buddhism. His master also taught him the *Vinaya* tradition, which Eisai would later make the foundation of Zen monastic life in Japan. Eisai finally received the formal approval (*inka*) to teach Zen, and upon returning to Japan in 1191, he built Shōfuku-ji, the first Zen temple in Japan.

Eisai met strong opposition from the Tendai School because they saw in his teachings the possibility for a personal, single-practice form of Buddhism that would challenge their more complex, ritual-based tradition. In 1199, Eisai traveled to Kamakura where he gained the support of the shogun. With this support, he established a temple, the Jufuku-ji, in Kamakura. Under Eisai's guidance, Jufuku-ji was at first a center for Tantric rituals, but later became one of the great centers for Zen practice. In 1202, Eisai was given some land in Kyōto where he founded another temple, the Kennin-ji, in which Tendai and esoteric practices were taught alongside Zen. Because of the resistance of the powerful Tendai School, Eisai was careful to present Zen only in the wider context of the older more accepted Tendai tradition. Therefore, while Eisai is considered the founder of the Rinzai (Chinese: Lin-chi) School of Zen Buddhism in Japan, he was primarily a Tendai priest who tried to reform that tradition. Eisai was also respected for his purity and simplicity, in accord with the Zen style of life, and for his personal kindness and generosity.

The following passages are taken from Eisai's *Propagation of Zen in Defense of the Country*, written in 1198 in an attempt to gain support for Zen in Japan in the face of Tendai resistance:

> The Mind is great. The height of heaven is immeasurable, but the Mind extends itself beyond heaven. The depth of the earth is also immeasurable, but the Mind extends itself below the earth. One cannot outdistance the light of the sun and moon, but the Mind does so. . . . Because of the Mind, heaven covers while the earth produces. Because of the Mind, the sun and moon move, the seasons pass one after the other, and all things come to be. The Mind is indeed great!
>
> We necessarily call it Mind, but it has many other names: the highest principle, the truth of innate wisdom, the one reality, the perfect Awakening. . . . Gautama Buddha, the greatest of teachers, transmitted the truth of this Mind to [Mahākāśyapa], saying it is a special transmission outside the scriptures. . . . Therefore, with the slightest turning of a flower, a thousand trees broke into bloom. From this single fountainhead, ten-thousand rivers of truth flowed.
>
> Just as in India, this teaching in China has attracted many followers and disciples. Like the Buddha, it propagates the truth . . . transmitting it from person to person. . . . This vision of the Dharma soon appeared in Korea . . . and the Oxhead School of Zen . . . has made its way to Japan. By studying it, one discovers the essential key to all forms of Buddhism. By practicing it, one's life is fulfilled in the realization of Awakening. In terms of externals, Zen stresses discipline over doctrine; internally, it brings one the highest inner wisdom. This is what the Zen School is all about.
>
> However, there are those who attack this teaching, saying that it is "the Zen of dark Awakening." Others question it saying that it is "utter nihilism." Still

others do not consider it suitable for the age of the Degenerate Dharma, saying it is not what our country needs now. Or they express their contempt for
our traveling from place to place, and the supposed lack of documented support for our ideas. Finally, some who have a low opinion of their ability to follow our way, consider Zen to be far beyond their power of attainment. In their
attempt to uphold the Dharma, these persons are actually suppressing the very
treasures of the Dharma. They condemn us without knowing what we are doing. They are not only blocking the Gate of Zen, but they are ruining the work
of our great forefather, [Saichō] of Mt. Hiei. What a pity! How sad and dis-
tressing! (*Kōzen gokoku ron*, Preface)

Eisai's foundation of Rinzai Zen was later advanced by certain Chinese
Ch'an masters and Japanese disciples in ways that purified the school of
Tendai and Shingon elements and produced the great single-practice Rinzai
Zen tradition in Japan. This process was aided by the fact that both the shōgunate and the imperial court patronized Zen monks. The purification of non-
Zen practices from Rinzai happened in the monasteries that were founded
by Eisai and by the later Chinese and Japanese developers of his school. One
of the greatest of these developers was Enni Ben'en (1202–1280), who studied in China and founded Tōfuku-ji in Kyōto. There, Zen was the major practice of the temple, and all other practices took a back seat. From Tōfuku-ji,
a broad Zen movement grew to include over fifty temples.

Another early Rinzai figure was Muhon Kakushin (1207–1298), who
founded the great Kōkoku-ji temple. The Chinese Ch'an Master Lan-hsi Tao-
lung (1213–1278), known in Japan as Rankei Dōryū, founded the Kenchō-ji
Temple in 1252. Daiō Kokushi (1282–1338) built the famous Daitoku-ji in
1324, as well as the Myōshin-ji in 1337. Kian Soen (1269–1313) established
what became the most influential Rinzai temple in Japan, Nanzen-ji. In each
of these monastic temples, any mixture of Zen with other forms of Buddhism
was avoided, and Zen meditation (*zazen*) was practiced with a strict program of *kōan* study. These temples became the core of over three hundred
official Rinzai temples throughout Japan. Today, Rinzai remains famous for
its strict monastic discipline and its use of *kōans* in meditation practice to
foster the sudden experience of Awakening (*satori*).

The second great Zen innovator of the Kamakura period was Dōgen
(1200–1253), the founder of the Sōtō School of Zen Buddhism. Dōgen's father died when Dōgen was only two years old, and his mother died when
he was seven. These difficult early circumstances had a strong effect on the
sensitive Dōgen. It is said that while in grief over the death of his mother,
Dōgen saw the incense ascending from a Buddhist temple and felt the desire to find Awakening. So, at the age of thirteen, Dōgen went to Mt. Hiei
and was ordained a year later. At Mt. Hiei, Dōgen confronted a serious religious paradox in the form of an existential question: If all living beings
have an innate Buddha-nature, why does one feel the longing for Awakening and have to engage in spiritual practice? Dōgen did not find a satisfying answer to this quandary on Mt. Hiei, and he left to pursue his spiritual
journey elsewhere. First, he went to a disciple of Hōnen, who felt that

Dōgen's quest could not be satisfied with Pure Land teachings. So, Dōgen was sent to Eisai, because the latter was teaching a strict method of Rinzai Zen that could produce a sudden Awakening in which Dōgen's question might find its answer. At Kennin-ji, Dōgen was trained in Zen by Eisai's disciple, Myōzen (1185–1225).

In 1223, Myōzen took Dōgen with him to China. After trying Lin-chi (Rinzai) and other forms of Ch'an practice, Dōgen studied under Ju-ching (1163–1268). Ju-ching was a master in the Ts'ao-tung (Japanese: Sōtō) School of Ch'an, which stressed the pure practice of meditation rather than *kōan* practice. One evening when the monks were sitting in night meditation, Ju-ching noticed that a monk had fallen asleep. He said, according to Dōgen, "In Zen, body and mind are cast off. Why do you sleep?" Hearing this, Dōgen gained Awakening. After staying for two more years to perfect his understanding, Dōgen returned home to Japan.

Upon his arrival in Japan, Dōgen returned to Kennin-ji, but was dissatisfied with the mixture of Zen practice and esoteric rituals. So in 1230, he moved to the south of Kyōto, where he founded a meditation center, the Kōshō Hōrin-ji. There, strict Zen meditation practice and observance of the precepts were taught, and Dōgen began to write his greatest work, the *Shōbōgenzō* (*The Essence of the Buddha's True Dharma*). However, because of pressure from the monks on Mt. Hiei, Dōgen retreated to a remote place deep in the mountains of Echizen. He lived in small rural temples until he settled in Eihei-ji, the temple that became known as the headquarters of the Sōtō Zen School. Dōgen lived out his last years teaching the single practice of *zazen* and completing the *Shōbōgenzō*.

While Dōgen recognized the usefulness of *kōan* practice, he emphasized the single practice of "just sitting" (*shikan-taza*). This emphasis reflected the answer to his existential question: Why does one practice meditation if one is originally enlightened? For Dōgen, the answer to that question is found in the experience that all things and actions, including sitting practice, are manifestations of original Buddha-nature. In this regard, practice and attainment are identical. Thus, when one practices sitting meditation, one is manifesting one's Buddha-nature. To realize this fact is to be aware that practice is attainment: One's practice manifests innate Awakening. Dōgen explains this in *A Lecture on Studying the Way*:

> Grass, trees and the land, which this teaching embraces, together radiate a great light. They endlessly teach the inconceivable and perfect Dharma. . . . This being true, one person's *zazen* at just one moment imperceptibly fits in with all things, fully radiating through all time. . . . Each moment of *zazen* is itself equally the wholeness of practice and Awakening. . . . It is like a hammer striking emptiness: both before and after, its wonderful sound permeates everywhere. . . . Things all manifest the original practice from the original face [Awakening], impossible to measure.
>
> It is heretical to think that practice and Awakening are not one. In the Dharma of the Buddha, practice and Awakening are the same. Practice is done in Awakening in this very moment. So, the beginner's practice on the Way is

itself the whole of original Awakening. Therefore, when we give instructions for practice, we teach that Awakening cannot be found outside practice, since practice itself is the immediate original Awakening. (*Bendōwa*, 6)

Dōgen felt that just sitting is the best means for nourishing the gradual awareness of this original condition of enlightened Buddha-nature. In just sitting, one gradually sees that one's present condition, no matter what that condition might entail, is already manifesting Buddha-nature. To make this point, Dōgen used the example of a fish swimming in the water without realizing the water is there. Similarly, people are already manifesting their Buddha-nature in each daily activity, like a fish swimming in water, even if they are not aware of that primordial fact. Just sitting quietly in meditation enables one to see what is presently the case, one's originally enlightened Buddha-nature reflected in the present moment. As a fish just swims, one just sits until he or she gradually realizes that this sitting practice is a manifestation of Buddha-nature. Therefore, Sōtō is called the "gradual" school of Zen, while Rinzai with its intense form of *kōan* practice is called the "sudden" school of Zen.

Further reflecting on his experience, Dōgen claimed, "All beings *are* Buddha-nature." This statement is different from the more traditional claim that all *living* beings *have* Buddha-nature. In the traditional sense, all sentient beings have a Buddha-nature like a Buddha statue covered by a dirty rag. For Dōgen, there are two problems with this traditional statement. First is the distinction or duality between living and nonliving beings. For Dōgen, all states of existence, be they mind or body, mental or physical realities, are manifestations of the one Buddha-nature. Second is the distinction or duality between one's Buddha-nature and one's ordinary mind/body that "has" that original nature within it. The rag/statue analogy implies that there is some eternal and pure spiritual status hidden within, yet separate from, one's transitory and suffering condition. In Dōgen's experience, the search for such a hidden spiritual essence is a misguided example of dualistic thinking. This is because all transient forms of existence are, for Dōgen, Buddha-nature. All the present forms of life, from mountains and trees to the ordinary states of one's own mind, are manifestations, or self-determinations, of Buddha-nature. To experience this nondualistic fact of true existence is to realize, according to Dōgen, the Buddha-nature that just *is* all beings.

The following passages from Dōgen's *Shōbōgenzō* convey his experience of Awakening. They were placed in the first chapter, suggesting that they are something like his statement of Awakening:

When all things are [experienced through] Buddha Dharma, there is delusion and Awakening, practice, birth and death, Buddhas and living beings. When the myriad things are [experienced] without self, there is no delusion, no Awakening, no Buddhas, no living beings, no birth and death. Since the Buddha's Way is itself, from the beginning, beyond fullness and lack, there are birth and death, delusion and Awakening, living beings and Buddhas. Though this is so, flowers fall when we are attached to them, and weeds grow when we dislike them.

To bring yourself to the myriad things in order to authenticate them is delusion. For the myriad things to come forward to authenticate yourself is Awakening. . . .

To study the Buddha's Way is to study oneself. To study oneself is to forget oneself. To forget oneself is to be enlightened by all things. To be enlightened by all things is the dropping away of one's mind and body, and the mind and body of others. No trace of Awakening remains, and this no-trace leaves traces endlessly.

When you first seek for the Dharma, you imagine that you are outside its boundaries. But when you see that the Dharma is already conveyed correctly within yourself, immediately you are your original self.

Awakening is like the moon reflected in water. The moon does not get wet, nor is the water broken. Though its light is vast and great, it is reflected in a tiny bit of water. The whole moon and the sky are reflected in dewdrops on the grass, or in just a drop of water. Awakening does not obstruct people, just as the moon does not break the water. A person does not obstruct Awakening, just as the drop of water does not obstruct the moon. The depth of the water is equal to the height of the moon. However long or short is the duration of the reflection, one realizes in the vastness or smallness of the water, the breadth and brightness of the moonlight in the sky. (*Shōbōgenzō, Genjō Kōan*)

After Dōgen's death, Sōtō Zen grew into a mass lay movement that eventually became the largest Zen sect in Japan. This evolution was due primarily to the Fourth Patriarch of Sōtō, Keizan Jōkin (1268–1325). Keizan modified Dōgen's austere Zen style, simplified Sōtō doctrine, and incorporated elements from Shintō and Shingon that were popular with the common and rural people of Japan. Keizan was also concerned with the problems of the common people. His Sōtō priests became involved in social issues and popular projects such as irrigation systems and medical treatment. There was an effort by the Sōtō priests to educate the people as well as rendering them spiritual, ritual, and social services. Some time later, priests of Keizan's tradition took up residence at Eihei-ji and made it the headquarters of the unified national Sōtō School that is today the second largest Buddhist organization in Japan.

Nichiren Buddhism

The third great tradition that began in the Kamakura period is Nichiren Buddhism, named after its founder, Nichiren (1222–1282). Nichiren was born in a small fishing village associated with the famous Shintō shrine of Ise, far from the cities of political and religious power. Given that the Ise shrine was connected to the imperial family, Nichiren began at an early age to wonder why the emperor had recently suffered disgrace at the hands of an uprising. If the Shintō gods were protecting the emperor, why did this happen to him? Also, by this time Nichiren had observed the many Buddhist sects, and wondered which one was the true form of Buddhism. Nichiren carried these two religious questions when he entered the nearby temple of the Tendai School, Kiyosumi-dera, to study Buddhism at the age of eleven.

At Kiyosumi-dera, Nichiren learned the basic Tendai teachings based on the *Lotus Sūtra* and prayed to Amida Buddha and other esoteric deities. But as his faith in the *Lotus Sūtra* grew, Nichiren abandoned his Pure Land piety. At the time Nichiren was studying at Kiyosumi-dera, the temple belonged to an esoteric branch of Tendai. There is a history of "title exegesis" in Tendai whereby one finds the doctrinal essence of the text in the title of a *sūtra* itself. Tendai also divides the *Lotus Sūtra* into two halves. The first half is seen as stressing the teachings of Gautama Buddha, and the second half is seen as more clearly revealing Gautama's eternal nature. Esoteric Tendai stresses this idea of the Eternal Buddha in the second part of the *sūtra*. Also, in esoteric Tendai, *mantras* are used to enable one to realize his or her innate Buddha-nature, and *maṇḍalas* assist one in refining his or her states of mind. In his mature thought concerning the Eternal Buddha and the *Lotus Sūtra*, Nichiren would utilize all of these ideas and practices from the Tendai tradition.

After four years at Kiyosumi-dera, Nichiren was ordained. Two years later, he traveled to Kamakura to further his study. Most likely, he focused on Zen and Pure Land Buddhism. However, he became uncomfortable with the contradictory claims of the schools and with the fact that many *sūtras* were being proclaimed. Eventually, Nichiren decided that the *Lotus Sūtra* taught the truest form of Buddhism, and so rejected Zen and Pure Land. Given his Tendai roots, and the fact that Tendai stresses the *Lotus Sūtra*, Nichiren decided at the age of twenty-one to go to Mt. Hiei. At Mt. Hiei, Nichiren concluded that Pure Land, Zen, Shingon, and the older Nara schools were all inferior to Tendai and that Tendai was the only sect that fully represented "true" Buddhism.

Nichiren became convinced that since the *Lotus Sūtra* was the most perfect presentation of the Dharma, it was the best hope for liberation in the age of the Degenerate Dharma. But more than this, he believed that if people gained liberation, their physical and social life would be so affected that the area in which those people lived would be transformed into a place of peace and prosperity. Reaching this conclusion, Nichiren was able to answer the two questions that led him to take up the religious life. He reasoned that the emperor had been abandoned by the gods because Japan had failed to honor the *Lotus Sūtra*, having instead embraced the lesser doctrines of the other Buddhist schools. Therefore, he felt that it was urgent that the *Lotus Sūtra* be preached in order to bring people to liberation and to bring peace and prosperity to Japan. With this new conviction, Nichiren left Mt. Hiei at the age of thirty-two to preach his views back at Kiyosumi-dera. However, his ideas irritated Pure Land followers in the region, and within a year's time Nichiren was forced to flee to Kamakura.

In Kamakura, Nichiren taught that he was preaching Tendai doctrine. However, he became more and more convinced that only the *Lotus Sūtra* could offer people true Buddhism, and the Japanese nation peace and prosperity. He concluded that the other schools of Buddhism should not be allowed to exist, and he developed a method of preaching called "confrontational conversion" (*shakubuku*). This method utilized shocking attacks of the other schools of Buddhism. For example, he preached that Zen Buddhists are devils and that Pure Land followers would not reach the heavenly Pure Land after death, but would fall into hells.

To understand Nichiren's radical approach, it is important to note that when he arrived in Kamakura, a number of calamities began: plagues, famines, droughts, earthquakes, and uprisings. There were also eclipses and comets seen in the sky. Nichiren was extremely concerned about the physical, social, and spiritual welfare of the Japanese nation. He also became convinced that only faith in the *Lotus Sūtra* could bring an end to Japan's problems. Since Buddhists were so wedded to their different views, shocking words were needed to get them to reevaluate and change their beliefs. Here are Nichiren's words justifying his approach:

> If a person was about to kill your parents, wouldn't you try to warn them? If a bad son insane with drunkenness threatens to kill his father and mother, wouldn't you try to stop him? If an evil person is trying to burn temples and pagodas, wouldn't you try to stop that person? If your child is seriously ill, wouldn't you try to cure him or her? To fail to do so is to act like those persons who do not try to stop Zen and *Nembutsu* followers in Japan. (*Kaimoku shō*, II)

As one could imagine, the reaction of many Buddhists in Kamakura to Nichiren's words was at first extremely negative. But in time he gathered some disciples. In 1260, Nichiren submitted a document to the government in Kamakura charging that the calamities befalling Japan were caused by its protecting gods leaving the nation because of the popularity of unsuitable Buddhist schools. Nichiren claimed that to save the nation, the rulers must give sole homage to the *Lotus Sūtra*. If not, he predicted that foreign invasions and civil disturbances would occur. The government did not respond, and Pure Land followers in Kamakura attacked Nichiren a year later. When he escaped, they convinced the government to exile him to the Izu Peninsula. During that exile, Nichiren took heart from the story in the *Lotus Sūtra* about a bodhisattva who was persecuted for practicing the *Lotus Sūtra*. Nichiren eventually came to identify with this bodhisattva, and he saw his sufferings as indicating that his destiny was to make Japan a Buddhist state based on the *Lotus Sūtra* and a springboard for a worldwide *Lotus* community.

When Nichiren was pardoned in 1263, he returned to Kamakura. Drawing on Tendai esotericism, he began to teach his growing group of followers to recite the title of the *Lotus Sūtra* as a *mantra*. This chanting of *Namu Myōhōrengekyō*, he taught, can itself bring realization of one's Buddha-nature. Like *nembutsu* in Pure Land Buddhism, this recitation would become central to Nichiren practice. Then in 1268, Nichiren saw the threat of a Mongol invasion as a confirmation of his prophecy six years earlier. He and his followers stepped up their efforts to convert Buddhist from other schools—efforts that in 1271 led to his second exile, this time to the remote island of Sado in the north.

It was on Sado Island that Nichiren became convinced that he was the emanation-body of Jōgyō Bodhisattva, the protector of the *Lotus Sūtra*. He also came to believe that in the age of the Degenerate Dharma, he was to be a new leader of the Buddhist faithful. While on Sado, Nichiren created the *Gohonzon*, a Great Maṇḍala that manifests his Awakening. In this *maṇḍala* are the characters of praise to the *Lotus Sūtra* (*Namu Myōhōrengekyō*) surrounded by figures of Buddhas and bodhisattvas, including Jōgyō. At a lower level are *arhats* and bodhisattvas, and on the lowest level are Shintō gods and names of Tendai masters. For Nichiren Buddhism, this *Gohonzon* became the principle image used in devotions.

During 1274, the year of his return from exile, Nichiren retired to a remote sanctuary on Mt. Minobu, convinced that his message had been ignored by the Japanese nation. There, Nichiren turned his attention to clarifying his philosophy and training his disciples. Meanwhile, two Mongol invasions of Japan were attempted. These were again viewed by Nichiren and his followers as the invasions predicted years ago. However, in both cases the invading ships were struck by typhoons, and the invasions were failures. Then in 1282, the year after the second Mongol invasion, Nichiren became ill. He chose the disciples to succeed him and passed away. His hermitage was enlarged into the famous temple of Kuon-ji. After Nichiren's death, his school spread in different parts of Japan and split into various sects.

Nichiren Buddhism is considered a single-practice school, like Zen and Pure Land, because it teaches that liberation is attainable by chanting the title of the *Lotus Sūtra*. Drawing on Tendai's title exegesis, Nichiren taught that the title of the *Lotus Sūtra*, namely *Myōhōrengekyō*, embodies the power of the Dharma presented in the text. Chanting an invocation to the *Lotus Sūtra*—*Namu Myōhōrengekyō*—concentrates this saving power of the Dharma into the life of the Nichiren practitioner. Along with this *mantra* chanting, Nichiren Buddhism also uses the *maṇḍala* that Nichiren created. This *maṇḍala* is believed to help draw forth from the practitioner the inner qualities of his or her pure Buddha-nature. It is as though the *maṇḍala* is like a mirror that reflects these inner qualities into one's conscious experience.

To explain this experience of personal transformation through chanting, Nichiren taught that the *Lotus Sūtra* contains Three Secret Teachings. First is that the Eternal Buddha, spoken of in the *Lotus Sūtra*, is an image of the innate Buddha-nature, or original Awakening. This enlightened life can be found within oneself by stripping away the layers of ignorance. Second is that the name of the *Lotus Sūtra* carries the reality and power of the Dharma that can overcome ignorance and reveal one's Buddha-nature. Third is that chanting is like an ordination platform. An ordination platform is where one is empowered to live the moral and spiritual virtues of Buddhism. Nichiren believed that since chanting embodies the power of the Dharma, it empowers one with the purity and positive qualities of Buddhahood.

To gain Awakening in this way was, for Nichiren, to realize one's "original Awakening" in the interrelatedness of all existence. Drawing on the Tendai notion that "one thought moment contains the three-thousand worlds," Nichiren taught that in the interpenetration of existence, each moment of life permeates all phenomena. This means one moment of chanting *Namu Myōhōrengekyō*, which embodies the "perfect truth" of one's true original nature, sets one anew in harmony with the positive dynamics behind the interrelated events of life. In this harmony, not only is one's spiritual condition affected, but also one's material conditions.

However, more important than these visible signs of the Dharma's power is growth in freedom from afflictive emotions, incorrect views, and unhealthy attachments. This moral and spiritual freedom fosters the more positive qualities of Buddhahood, such as wisdom, courage, purity, and compassion. Nichiren believed that given the interpenetration of life, as these material, moral, and spiritual conditions of people's lives change for the better, society will also change for the better. Thus, Nichiren saw Japan as the center of a world-transforming community of followers of the *Lotus Sūtra*. Following this insight, Nichiren Buddhism has seen itself as working for a more enlightened, peaceful, and happy world civilization. The following words of Nichiren express this kind of experience:

If you want to be free from the sufferings of birth and death that you have undergone since beginningless time, and if without fail you want to attain supreme Awakening in this very lifetime, then you must realize the inherent, original perfect truth in all living beings. This truth is *Myōhōrengekyō*. Therefore, chanting *Myōhōrengekyō* will enable you to realize the innate perfect truth in all life.

Among the *sūtras*, the *Lotus Sūtra* is king. It is true and correct in both its words and the principle it teaches. Its very words themselves are ultimate reality. This ultimate reality is the ultimate Dharma. It is called the ultimate Dharma because it reveals the principle of mutual interrelatedness of a single moment of life and all phenomena. Therefore, this *sūtra* is the very wisdom of all the Buddhas.

Each moment of life includes body, mind, personhood, the environment of all living beings in the Ten Worlds, the non-living beings in the 3,000 realms from the plants, sky and earth to the tinniest dust particles. Each moment of life permeates the whole realm of phenomena, and is therefore found in all phenomena. Awakening to this principle is itself the mutual interrelatedness of life in each moment including all phenomena.

However, even if you chant and believe in *Myōhōrengekyō*, if you think that the Dharma is outside yourself, you are not accepting the ultimate Dharma, but an inferior teaching. . . . Therefore, when you chant . . . you must have a deep faith that *Myōhōrengekyō* is your very life. . . . Your practice of Buddhism will not at all free you from the sufferings of birth and death unless you realize the true nature of your life.

The *Vimalakīrti Sūtra* says that when you seek the liberation of the Buddhas in the minds of ordinary beings, you will find that they are enlightened beings, and that the sufferings of birth and death are Nirvana itself. The *sūtra* also states that if one's mind is impure, one's land is impure; but if one's mind is pure, one's land is pure. There are not two lands, one pure and the other impure. The difference is solely found in the good and evil of one's mind.

This is true of Buddhas and ordinary beings. Deluded, one is called an ordinary being. Enlightened, one is called a Buddha. This can be likened to a dirty mirror that can shine like a jewel when cleaned. A mind clouded by the illusions of the inherent darkness of life is likened to a dirty mirror. When this mind is cleaned, it will surely be like a clear mirror that reflects the essential nature of all phenomena, the truth of reality. So, arousing a deep faith, diligently clean your mirror night and day. How should you clean it? Only by chanting *Namu Myōhōrengekyō*. . . . If you chant with deep faith in this inner principle, you will certainly attain Buddhahood in this very lifetime. (*Isshō jōbutsu shō*)

THE MUROMACHI PERIOD (1338–1573): ZEN AND JAPANESE CULTURE

From the end of the Kamakura Period in 1333 to the rise of the Tokugawa Period in 1603, Buddhism faced radical cultural changes in Japanese society, and eventually even tragic religious persecution. From the beginning of the Muromachi Shōgunate (1338–1573), the status of Buddhism was uncertain. The society was becoming more and more secularized, and intellectual interest was turning to China, especially to a popular form of Confucianism called Neo-Confucianism. However, Rinzai Zen held on to a special position in relation to the government that made it a kind of state religion. This relationship was forged by Musō Soseki (1275–1351), who was the religious advisor of the first shōgun. Zen was thus able to affect Japanese culture, in a society that was less open than in the past to direct religious teachings, through certain artistic forms that expressed Zen's subtle spirit.

Zen impacted Japanese culture through a number of different avenues. Zen temples, which were originally inspired by Chinese counterparts, became models for Japanese architecture. Temple gardens, especially the stone gardens of the late Muramachi Period, also created a new style of gardening that spread across Japan. In this artistic style, boulders represent mountains or islands, while a plane of moss or sand symbolize the boundless sea of life. But more than this, the gardens themselves have a strong spiritual affect on the viewers. In Zen calligraphy and painting, an enlightened artist can display his or her attainment through a certain vitality expressed in the work of art. The creative brushwork of the calligraphy or ink-painting portrays the spirit of Zen in ways that were appreciated by the Japanese people. Often the strong personalities of Zen masters could be gleaned from the calligraphy or seen more directly in the ink-portraits that seem to stare back at the viewer with extraordinary intensity.

Another avenue of Zen cultural influence is to be found in the Noh drama. The Noh drama was influenced by a subtle Zen aesthetic sensitivity. There is very little external action in these dramas. Rather, what is portrayed are the inner thoughts, feelings, and states of mind and heart that are in the deepest sense unspeakable. The actors' expressions and body movements allow the interiority of life to surface in subtle ways.

Tea gardens provided another unique bridge between Zen and the secular Japanese society, especially in the following Tokugawa Period. A path of irregular stepping stones leads through trees and thick shrubbery to a small teahouse. Walking this way past a stone lantern, water flowing from a bamboo pipe, and a stone water basin for rinsing one's mouth, a person is led from the busy world into a quiet place where worldly cares and concerns are put aside. The quiet tea ceremony, with only little verbal exchange, creates a deep and lasting experience of affirmation, friendship, and peace. The tea garden became a beloved and lasting tradition throughout Japan.

While Buddhism was influencing the broader Japanese culture, the secular nature of that society was also influencing Buddhism. For example, the most important figure in Pure Land Buddhism during this era was Rennyo (1415–1499). Rennyo was known as the "Restorer of Shinshū." He traveled to cities and towns, converting to his ideas not only Jōdo Shinshū followers, but also members of other traditions like Tendai and Shingon. In his preaching, a central theme was the distinction between the inner and outer aspects of a person's life. In one's heart, he said, one should hold to a strong faith in Other power. With this inner commitment, one can turn his or her attention to the secular affairs of daily life, such as one's family and occupation. In dealing with everyday issues, the values of one's faith should be guides for how to behave properly. When talking about these values, Rennyo spoke of the Confucian virtues, an ideology that was becoming popular in secular society.

In this and other ways, Rennyo redesigned Pure Land theory and practice in a way that attracted a vast number of common people throughout Japan. Eventually, Rennyo's sect of Jōdo Shinshū Buddhism, the Hongan-ji sect, became a powerful feudal institution popular with the masses. Then in the sixteenth century, the Hongan-ji split into two schools: the Nishi (Western) Hongan-ji and the Higashi (Eastern) Hongan-ji, both headquartered in Kyōto. This split is institutional rather than doctrinal, and both schools combine to form the largest Buddhist school in Japan.

In the fifteenth century, the fabric of Muromachi society was coming apart. The shōgunate was divided by power struggles, and the populace was plagued by civil uprisings. The Ōnin War (1467–1478) brought an end to central government control in Japan, leading to the independence of provincial warlords. In this social chaos, the Pure Land and Nichiren sects created their own feudal states protected by peasant armies. A leader in this Buddhist movement was Rennyo, whose Hongan-ji sect became a powerful force in Japan. Nichiren Buddhist temples in Kyōto held great influence in the southern part of the city. These temples followed the Pure Land example and formed self-defense militias that later developed into armies. After some clashes with armies backed by the Pure Land tradition, a massive army from Mt. Hiei destroyed the Nichiren temples and community in Kyōto. However, this did not stop Nichiren Buddhism from continuing to grow. Later, it would organize into seven sects and remain one of the important forms of Buddhism in Japan.

BOX 9.2

THE FIRST BOOK

Many serious intellectuals had a "first book," which, in a time of youthful crisis, set their lives on course. For some of my friends, searching for meaning in their confused adolescence, it was Thoreau's *Walden*. For Dorothy Day, in anguish over social injustice and an unresponsive church, it was *The Brothers Karamazov*. For me, interned in Japan during World War II, it was R. H. Blyth's *Zen in English Literature*.

That was fifty-seven years ago. I'm a retired teacher of Zen Buddhism now, and looking through those old pages, I find many points where I disagree. Nonetheless, I am still mining the riches of this remarkable work.

Fundamentally, *Zen in English Literature* is not so much about Zen Buddhism, the religion, with its practice of meditation and its course of *kōan* study, as it is about language and the thought and attitudes that produce language.

Blyth quotes Tennyson, speaking of a woman staring hopelessly out of a window:

> Fixed like a beacon tower above the waves
> Of tempest, when the crimson-rolling eye
> Glares ruin, and the wild birds on the light
> Dash themselves dead.

Metaphor vividly exposes the net and indeed the hologram of people, animals, plants, mountains, rivers, the great Earth, sun, moon, and stars in all their infinite variety that is our personal life. Paul Shepard has shown how our language is charged with animal metaphor to describe human qualities and conditions: dogged, foxy, mousey, mulish, owlish, sheepish, and so on. There are countless similar metaphors in daily use from plants, minerals, mountains, the weather, and so on. All expose the net, the unity, the great "cooperative"—in Buddhadāsa's words:

> The entire cosmos is a cooperative. The sun, the moon, and
> the stars live together as a cooperative. The same is true
> for humans and animals, trees and soil. Our bodily parts
> function as a cooperative.

"Great wits jump" to personalize this cooperative. Blyth quotes Shelley's *Skylark*:

> All the earth and air,
> With thy verse is loud.

And comments: "That is, not only the skylark is singing but the trees and stones and rivers, the clouds, winds and air—all is singing, singing with the voice of the skylark."

This kind of example and explication, woven with such genius in my "first book," brought me to Zen Buddhist practice, where metaphor brings forth deepest understanding:

> Yün-men said to his assembly, "Within heaven and earth, through space
> and time, there is a treasure hidden inside the mountain of form. It takes

a lantern and goes to the Buddha hall. It takes the great triple gate and puts it on the lantern.

And it brought me to social action, to sit down squarely in the way of obscene defilements of the cooperative.

ROBERT AITKEN
Retired Master of Honolulu Diamond Sangha
A Zen Buddhist Society

In the sixteenth century, these Buddhist armies were seen by the warlords as standing in the way of the reunification of Japan. Oda Nobunaga (1534–1582) played a leading role in this reunification effort. In so doing, he was especially ruthless in his drive to strip Buddhism of any political power. His army burnt down all the Tendai temples on Mt. Hiei, attacked the Shingon headquarters on Mt. Hōya, and suppressed the Pure Land and Nichiren armies throughout the countryside. The Zen schools escaped this suppression because they had not formed any kind of armed forces. Nobunaga's successor, Toyotami Hideyoshi (1536–1598), was able to steer a more moderate course because Buddhist political power was essentially broken. Hideyoshi rebuilt temples on Mt. Hiei and aided the construction of the Hongan-ji monastic complex in Kyōto. He also supported the Zen schools to which he felt indebted for their cultural contributions. The full unification of Japan came under Tokugawa Ieyasu (1542–1616), who moved the capital to Edo (modern Tokyo). Thus began the Tokugawa Shōgunate (1603–1868), which is referred to as Japan's modern period.

THE TOKUGAWA PERIOD (1603–1868): STRUGGLE AND REFORM

Japan's "modern period" began with the establishment of the Tokugawa Shōgunate in 1603. This new period advanced the secularization of Japanese society and provided national unity. The government no longer granted Buddhism the leading role in the affairs of the country that it had enjoyed in medieval times. In fact, the shōgunate adopted a Confucian ideology based primarily on the Neo-Confucianism that had successfully contributed to the unity of China achieved during the Ming Dynasty (1368–1644). While the Buddhist schools were allowed to freely practice their religion if they did not criticize the government, they no longer exercised significant influence over the rulers or the educated classes.

The Tokugawa government did use Buddhism to enforce its tight control over Japanese society. All religious bodies were organized under the state. The Buddhist temples were registered, and all Buddhist schools were associated with either main or branch temples. All families in Japan were also registered with local Buddhist temples in order for the government better to keep track of the population. The Buddhist schools were forbidden to proselytize since people switching from one temple to another would disrupt the state census. The government did not support Buddhism financially, so the temples had to be financed by their official members.

As Buddhism was stripped not only of its political power but also of its intellectual and moral influence in society, Neo-Confucianism provided Japan with its prevalent worldview and moral code. In presenting their ideas and values, Confucian scholars in Japan also criticized Buddhism for being socially harmful due to its monastic religiosity, which seemed to them to have little social relevance. The Confucian challenge was strengthened by the fact that Buddhism at the time was torn by a sectarianism that had a divisive social impact and by the fact that there was a moral decline among the clergy.

A number of innovative and significant Buddhist responses to this Confucian challenge arose. One prominent example was a Buddhist reform movement founded by Jiun Sonja (1718–1804). Jiun was ordained a Shingon monk, but was also trained in Confucianism and Sōtō Zen. As he matured as a Buddhist practitioner, Jiun became more and more aware of the need for a revival of Buddhist thought, practice, and morality that was not limited by sectarianism. With a small group of disciples, Jiun developed a discipline of study, practice, and strict observance of the *Vinaya*. He called this new reform movement *Shōbōritsu*, or "Vinaya of the True Dharma." Taking the historical Buddha as a model, Jiun proposed that the Buddha's wisdom into emptiness as the interrelatedness of all things shows that all living beings are "one's own body." With this insight, one is inspired to treat all living beings as one would his or her own body. For Jiun, this kind and compassionate treatment of others is best defined in the Ten Good Precepts that are recognized by all forms of Japanese Buddhism.

Jiun believed that this view of the connection of wisdom with morality provided Buddhists with a common ground that transcended sectarian divisions. It also provided Buddhism with a rebuttal to the Confucianist claim that Buddhism is socially irrelevant. Jiun taught that the morality of the Ten Good Precepts gave all people a moral guide for family life, business practices, and government policymaking. Juin did not call for the abolition of the Buddhist sects, but taught that each sect should focus on what in its tradition is in accord with the True Dharma and the Ten Good Precepts. They should then live those fundamental aspects of Buddhism shared in common with members of other Buddhist schools.

Another more institutional example of making Buddhist religiosity relevant to the secular world can be seen in the Sōtō School at this time. Many of the Sōtō monks during the Tokugawa Period preached the Buddha's Dharma to the common people in rural areas. They stressed the connection between Zen practice and the daily needs of the people by teaching that secular actions can have religious import if performed in the true spirit of the bodhisattva. When a person has the heart of the bodhisattva and works with that attitude for the welfare of others, then his or her actions are as religious as those performed in the temple.

Besides these kinds of internal Buddhist reforms in Japan, another kind of attempt to renew Japanese Buddhism came from China. Around the beginning of the seventeenth century, an influx of Chinese Ch'an (Zen) masters brought new inspirations to the Zen world in Japan. Among these masters was Yin-yüan (1592–1673). Yin-yüan arrived in Japan in 1654, and at first settled in the port city of Nagasaki. He then moved to near Kyōto, and was eventually given some property in Uji, also near Kyōto. There he had a new temple built that he named *Mampuku-ji*. He also called the hilly site for the temple *Ōbaku-san* after the region in China that he had left behind. This new monastic foundation would become the home of a third school of Zen in Japan, the Ōbaku School.

Ōbaku Zen combined *zazen* and *kōan* practice with Tantric ritual, *nembutsu*, and the ritual recitation of *sūtras*. Chinese customs of dress and etiquette were also used in everyday monastic life, and the strict monastic rules as observed in China were also introduced. This particular reform was at first somewhat popular. Before Yin-yüan died, he had expanded his movement to include some twenty-four Ōbaku monasteries around Japan. However, after a few decades, the growth of Ōbaku slowed because it never became fully inculturated. In 1876, the Ōbaku School was recognized as an independent Zen sect. Today, Ōbaku has about five hundred affiliated temples.

The traditional schools of Japanese Zen were not receptive to the complex and sophisticated innovations introduced by the Ōbaku School. Instead, Japanese Zen often focused on the ordinary, everyday experiences of life, especially those found in nature. For example, Bashō Matsuo (1644–1694) was one of the greatest poets of Japan. Bashō brought the spirit of Zen into the world of poetry with his famous *haiku*. This simple and direct style of poetry provided him with a vehicle for expressing his Zen contemplation of nature. While not a monk, Bashō was a lay disciple, who, from the age of forty, traveled around Japan writing about his aesthetic/spiritual experiences. Certain themes such as solitude and silence, simplicity and ordinariness, seasons and sounds are presented in poems that lack any note of ego. The following poems by Bashō draw on the spirit of Zen:

Only Silence alone!
Into the rock cliff penetrates
The sound of the cicada.

An old pond, Ah!
A frog jumps in
The sound of water.

The light of the moon!
The four gates and four sects
Yet only one.

Another important figure from this period who also stressed the simplicity of Zen was Bankei Yōtaku (1622–1693). Bankei was a Rinzai master who lived and taught in the provinces where he was close to the common people. His message was simple and clear. All people have the innate "Unborn

Buddha Mind." It is this innate reality that is the source of enlightenment. In that Unborn Buddha Mind, all things have their proper place and enjoy their true harmony. In discovering that reality, all of one's ordinary daily activities become acts of the Buddha. Instead of quoting the *sūtras* or patriarchs and masters from the past, stressing formal *kōan* practice, or emphasizing the importance of experiences in Zen, Bankei simply directed his followers to become aware of the Unborn Buddha Mind within them. For Bankei, the clarity of this Mind develops in a constant process along the way to Buddhahood.

While Bankei's Zen was influential and continues to be so, the most famous Rinzai master from this time was Hakuin Ekaku (1686–1769). Hakuin agreed with Bankei about the importance of the process of Zen growth. But unlike Bankei, Hakuin focused on how this process can be nourished by proper *kōan* practice. Hakuin created a comprehensive *kōan* system with 1700 anecdotes that remains the core of Rinzai training today. There are five types of *kōans* in Hakuin's system. *Kōans* of the first type are designed to bring the Zen student to an initial insight of Zen experience called *kenshō* ("insight into one's True Self"). Hakuin, like Tsung-mi in China and Chinul in Korea, understood from his own experience that this initial insight must be deepened into full enlightened living. After *kenshō*, this growth is achieved by working with the four other types of *kōans*, which are designed for that exact purpose. In this way, one cultivates freedom, wisdom, and compassion in a process of growth in the Dharma that continues to the end of one's life.

Drawing on his own life experience, Hakuin revitalized Rinzai Zen with his writings, which give us a most detailed description of the process of growth in the Zen experience from beginning to end. Hakuin discusses his personal struggle in what he calls the "Great Doubt" as it was produced by his *kōan* practice. Based on his experience, Hakuin taught that *kōans* are used initially in meditation and daily life to generate the Great Doubt, or an existential questioning of the suffering condition of oneself and the world. This Doubt is called "Great" because it is not an objective doubt concerning a particular question or some particular phenomenon in the world. Rather, it is a "mass of Great Doubt" in which oneself and the world are no longer separate realities.

This Great Doubt is, Hakuin says, in tension with one's belief in "self power," the power of one's True Self or Buddha-nature to break this mass of Great Doubt and produce Awakening. In this intense process, one works on his or her *kōan* with the guidance of a master. The master moves the disciple beyond thinking about his or her *kōan* in a dualistic and rationalistic way. Eventually, moving beyond such ordinary thought processes, there comes a moment in which suddenly and without willful effort, of itself the True Self realizes itself. One therein finds Awakening in a flash of "Great Enlightenment," or "Great Joy." Here are some of Hakuin's own words about the experience of this Great Doubt:

A person confronted with the Great Doubt sees in the four directions only wide and empty land, without birth and death, like a plain of ice 10,000 miles in expanse. . . . In his heart, there remains not a trace of desires or concepts, only the word "emptiness" as if one is standing in the wide-open dome of heaven. . . . If one progresses in this Way, without turning back, he or she will suddenly experience something like the breaking of an ice cover, or the collapse of a tower made of crystal. . . . Nothing gives one more joy than to break through the many-storied gate of endless rebirths in *saṃsāra*. This is the inner realization of original Awakening of all the perfected ones in the four directions. (*Orategama*, Appendix)

THE MEIJI PERIOD (1868–1912) AND RECENT DEVELOPMENTS

The Meiji Restoration marked the end of Japan's long period of isolation under the Tokugawa government. Japan opened up to the outside world, and the Tokugawa Shōgunate was replaced with the emperor system. Among the first decrees of the new Meiji government were those that established a new government office for Shintō, and separated Shintō from Buddhism. Within the first few years of the Meiji Period, the government also denounced Buddhist traditions and expropriated some temple lands. Buddhist monks serving Shintō shrines had to become Shintō priests or return to the lay state. Another decree permitted Buddhist monks to marry. In fact, today most Japanese monks are married. On the other hand, the women's orders have remained celibate. Fortunately for Buddhism, these policies were soon tempered, and it was clear that the government's intention was not to destroy Buddhism, but to make Shintō the national religion for its political advantage.

Along with the political and economic opening of Japan came an intellectual opening to the modern Western world. After the difficulties of the first few years, Buddhist religious leaders understood that the future of Buddhism depended on adapting to this new intellectual climate. To foster this adaptation, Buddhist institutions expanded the curricula of their monastery schools to include such subjects as modern mathematics and science, Western philosophy and literature, and comparative religions and foreign languages. In some cases, these schools evolved into universities; for example, a Sōtō monastic school became Komazawa University of Tokyo and a Rinzai monastic school became Hanazono Univeristy of Kyōto.

As Japanese Buddhism sought enrichment from contact with Western perspectives, the West was becoming interested in Buddhism. Indeed, Buddhism throughout Asia was being stimulated by Western scholars, who were studying their religion. Many Japanese Buddhist schools sent some of their young monks to study in the West. As they did so, they provided the West with Buddhist teachings as well as the opportunity to practice Buddhism. We will discuss this kind of contact in the last chapter of our story of Buddhism.

Through these kinds of contacts with Western culture, Buddhism produced a new generation of scholars and leaders who sought to redefine their religion in ways that are intellectually respectable, spiritually viable, and socially responsible. This task was at times a real struggle. One example of how this was so is found in the work of Kiyozawa Manshi (1863–1903), commonly referred to by his first name. Manshi was a Pure Land Buddhist educated at the University of Tokyo, where he studied the full range of Western thought. After his education was complete, he settled in Kyōto, where he was an educator. While he valued his modern education, he also treasured his Pure Land faith. The existential problem he faced was how to reconcile the modern view of the world with his personal religious faith. Influenced by German Idealism and Kegon Buddhism, Manshi concluded that the universe is an organic whole in a state of constant evolution and dissolution. Faith that each entity in the cosmos is a dynamic expression of this organic whole brings inner peace as one exercises reason to understand life and live morally. Without this faith, one's rational study and moral reasoning become matters of anxiety and undue exertion.

There were some missteps in this effort to redefine modern Buddhism. During the time of Japan's military expansionism at the turn of the twentieth century, some Rinzai Buddhist intellectuals proclaimed the spiritual superiority of Rinzai Zen. They taught that Rinzai was the highest embodiment of the essence of Buddhism, and of all forms of religion. These Zen writers stressed the tie between Zen and the Way of the Warrior (*bushidō*) with its one-pointed conviction without doubts or questions, fearless discipline, and self-sacrifice for the good of the Japanese nation. Thus, some Rinzai leaders extended the claim for spiritual superiority to one of cultural and racial superiority. This "New Buddhism" was used by the government to bolster national pride, militarism, and the war effort during World War II.

On the other hand, one very positive Japanese Buddhist contribution to the world during the twentieth century was the Kyōto School. As Japan opened to the West, Nishida Kitarō (1870–1949) studied Western philosophy and religion and went on to write highly sophisticated philosophical works drawing on both Buddhist and Western thought. He founded the Kyōto School as an intellectual movement, giving both Zen and Pure Land Buddhism a new and highly respected voice in the international philosophical and theological worlds. The Kyōto School's work was brought forward by such persons as Tanabe Hajime (1885–1962), Nishitani Keiji (1900–1990), Takeuchi Yoshinori (1913–present) and Abe Masao (1915–present). Also influenced by Nishida, the great Zen master Hisamatsu Shin'ichi (1889–1980) founded the F.A.S. Society dedicated to the realization of the "Formless Self" (F.) that embraces "All Humankind" (A.) in order to transform modern society "Superhistorically" (S.), that is, on a spiritual basis. In opposition to New Buddhism, Hisamatsu opposed any kind of racism, nationalism, or any ideology that stands in the way of realizing a more united and peaceful world community.

After World War II, a secular government and society in Japan turned its attention toward rebuilding the nation into one that is technologically and economically progressive. Interest in traditional forms of Buddhism began to wane. However, this meant that certain spiritual needs were left unmet by older religious forms. After the Korean War, new forms of religiosity began to become popular in Japan. What are called the "New Religions" grew in membership as literally millions of Japanese laypeople joined their ranks. More recently, even newer religious groups continue to be founded by charismatic figures. Among the New Religions are a number of influential Buddhist lay movements that have sought to balance personal healing and transformation with social engagement. Some are working in ways that better human society, not only in Japan but also around the world. They see themselves as living and sharing the values of Buddhism for the good of humankind. Two of the best-known of these Buddhist lay organizations are the Sōka Gakkai and the Risshō Kōsei-kai, which we introduce along with other types of modern Buddhism in the next chapter.

SUGGESTIONS FOR FURTHER READING

Abé, Ryuchi. *The Weaving of Mantra: Kūkai and the Construction of Esoteric Buddhist Discourse.* New York: Columbia University Press, 1999.

Andreason, Esben. *Popular Buddhism in Japan: Shin Buddhist Religion and Culture.* Honolulu: University of Hawaii Press, 1998.

Baroni, Helen J. *Ōbaku Zen: The Emergence of the Third Sect of Zen in Tokugawa Japan.* Honolulu: University of Hawaii Press, 2000.

Colcutt, Martin. *Five Mountains: The Rinzai Zen Monastic Institution in Medieval Japan.* Cambridge: Harvard University Press, 1981.

Cook, Francis H. *Sounds of Valley Streams: Enlightenment in Dōgen's Zen— Translation of Nine Essays from* Shōbōgenzō. Albany, NY: SUNY Press, 1989.

de Bary, Wm. Theodore, ed., with Ryusaku Tsunoda and Donald Keene. *Sources of Japanese Tradition.* 2 vols. (Second Edition of Vol. 1 edited by Donald Keene, George Tanabe and Paul Varley.) New York: Columbia University Press, 2001, 1964.

Dumoulin, Heinrich. *Zen Buddhism: A History.* Vol. 2, *Japan.* New York: Macmillan, 1990.

Franck, Frederick, ed. *The Buddha Eye: An Anthology of the Kyōto School.* New York: Crossroad, 1982.

Groner, Paul. *Saichō: The Establishment of the Japanese Tendai School.* Berkeley, CA: Berkeley Buddhist Studies Series, 1984.

Hakeda, Yoshito S, trans. *Kūkai: Major Works.* New York: Columbia University Press, 1972.

Heine, Steven, and Dale S. Wright, eds. *The Kōan: Texts and Contexts in Zen Buddhism.* New York: Oxford University Press, 2000.

Hirota, Dennis, trans. *The Collected Works of Shinran.* 2 vols. Kyoto: Shin Buddhism Translation Series, 1997.

Kasulas, Thomas P. *Zen Action, Zen Person.* Honolulu: University of Hawaii Press, 1981.

Kitagawa, Joseph M. *On Understanding Japanese Religion.* Princeton, NJ: Princeton University Press, 1987.

LaFleur, William R. *The Karma of Words: Buddhism and the Literary Arts in Medieval Japan.* Berkeley, CA: University of California Press, 1983.

Sanford, James H. *Flowing Traces: Buddhism in the Literary and Visual Arts of Japan.* Princeton, NJ: Princeton University Press, 1992.

Senchakushū English Translation Project, trans. *Hōnen's* Senchakushū: *Passages on the Selection of the Nembutsu in the Original Vow.* Honolulu: University of Hawaii Press, 1998.

Stone, Jacqueline I. *Original Enlightenment and the Transformation of Medieval Japanese Buddhism.* Honolulu: University or Hawaii Press, 1999.

Tanabe, George, Jr, ed. *Religions of Japan in Practice.* Princeton, NJ: Princeton University Press, 1999.

Tanahashi, Kazuaki, and David T. Schneider, eds. *The Essential Zen.* San Francisco: HarperSanFrancisco, 1995.

Yampolsky, Philip B., trans. *The Zen Master Hakuin: Selected Writings.* New York: Columbia University Press, 1971.

TEN

Modern Buddhism
in Asia

Asia has experienced many acute crises in the twentieth century that have seriously influenced the Buddhist world. Some of these crises include lingering effects of colonialism, especially in Sri Lanka and Vietnam; modern warfare in China, Korea, Japan, and Southeast Asia; foreign invasion and occupation, especially in Tibet; genocide in Cambodia and cultural genocide in Tibet; poverty, social problems, and ecological devastation in Southeast Asia caused by the postcolonial effects of global economics and social-cultural Westernization; Western consumerism, materialism, and secularism in developed Asian countries such as Korea, Japan, and Taiwan; and political oppression in Burma and communist-controlled countries. These kinds of crises have led to new forms of Buddhism that seek not only personal Awakening but also to affect society.

Some of these new Buddhist movements are problematic. We have already mentioned the nationalistic propaganda of early twentieth-century Rinzai in the last chapter. Today, there are also fundamentalist and nationalistic Buddhist organizations in such places as Sri Lanka and Thailand. In this chapter, we prefer to focus our attention on the more positive Buddhist reform movements in Asia, which are concerned with the physical, social, and political as well as the mental, emotional, and spiritual dimensions of human existence. We focus on how they are seeking to give a positive answer to the question: Can the Dharma of the Buddha contribute to building a better world for the good of all humankind, indeed of all forms of life?

New Buddhist Movements in Asia

Buddhism in Asia is today experiencing new growth in which innovative Buddhist reform movements are attempting to address the personal, social, political, economic, and environmental ills that plague that part of the world. These new forms of Buddhism reinterpret their scriptures and lineage experience in ways that confront and address the *duḥkha* of our modern world.

In particular, Buddhist movements and organizations referred to as "socially engaged Buddhism" seek to complement the ancient contemplative search for inner peace, Awakening, Nirvana, and Buddhahood with an active engagement of the many problems facing our world today. They balance pursuing the personal goal of inner peace with contributing to the collective goal of social peace.

In Buddhism, a peaceful society is not understood as one that enjoys just the absence of war, injustice, and social and environmental ills, but as a social expression of the Dharma. In this section, we revisit the traditions of Asian Buddhism to see how some of their reform movements have sought to interpret the Dharma to address the problems of the modern world and to build a more united and peaceful global community for the benefit of all living beings. In the concluding section, we end this chapter with a look at one particular issue that has emerged throughout Asia—the status of women in the Saṅgha.

India

Bhimrao Ramji Ambedkar (1891–1956) was the Hindu leader of the Untouchables in India prior to Indian independence. As a boy, because of his untouchable status, Ambedkar endured terrible persecution at school and in his community. His notebooks could not be touched by his teacher, a drink of water had to be poured into his mouth for fear of polluting contact, and he was beaten when he inadvertently stepped where he was not wanted. However, through his intelligence and perseverance, Ambedkar became only the second Untouchable to graduate from high school in India. Then with support from a liberal Hindu leader, he went on to attend college and gained doctorate degrees from Columbia University and the University of London.

Even as an academic and elected leader in India, Ambedkar continued to experience caste violence. He was evicted from his home and subjected to beatings. Eventually, Ambedkar became convinced that mere reform of the Hindu caste system would never solve the problem of untouchability. So in 1935, he decided to give up Hinduism and thereby his status as an Untouchable by converting to another religion. After exploring a number of religions, Ambedkar decided on Buddhism. On October 14, 1956, during the celebration of the 2500th anniversary of Buddha's *parinirvāṇa*, he and his wife took vows for the Three Refuges. Six weeks later, Ambedkar died, having opened the way for his Untouchable brothers and sisters to enter and forge a new form of Indian Buddhism. In just five years, over three million Untouchables followed Ambedkar's lead and became Buddhists.

Before his conversion to Buddhism, Ambedkar wrote *The Buddha and His Dhamma*, in which he applies the Dharma of the Buddha to the suffering condition of Untouchables in India. Indeed, Ambedkar saw the teachings of the Buddha as having the precise purpose of eliminating this type of suffering endured by so much of humankind:

[His] path which is his Dhamma (religion) had nothing to do with God or Soul. His Dhamma had nothing to do with life after death. Nor has his Dhamma any concern with rituals and ceremonies. The center of his Dhamma is man and the relation of man to man in his life on earth. This he said was his first postulate. His second postulate was that men are living in sorrow, in misery and poverty. The world is full of suffering and that how to remove this suffering from the world is the only purpose of Dhamma.[1]

In interpreting this Dharma, Ambedkar set aside certain central teachings of the Buddha such as the Four Noble Truths, karma and rebirth, and the monastic life. The Four Noble Truths, Ambedkar felt, speak only about one's own ignorance and selfishness as the causes of suffering, not the heartless actions of others and the systemic injustice of such social arrangements as the caste system. The idea of karma, he believed, would only accentuate the self-blame of the Untouchables instead of placing the blame on the caste system itself. Also, the monastic life would be of little or no use to the poor masses of India.

On the other hand, Ambedkar believed that the virtues taught by the Buddha do in fact provide a basis for a liberating social life that can uplift those bound by poverty and oppression. The Four Divine Abodes of loving kindness, compassion, sympathetic joy, and equanimity provide the attitudes that lead to working together to address the suffering of poverty. Wisdom enables one to understand one's condition and the steps that one must take to change that situation. The Eightfold Path defines those steps that can bring the self-respect and social-political change needed such that the social structures that produce poverty and suffering are removed. The overcoming of human passions such as hate, anger, and greed can aid in eradicating the roots of class struggle and social inequality, and thereby the suffering they engender.

By converting to Buddhism, the plight of the ex-Untouchables was not changed overnight. There is still much work to be done today to raise their lives out of abject poverty. Therefore, the "New Buddhists" in India, those converts inspired by Ambedkar, founded a number of organizations based on his call for social transformation through Buddhist principles. One such organization is the Trailokya Bauddha Mahasangha (literally the "Buddhist Order of the Three Realms"), or TBM. Lay and monastic members of TBM participate in what is called the "Dharma Revolution," by which New Buddhists can transform their own lives, and work with each other to transform society.

TBM has developed three ways of facilitating this Dharma Revolution. First is through "public centers," one- or two-room huts where Dharma talks and classes are given on Buddhist principles for living and on the practice of meditation. The Dharma is applied to particular problems such as domestic violence, lack of self-esteem, and the effects of poverty. Meditation focuses on mindfulness of breathing and loving-kindness meditation. The second part of TBM work is done at rural "retreat centers" in retreats intended to deepen what is begun at the public centers. The third part of the movement's work is done in "residential communities," where members learn to develop spiritual friendships, live harmoniously with each other, and work together for their common good. To address specific problems of ex-Untouchables, TBM has also set up a number of social projects that include kindergartens, residential schools, women's literacy classes, vocational classes, health-care outreach programs, and outpatient clinics for slum dwellers.

Sri Lanka

In Sri Lanka, many Buddhist leaders have been concerned with the effect of the capitalist model of economic development on the people and environment of their country since the colonial period. Production-centered development defines the well-being of the country in purely quantitative terms, and thus it creates desires through the media for more consumer goods. Buddhist leaders point out that in working for the wealth needed to purchase these objects, many Sri Lankans forget the well-being of their less fortunate neighbors, as well as the spiritual wealth offered by Buddhism. In part to counter this influence of Westernization on Sri Lanka, A. T. Ariyaratne founded the Sarvodaya Shramadana Movement. *Sarvodaya* is a term first coined by Mahātmā Gandhi to mean "the well-being of all." *Shramadana* is interpreted to mean "the gift of sharing one's time and labor." As a social movement in Sri Lanka, Sarvodaya Shramadana seeks to live the Dharma by sharing both time and labor for the well-being of all in order to create a society where there is "no poverty and no affluence."

Sarvodaya members live out the experience of no-self (*anattā*) by sharing what they can with all persons in need. They see this selfless service to others as a way of changing their own consciousness into a more awakened and compassionate state on the way to Nirvana. When organized properly, such service can also contribute to social and economic changes that will help those who are served to better understand and live the Dharma. It has been pointed out that the Buddha once did not deliver a Dharma talk until a poor laborer was fed, because, as the Buddha said, no one suffering from hunger can comprehend the Dharma. To guide this work for those in need, Ariyaratne interprets the Four Divine Abodes in the following manner: Loving kindness means a love and respect for all persons. This leads to compassion for those persons one loves who are in need. Sympathetic joy comes from seeing how compassionate service to the needy has helped them. Equanimity aids one in continuing this life of service undeterred by praise or blame, gain or loss.

Concretely, Sarvodaya directs a village-renewal program by which members assist villagers in Sri Lanka with their particular problems by applying the Four Noble Truths. First, what is the problem to be addressed? Second, what are the causes of that problem? Third, how can the problem be resolved? And fourth, what are the steps that need to be taken to resolve it?

Then, to solve a problem, for example the need for clean drinking water, villagers join Sarvodaya members in a "project working camp" for a week or so. During that time not only is work done, but a positive spiritual atmosphere is created by living together practices and values of Buddhism. Work is both planned and concluded each day in a "family meeting" during which these values are discussed and applied to the task at hand. The work is done in the spirit of the Four Grounds of Kindness: generosity, kindly speech, useful work, and equality. Ariyaratne believes that these four Buddhist virtues can combat the materialism, individualism, and unbridled competition of modern economic life. In so doing, these virtues cultivate spiritual friendship, community, and sharing in ways that foster personal Awakening and social development.

Given this moral and spiritual dimension of Sarvodaya, besides the reconstruction of the village, the reconstruction of the minds and spirits of the people participating in this work is of prime importance. As the working groups achieve this end, the villages move to a community-building stage guided by an elected village committee comprised of men, women, and children. Each village also joins a network of villages that builds trust between people of different religions, races, and ethnic backgrounds. They confront basic problems like poverty, environmental degradation, crime, and other social ills together in ways that contribute to national peacemaking. The latest innovation of Sarvodaya is Vishwa Niketan, a peace center where persons of all nationalities come together to learn the universal teachings of the Buddha and cultivate inner peace and spiritual growth for service to humankind.

Ariyaratne began this program of village renewal in the 1950s, and by the end of the 1970s his movement was working in over two thousand villages. In the 1980s there were not only working camps but also vocational training schools, preschools, and even communal farms; over eight thousand villages (one-third of the island's villages) were involved. In response to the tension between the Tamil Hindus and the Sinhalise Buddhists in Sri Lanka, Ariyaratne translated his Buddhist values into a universal language that could be shared by Hindus, Buddhists, and Christians. Thus, his movement could provide an interfaith force for unity and peace in Sri Lanka. Sarvodaya has sponsored peace walks and peace conferences seeking to reconcile all sides of the conflict on the basis of their common values. When Ariyaratne received the Niwano Peace Prize in 1992, he said that now is the time to guide science and technology with our shared spiritual wisdom so that we can create by kindness, compassion, and sharing a nobler, more just, and peaceful world community. Here are his own words reflecting on the Sarvodaya experience:

> There was a time in our history when there was total peace and harmony in our country. In modern times, why do children take to violence as they grow to adulthood? Why do we have a society today which is far from peaceful?. . . . One of the unique teachings of the Buddha is the theory of dependent arising.

Everything is related to every other thing. If there is no peace in a society, there should be a variety of interdependent and interrelated causes that bring about such a situation. All of these causes have to be attacked simultaneously and removed to make a reversal of the processes that have brought about a loss of peace in our society so that we can rebuild a culture of peace. The Sarvodaya Shramadana Movement in Sri Lanka has evolved . . . an integrated self-development approach to counteract the causes that bring about conflicts, crime, and war. . . . People expect quick solutions to the culture of violence that prevails today. They forget that this culture has been caused over a long period of time by multifarious factors. . . . Sarvodaya is patiently and silently rebuilding the foundations of the required new social order. . . . We in Sarvodaya believe that religions should assist human beings and human groups to overcome internal defilements such as greed, ill will, and egotism, and promote internal spirituality so that beneficence, sharing, morality, and enlightenment will evolve within them. The ultimate objective of Buddhists and other religious individuals should be building a critical mass of spiritual consciousness on this planet—which is the surest way to live in a culture of peace.[2]

Thailand

One of the greatest critics of modern social and economic structures that have influenced Thailand has been Buddhadāsa Bhikkhu (1906–1993). At the age of ten, Buddhadāsa entered a temple in his small hometown six hundred miles south of Bangkok. There he learned to read and write, celebrate Buddhist ceremonies, and collect medicinal herbs in the forest. Later, he was ordained a monk and took advanced Dharma studies in Bangkok. Missing the peace and simplicity of his hometown, Buddhadāsa returned to the south, where he moved into an abandoned temple and founded *Suan Mokkh*, "The Garden of Liberation." For the first three months, Buddhadāsa remained alone in silence; it was only after five years that three monks came to join him. During those first five years, Buddhadāsa developed a balanced way of Buddhist practice and study. Until that time, it was common for city monks to study the scriptures, while forest monks practiced meditation.

Buddhadāsa taught that personal and social transformation go hand in hand. Both involve cleansing any attachment to self and possessions. The egoism and selfishness that make individuals unsatisfied are the same realities that define social, economic, and political structures and processes in ways that lead to an unsatisfied society. Letting go of egoism and selfishness can quench *duḥkha* for individuals and society. To achieve this letting go, people must find a "right understanding" of life, the first step in the Noble Eightfold Path. For Buddhadāsa, this right understanding involves the experience of emptiness, the voidness of independent selfhood. To see and judge the world in relation to oneself is the "ordinary view" of things. True insight reveals what Buddhadāsa calls "Nature," or the interdependent wholeness of existence in which every being is connected to all other beings. This insight into dependent arising is achieved, Buddhadāsa teaches, by study and strong concentration (*samādhi*) practice. It brings a right understanding that fosters the experience of freedom from self-concern and freedom to live for others in ways that quench both personal and social *duḥkha*. In the words of Buddhadāsa:

> Buddhists aim to penetrate deeply into the inner Nature, the spiritual Nature, the Nature which is the Law of Nature, which is the source of everything. We try to study so that we realize the Nature within which is called "Dhamma-element" (*dhammadhātu*), namely, the law of dependent coorigination or conditionality. If we realize this Nature, we have no way that selfishness can happen.[3]

For Buddhadāsa, capitalism is an economic system that reinforces inner egoism and selfishness, and thereby the negative states of consciousness that produce personal and social *duḥkha*. Capitalism is based on competitive individualism that ignores the mutually interdependent world and the value of selflessness. Instead, it pits one person against another in the struggle for personal gain. Buddhism, Buddhadāsa taught, implies a life dedicated to mutual benefit and support, caring for the needy and the poor, and working together unselfishly for peace and prosperity for all beings. So, being mindful of the negative effects of capitalism on society and following the Buddhist way of wise and compassionate living can bring both social and personal transformation. Buddhist practices, such as mindfulness and loving kindness, can help persons discover their wholesome mind and society regain its healthy peacefulness. By establishing more positive forms of social living, one is not only changing society for the better but is also overcoming the inner egoism that produces personal *duḥkha* and blinds one to the liberating truth about life.

One of Buddhadāsa's students who has sought to build healthy communities based on his teachers principles is Sulak Sivaraksa. Sulak is especially concerned about the effect of powerful national and international economic interests on Thai cities and villages and on the environment throughout the countryside. These interests have created an economy that has driven subsistence farmers and fishermen from their villages into the cities where they live in slum conditions. These same interests have deforested much of Thailand. Forty years ago, 80 percent of Thailand was forest; today that number has been seriously reduced. The loss of topsoil by erosion and the destruction of water sources have worsened the plight of those living in the countryside. Some families are driven to sell their daughters to the prostitution industry that is thriving in Bangkok.

As a leading Thai lay Buddhist intellectual, Sulak has founded a number of organizational networks that seek to address these problems. The Asian Cultural Forum on Development (ACFD) was founded in 1977 as an international interfaith network for human development among the urban and rural poor. The focus of their human development programs is not on economic growth that serves only the interests of investors in the Thai economy. Rather, for the ACFD, human development means linking the Thai

---

BOX 10.1

A Socially Engaged Buddhist

The Assembly of the Poor in Siam (Thailand) is what we call a "people's organization," a type of movement with increasing influence among NGOs. The Assembly of the Poor unites the villagers, fishermen and -women, small-scale farmer families, and crafts folks who lost their livelihood because of a series of dams now obstructing their Pak Moon River. The homes of some thirty thousand persons have been flooded. Not far from the point where the Pak Moon River joins the Mekong River, near the border with Laos, the major giant dam has been constructed. At this place, the villagers who organized themselves as the Assembly of the Poor erected a bamboo protest-village.

The World Commission on Dams, an independent commission that scientifically assesses the impact of this type of mega-project, found that the series of Pak Moon dams would not fulfill their purpose, namely, providing energy production for urban-industrial needs and irrigation for chemical farming. Soon after that finding, the protest-village of the Assembly of the Poor was set afire.

But, direct violence is not my main worry. My deepest concern is "structural violence." Our world is ruled by anonymous powers systematically manipulating our consciousness to believe that material growth is the ultimate goal in life. Global corporate structures have become more powerful than many nations. Nations have been made to compete amongst each other in seeking ever greater economic development, no matter what the cost to people's lives. The poor nations compete to provide cheap labor in what is called a "race to the bottom." This global development has destroyed most of the traditional, self-sufficient, and sustainable rural community-life on earth. The Assembly of the Poor is but one example.

What can we do? In "Engaged Buddhism," we try to practice interrelatedness or "inter-being." I know that I am part of the struggle of the villagers. Our growing group of spiritual friends attempts to support the villagers. I also know that I am part of the suppressing powers: the rich middle class and elites seeking an increasingly greedy urban lifestyle. So, we must try to change minds and seek new and more just alternatives for the good of all people. This can be done through self-critical awareness and dialogue, through critical, direct, spiritual dialogue among human beings across all social and cultural boundaries.

For example, in our Ariyavinaya project, Buddhist monastics (monks and nuns), laypersons, students, artists, media experts, environmentalists, and business people engage in critical dialogue. Together we rethink the *Vinaya* (code of conduct; discipline) within a contemporary perspective and an intercultural context. We also include like-minded friends from other religious traditions in the process.

There are alternatives to what is going on in the world today. We just have to change our minds and hearts through dialogue across all boundaries. Then, we can work to realize our future together.

SULAK SIVARAKSA

Director, Santi Pracha Dhamma Institute
Bangkok, Thailand

people together in ways that provide for their economic needs, while conserving their resources, protecting their environment, and promoting cultural values and social harmony. Other network organizations founded by Sulak pursue these ideals through educational programs for children in slums, rice banks for farmers, urban community health work, human rights activities, and protecting forests from more clearcutting.

To guide these efforts, Sulak proposes a modern reinterpretation of the principles of Buddhism. One example has to do with the Five Precepts. The first precept, not to take life, is interpreted to mean not to deprive people of a decent living, deplete the soil, contaminate the water, pollute the air, destroy the forests, or consume wastefully while people die of starvation. The second precept, not to steal, is extended to mean opposing inappropriate development that robs people and their land and rejecting economic systems that produce poverty and exploitation of the poor. The third precept, no sexual misconduct, is expanded to mean opposing the widespread exploitation of women in Thailand, especially as prostitutes. The fourth precept, no lying, is said to mean not to use false and misleading statements in the media and hedonistic images in advertising, which generate a consumer culture that believes in the lie that happiness can be found in obtaining consumer goods. Finally, the fifth precept, no intoxicants, is interpreted to mean overcoming social and economic factors, such as unemployment, poverty, and unequal opportunity, which lead to despair and thereby spawn addictive behavior.

Sulak, like Ariyaratne, sees the Four Grounds of Kindness—generosity, kindly speech, useful work, and equality—as guidelines for restructuring one's consciousness for responsible social action. This restructuring of consciousness, Sulak says, brings emotional and intellectual freedom from the three roots of *duḥkha*: greed and materialism, hatred and violence, and delusion about the interrelated nature and value of life. Such inner freedom not only helps one advance to the ultimate spiritual experience of Nirvana but can also be put into practice in seeking social freedom. This restructuring of human consciousness with wisdom insight and compassion is also, for Sulak, the essence of Buddhism:

> You don't have to profess . . . faith, you don't have to worship the Buddha, you don't have to join in any ceremonies. What is important is that you grow in mindfulness and awareness. You try to restructure your consciousness to become more selfless, to be able to relate to other people more meaningfully in order that friendship will be possible and exploitation impossible. To me the essence of Buddhism is this.[4]

Cambodia

During the rule of the Khmer Rouge from 1975 to 1979, two to three million Cambodians died of starvation, disease, overwork, torture, or execution. All of Cambodia's 3600 Buddhist temples were destroyed, and afterwards only three thousand of its fifty thousand Buddhist monastics survived. During those years, Samdech Preah Maha Ghosananda, now the Supreme Patriarch of Buddhism in Cambodia, established temples in each of the Cambodian refugee camps in Thailand. Since that time, he has also established temples in each of the major Cambodian resettlement communities around the world. Called the "Gandhi of Cambodia," Ghosananda has organized "peace walks" against land minds, peace and reconciliation initiatives with the Khmer Rouge, and other activities that have earned him recent nominations for the Nobel Peace Prize. He presently directs the Dhammayietra Center for Peace and Nonviolence in Cambodia.

Ghosananda teaches that the whole human family is progressing toward peace, humankind's "fullest flowering." For this social goal to be reached, each person of every religion must begin his or her journey to peace each day by experiencing peace in his or her heart and then sharing it with others. When asked what he was doing when he was meditating in a temple-hut in a refugee camp, he answered that he was finding peace in his heart to share with others. For Ghosananda, this sharing of peace should be directed to everyone, even one's "unwholesome" enemies, who, he says, need it most. By loving one's enemies with peacemaking, one can stop the cycle of violence and retaliation. The loving service of peacemaking can, Ghosananda believes, lift the ignorant world into the light of liberating truth. So for him, living the Dharma today involves both the development of inner peace and the sharing of that peace with others through loving kindness.

To those who say that Buddhist monks and nuns should stay in their temples and not become involved in social action, Ghosananda replies:

> Many Buddhists are suffering—in Tibet, Cambodia, Laos, Burma, Vietnam, and elsewhere. The most important thing that we Buddhists can do is to foster the liberation of the human spirit in every nation of the human family. We must use our religious heritage as a living resource. . . . We Buddhists must find the courage to leave our temples and enter the temples of contemporary human experience, temples that are filled with suffering. . . . The refugee camps, the prisons, the ghettos, and the battlefield will become our temples. . . . [W]e monks must respond to the increasing loud cries of suffering. We only need to remember that our temple is with us always. We *are* our temple.[5]

Those who follow Ghosananda teach peacemaking and loving kindness by example, through caring for the sick, the dying, prisoners, and the hungry. They also teach those who are the victims of oppression and injustice that the very anger and desire for revenge that they feel is what caused the injustice in the first place. Therefore, one must cultivate inner peace and loving kindness to combat the roots of injustice—ignorance and selfish desires—as a prelude to true social engagement. To achieve this cultivation, Ghosananda recommends the practice of insight meditation. This practice enables one to see how the unwholesome factors of mind, like anger, hatred, and lustful desire, arise from perceptions interpreted through the lenses of ignorant viewpoints. This insight gives one freedom from being caught in patterns of thoughts, words, and actions that produce violence. Along with insight meditation, Ghosananda recommends that one meditate on the Four Divine Abodes. Then one can meditate on the body in a way that brings about self-control, overcomes fear for one's self, and produces vigilance. One is thereby more enabled to share peace and love vigilantly for others, being freed from hurtful thoughts about others and free from fearfulness about oneself.

Vietnam

At the age of seventeen, Thich Nhat Hanh entered a Thiên (Zen) monastery in Hue, Vietnam. His training included aspects from both the Theravāda and Thiên traditions with emphasis on mindfulness and *kōan* practice. Nhat Hanh also studied at Saigon University and Princeton. After his studies in the West, he returned to Vietnam and founded the School of Youth for Social Service, which would become one of the primary organizations for Buddhist social engagement during the Vietnam War. In 1965, he founded the "Order of Interbeing" as a new branch of Thiên Buddhism. This Order has brought together lay and monastic Buddhists for training in liberating practice and social engagement. Nhat Hanh's work for peace, healing, and reconciliation and his refusal to take sides in the war were seen as threatening by the governments of both North and South Vietnam. While traveling in the West in the late 1960s, Nhat Hanh was advised not to return to Vietnam. So he directed the Vietnamese Buddhist Peace Delegation in Paris until the end of the war. After the war was over, Nhat Hanh spent several years in retreat in southern France before continuing his leadership of the Order of Interbeing and an active life of publishing, lecturing, and offering workshops throughout the world. While he would like very much to return to his beloved Vietnam, until now the Vietnamese government has not given Nhat Hanh a visa.

During the Vietnam War, Nhat Hanh and the Buddhist social movement in Vietnam refused to side with either the North or the South. Instead they called for a negotiated political, rather than military, solution to the war. This position was embraced by the vast majority of the Vietnamese people in the South, but not by the American government or the government of the South. It was a position that Buddhist leaders took in solidarity with the peasants and masses of people of Vietnam, who were victims of an ideological fight between communism and anti-communism that they did not understand. For example, peasants in villages were told by the Viet Cong to dig caves for their soldiers. If they did not, they were punished. But if they did, they were punished by the South Vietnamese government forces. The Buddhists also saw the American servicemen and servicewomen as victims of the war. For the good of all involved, they felt that the war must come to a negotiated end as soon as possible.

Working for an end to the war, Buddhists practiced many forms of humanistic action. They evacuated villagers caught in cross-fire; they established cease-fire lines outside villages; they worked to reconstruct villages and rebuild buildings destroyed in battles; they cared for orphans and provided basic medical care for everyone. The most dramatic act was self-immolation. While not sanctioned by any Buddhist group, and not part of any Buddhist program of action, these acts occurred at unexpected moments when a person was unable to bear the suffering of those around him or her and wanted to do something to move the hearts of those causing the suffering.

The various actions on behalf of the suffering victims of the war supported by Buddhist activists were motivated by an empathy stemming from the Buddhist insight that there is no separation between oneself and the person who is suffering. They believed that given the interdependence of life, all persons, including the Viet Cong, the innocent villagers, and the American soldiers, are intertwined victims in the web of violent suffering. Inspired by mindfulness of this interrelatedness, and by meditation generating selfless loving kindness and compassion, Buddhists sought to be makers of peace for the mutual benefit of all. After the war was over, the Buddhist activists hoped they could cooperate with the new communist regime in healing and reconciling the country. However, the new rulers, fearful of the influence Buddhists had over the population, suppressed their organizations and activities, and Buddhist leaders were often detained and even tortured and imprisoned.

In the West, Nhat Hanh continues to share with the world the Vietnamese experience of engaged Buddhist spirituality through his Order of Interbeing. Nhat Hanh has helped people see that experiential insight into the interbeing of life, or the dependent arising of life, frees one from preoccupation with one's own suffering and releases one's loving kindness and compassion for others. This message is expressed in one of the often-quoted poems of Nhat Hanh, "Please Call Me By My True Names":

Do not say that I'll depart tomorrow
because even today I still arrive.

Look deeply: I arrive in every second
to be a bud on a spring branch,
to be a tiny bird, with wings still fragile,
learning to sing in my new nest,
to be a caterpillar in the heart of a flower,
to be a jewel hiding itself in a stone.

I still arrive, in order to laugh and to cry,
in order to fear and to hope,
the rhythm of my heart is the birth and
death of all that are alive.

I am the mayfly metamorphosing on the
surface of the river,

and I am the bird which, when spring comes,
arrives in time to eat the mayfly.

I am the frog swimming happily in the
clear water of a pond,
and I am also the grass-snake who
approaching in silence,
feeds itself on the frog.

I am the child in Uganda, all skin and bones,
my legs as thin as bamboo sticks,
and I am the arms merchant, selling deadly
weapons to Uganda.

I am the 12-year-old girl, refugee
on a small boat,
who throws herself into the ocean after
being raped by a sea pirate,
and I am the pirate, my heart not yet capable
of seeing and loving.

I am a member of the politburo, with
plenty of power in my hands,
and I am the man who has to pay his
"debt of blood" to my people
dying slowly in a forced labor camp.

My joy is like spring, so warm it makes
flowers bloom in all walks of life.
My pain is like a river of tears, so full it
fills up the four oceans.

Please call me by my true names,
so I can hear all my cries and my laughs
at once,
so I can see that my joy and pain are one.

Please call me by my true names,
so I can wake up,
and so the door of my heart can be left open,
the door of compassion.[6]

To foster this insight into interbeing, Nhat Hanh recommends mindfulness as pure observation of the present moment by which one sees through
the pain in life to the hidden wonder of interrelatedness. One of the ways
to bring one's mindfulness into the present moment with pure observation

is, according to Nhat Hanh, by attending to one's breathing. Then, deeper
forms of meditation lead one to a fuller insight into one's mind, a letting go
of the burdens one finds and discovering there the interbeing of life. Thereby,
one is in touch not only with humanity's shared suffering existence, but also
with an even deeper source of inner peace to give to others. Nhat Hanh, like
Ghosananda, stresses that the peace experienced in one's mind and heart is
to be lived with one's body. Being peace for others requires inner healing;
and that peace given to others is also healing for them.

This journey of healing experience and social ministry is guided in the Order of Interbeing by the Fourteen Precepts, which can be summarized in the
following way. First is not to absolutize any belief in a way that blocks
growth in understanding and leads to fanaticism. Second is always to continue to learn by observing self and world. Third is not to force anyone to
adopt one's own viewpoint. Fourth is to be aware of suffering in oneself and
others. Fifth is to live simply and avoid greed, the pursuit of fame and sensual pleasure. Sixth is to let go of anger and hatred by the practice of meditation and to live compassionately for others, especially those who have
wronged one. Seventh is to return to one's true self by breathing practice,
meditation, and mindfulness. Eighth is to use language to build unity and
not to divide people. Ninth is to purify speech with truthfulness. Tenth is
not to use the community for personal gain or for political purposes.
Eleventh is to pursue a livelihood that does not harm life. Twelfth is not to
kill living beings. Thirteenth is not to possess things that belong to others.
Fourteenth is to preserve the vital energies of our body for the realization
of the Dharma. These precepts, fashioned from the Noble Eightfold Path in
the violent experience of Vietnam, give the world a Buddhist guide for spiritual growth, healing, reconciliation, and peacemaking in the midst of the
many difficulties of modern life.

Tibet

Since the Chinese military overthrow of the Tibetan government in 1959, the
Dalai Lama has lived in the village of Dharamsala in northern India. There
are now almost one hundred thousand Tibetan refugees in northern and
southern India who have escaped the dire situation in their homeland. This
tragic situation, which we introduced in Chapter 6, includes the death of
more than one million Tibetans; two five-year periods of famine and starvation; the pillage and sale of much of Tibet's cultural, religious, and artistic treasures; the destruction of more than six thousand monasteries, temples, and religious sites; the systematic torture of Tibetan prisoners including
monks and nuns; the clearcutting of Tibetan forests; the depletion of Tibet's
wildlife; and the massive repopulation of Tibet with Chinese immigrants.

In light of this experience of ethnic and antireligious violence against the
Tibetan people, the Dalai Lama with his government in exile has used Buddhist ideals to guide the global Tibetan liberation movement. Rejecting coun-
terviolence, the Dalai Lama has sought to engage the Chinese government

in negotiations. He has suggested what is now his famous Five Point Peace Plan:

1. Transformation of the whole of Tibet into a zone of peace.
2. Abandonment of China's population transfer policy that threatens the very existence of the Tibetans as a people.
3. Respect for the Tibetan people's fundamental human rights and democratic freedoms.
4. Restoration and protection of Tibet's natural environment and the abandonment of China's use of Tibet for the production of nuclear weapons and dumping of nuclear wastes.
5. Commencement of earnest negotiations on the future of Tibet and of relations between the Tibetan and Chinese peoples.[7]

Although China has not given any positive response to this plan, the Dalai Lama was awarded the Nobel Peace Prize in 1989.

What are the Buddhist ideals that guide the Tibetan liberation movement's peacemaking? The virtues of loving kindness and compassion challenge the movement to have compassion for the Chinese, who are bringing karmic harm to themselves by oppressing the Tibetans. Also, one's enemies can provide an opportunity to expand one's loving kindness to all living beings. Thus, the movement pursues options that embody care for the Chinese as well as for the Tibetan people. The ideal of living the Dharma guides the movement's attempt to bring the truth of what their people are undergoing to all nations. The Dharma implies a faith that insight into the truth can expose and overcome evil, both in one's own mind and in society. This belief supports the movement's hope, against great odds, for a peaceful and equitable solution to the Tibetan problem. Many people feel that this hope is dependent on international support that can influence the Chinese government. In the meantime, the Tibetan diaspora is attempting to preserve Tibetan culture and religion by finding safe havens elsewhere in the world.

The Buddha taught that misery comes from within the human mind and heart when they are influenced by greed and ignorance. Therefore, the Dalai Lama teaches that each religion must provide an inner transformation of mind for its members in ways that stress a sense of universal fellowship, attitudes of compassion and love for all persons, and insight into the oneness of humankind. When people of all faiths realize the unity of the one human family, extend a sense of fellowship to all persons, and develop the virtues of love and compassion, they will have a moral foundation on which to live and work together for the well-being of all humankind through interfaith collaboration. Indeed, most of the recent Buddhist reformers agree that Buddhism alone cannot solve all the problems facing humankind. So, people like Ariyaratne, Buddhadāsa, Sulak, Ghosananda, and others emphasize the importance of interfaith dialogue leading to mutual understanding and respect as a basis for interfaith collaboration for the good of all peoples.

The Dalai Lama also believes that the particular Buddhist experience of the emptiness of any independent entities also supports peacemaking. While one may distinguish different peoples and their cultures, they are all equal in that they are diverse parts of the wholeness of life. All people are equally entitled to be free from suffering and to enjoy happiness. With this insight into the equality of self and other, one can, the Dalai Lama teaches, find the basis for mutual recognition of human rights and mutual cooperation for the good of all persons. A corollary to this view is that any violence against others is to be rejected. While anger-motivated violence may remove the offending party, it does not produce the ethical mutuality that is needed for reconciliation and peace. Violent action may be a short-term answer to a problem, but violence cannot sow the seeds of peace, just the seeds of resentment and more violence. What can bring a more lasting peace is the right understanding of the problem along with a wise and compassionate program of responsible and just change for all involved. While this program of the Dalai Lama may take longer to realize, he believes that it will provide a more lasting peace for everyone.

The following are the words of the Dalai Lama regarding traditional Buddhist experience and modern peacebuilding:

> When we rise in the morning and listen to the radio or read the newspaper, we are confronted with the same sad news: violence, crime, wars, and disasters. I cannot recall a single day without a report of something terrible happening somewhere. . . . According to Buddhist psychology, most of our troubles are due to our passionate desire for and attachment to things that we misapprehend as enduring entities. The pursuit of the objects of our desire and attachment involves the use of aggression and competitiveness as supposedly efficacious instruments. These mental processes easily translate into actions, breeding belligerence as an obvious effect. Such processes have been going on in the human mind since time immemorial, but their execution has become more effective under modern conditions. What can we do to control and regulate these "poisons"–delusion, greed, and aggression? For it is these poisons that are behind almost every trouble in the world. . . . [C]ompassion is what we must strive to cultivate in ourselves, and we must develop it from a limited amount to the limitless [compassion for all sentient beings]. . . . Further, the Tibetan Buddhist tradition teaches us to view all sentient beings as our dear mothers and to show our gratitude by loving them all. For, according to Buddhist theory, we are born and reborn countless times, and it is conceivable that each being has been our parent at one time or another. In this way all beings in the universe share a family relationship. . . . When you train in this sort of outlook, a true sense of compassion—a true sense of love and respect for others—becomes possible. . . . Another result of spiritual development, most useful in day-to-day life, is that it gives a calmness and presence of mind. . . . When faced with a calm and clear mind, problems can be successfully resolved. . . . Thus the practice of compassion and wisdom is useful to all, especially to those responsible for running national affairs, in whose hands lie the power and opportunity to create the structure of world peace.[8]

China

In 1949, when the Republic of China was established in Taiwan, some of the senior Buddhist leaders in mainland China moved to the island. Since that

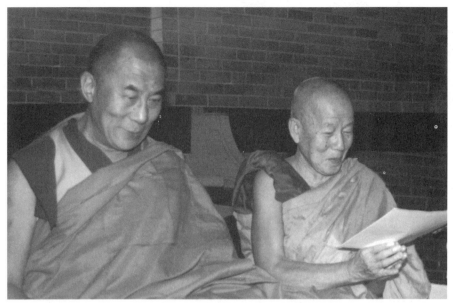

Figure 10.1. His Holiness Tenzin Gyatso, The Fourteenth Dalai Lama, and Samdech Preah Maha Ghosananda, the Supreme Buddhist Patriarch of Cambodia at Gethsemani Abbey in 1996, Trappist, Kentucky.

time, Taiwan has experienced a Buddhist revival. There are now thousands of Buddhist temples and organizations in Taiwan, and many of these organizations have been sending missionaries overseas. Over ten thousand men and women monastics have been ordained between 1951 and 1987. Of these new monastics, between 60 and 70 percent are women.

Perhaps the best known of these woman monastics is the Ven. Cheng Yen, founder of the largest charitable organization in Taiwan, the Compassion Relief Tzu Chi Foundation. When Cheng Yen was twenty-three years old, she left home to become a Buddhist nun. Her master was the highly revered Dharma Master Yin Shun. Living simply and pursuing a life of helping the poor, Cheng Yen became convinced and taught that the reason there is so much strife in the world is that people have not awakened to an innate and universal love. If they did awaken to and act out that love, this world, she teaches, will become a "Pure Land of peace and joy." Cheng Yen says, "If we remember that all creatures in the universe are one, we will know how to let go of our egotism. . . .We will then return to the true, clear essence of our human nature, and from the depths of our hearts will arise a reverent love for all beings."[9]

In 1966, Cheng Yen founded the Tzu Chi Compassion Relief Association to help the poor. In 1980, she founded the Tzu Chi Foundation with its eight missions. First is charity work, whereby the members provide food and other necessities as well as medical care and spiritual support to those in need. Second, the Tzu Chi medical care network includes four hospitals in Taiwan, with two more under construction, and a system of mobile free clin-

---

BOX 10.2

RELIGION AND LOVE

Whenever someone asks me for a definition of religion, I reply that it is an education in the purpose of life. What we call Buddhism is in fact the teachings of the enlightened sage Śākyamuni Buddha that guide us along the path toward attaining release, peace, and joy.

Far from stressing the abstruse or esoteric, these teachings instruct us to "actually go and do." While caring for humanity and all living beings we become aware of our own shortcomings and learn bravely to face worldly suffering. From this, love and wisdom arise, and the long-indifferent heart softens.

Therefore, all Tzu Chi people and I make the same wish each year, asking not for good health, but for wisdom and clarity; asking not for a lighter burden, but for greater strength; asking not for everything to go as one wishes, but for perseverance and courage.

Life without love is swathed in darkness. Only love equally and selflessly given can transcend political, racial, cultural, and religious boundaries. Hence, I sincerely want to extend my gratitude and respect to all those who have made contributions and have striven for a better world. Respect for the glory of all life immediately allows every person to become a compassionate living Buddha.

When a drop of water falls in the midst of a desert, it quickly evaporates without a trace. However, were it to fall into an ocean, that same drop of life would never dry up. May the love in each of us converge into a vast ocean of love, which can then be given to everyone in the world without end.

DHARMA MASTER CHENG YEN

Buddhist Compassion Relief Tzu Chi Foundation
Taiwan

---

ics in many other countries as well. Their doctors are trained to treat the whole person as they would a member of their own family.

The third mission is education. Besides teaching young people about caring for others, the foundation is building an educational system from kindergarten to graduate schools. Tzu Chi also works at educating the wealthy in Taiwan society by showing how giving to those in need and devoting one's life to the service of others are more meaningful than pursuing fame and fortune. Fourth is a cultural mission, which is also related to education. The Tzu Chi Foundation publishes books, magazines, and newspapers that bring their values to a broader audience. They also have a cable television station in Taiwan that broadcasts true stories of compassion and service.

The fifth mission of Tzu Chi, their bone-marrow donor registry, is now the world's third largest. Tzu Chi as of this writing has handled over 250 transplants worldwide. The sixth mission of the Tzu Chi Foundation is their international relief work. Relief teams travel to disaster areas around the world, where they distribute relief supplies. They have traveled to Mainland China, Cambodia, Rwanda, Ethiopia, Afghanistan, Kosovo, and over fifty other countries.

The final two mission areas are environmental protection and community volunteerism. In all these areas, Tzu Chi members are inspired by the bodhisattva ideal and try to live by the teachings of the Buddha. They seek to change the world by starting with themselves. For example, in their environmental work, members collect, sort, and recycle garbage. They are not only trying to help the environment and keep it clean, but are also humbling themselves in order to overcome pride. From just thirty original members in Taiwan, Tzu Chi now includes four million members throughout the world.

Another large new Buddhist organization in Taiwan is the Fo Guang Shan Buddhist Order. Founded by Grand Master Hsing Yün, Fo Guang Shan has millions of followers and has established 120 temples in Taiwan and other countries. In the United States, their central site is the Hsi Lai Temple in Hacienda Heights, California.

Hsing Yün entered Buddhist monastic life at the age of twelve. He went on to become the forty-eighth Patriarch of the Lin-chi lineage of Ch'an Buddhism in China. When Hsing Yün went to Taiwan, he did not just propagate traditional Ch'an Buddhism. Given his experience of war and poverty in China, he sought to revitalize Buddhism, making it more responsive to the needs of the modern world. Hsing Yün developed what he calls "Humanistic Buddhism," which seeks to link religious practice with ethical daily living and working for positive social change. For example, meditation and chanting are balanced with integrating the human qualities of the Four Divine Abodes into daily life, whether one is a monastic or a layperson. This spiritually based moral living then is given expression in social action that seeks to change the world and build the Pure Land in our midst. Humanistic Buddhism grounds and guides this task through the cultivation of the experience of wisdom, whereby one can see more clearly the Buddha-nature in all one serves. In this grounding, we see a joining of contemplation with action, a balance between moral living, social service, and inner growth that is central to many forms of modern Buddhism in Asia.

The following are Hsing Yün's words about his approach to Buddhist living and its relationship to Humanistic Buddhism. Note his reference to T'ai Hsü, whom we introduced in Chapter 7.

> Living in our bustling, intense, turbulent, and chaotic contemporary society, we need to find something that can set our impetuous minds at ease. . . . Ch'an reflects wisdom, humor, and compassion. It can prevent the formation of wishful and vexing thoughts. Guided by the ease, humor, profundity, and liberating nature of Ch'an, one will not be bothered by unkind words, awkward behavior, or painful memories of the past. They will simply vanish like mist and smoke.
>
> Ch'an raises life to the level of art. It manifests the perfection of life by revealing the original nature that underlies all phenomena. Ch'an's exquisite teaching is not confined to temples. . . . It belongs to every family and to every

human being. Everyone is in need of its wisdom, spontaneity, freedom, and ethics in his or her daily life.

Ch'an, if applied in our daily lives, would be like a ship in the sea of suffering. It would be like a bright light in the darkness. At the same time, it would serve as true medicine for the illnesses of our world.

People in the world focus their lives on materialism, personal interests, fame, and power. They do not realize that all such matters are in constant flux. Therefore, how can they dwell in peace?

Ch'an is not a theory, but rather, it is life. When Ch'an is implemented into daily life, people will respect and dwell in harmony with each other.

Where is the Pure Land for a Ch'an practitioner? It is in the performing of lowly tasks. It is in the love for and salvation of others. It is also in the transformation of one's surroundings.[10]

Humanistic Buddhism is not a new kind of Buddhism: it is simply a name used to emphasize the core teachings of the Buddha. The Buddha taught wisdom and compassion. These teachings always lead us back to the lives of other sentient beings. To not understand the unity of human nature and Buddha nature is to not understand the teachings of the Buddha. Humanistic Buddhism encourages us to participate in the world and be a source of energy that is beneficial to others. Our enlightenment depends on others, just as their enlightenment depends of us. Master T'ai Hsü said that we can achieve Buddhahood *only* by fulfilling our humanity.[11]

Fo Guang Shan emphasizes the need for Buddhism to meet people's spiritual and physical needs here and now to build the Pure Land in this world. Thus in Taiwan, thousands of monks and nuns of the order work together with committed and well-educated lay members in a number of projects for the betterment of Taiwan society and for world peace. They have a free medical clinic with mobile units to reach remote villages. They also have founded orphanages, homes for the elderly, social service agencies that provide food and clothing to the poor, and wildlife areas for the benefit of other living beings. Given their belief that education is a way to better people's lives, they have twelve libraries, four Buddhist universities, thirteen Buddhist colleges, elementary and high schools, as well as Sunday schools, adult education programs, and summer education camps for youths.

Hsing Yün has also revised the traditional Buddhist monastic educational system to make it more responsive to the modern world. This system of education is said to focus on the head, heart, and hands: to learn the Dharma, to develop the wise and caring qualities of the Buddha, and to serve society compassionately in practical ways. In terms of learning the Dharma, Fo Guang Shan teaches both Theravāda and Mahāyāna Buddhism to both monastics and lay Buddhists. It blends traditional Buddhist subjects with modern subjects such as psychology, sociology, and literature. It also provides internship programs in such practical areas like public relations, business administration, and social services. In terms of religious practice for the mind and the heart, Fo Guang Shan offers different traditions of Buddhist practices for laypersons as well as monastics. Commonly, practice entails *sūtra* recitation, chanting and meditation (including both Ch'an and insight meditation), seven-day meditation retreats, pilgrimages to holy sites, guidance in the precepts, and biweekly repentance ceremonies. These first two parts of Fo Guang Shan's educational curriculum can be seen as combating the materialism and secularism of modern society.

In terms of using one's hands for the benefit of others, Fo Guang Shan administers many social services in Taiwan. Through their Buddha's Light International Society (BLIS), they also support human development internationally. This international action is seen by them as a way of contributing to the Pure Land here on earth. To achieve this worldwide ideal, BLIS stresses the need to work together with all forms of Buddhism in a kind of Buddhist ecumenism that respects diversity while emphasizing harmony between different traditions and practices. BLIS recognizes that while Buddhists can build unity with each other for the good of humankind, they also need to build unity with other religious traditions that are working for world peace. Therefore, Fo Guang Shan stresses the importance of interfaith dialogue and collaboration.

Korea

It is said that in 1916, Pak Chŏng-bin (1891–1943), better known as Sot'aesan, attained a great spiritual Awakening after many years of ascetic practice. Part of his experience was a vision of the future in which he saw many people in the twentieth century enslaved by the power of materialism, turning to violence, and forsaking moral and spiritual living, thus putting modern civilization in danger. Sot'aesan believed from what he saw that there was a need for a spiritual power based on enlightenment, faith, and morality to protect the dignity of humankind and justice in society. Upon reading the *Diamond Sūtra*, Sot'aesan concluded that the Dharma needed to be reformulated in order to be an effective force for modern spiritual renewal.

Sot'aesan presented an outline of his proposed doctrinal reforms and exchanged ideas about this reform with Buddhist monastics in Korea. Deciding that his reform required a new Buddhist order, the headquarters for such a reform order was begun in Iri, Korea, in 1924. The new order was named "The Research Society of the Buddha Dharma." In 1935, the Great Dharma Hall was built on the grounds of the headquarters, and the *Irwŏn-sang* was enshrined. The *Irwŏn-sang* is a unitary circle symbolizing *Dharmakāya* Buddha, which is seen to be the origin and original enlightened nature of all sentient beings, Awakening, and Nirvana. Branch temples were also established throughout Korea to bring this new movement to the general public. Later, renamed "Won Buddhism," referring to the unitary circle symbolizing the *Dharmakāya*, it became a major religion in Korea with over four hundred temples. Won Buddhism also has over thirty branch temples in Europe and the United States. Advocating interfaith cooperation between world religions to foster peace and unity, Won Buddhism has been a major contributor to international interfaith activities.

The Won Buddhist experience entails "Four General Platforms" as the bases for dealing with the social ills of modernity. First is "Right Enlightenment and Right Conduct." For Won Buddhism, the essence of the Buddha's enlightened mind, the *Dharmakāya*, is the pure and unchanging essence of all the ordinary and changing things in the universe. "Right Enlightenment" is the realization of this ultimate reality. In "Right Conduct," one reflects this reality that is clear, impartial, and compassionate in dealing with situations that would ordinarily make one greedy, angry, or confused. Thereby, one can use the power of the *Dharmakāya* to escape modern forms of delusion, overcome the temptations of modern materialism, and confront modern types of violence to humanity and the environment.

How does one attain this spiritual experience of *Dharmakāya* and its ethical power according to Won Buddhism? It is suggested that one follow the "Threefold Practice" of spiritual discipline. These three practices relate to the three parts of the Buddha's Noble Eightfold Path: morality, concentration, and wisdom. The first practice, "Mindful Karma Creation," is moral discipline cultivated in daily life and in formal sessions at training institutes. This formal training includes calling on the name of Amitābha Buddha, study of scripture, lectures, discussions, keeping a diary, repentance, and exercise of the precepts. The second practice, "Cultivation of Spirit," is meditation for the development of clear awareness and tranquillity, which are aspects of the essence of one's true mind, the *Dharmakāya*. By practicing Sŏn (Zen) meditation along with chanting to Amitābha Buddha, one can realize this clear and calm reality so as not to be blinded or disturbed by the materialistic desires and violence that attract and attack our modern world. The third practice, "Inquiry into Facts and Principles," is wisdom development that guides proper action. One can gain wisdom by studying the functioning of the *Dharmakāya* in the world. By pondering the seasons; the faces of nature; the realities of illness, birth, and death; and the qualities of goodness and peace, one can discern the *Dharmakāya* and better distinguish truth and goodness in daily affairs.

The second platform is called "Awareness of Beneficence and Its Recompense." Sot'aesan is said to have seen that in the modern world there would be a lack of respect and gratitude for life in its many forms. There would especially be discrimination against people based on social status, age, gender, and race. Won Buddhism teaches that the *Dharmakāya* is the source of the "Fourfold Beneficence" to which one owes his or her life. It says that by recognizing this fact, one can build peace and reconciliation in our modern world. The first beneficence is heaven and earth, which support all life forms with an impartial embrace that cares for all living beings. Gratitude to heaven and earth turns into a practice of grateful care for all people and other living beings. Second is the beneficence of parents, who gave life to their children. Gratitude in this case means to support one's own parents and the parents of all peoples as one would do for one's own. Third is the beneficence of one's fellow humans, animals, and plants. Gratitude for the support of our life by people, animals, and plants means to share with all living beings whatever one can to better their lives. Finally, the fourth beneficence is the law. "Law" here means religious and moral teachings, the principle of justice, and the particular laws that support a just and peaceful social order. Gratitude in this case means to follow the ways of spiritual and moral cultivation, live justly, and support social harmony and world peace.

The third platform is "Practical Application of the Buddha Dharma." Won Buddhism believes that today Buddhist principles must have practical application to daily affairs for the good of one's self, family, nation, and world. Therefore, Buddhism should become a powerful tool for both personal and social transformation. Finally, the fourth platform is "Selfless Service for Public Well-Being." This means living out the third platform in the spirit of Buddhist compassion embodied in the *bodhisattva* as an antidote for modern egoism, materialism, and consumerism. This bodhisattva-like selfless service is the inspiration for Won Buddhism's social engagement of the modern world.

In his *Scriptures of Won Buddhism*, Sot'aesan presents "The Essentials of Daily Cultivation." They begin with an explanation of how the Threefold Practice relates to the experience of *Dharmakāya*:

> Although there is no disturbance in the mind-ground [*Dharmakāya*] in its original nature, disturbances arise in accordance with the mental spheres; hence, set up the calmness (*samādhi*) of self-nature by keeping disturbances from arising.
>
> Although there is no delusion in the mind-ground in its original nature, delusions arise in accordance with the mental spheres; hence, set up the wisdom (*prajñā*) of self-nature by keeping delusions from arising.
>
> Although there is no defilement in the mind-ground in its original nature, defilements arise in accordance with the mental spheres; hence, set up the precepts (*śīla*) of self-nature by keeping defilements from arising.[12]

This Threefold Practice is complemented in The Essentials of Daily Cultivation with the practice of the Fourfold Beneficence and Selfless Service for Public Well-Being. Failure to pursue or achieve these ideals leads one to personal confession and prayer, and then to a return to further socially engaged practice.

Japan

One of the most successful and yet controversial modern Buddhist movements is Sōka Gakkai (Value Creation Society) of Japan. Tsunesaburō Makiguchi (1871–1944) and Jōsei Toda (1900–1958) founded what would become Sōka Gakkai before World War II, when both men were educators interested in value education.[13] During the war, they were imprisoned for refusing to participate in nationalistic Shintō worship. While Makiguchi died in prison, Toda spent his prison time reading and chanting the *Lotus Sūtra*. During that time, Toda felt that he was being chosen to spread the teachings of Nichiren for the good not only of Japan but the whole world. After the war, Sōka Gakkai was eventually developed as a lay movement associated with one of the smaller Nichiren sects, Nichiren Shōshū. As a lay movement, Sōka Gakkai offered a way of bettering one's life and a new and positive vision of the future to many struggling and disillusioned people in postwar Japan. However, many of the new Sōka Gakkai converts practiced an intense form of proselytizing of other Japanese Buddhists, an activity that contributed to the controversial status of Sōka Gakkai in Japan. Despite this, Sōka Gakkai's membership grew at an incredible rate; today it claims between eight and ten million adherents with over one million outside of Japan.

Sōka Gakkai uses Buddhism as a foundation for its projects for personal and global betterment. It believes that all persons possess Buddha-nature, but that people's minds and hearts are affected by the fact that they live in the age of the Degenerate Dharma. In other words, the negative karma of the modern age dominates people's lives. People can experience ten levels of consciousness that range from hellish states of anger, hatred, and greed on the one hand, to states of peace and happiness associated with Buddhahood on the other. While we have the potential for the latter, because of negative karma, our world is full of violent, ignorant, and tragic conditions fueled by the hellish states of people's minds. To build true peace in the world, one cannot just address particular social or political crises; one must also address the problems at their roots, in the human mind. One must free oneself from the lower states of mental bondage and achieve the higher states of mental freedom and Buddhahood by realizing one's Buddha-nature.

The methods of Nichiren Buddhism that Sōka Gakkai believes are strong enough to break this mental bondage include chanting of Nichiren's *mantra* to the *Lotus Sūtra* and using Nichiren's *maṇḍala* (the *Gohonzon*). The *mantra* is said to awaken a spiritual power in one's life that changes the mental and physical conditions in which one finds oneself. The *maṇḍala* is said to bring about an awareness of one's Buddha-nature that is ultimately the source of these positive mental and physical changes. Since one's Buddha-nature is shared by all living beings, its realization brings about a sense of connection to other people and to the natural environment. This sensitivity to others, and especially to the needs of others, impels one to work together with other persons to establish a peaceful and harmonious world in which all can be happy and prosper. This achievement, Sōka Gakkai teaches, will bring an end to the present cultures of division and violence by cutting their roots in the human mind and heart, as well as their expressions in such realities as war, unjust societies, economic poverty, and environmental exploitation.

Sōka Gakkai has attracted many modern urban people who are searching for fellowship in an impersonal secular world and are interested in crafting a better life for themselves and for humankind. Members meet in neighborhood groups that tend to each other's needs, giving advice and support with the problems of daily life. The different official organs of the international Sōka Gakkai movement, Sōka Gakkai International (SGI), present members in many countries with avenues to help build a better world. One such project in the United States is the Boston Research Center for the 21st Century, which sponsors programs with world experts on social, political, economic, and environmental problems and publishes materials that explore these problems and possible solutions. In regard to this goal, SGI has established peace education programs to foster face-to-face relations between peoples of opposing cultures and ideologies, programs to address environmental problems such as global warming and deforestation, and humanitarian programs to aid refugees, feed the hungry, and meet the needs of the poor.

In addressing these social and environmental issues, Sōka Gakkai stresses the need to change the way people experience themselves and the world. This personal change, Sōka Gakkai teaches, should lead to structural changes in society. To this end, Sōka Gakkai has entered the world of politics in Japan by forming, for example, the Kōmeitō Party. This move into politics is limited to Japan, and SGI does not become involved in politics in other countries, where it simply emphasizes value education and contributes to public awareness of social issues. In its social thought in Japan, the Sōka Gakkai proposes a "Buddhist Democracy" that affirms the freedom of capitalism, but balances it with a "human socialism." This human socialism recognizes the equality of all human beings and seeks to protect everyone from the negative effects of unchecked competitive capitalism. This, they believe, can be done by sharing the wealth of a nation with those in need through providing such benefits as adequate health care and housing and good education and job training. Again, convincing people that sharing with the less fortunate is a social good demands that they begin to experience the world from a less individualistic point of view. Hence the need for spiritual transformation.

The president of SGI, Daisaku Ikeda, describes the experience of spiritual transformation in function of world peace as follows:

> The practice of Buddhism is based on compassion. . . . [I]n Buddhism, compassion signifies the sublime endeavor to share the suffering of another from the stance of our common humanity and to create an expanding network of genuine friendship and trust.
>
> I perceive in Shakyamuni's compassion—elaborated and extolled in the Mahayana tradition as the Bodhisattva Way—a profound and unshakable humanism. The SGI is a body committed to developing activities in the areas of peace, culture and education based on this Buddhist humanism. The bedrock of the Buddhist spirit of humanism is reverence for all life, which discerns an incomparably precious "Buddha nature" inherent not only in humankind but in all living beings. . . .
>
> The bodhisattva, as a world citizen, is someone who is constantly challenging egotism and is engaged in the race to transform what Buddhism refers to as deluded impulses (represented by the three poisons of greed, anger, and stupidity) into enlightenment. Bodhisattvas, refusing to be engulfed in the consumerism and materialism of contemporary society, embrace a noble spirit of serving others, and pledge to make this their mission in life. This process sets in motion a fundamental change in life orientation—from egotism to the desire to create happiness for oneself and others.
>
> I believe that every religion should be promoting, according to its own methods, this kind of fundamental change in life from our contemporary materialism to a highly spiritual and humanistic culture. . . . Finally, I strongly hope

that the world's religions will use dialogue and exchange to resolve the multitude of problems that threaten the survival of humanity, and stress harmony and cooperation with the aim of creating a culture of peace.[14]

Another important Japanese movement is the Risshō Kōsei-kai (RKK). This lay Buddhist movement was founded in 1938 by Nikkyō Niwano (1906–1999) and Myōkō Naganuma (1989–1957). Its name means "Society for the Establishment of Righteousness and Friendly Relations." While under the guidance of Nikkyō Niwano, RKK emerged from a loose-knit Nichiren reform movement named Reiyukai, and has grown into a large international lay organization of over five million members dedicated to a broader understanding and application of the *Lotus Sūtra*. Niwano felt that the *Lotus Sūtra* presents the culmination of Gautama Buddha's teachings in a way that is universal, and therefore compatible with the world's religions. RKK concludes that by living the *Lotus Sūtra* in daily life, they can contribute to bringing all humankind to unity and peace. Indeed, Niwano was instrumental in the foundation of the World Conference on Religion and Peace (WCRP), the most important worldwide interfaith organization working for the betterment of humankind. Niwano also established the Niwano Peace Foundation in Japan and the Niwano Peace Prize at the United Nations.

RKK teaches that all persons have the Buddha-nature and can attain Buddhahood through faith and practice. One is enabled through RKK practice to deepen one's experience of wisdom, reflecting the Dharma in one's own life and by compassion into the lives of others. In terms of particular practices, the RKK stresses the Six Perfections and the Bodhisattva Path to liberation. One seeks guidance on this path in the *Lotus Sūtra*. To strengthen this practice, one can turn in faith to the Eternal Buddha. Chapter 16 of the *Lotus Sūtra* states that the historical Buddha was a manifestation of the Eternal Buddha, who has appeared in different forms over the ages to guide and aid beings toward liberation. While some Nichiren groups worship the sacred *maṇḍala*, RKK reserves worship for the Eternal Buddha and uses a *maṇḍala* only for liturgical focus. They also use *mantra* chanting not for obtaining any special power, but as an expression of prayerful gratitude to the Eternal Buddha. RKK believes that the Eternal Buddha fills the universe with his spiritual presence, communicating his mercy to all beings in need.

Community life is central to RKK. As one experiences his or her ignorance and selfish nature, one is led to repentance (*zange*) before the Eternal Buddha and the community. This act of faith entrustment unites the person with both the Eternal Buddha and the community in ways that heal and transform one's mind, speech, and action. The healing and transforming experience of the individual is strengthened by the RKK practice of *hōza*, or "Dharma sitting." People sit in circles to discuss their problems and questions and seek solutions in the principles of Buddhism presented in the *Lotus Sūtra*. Guided by a trained facilitator, the *hōza* circle addresses issues having to do with work, family life, relationships, religion, and ethics. For *hōza* members, the Four Noble Truths are the "key" to this process. All members take on them-

Figure 10.2. The Great Sacred Hall; at the Risshō Kōsei-kai headquarters, Tokyo, Japan.

selves the problem of the troubled person. Then they seek together, from their own experience, the cause of the problem. With the help of the facilitator and the scriptures, they find a path to liberation from the problem, a liberation that brings extinction of the suffering. In the main temple in Tokyo alone, there are over two hundred *hōza* groups that meet each day.

Hōza practice gives people the opportunity to grow in wisdom in the context of compassionate community relationships. By making themselves one with those in need who share their troubles, RKK members move beyond self-centeredness, discover their interrelatedness, and compassionately connect with others. In this manner, they grow in their compassionate awareness of their own Buddha-nature, the Buddha-nature of the troubled person, and the Buddha-nature of all living beings. This communal way of developing enlightened awareness, compassion, and practical insight into solving the problems of modernity has become a model for RKK's activities of social engagement. That is, RKK has sought ways of helping people come together to address national and international problems with wisdom and compassion. This can be seen in the operational style of WCRP as well as in RKK's other projects such as the Overseas Assistance Program, which provides aid to persons in need of food, clothing, or shelter, especially in Southeast Asia.

Another good example of communal problem solving is RKK's Brighter Society Movement developed in the late 1960s. This movement is dedicated to bringing together leaders from the worlds of business, government, and religion in order to promote humanitarian activities. Some of these activities include blood donations, fund-raising for established charities, neighborhood renewal programs, and training for parents in crisis. For RKK, personal faith and practice are linked to collective collaboration for human betterment among religious leaders and all persons who are concerned about the many personal and social sources of suffering in the modern world. Nikkyō Niwano described his personal religious experience and his views concerning peace this way:

> Listening to lectures on the *Lotus Sūtra*, I realized that I had found what I had been looking for. The *Lotus Sūtra* was the perfect net in which to save everyone in the world. Physically and spiritually it could help both the individual and all of society. I was profoundly shaken by what I had learned. The impression made on me was of astonishing, vibrant freshness. It has remained fresh for over forty years. During that time, I have not missed reading the *Lotus Sūtra* a single day. And the text has lost none of its subtlety, none of its ability to reverberate in my heart and sink deeply into my spirit. On the contrary, the more I read the *sūtra*, the more impressive and profound it seems.[15]

> The practice of the Risshō Kōsei-kai is to seek to incorporate [the] Eightfold Path into their daily lives and to endeavor to be a motive force in bringing peace to the world. . . . To encourage others to develop peace in their hearts, we must dismantle the armor around our own hearts. . . . When we can face others with an open mind, they will relax . . . and open their hearts to us. Buddhism teaches this in its doctrine that all phenomena lie within a single thought, the doctrine of the Three Thousand Realms in One Mind. The thoughts we embrace, whether good or evil, are transmitted just as they are to others. . . . [T]he doctrine of Three Thousand Realms in One Mind [is] an expression of the essence of the Buddha's teachings in the *Lotus Sūtra*: all sentient beings can attain perfect enlightenment-Buddhahood, and the appropriate goal of believers is to attain enlightenment not only for themselves but for all sentient beings since individual salvation is not true salvation because no individual exists apart from the whole—all things are interconnected. Risshō Kōsei-kai members try to understand at the deepest level the practical doctrine of Three Thousand Realms in One Mind, that is, that it is necessary to improve themselves and practice this doctrine in order to help others.[16]

WOMEN'S EXPERIENCE OF BUDDHISM IN MODERN ASIA

We have now seen that Buddhism throughout Asia is facing a new era of challenges in the modern, often Westernized world. The socially engaged Buddhist movements throughout Asia that we have introduced in this chapter testify to the ongoing vitality of the Dharma and its ability to meet the challenges of modern life. These movements indicate that as Buddhism takes on new forms in the modern world, these forms are helping to redefine Buddhism, its contribution to building a better world, and its relationship with other religious traditions. In many of these movements, the role of women is also being redefined in ways that enable women to partake more fully of the Buddhist experience and give women greater opportunities to contribute to the institutional life of the Saṅgha.

For example, Fo Guang Shan has provided equal opportunities to men and women for education, training practice, and leadership. In Won Buddhism, men and women priests have equal status and independently establish and lead local temples. These kinds of changes support the voices of those who challenge the more traditional role of women in institutional Buddhism. These challenges in Asia are primarily two. First is the challenge to improve the status of women in the Saṅgha and to establish the full *bhikṣuṇi* (fully ordained women monastic) lineage where it has died out or has never been established. Second is the challenge to reform practices, teachings, and institutional structures that support sexist ideas or customs. To understand the force of these challenges, we need to look more closely at the experience of women in the Asian Saṅgha historically, especially in the modern world.

The women's order flourished in India until Buddhism's demise. From there, it was transmitted to Sri Lanka, Burma, and China. From China it was transmitted to Korea, Japan, and Vietnam. However, today it only survives intact in East Asia and Vietnam. In Sri Lanka, as we saw in Chapter 3, in the eleventh century both orders were devastated by war. When peace again returned to the country, the Sri Lankan king reinstated the men's but not the women's order. There is also no record of the women's order in Burma after the end of the thirteenth century, and there are no records of the women's order ever being introduced to other parts of Southeast Asia such as Thailand. There is debate as to whether the women's order was ever transmitted to Tibet, but most Tibetan scholars conclude that is was not.

On the other hand, even without the fully ordained women's order there have been women renunciants in recent centuries in Sri Lanka, Burma, Thailand, and Tibet. In Sri Lanka during the nineteenth century, some women took the Ten Precepts, shaved their heads, put on saffron and white robes, and lived in women's communities. These women, neither lay nor ordained, are called "Ten-Precept Women." As part of the Buddhist renewal in Sri Lanka in reaction to colonialism, these women not only studied and practiced meditation but also opened schools to educate young girls, counseled laypeople, cared for the sick, chanted Buddhist texts for the laity, and assisted at religious ceremonies. Recently, some have hoped that these women would become fully ordained monastics. However, most of Sri Lanka's two thousand Ten-Precept Women today are not interested in this because it would mean that they would become institutionally subordinated to the men's order and would be supervised by the government.

In Burma, there are thousands of women renunciates who keep either the Eight or the Ten Precepts. Called "Precept Keepers," these women, who shave their heads and wear robes, include a number of famous teachers and scholars. In 1961, there were an estimated eight thousand such women. Today, most live together in women's communities, practice chanting and meditation, study the Dharma, and collect alms. In Thailand, there are around ten thousand women renunciates who take the Five or Eight Precepts. These women are poorer and less organized than their sisters in Sri Lanka and Burma. Shaving their heads and wearing special white robes, they seek to renounce the world and devote themselves to serious practice and devotion. In 1969, an institute was founded dedicated to organizing these women, educating them more fully in the Dharma, and providing for their welfare. Finally, for centuries in Tibet, there have been renunciate women who have taken precepts and are regarded as permanent novices since there is no tradition of full ordination for women in Tibet. In 1959, there were twelve thousand such women, called *ani*, meaning "aunt." Like their Thai sisters, the *ani* have been more uneducated and live in poorer conditions than male monastics. However, in recent years Tibetan religious leaders have given them more training and have even encouraged them to seek full ordination as a way of raising their condition in the Saṅgha.

In terms restoring the women's order, there are a number of problems currently being addressed in Sri Lanka and Southeast Asia. For a woman to be ordained, she needs to go through a ceremony with a quorum of ten fully ordained women monastics, and then the same ceremony with a quorum of ten fully ordained men monastics. Many Sri Lankan and Southeast Asian monastic leaders claim that there are no fully ordained women monastics of the Theravāda lineage in the world. They do not accept the women's orders in Vietnam and East Asia as carrying on the Theravāda lineage. So, they argue, there cannot be any women's quorum, making it impossible to reestablish the woman's order. Other Buddhist leaders in those countries are more accepting of the existing East Asian women's orders and support using them to reestablish the women's order in their own countries. Since Tibetan Buddhism is Mahāyāna, this issue does not apply, and many Tibetan leaders are encouraging women to take ordination in East Asian women's orders.

In places where the Buddhist women's order does exist in the modern world, it is often flourishing. This is especially true in Korea and Taiwan, where women monastics are given much freedom and education, as well as opportunities to teach, engage in social services, and hold leadership positions. In the words of one such monastic, the Ven. Yifa:

> In Taiwan, Mahayana Buddhist nuns receive higher education, establish temples, give Buddhist lectures, conduct research, transmit Buddhist disciplinary precepts, manage temple economics, as well as manage and participate in various charitable programs such as free medical care, child care and services for senior citizens. These nuns have not only reformed the old traditional Buddhist monastic system, but have also proved to be equal with the male Buddhist practitioners. Consequently, in addition to advancing within the monastic hierarchy, the nuns have made many religious, educational and social contributions to society. Thus, they have helped to propel Buddhism into people's daily lives and thereby to purify Taiwan society.[17]

The lives and work of women like these provide models for those who call for the restoration of the women's order in other parts of the world. Rita M. Gross, a Western scholar and practitioner of Buddhism, makes it clear why the life of a woman Buddhist monastic can be very fulfilling in the modern world:

Contrary to outsiders' impressions of the limitations of being a nun, most nuns stress the freedom inherent in their lifestyle. . . . [T]hey can develop themselves fully and be available freely and as needed to provide service and support. The emphasis is not on losing an immediate family and a primary relationship, but on taking on a much wider, more inclusive network of relationships that will be healthier and less prone to conflict. Furthermore, nuns live in a supportive community of like-minded and like-spirited companions. . . . Nuns live a lifestyle dedicated to study and spiritual discipline. . . . The opportunity to pursue these goals single-mindedly in a community dedicated to such vocations sometimes seems almost utopian.[18]

In response to this possibility and the concerns and needs of Buddhist women monastics and renunciates, an organization was founded in 1987 named *Sakyadhītā* ("Daughters of the Buddha"). This International Association of Buddhist Women engages in many activities, including researching the *Vinaya* rules to find a way to restore the women's order in Theravāda countries and in Tibet. In the meantime, modern Buddhism in Asia continues to expand its diverse experience of inner and social transformation, building on enlightened insight and compassion for all forms of life and working with persons of all religions for a more united and peaceful global community. As we shall see in the next and final chapter, this spirit of renewal is also at work in Buddhist communities in the West.

Notes

1. B. R. Ambedkar, *The Buddha and His Dhamma*, Third Edition (Bombay: Siddharth Publications, 1984), p. 83.

2. A. T. Ariyaratne, "Sarvodaya Shramadana s Approach to Peacebuilding," in David W. Chappell, ed., *Buddhist Peacework: Creating Cultures of Peace* (Somerville, MA: Wisdom Publications, 1999), pp. 69–70, 75, 77.

3. Buddhadāsa, *Buddhists and the Conservation of Nature* (Bangkok: Komol Kimtong, 1990), p. 12; trans. Santikaro Bhikkhu in "Buddhadāsa Bhikkhu: Life and Society through the Natural Eyes of Voidness," in Christopher S. Queen and Sallie B. King, eds., *Engaged Buddhism: Buddhist Liberation Movements in Asia* (Albany, NY: SUNY Press, 1996), p. 162.

4. Sulak Sivaraksa, *A Socially Engaged Buddhism* (Bangkok: Thai Inter-Religious Commission for Development, 1988), p. 185.

5. Maha Ghosananda, "The Human Family," in Donald W. Mitchell and James Wiseman, O.S.B., eds., *The Gethsemani Encounter: A Dialogue on the Spiritual Life by Buddhist and Christian Monastics* (New York: Continuum Publishing Co., 1997), p. 139.

6. Thich Nhat Hanh, *Call Me By My True Names: The Collected Poems of Thich Nhat Hanh* (Berkeley, CA: Parallax Press, 1999), p. 72.

7. *Tibet Briefing* (New York: The Office of Tibet, 1991), pp. 10–11.

8. His Holiness Tenzin Gyatso The Fourteenth Dalai Lama, *A Human Approach to World Peace* (London: Wisdom Publications, 1984), pp. 3, 10–12.

9. Venerable Shih Cheng-yen, "A New Millennium of Goodness, Beauty, and Truth," in Chappell, ed., *Buddhist Peacework*, p. 48.

10. Venerable Master Hsing Yün, *The Lion's Roar: Actualizing Buddhism in Daily Life and Building the Pure Land in Our Midst* (New York: Peter Lang, 1991), pp. xv, 8, 11, 129, 136.

11. Master Hsing Yün, *Lotus in a Stream* (New York: Weatherhill, 2000), p. 154.

12. Bongkil Chung, *An Introduction to Won Buddhism* (Iri, Korea: Won Buddhist Press, 1994), p. 36.

13. For contemporary Japanese names, we do not put the last name first, as was done in the previous chapter.

14. Daisaku Ikeda, "The SGI's Peace Movement," in Chappell, ed., *Buddhist Peacework,* pp. 130, 136–137.

15. Nikkyō Niwano, *Life Time Beginner* (Tokyo: Kōsei Publishing Co., 1978), p. 76.

16. Nikkyō Niwano, *Some Thoughts on Peace* (Tokyo: Kōsei Publishing Co., 1984), pp. 17–18, 20.

17. Ven Dr. Yifa, "The Woman's Sangha in Taiwan," in Mitchell and Wiseman, eds., *Gethsemani Encounter,* p. 108.

18. Rita M. Gross, *Buddhism after Patriarchy: A Feminist History, Analysis, and Reconstruction of Buddhism* (Albany, NY: SUNY Press, 1993), p. 242.

SUGGESTIONS FOR FURTHER READING

Bartholomeusz, Tessa J. *Women under the Bo Tree: Buddhist Nuns in Sri Lanka.* Cambridge: Cambridge University Press, 1994.

Bond, George. *The Buddhist Revival in Sri Lanka: Religious Tradition, Reinterpretation, and Response.* Columbia, SC: University of South Carolina Press, 1988.

Chappell, David, ed. *Buddhist Peacework: Creating Cultures of Peace.* Boston: Wisdom Publications, 1999.

Ching, Yu-ing. *Master of Love and Mercy: Cheng Yen.* Nevada City, CA: Blue Dolphin Publishing, 1995.

Chong, Key Ray. *Won Buddhism: A History and Theology of Korea's New Religion.* Lewiston, NY: Edwin Mellen Press, 1997.

Goldstein, Melvyn C. *The Snow Lion and the Dragon: China, Tibet and the Dalai Lama.* Berkeley, CA: University of California Press, 1997.

Kabilsingh, Chatsumarn. *Thai Women in Buddhism.* Berkeley: Parallax Press, 1991.

Keyes, Charles F., Laurel Kendall, and Helen Hardacre, eds. *Asian Visions of Authority: Religion and the Modern States of East and Southeast Asia.* Honolulu: University of Hawaii Press, 1994.

Kotler, Arnold, ed. *Engaged Buddhist Reader.* Berkeley, CA: Parallax Press, 1996.

Kraft, Kenneth, ed. *The Wheel of Engaged Buddhism: A New Map of the Path.* New York: Weatherhill, 1999.

Lopez, Donald S., Jr., ed. *Curators of the Buddha: The Study of Buddhism under Colonialism*. Chicago: University of Chicago Press, 1995.

Metraux, Daniel. *The History and Theology of Sōka Gakkai: A Japanese New Religion*. Lewiston, NY: Edwin Mellen Press, 1988.

Nhat Hanh, Thich. *Vietnam: Lotus in a Sea of Fire*. New York: Hill and Wang, 1967.

Queen, Christopher and Sallie B. King, eds. *Engaged Buddhism: Buddhist Liberation Movements in Asia*. Albany, NY: SUNY Press, 1996.

Seneviratne, H. L. *The Work of Kings: The New Buddhism in Sri Lanka*. Chicago: University of Chicago Press, 1999.

Swearer, Donald K. *Me and Mine: Selected Essays of Bhikku Buddhadāsa*. Albany, NY: SUNY Press, 1990.

Tsomo, Karma Lekshe. *Sakyadhita: Daughters of the Buddha*. Ithaca, NY: Snow Lion Publications, 1988.

Victoria, Brian Daizen A. *Zen at War*. New York: Weatherhill, 1997.

ELEVEN

BUDDHISM IN
THE WEST

The religious tapestry of the West has been, for the most part, woven from Christianity and Judaism. Recently, new strands of religiosity have been introduced, especially from Islam, Hinduism, and Buddhism. Buddhism's introduction into the West actually began a number of centuries ago. In the sixteenth and seventeenth centuries, Jesuits in India, China, Japan, and Tibet wrote detailed studies of Asian religions, including Buddhism. Matteo Ricci (1552–1610), the famous Jesuit scholar and missionary in China, used his studies to accommodate Christianity to a Chinese culture infused with Buddhism. However, these writings and experiments never made any significant impact on the West. On the other hand, in the eighteenth century, European Protestant merchants wrote of their travels in Asia in such glowing terms that some European intellectuals began to look more positively at Asian religions. This interest led to the beginnings of Buddhist scholarship in Europe in the early nineteenth century as intellectuals began to translate and study Buddhist texts being brought back from Asia.

Early scholars involved in this endeavor include Michel François Ozeray, Henry Thomas Colebrooke, Brian Houghton Hodgson, Alexander Csoma de Körös, and Eugene Burnouf. Burnouf is often credited with showing that the many forms of Buddhism found throughout Asia are in fact branches of a single tradition going back to the Buddha in India. Burnouf and other European scholars laid the foundations for modern Buddhist studies, and their work also influenced the intellectual world both in Europe and America. Examples of such intellectuals in Europe include Arthur Schopenhauer, Richard Wagner, and Friedrich Wilhelm Nietzsche, while in the United States, there were Ralph Waldo Emerson, Walt Whitman, and Henry David Thoreau. Other important later nineteenth- and early twentieth-century scholars who brought Buddhist studies forward include such people as Thomas William Rhys Davids, founder of the Pali Text Society in 1886 and the Buddhist Society in 1907 in England; Hermann Oldenberg in Germany; Louis de La Vallée Poussin and Étienne Lamotte in Belgium; Theodore

Stcherbatsky in Russia; and Paul Carus, Henry Clarke Warren, and Charles Rockwell Lanman in the United States.

One work from this time period that had a significant impact on the West's perception of Buddhism was Edwin Arnold's 1879 poem on the life and teachings of the Buddha, *The Light of Asia*. The following are some verses from that famous work:

> As one who stands on yonder snowy horn
> Having nought o'er him but the boundless blue,
> So, these sins being slain, the man is come
> NIRVANA'S verge unto.
>
> Him the Gods envy from their lower seats;
> Him the Three Worlds in ruin should not shake;
> All life is lived for him, all deaths are dead;
> Karma will no more make
>
> New houses. Seeking nothing, he gains all;
> Forgoing self, the Universe grows "I";
> If any teach NIRVANA is to cease,
> Say unto such they lie.
>
> If any teach NIRVANA is to live,
> Say unto such they err; not knowing this,
> Nor what light shines beyond their broken lamps,
> Nor lifeless, timeless bliss.
>
> Enter the Path! There is no grief like Hate!
> No pains like passions, no deceit like sense!
> Enter the Path! far hath he gone whose foot
> Treads down one fond offence.
>
> Enter the Path! There spring the healing streams
> Quenching all thirst! there bloom th' immortal flowers
> Carpeting all the way with joy! there throng
> Swiftest and sweetest hours![1]

Besides the rise of Buddhist scholarship in the West and its impact on the intellectual scene, two other events in the late nineteenth century deserve mention. First was the founding of the Theosophical Society in New York City in the 1870s. Its two founders, Henry Steel Olcott and Helena Petrovna Blavatsky, converted to Buddhism and moved to Sri Lanka. There, Olcott helped the Sri Lankan Buddhist community redefine itself in a way that contributed to a Buddhist revival in reaction to European colonialism. The Theosophical Society also helped to disseminate Buddhist ideas in the West.

The second event was the World's Parliament of Religions held in Chicago in 1893. At this Parliament, articulate Asian spokespeople presented lectures about different schools of Buddhism so that the American audience could appreciate the sophisticated and diverse nature of Buddhism as an attractive living tradition. The interest sparked by the Parliament led to important Buddhist missions in the United States. Anagarika Dharmapala, the Theravāda representative and protégé of Olcott, made a number of lecture tours in the United States after the Parliament. So did the Zen representative from Japan, Shaku Sōen, who later sent some of this students, Nyōgen Senzaki, Shaku Sōkatsu, and D. T. Suzuki. As we shall see in the next section, these three figures played major roles in bringing Zen to America. The Parliament also fostered interfaith dialogue between Buddhism and other religions, which, as we shall also see, has aided Buddhists in their efforts to enter American's religious mainstream.

Turning further to the American scene, a watershed in the history of Buddhism in the West began during the 1950s. Leaders of the Beat movement such as Jack Kerouac, Allen Ginsberg, and Gary Snyder, along with other figures such as Alan Watts, D. T. Suzuki, and Thomas Merton, began to popularize Zen Buddhism through their writings. For example, the following is from Kerouac's *Dharma Bums*:

> The little Saint Teresa bum [a "thin old little bum" with a prayer by Saint Teresa in his pocket] was the first genuine Dharma Bum I'd met, and the second was the number one Dharma Bum of them all and in fact it was he, Japhy Ryder, who coined the phrase. Japhy Ryder was a kid from eastern Oregon brought up in a log cabin deep in the woods with his father and mother and sister, from the beginning a woods boy, an axman, farmer, interested in animals and Indian lore so that when he finally got to college by hook or crook he was already well equipped for his early studies in anthropology and later in Indian myth and in the actual texts of Indian mythology. Finally he learned Chinese and Japanese and became a Oriental scholar and discovered the greatest Dharma Bums of them all, the Zen Lunatics of China and Japan. . . .
>
>   "Where did you meet Ray Smith?" They asked him when we walked into The Place, the favorite bar of the hepcats around the Beach.
>
>   "Oh, I always meet my Bodhisattvas in the street!" he yelled.[2]

During the 1960s, Buddhism in the United States grew into a more diverse phenomenon. Besides turning to Zen, many Americans began to practice other forms of Buddhism such as Nichiren, Tibetan, and Theravāda. Soon, there was a significant growth of new Buddhist communities and organizations not only in a few major cities, but also in urban and rural areas across the American landscape. This proliferation of active Buddhist lineages in the United States was aided by the 1965 changes in the U.S. immigration laws that allowed a much larger wave of Asian immigration. During the next decade, it was common to find Euro-American laypersons, men and women, being taught Buddhism by Asian monastic-trained teachers. In the 1980s and 1990s, many of these Western students became teachers themselves. Under both Asian American and Euro-American leadership, the

American Buddhist communities had by the end of the twentieth century produced many creative innovations, some of which we introduce in this chapter.

As these changes were taking place in the religious culture of the United States, the academic study of Buddhism was also developing in ways that have added not only to Western understanding of Buddhism, but also to the maturity of Buddhism in the West. After the new interest in Buddhism in the 1960s, Buddhist Studies began to be accepted as a significant academic discipline in American universities and by university presses. The University of Wisconsin instituted a formal graduate program in Buddhist Studies. Soon, other graduate programs offering specializations in Buddhism began at such places as the University of California at Berkeley, Columbia University, Harvard University, the University of Chicago, the University of Hawaii, the University of Virginia, and the University of Michigan. At the end of the twentieth century, these and other universities were producing a new generation of Buddhologists that continues to contribute to the objective and critical study of Buddhism as a multifaceted, historical phenomenon.

MAJOR BUDDHIST TRADITIONS IN THE WEST

We conclude our study of Buddhism first by introducing the ways that Buddhism has been forming and reforming itself in the West, especially in the United States. In the final section of this chapter, we consider some of the important issues that have arisen in this process of Buddhist inculturization, which are defining the Western experience of Buddhism at the beginning of the twenty-first century. In so doing, we can hopefully glimpse something of Buddhism's future in the West as it writes a new chapter in the ongoing story of Buddhism.

Theravāda Buddhism

One of the first forms of Buddhism to be introduced to the West through nineteenth-century Buddhist scholarship was Theravāda. However, the first Theravāda temple in the United States, the Buddhist Vihāra Society, was not established until 1966 in Washington, DC. On the other hand, by 1996 there were 150 Theravāda temples in over thirty states, with about five hundred resident monastics. Indeed, throughout the West during the later part of the twentieth century, many Sri Lankan, Thai, Cambodian, Lao, and Burmese immigrant communities founded temples and staffed them with monastic teachers. These temples not only serve the Asian immigrant communities but also provide Euro-Americans with Buddhist study centers, as well as guidance in the practice of mindfulness and meditation.

One of the most influential Sri Lankan monastics to reach out beyond the immigrant community is Henepola Gunaratana, who came to the United

States in 1968 to serve the Washington Buddhist Vihāra Society. In 1982, Gunaratana founded the Bhavana Society in West Virginia as a residential
retreat center devoted to meditation training and study for Asian and Western laypeople and monastics. Another highly successful Theravādin monastic in the United States was Havanpola Ratanasara (1920–2000). Ratanasara
entered the monastic life at age eleven and went on to receive a doctorate
from the University of London. He was Sri Lanka's delegate to the United
Nations in 1957, the first Buddhist monk to hold such a position. Emi-
grating to the United States in 1980, he helped found the Dharma Vijaya
Buddhist Vihāra in Los Angeles, the Interreligious Council of Southern California, and the American Buddhist Congress. This latter organization
sought to provide a kind of national-level Saṅgha council for the United
States.

Monastic Theravāda has not drawn many Western converts into their
monasteries; there are only a dozen or so non-Asian monastics in U.S. Theravāda temples as of this writing. Therefore, some Theravāda Buddhist
groups have developed lay initiations and ordinations for those people who
are interested in participating more fully in the Buddhist way of life, but do
not wish to enter fully into the monastic community. These new lay programs provide a unique partnership between Asian monastics and Western
converts in the development of Buddhism in the West. An example of such
lay vocations can be seen in the five-level system devised at the Dharma Vijaya Buddhist Vihāra. The first level involves initiation into the Five Precepts. The second level includes initiation into the Nine Precepts, formal
daily practice, and training for leadership roles so that one can give Dharma
talks and conduct meditation classes. The third level involves more stringent Buddhist precepts. The fourth level carries the status of lay minister
and gives the possibility of conducting certain religious services, being a
chaplain, and initiating laypeople at the three lower levels. This fourth level
involves ordination, taking the precepts of the Ten Perfections, and a more
detailed daily regimen. The fifth and final level adds the vow of celibacy.

One important movement in the West that has grown out of the Theravāda tradition is called the "Insight Meditation" movement. This movement, which emerged in the late 1970s, is now one of the fastest growing
forms of Buddhism in the West. As a loose-knit lay movement, it teaches insight meditation (Pali: *vipassanā*) along with mindfulness and other Theravāda forms of mental culture. The Western founders of this movement were
trained mainly by Burmese and Thai meditation masters who refined their
methods to be of use to laypeople. A pioneer of this movement is Ruth Deni-
son. She studied Theravāda meditation in Burma in the 1960s and began
teaching in the United States in 1973. In 1977, she began what became
Dhamma Dena, a retreat center near Joshua Tree, California.

Also in the late 1960s, Sharon Salzberg, Jack Kornfield, and Joseph Goldstein, among others, took training in insight meditation in Southeast Asia
and returned to teach in the United States. In 1975, they founded the Insight
Meditation Society (IMS), which has retreat centers in Barre, Massachusetts,

and, more recently, Spirit Rock in Marin County, California. At these centers, teachers offer short- and long-term retreats focusing on such practices as mindfulness of breathing, insight meditation, and loving-kindness meditation. Today, their practitioners have opened over 150 independent centers around the country. With its practical focus on training, healing, and Awakening, the movement does not emphasize participation in traditional Theravāda institutions. Given this freedom, students of other forms of Buddhism, and even other religions, have trained at IMS centers to complement their own practice with mindfulness and insight meditation. This blending of practice has lessened some of the sharp divisions between schools of Buddhism in the West, and has also fostered positive interfaith relations.

Joseph Goldstein explained the attraction of insight meditation for many Westerners:

> We practice the Dharma in order to understand [the way to Awakening], in order to be free. That is the heart of all the effort we make, because from freedom comes connectedness, compassion, lovingkindness, and peace.
>
> The Buddha saw with such clarity how different states of mind and courses of action lead to different results. Unwholesome mind states have certain consequences. Wholesome mind states have results of their own. As we begin to understand the truth of how things are, we see for ourselves what brings suffering in our lives, and what brings happiness and freedom.
>
> Although at first our mind might feel like a whirlwind of activity, the amazing path of Dharma practice helps us begin to sort things out. We establish some stability and focus in our mind and see which elements in it lead to greater peace, which to greater suffering. All of it—both the peace and the suffering—happen lawfully. Freedom lies in the wisdom to choose.
>
> As we walk the way of awareness, we see that the deepest purpose we all have is to perfect the qualities of our heart and mind. The spiritual path transforms our consciousness, purifying it of greed, hatred, ignorance, fear, envy, jealousy—those forces that create suffering in us and in the world.
>
> We all share this most fundamental purpose of freedom. It is the universal potential of the mind itself. . . . Everyone shares the basic commonality of being alive, of having a mind and heart. Our task is to awaken and purify this mind-heart for the benefit of all.[3]

Vietnamese Buddhism

After the Vietnam War, Vietnamese Buddhist monastics came to the West to establish temples in Vietnamese neighborhoods. At first they did so in homes or small storefronts. Today, more traditional temples have been erected, and there are now over 160 Vietnamese Buddhist temples in the United States alone. As has been traditionally the case in Vietnam, the temples operate quite independently, with decisions on doctrine and activities made on the local level. Since Vietnamese Buddhism is primarily Mahāyāna, the temples' Sunday services entail chanting *sūtras*, meditation, reciting Buddhas' names, and praying to Amitābha Buddha for rebirth in the Pure Land. While meditation is practiced to some degree, it is felt that Awakening must be assisted by Buddhas and bodhisattvas. Thus Zen and Pure Land are seen as complementary in typical Vietnamese Buddhist practice. Vietnamese temples in the West also provide Vietnamese language lessons, Dharma classes for children, and adult education. The temples commemorate special Buddhist holidays, perform daily rituals that can be joined by laypeople, and celebrate rituals for funerals and weddings.

While some Vietnamese laypeople take the Three Refuges and even hold bodhisattva vows, few Westerners have become vowed members of this kind of ethnic Buddhism. However, a number of Vietnamese Buddhist leaders have reached out beyond their ethnic communities. For example, Thich Thien-An (1926–1980), a monk trained also in the Japanese Rinzai tradition, founded the International Buddhist Meditation Center in Los Angeles in 1971. His center is now directed by Karuna Dharma, said to be the first fully ordained American woman. Also, Thich Nhat Hanh has been successful in attracting many Westerners with his form of socially engaged Buddhism. His books are quite popular in the West, and a number of Westerners have been ordained in his Order of Interbeing. In 1983, the Community of Mindful Living was created in Berkeley, California, in order to support Nhat Hanh's work and to encourage the founding of retreats centers around the world based on his teachings. Today there are over two hundred such centers, mostly in the United States. Setting aside the ritual practices of Vietnamese Buddhism, Nhat Hanh's movement balances inner practice with outer action, personal transformation with social change. This balanced style of Buddhist spirituality has made Asian socially engaged Buddhism appealing to many Westerners.

Tibetan Buddhism

In the 1950s, the first Tibetan lamas in exile began arriving in the West. In the 1960s, two major efforts were undertaken to preserve and pass on the traditions of Tibetan Buddhism. First, some lamas and their students collected, translated, and disseminated Tibetan texts. Two presses have aided in this work in the United States: Shambhala Publications, founded in 1969, and Snow Lion Publications, formed in 1980. Second, centers associated with the various schools of Tibetan Buddhism were founded in Europe and America, and began to draw students who wished to become practitioners of Tibetan Buddhism.

In terms of the Geluk Order in the United States, Geshe Ngawang Wangyal (1901–1983) arrived in the United States in 1955. Wangyal lived in Freewood Acres, New Jersey, where he founded the Lamaist Buddhist Monastery of America, later renamed the Tibetan Buddhist Learning Center. Wangyal attracted such students as Jeffrey Hopkins and Robert Thurman, both of whom went on to become Buddhist scholars. Thurman is now the Jey Tsong Kha Pa Professor of Buddhist Studies at Columbia University. Hopkins founded the Buddhist Studies Program at the University of Virginia. Wangyal also brought a number of important Tibetan scholars to his monastery. One was

Geshe Lhundrup Sopa, who later became professor at the University of Wisconsin and founded the Deer Park Buddhist Center in Madison, Wisconsin, in 1975.

The Sakya Order was first represented in the United States by Deshung Rinpoche (1906–1987), who taught at the University of Washington beginning in 1960. One of the first Sakya centers in the United States, the Ewam Choden Tibetan Buddhist Center in Kensington, California, was founded in 1971. In 1974, the Sakya Monastery of Tibetan Buddhism was founded in Seattle. This latter institution takes an ecumenical approach, hosting lamas from all Tibetan traditions, including the Dalai Lama. On the East Coast, the Sakya Center for Buddhist Studies and Meditation was founded in Cambridge, Massachusetts, in 1980, and the Sakya Phuntsok Ling Center for Tibetan Buddhist Studies and Meditation was founded in Silver Springs, Maryland, in 1986.

The Nyingma Order was introduced by Tarthang Tulku Rinpoche, who arrived in the United States in 1968. With an emphasis on Tantric training, Tarthang founded the Tibetan Nyingma Meditation Center in Berkeley in 1969. There, he trained Westerners in rigorous practice, but also helped them integrate that practice into their normal Western life at work and in the family. More recently, Lama Surya Das (Jeffrey Miller) founded the Dzogchen Foundation in Cambridge, Massachusetts, in 1991 to give Western students greater access to *dzogchen* practice. Another recent Nyingma teacher in the West is Sogyal Rinpoche. Trained in Tibetan studies in India and comparative religion at Cambridge University, Sogyal first founded centers in Europe. Then he established the Rigpa Fellowship with a center in Santa Cruz, California. Giving death and dying an important place in his teachings, Sogyal published *The Tibetan Book of Living and Dying*, from which the following passages are taken:

So whatever our lives are like, our buddha nature is always there. And it is always perfect. . . . Our true nature could be compared to the sky, and the confusion of the ordinary mind to clouds. Some days the sky is completely obscured by clouds.

So where exactly is this buddha nature? It is in the sky-like nature of our mind. Utterly open, free, and limitless, it is fundamentally so simple and so natural that it can never be complicated, corrupted, or stained, so pure that it is beyond even the concept of purity and impurity.

The purpose of meditation is to awaken in us the sky-like nature of mind, and to introduce us to that which we really are, our unchanging pure awareness, which underlies the whole of life and death. In the stillness and silence of meditation, we glimpse and return to that deep inner nature that we have so long ago lost sight of amid the busyness and distraction of our minds. . . . Meditation is, then, bringing the mind home.

[T]his practice unveils and reveals your essential Good Heart, because it dissolves and removes the unkindness or the harm in you. . . . Through the practice, then, by slowly removing the unkindness and harm from ourselves, we allow our true Good Heart, the fundamental goodness and kindness that are

our real nature, to shine out and become the warm climate in which our true
being flowers.

That is why in our tradition we see compassion as the source and essence
of enlightenment, and the heart of enlightened activity. . . . Compassion is the
wish-fulfilling gem whose light of healing spreads in all directions.[4]

As for the Kagyü Order, Kalu Rinpoche (1939–1987) was one of the earliest Kagyü lamas to teach in the West. He founded centers in Canada and
France and taught in the United States from 1971 until his death. In 1979,
the Sixteenth Gyalwa Karmapa, head of the Karma Kagyüs, founded the
Karma Triyana Dharmachakra in Woodstock, New York. This center, a
monastery with a staff and class offerings for laypeople, has dozens of branch
meditation centers in many states. The most famous of the early Kagyü teachers in the United States was Chögyam Trungpa Rinpoche (1939–1987).
Trungpa moved to the United States in 1969 and settled at Tail of the Tiger
in Barnet, Vermont. Later, Trungpa founded Shambhala International, which
now has its headquarters in Halifax, Nova Scotia. Its main monastic facility
is the Rocky Mountain Shambhala Center in Colorado, where training in
Kagyü and Nyingma practice is offered. A network of local centers, called
Shambhala Meditation Centers, are also present around the United States.
Part of Shambhala's educational branch is Naropa University in Boulder, the
first fully accredited Buddhist liberal arts college in the United States.

In Tibet, it is rare for laypeople to pursue in-depth study of Buddhism or
to participate in intensive monastic practice, especially Tantric practice. In
the West, however, the Tibetan orders have created ways for laypeople to
study Tibetan Buddhism and to be initiated and trained in its practices. Most
Tibetan Buddhist centers offer formal and informal courses of study on Tibetan Buddhism to the general public, sometimes through local universities.
In terms of practice, nonmonastic intensive retreats of longer or shorter duration are now offered for laypeople, especially in the Kagyü and Nyingma
lineages. Weekend meditation workshops are also offered to the general public with innovative programs of Dharma teaching and guided meditative
practice. For example, the Dalai Lama's personal monastery in the United
States is Namgyal Monastery in Ithaca, New York. There, the Namgyal Institute offers a traditional Tibetan curriculum to Western lay students.

In the 1990s, Western support for Tibet and its culture and religion was
galvanized by the Dalai Lama and Tibetan monastics around the world. In
New York City, the U.S. Tibet Committee promotes public awareness of Tibet, and the International Campaign for Tibet works with elected officials
in Washington, DC. The Students for a Free Tibet has grown from 45 chapters in 1994 to 350 in 1997. The Tibet House in New York City was founded
by the Dalai Lama as a cultural center to educate the public about Tibet's
endangered living culture. Support for the Tibet cause has also been received
from the entertainment industry. Adam Yauch of the Beastie Boys sponsored
a series of Concerts for a Free Tibet, and in 1997 two film about Tibet were
released: *Seven Years in Tibet* with Brad Pitt and *Kundun,* directed by Mar-

tin Scorcese. The public concern for and interest in Tibet, along with serious scholarship and the development of practice and study centers, have made Tibetan Buddhism one of the fastest growing forms of Buddhism in the West.

Chinese Buddhism

Chinese Buddhist temples began to be built in the West in the nineteenth century in order to serve Chinese immigrant families. The first such temple in the United States was built in San Francisco in 1853. By 1875, there were hundreds of Chinese Buddhist temples throughout the western states. However, as Chinese people assimilated into Western culture, many lost interest in their religious heritage, and temples in Chinatowns were often abandoned. Then came the changes in immigration laws in the 1960s, and Chinese communities experienced the influx of immigrants from mainland China, Taiwan, Hong Kong, and other areas around the Pacific Rim. Along with this sociological change, a number of Chinese Buddhist organizations and individual masters from Taiwan came to the West to minister in these expanded communities. By 1990, there were more than 150 Chinese Buddhist organizations, temples, and centers in the United States alone. The result has been a new flourishing of Chinese Buddhism in the West.

Buddhist Pure Land and Ch'an practices have not been as institutionally separated in China as they were in Japan. So, chanting and meditation are taught at numerous Chinese Buddhist organizations in the West. For example at his New York Ch'an Meditation Center, highly regarded Master Sheng-yen of Dharma Drum Mountain in Taiwan teaches Ch'an meditation along with recitation sessions. Chanting or recitation is seen as a powerful means of concentrating the mind and generating peacefulness in a world of distractions. Also, Chinese Buddhist organizations often have *sūtra* study groups in order to help members understand the teachings of their tradition and to apply them to daily life. They present the Buddhas and bodhisattvas as models of compassion to be emulated in everyday living. Many Chinese Buddhist organizations in the West have taken these models of compassion seriously and have, like their socially engaged Buddhist counterparts in Asia, provided goods for the poor in their cities, health fairs offering free physical examinations, and meditation lessons to prisoners.

The Eastern States Buddhist Temple of America was founded in the early 1960s in New York's Chinatown. It played an important role in bringing Chinese monastics to the United States and has a retreat center in the Catskills named Temple Mahāyāna. Taiwan Master Cheng Yen's Tzu Chi Foundation, devoted to charitable work, now has some sixteen thousand members in the United States. Master Hsüan Hua (1908–1995) moved to the United States in 1962, and founded the Gold Mountain Dhyana Monastery in San Francisco, and later the City of Ten Thousand Buddhas in northern California. The City of Ten Thousand Buddhas seeks to institute a fully ordained and well-educated monastic Saṅgha. It now has about 350 residents, including 150 monastics. The Buddhist Association of the United States was

Figure 11.1. Hsi Lai Temple; Fo Guang Shan Buddhist Order, Hacienda Heights, California.

founded in 1964 in New York City. It has the Temple of Enlightenment in the Bronx and the Chuang Yen Monastery in Kent, New York. The Buddha Hall at Chuang Yen holds two thousand people and has a thirty-seven-foot statue of Vairocana Buddha.

One of the largest Chinese Buddhist movements in the United States is Fo Guang Shan, which opened the Hsi Lai Temple in Hacienda Heights, California, in 1988. Hsi Lai houses more than one hundred monastics and serves as the world headquarters of the Buddha's Light International Society (BLIS). This organization alone has over one hundred regional chapters, and Hsi Lai has branch temples in a number of major cities in the United States. Also present at the Hsi Lai complex is Hsi Lai University, which began classes in 1994. While Hsi Lai is a cultural center for Chinese American Buddhists, it also has outreach programs for Euro-Americans. Indeed, nearly all of its meditation students are Euro-Americans. Some of these Western students have gone on to take Buddhist precepts, and even to become Buddhist monastics.

Korean Buddhism

Korean Buddhism has come to the West through at least two major movements. The first movement is made up of the Korean men and women monastics, who have been invited by local Korean Buddhist communities in America and Europe. These monastics serve educational, ritual, and cultural functions in the immigrant communities that allow members of those communities to maintain a connection with their Korean heritage and pass that heritage on to their children. Most Sunday temple services include readings from scriptures, chanting, formal ceremonies, and Dharma teachings. While many of the temples are affiliated with the Chogye Order in Korea, Won Buddhism also serves the Korean communities through their own temples and participates in interfaith activities and organizations at the local and national levels.

The second movement of Korean Buddhism to the West involves those Sŏn (Zen) teachers who have opened centers in the West that appeal to Westerners. In welcoming Westerners, these teachers have adapted to the diverse cultures of America and Europe. They blend such practices as prostrations, Pure Land chanting, and formal liturgies with *sūtra* study and meditation practice. This holistic approach to Buddhist practice is intended to foster a sense of community among its members and to encourage daily living in the spirit of bodhisatvahood. These Sŏn organizations in the West follow the Korean pattern of a head temple with many branch temples. One of the first such teachers in the United States was Kyung Bo Sunim (Korean *sunim*: monk). Kyung Bo came to Columbia University in 1964 and remained in the United States for the next six years lecturing on Korean Buddhism. His disciples founded meditation centers on the East Coast.

More recently, two Korean teachers have been particularly successful. Seung Sahn Sunim arrived in the United States in 1972 and settled in Providence, Rhode Island. He developed a form of Buddhism combining meditation with Dharma talks, chanting, and prostrations that appealed to Western students at what is now the Providence Zen Center. In 1983, Seung Sahn founded the Kwan Um School of Zen, which in 1998 had over sixty centers worldwide. Samu Sunim arrived in New York in 1967, and moved to Canada the next year. After four years of personal practice, he visited Buddhist centers throughout Canada and the United States. Based on his experience, he eventually founded the Zen Lotus Society, now called the Buddhist Society for Compassionate Wisdom. Centers in this society are located in cities in Canada, the United States, and Mexico. Given his interest in Buddhism in the West, Samu Sunim and Luis Gómez hosted the landmark Conference on World Buddhism in North America at the University of Michigan and his Ann Arbor temple in 1987. The following reflections of Samu Sunim stress the importance of socially engaged Buddhism in the West:

> [T]he majority of Western Buddhists practitioners pursue their *Dharma* life actively engaging the world while also being seriously involved in Buddhist spiritual practice. . . . *Dharma* work in the world today requires *bodhisattvas* with boundless hearts . . . ordinary persons with "great hearts," who involve themselves enthusiastically in world affairs. . . . With such great hearts, they bring charity to the needy, peace and calm to the troubled, comfort to the afflicted, smiles and forgiveness to the angry, and clarity and wisdom to the confused and perplexed.

Zen is an endless journey where there is no goal aside from the daily living of our life responsibly and full-heartedly. As the new travelers acquire *Dharma* habits and begin to lead a mindful life, an awakening of the "great heart" begins . . . and a new peace of mind and gratitude take hold. . . . The peace and happiness we experience inside through personal transformation must find an expression outside through social transformation. . . . We are a universal family, and as such, we depend on one another for peace, harmony and equilibrium. We all participate in the unity of this family. . . . Therefore, the awareness of this unity through Zen awakening also helps us awaken to our global responsibility and planetary consciousness.[5]

Japanese Buddhism

Japanese Pure Land Buddhism came to the West to minister to the needs of Japanese immigrant communities, and Pure Land temples have been in the United States for over one hundred years. In 1914, Pure Land priests of Jōdo Shinshū founded the Buddhist Mission of North America (BMNA), with twenty-five branch fellowships dedicated to serving the religious and social needs of Japanese immigrants. They provided Dharma schools for children, youth activities, adult education programs, and community support in the face of anti-Japanese attitudes and actions. When during World War II over one hundred thousand Japanese living on the West Coast were removed from their homes and taken to inland concentration camps, the BMNA made its headquarters in the Utah Topaz Camp. There, it changed its name to Buddhist Churches of America (BCA), which now has over sixty churches and fellowships around the country. The BCA presently offers courses at their American Buddhist Academy in New York City and their Institute of Buddhist Studies in Berkeley, California.

With its focus on faith in the grace of Amida Buddha, on family unity and community support, and on a life of kindness, compassion, and service to others, Pure Land Buddhism has given its Western Japanese members a link to their spiritual heritage that can also be lived in their adopted countries. Recently, young Pure Land members in the West have become interested in addressing pressing social concerns and want to expand the scope of their religion to be more universal in order to attract more non-Japanese members. The problem now is how to maintain Pure Land Buddhism's traditional and cultural function in the Japanese community, while sharing its experience and values with the broader non-Japanese society. One avenue for achieving this goal has been the Buddhist-Christian dialogue that has involved many Pure Land scholars in the West. This dialogue is said by some to be helping Pure Land Buddhism share its faith and, thereby, to discover a broader mission to the West.

The first Japanese Rinzai Zen master to visit America was Shaku Sōen (1859–1919), who attended the 1893 World's Parliament of Religions in Chicago. Sōen returned to lecture in the United States in 1905, and eventually brought three disciples to teach Rinzai Zen. First was Nyōgen Senzaki (1878–1958), who founded Zen centers in Los Angeles and San Francisco in the 1920s. The second disciple was Shaku Sōkatsu (1869–1954), who lived in the United States twice between 1906 and 1910. When Sōkatsu finally returned to Japan for good, he left behind a lay student named Shigetsu Sasaki (1882–1945). Sasaki eventually became ordained and took the name Sokei-an. In 1930, Sokei-an founded the Buddhist Society of America in New York City, which was later renamed the First Zen Institute of America.

The third disciple of Sōen was by far the best known. He was D. T. Suzuki (1870–1966), who, through his many writings, brought Zen to the awareness of the broader Western society. Suzuki lectured at different universities, especially at Columbia, and in 1956, the Zen Studies Society of New York was established to support his efforts. Suzuki's younger friend from Japan, Masao Abe, has also traveled and taught Zen philosophy and religion at universities throughout the United States and Europe, earning himself the title of Suzuki's heir.

Four more recent Rinzai masters have been active in bringing Zen to the United States. First is Nakagawa Sōen (1909–1983), a friend of Nyōgen Senzaki and a pioneer of Zen on the West and East Coasts. Sōen gave Dharma transmission to another important Rinzai leader, Maurine Stuart (1922–1990), who led the Cambridge Buddhist Association. A third influential Rinzai teacher is Kyozan Joshu Sasaki, who founded the Cimarron Zen Center in Los Angeles in 1966 and the Mt. Baldy Zen Center in 1971. Finally, there is Eidō Tai Shimano, who in the 1960s revitalized the Zen Studies Society of New York, which had been inactive since D. T. Suzuki returned to Japan. Shimano also founded the International Dai Bosatsu Monastery in the Catskills.

Sōtō Zen did not begin to appear in the United States until after World War II. In 1949, Soyu Matsuoka founded the Chicago Buddhist Temple, now named the Zen Buddhist Temple of Chicago. The best-known Sōtō Zen master in the United States was Shunryu Suzuki (1904–1971). He founded the San Francisco Zen Center in 1961 and established the Zen Mountain Center at Tassajara Hot Springs near Carmel, California, in 1967. In 1972, following the death of Suzuki, the Zen Center opened Green Gulch Zen community in Marin County. Daimin Katagiri (1928–1990) came to the United States in 1964 to assist Suzuki, and then went on to lead the Minnesota Zen Meditation Center with regional centers in the Midwest area. Jiyu Kennett (1924–1996), an English woman, was the first woman since the fourteenth century to be admitted to one of the chief Sōtō training temples in Japan. She came to America in 1969 and founded Shasta Abbey in 1970 for the training of Zen priests.

Shinryu Suzuki's informal Dharma talks in *Zen Mind, Beginner's Mind* have had a great influence on may Zen practitioners in the West. The following passages are from one such talk about Dōgen:

> The purpose of studying Buddhism is not to study Buddhism, but to study ourselves. It is impossible to study ourselves without some teaching. If you want to know what water is you need science. . . . It is the same thing with us.

---- **BOX 11.1** ----

THE RIOT POLICEMAN AND THE ZEN MASTER

My first forty years were greatly influenced by my deep love and admiration of my father. He was a humanist and an atheist, with a passionate concern for the suffering of poverty and racial discrimination so vividly apparent in Alabama, where we lived. When I was forty-two, I had a meeting with a riot squad policemen and a Zen Master which radically changed the direction of my response, but not my deep concern about suffering.

My parents were both professors at the University of Alabama at Tuscaloosa, where we lived until I was eight. My father became more and more concerned about the social injustice all around us, and our comfortable home in the pine woods outside of town became a "rest and recuperation" stop for labor and civil rights organizers who had been beaten up in the course of their organizing efforts. In 1934, he left the university to become a full-time civil rights organizer, and we moved to Manhattan, where he raised funds to support the organizing work he was doing at home. In 1935, he was beaten and left for dead in a field near Birmingham by a group of men working for the leading industrial conglomerate there. When he recovered, we moved back to Birmingham, where he continued his radical social activism.

During the war we moved to California, where my father was serving in the army. After the war, I became very active in efforts to ban atomic bombs and to promote civil rights. I became convinced, as my father had been, that the economic theories of Karl Marx were the most rational and fair way to organize economic life. The communist slogan, "from each according to his ability, to each according to his need," spoke to my idealistic passion for fairness. I became a very self-righteous social activist, "fighting for" peace, civil rights, civil liberties, and economic justice as I understood it.

In 1957, I became very disillusioned with the Soviet Union after the uprising and repression in Hungary, and resigned from the Communist Party. In the same year, my husband was subpoenaed by the House Committee on Un-American Activities and was blacklisted from his profession of more than twenty years. In 1967 my best friend complained of a very bad headache, was diagnosed with a brain tumor, and soon died. She was my age, with small children the age of my children. I was shaken by her sudden and unexpected death. Soon after, I developed an almost fatal septicemia. After my recovery, I realized that my life was changed. All those things about which I had been certain were open to question, and most of all, I was faced with the truth of impermanence.

At this time of deep uncertainty and questioning about the meaning, purpose, and direction of my life, there was a black students' strike at San Francisco State University where my son was a student. The first day of the strike was described by the newspapers as a "police riot." The riot squad police had arrested and beaten many students. Leaders of the black community called for citizens to come to the campus the next day to interpose themselves between police and students to prevent further violence. I went to the campus and noticed that some of the picketers were harassing some of the students who were entering a classroom building. Some athletic-looking white students were taking pictures and harassing the strikers. Then one of the picketers grabbed the camera and threw it hard on the ground. By this time I had become pretty much a pacifist. I had also become uneasy with the contradiction of "fighting for peace." There was no peace *in me*. As I watched the scene unfolding, I heard myself say, "Where's *my* side?"

In time we all began to congregate on the Quadrangle for a planned rally. A loudspeaker announced, "This is an illegal assembly!" A shoulder-to-shoulder phalanx of policemen in full riot gear emerged from behind some buildings and began to sweep across the Quadrangle with nightsticks extended, poking people who moved too slowly. People were breaking and running behind me in confusion. With no thought I interposed myself between police and students. Just then, someone blew a whistle and the police stopped poking with their nightsticks, and held them horizontal to their bodies with both hands. I looked up and my eyes met those of the policeman in front of me, perhaps eighteen inches away.

At that moment, there was no me, and no policeman. There was only a falling away of all boundaries and a profound experience of identity with the policeman which expanded to include everything. The reality of this experience was stunning beyond any discussion or speculation. Although I had absolutely no conceptual framework with which to understand what I had experienced, I knew that it was more authentic than any ideas I had about the world. I thought, "The world is different than I thought it was; I have to change my life."

Now I had read books on Zen and encountered sayings such as, "Self and other are not two." But at the time of the encounter with the policeman, my world was my family, the mathematics and chemistry of my profession, and politics. In my world then, a riot squad policeman was the epitome of "not me." To have such a profound experience of identity with him, together with the previous experiences of impermanence and uncertainty, started me on a search for someone who understood the world in which a riot squad policeman and I are not two.

In the course of my search, I had the good fortune to meet Shunryu Suzuki Roshi, a Sōtō Zen Master then living and teaching in San Francisco. He often used the phrase, "not one, not two," which resonated with my experience. When I met him face to face in a private interview, I knew when my eyes met his, *"He understands my experience with the policeman!"*

I understood that Suzuki Roshi had become the extraordinarily compassionate person I experienced him to be because of his many years of Zen practice. So, I began and have never stopped sitting *zazen* (Zen meditation) daily.

ZENKEI BLANCHE HARTMAN

Co-Abbot
San Francisco Zen Center

We need some teaching, but just by studying the teaching alone, it is impossible to know what "I" in myself am.

When you do not hear anything from the teacher, but just sit, this is called teaching without teaching. But sometimes this is not sufficient, so we listen to lectures and have discussions. But we should remember that the purpose of practice in a particular place is to study ourselves.

Dōgen zenji said, "To study Buddhism is to study ourselves. To study ourselves is to forget ourselves." When you become attached to a temporal expression of your true nature, it is necessary to talk about Buddhism, or else
you will think the temporal expression is it. But this particular expression of
it is not it. And yet at the same time it *is* it!

[T]he purpose of studying Buddhism is to study ourselves and to forget ourselves. When we forget ourselves, we actually are the true activity of the big
existence, or reality itself. When we realize this fact, there is no problem what-
soever in this world, and we can enjoy our life without feeling any difficulties.
The purpose of our practice is to be aware of this fact.[6]

Another strong link between Japanese Zen and the West has been forged
by what is called the Harada-Yasutani lineage of Zen in Japan. Daiun Harada
(1871–1961) developed a method of Zen training that tailors both Rinzai and
Sōtō practices to students' needs. Harada's student Hakuun Yasutani (1885–
1973) established a Zen center near Tokyo which made this training method
available to laypersons. Soon, it became a favorite training center for Westerners, and in 1954, Yasutani named this lineage Sanbo Kyodan, "The Order of the Three Treasures." From 1962 until he passed away, Yasutani often taught and led retreats in the United States. In Japan, Yasutani was
succeeded by Koun Yamada (1907–1989). Under Yamada's leadership, Sanbo
Kyodan has become known for training Christians, mainly Catholic priests
and nuns, so that they are able to attain *kenshō* and teach Zen as Christians.
In the United States, Yasutani's heirs include Eidō Tai Shimano, who is also
in the Rinzai lineage; Philip Kapleau; Robert Aitken; and Taizan Maezumi
(1931–1995).

Philip Kapleau attended D. T. Suzuki's lectures at Columbia and took up
formal Zen practice in Japan under Nakagawa Sōen, Harada, and finally Yasutani. Following this training, Kapleau published *The Three Pillars of Zen*, a
American Zen classic, based on his work with Yasutani. Kapleau also
founded the Zen Meditation Center in Rochester, New York, in 1966. Robert
Aitken was interned in Japan during World War II. There, he met Reginald
Blyth, a Zen practitioner and friend of D. T. Suzuki. After the war, Aitken
first trained in Zen practice under Nyōgen Senzaki in California, and then
with Nakagawa Sōen in Japan. In 1959, he and his wife Anne began a Zen
meditation group in Hawaii, which became the Diamond Saṅgha. Later,
Aitken trained under Yasutani and then Yamada, from whom he received
Dharma transmission in 1974. The Diamond Saṅgha has affiliated Zen centers in the United States and Australia. Aitken has been recognized by many
as a patriarch of Zen in America for his strong leadership since the 1960s.

Taizan Maezumi was ordained in the Sōtō School, but also gained Dharma
transmission in Rinzai and from Yasutani. Maezumi came to the United
States and founded the Zen Center of Los Angeles in 1956. In 1976, Maezumi
established the Kuroda Institute for the Study of Buddhism and Human Values, devoted to furthering Buddhist scholarship. Over the years, Maezumi
gave Dharma transmission to twelve of his students, who now have Zen
centers throughout North America, Europe, and New Zealand. They belong

Figure 11.2. Zendō of the Diamond Sangha; post-*sesshin* photo taken in 1965 with Philip Kapleau, Katsuki Sekida, and Hakuun Yasutani (front row, left to middle) and Robert and Anne Aitken (back row, far right), Honolulu, Hawaii.

to a network founded by Maezumi and his students called the White Plum Sangha. One of Maezumi's students is Bernard Tetsugen Glassman, who established the Zen Community of New York. Glassman has created innovative forms of Buddhist social engagement, which we introduce in the next section.

Thanks to these and other teachers, Japanese Zen centers have grown up all over North America and Europe. For the most part, the focus of Zen in the West has not been to create a Western Zen Buddhist monasticism but to establish Zen centers that mainly train both men and women lay students. These centers offer Zen training on a regular basis and hold *sesshin*, weeklong intensive retreats, during each year. Some of the centers have resident practitioners who follow a daily schedule that involves meditation, rituals, work, study, and community life. A few of these communities are now led by Christian Zen teachers. Ruben Habito, having received Dharma transmission from Yamada, leads the Maria Kannon Zen Center in Dallas. Robert E. Kennedy, a Jesuit priest, received Dharma transmission from Glassman and leads the Morning Star Zendo in New Jersey. Kennedy also has twentyeight affiliated Zen groups in the United States and Mexico.

Another form of Japanese Buddhism that has been successful in the West has come from the Nichiren tradition. Inspired by his travels to the West in the 1960s, the president of Sōka Gakkai, Daisaku Ikeda, encouraged his movement to reach out to Westerners. In the United States, the Sōka Gakkai movement was first known as Nichiren Shōshū of America (NSA). It spread rather quickly, attracting people with its promise of giving them the power to change their lives for the better and offering avenues to work together for world peace. While its proselytizing encountered some resistance, by the late 1970s, NSA was said to have had a half-million members in the United States alone.

In the 1980s, NSA began to adapt its structure and activities to Western culture. Some activities were scaled back, more serious regional meetings replaced glitzie national conventions, and eventually its name was changed to Sōka Gakkai International (SGI). In 1991, there was a split between Nichiren Shōshū and Sōka Gakkai in Japan. In the West, this meant that the SGI-run temples, six of which are in the United States, were taken control of by Nichiren Shōshū. These temples then organized lay communities to replace SGI communities. However, the vast majority of the lay members stayed with SGI.

Also, SGI has continued its inculturation by developing a more democratic model of leadership whereby its national organizations are led by executive committees appointed for one-year terms. Local communities have taken over the ministerial tasks once performed by the Nichiren Shōshū priests. Today, SGI sees itself more as a Buddhist lay movement dedicated to serious Nichiren practice for its members and to working with others for world peace. In regard to this latter goal, SGI has recently begun to develop more positive relations with other Buddhist lineages and constructive interfaith relations, both of which were not possible when it was part of Nichiren Shōshū.

The other new form of lay Buddhism in the West that has emerged from the Nichiren fold in Japan is Risshō Kōsei-kai (RKK). Unlike Sōka Gakkai, RKK has not sought to convert Westerners into its membership. Rather, it has worked within the Japanese American communities in the West in ways that have provided it with a local presence through which it participates in interfaith organizations and activities. This is especially the case with the World Conference on Religion and Peace (WCRP). Recently RKK has developed into a multipractice Buddhist movement more in line with the broader East Asian *Lotus Sūtra* tradition. This provides a unique opportunity for Westerners to encounter an important traditional form of Japanese Buddhist practice and thought.

THE EXPERIENCE OF BUDDHISM IN THE UNITED STATES

In the West, Buddhism is now facing the challenge of adapting to cultures that have already been molded over centuries by other religions and philosophies. Buddhist movements and organizations in the West today are in the process of establishing themselves as viable religious institutions that are able to contribute to the societies in which they find themselves. It should now be clear that in the United States, Buddhism is taking shape not as a single religious entity, but as plurality of temples, practice centers, monasteries, fellowships, activist groups, and study facilities. As Buddhists in the United States continue to found new communities and reform older ones, a number of issues have arisen that are presently being addressed. The ways in which these issues are resolved will determine to a large extent what kinds of American Buddhism will take shape in the future. Here, we introduce some of the key issues being addressed at this time in the United States.

Ethnicity, Identity, and Practice

Scholars have pointed out that there are certain differences of structure, purpose, and practice between communities founded for Asian American immigrants and communities created for European American converts. For example, ethnic temples serve the social, cultural, and educational as well as the religious needs of the community, while convert communities focus mainly on religious practice. This means that Euro-American converts typically identify with Buddhism through a particular single practice, such as chanting, insight meditation, *kōan* practice, or *dzogchen* training, rather than the broad range of doctrinal and cultural aspects of Buddhism so important to Asian American Buddhists.

For some in the Asian American Buddhist communities, there is a concern that this exclusive focus on practice in the convert communities could lead to a certain impoverishment of Buddhist identity in America. The concern here is that converts may not appreciate the full implications of what it is to be a Buddhist at the moral, intellectual, and cultural levels of self-understanding. However, for some in convert communities, not appropriating a Buddhist identity as it has been defined in Asia leaves open the possibility of new directions for the development of unique forms of Western Buddhism. While there is no real animosity between the immigrant and convert Buddhist communities in this regard, Kenneth K. Tanaka points out the following:

> Some Asian American Buddhists are offended at the suggestion that [Euro-American] Buddhists are the sole contributors to the creation of American Buddhism, while ethnic Buddhists are seen as having played virtually no role in it. Such perception, in their view, ignores the contributions made by the Asian American Buddhists with much longer history, some entering their second century on American soil. What is often implied, according to Asian American critics, is that Buddhism becomes truly American only when [Euro-]Americans become seriously involved. This form, then, is called "American Buddhism," distinguished from simply "Buddhism in America," as practiced by Asian American Buddhists.[7]

Drawing the distinction between "Buddhism in America" and "American Buddhism" in this way is certainly premature. As we saw in the histories of Tibet and East Asia, the formation of a fully inculturated Buddhism is some-

BOX 11.2

HOMECOMING

Why would someone born a farm girl in the conservative Christian climate of northern Wisconsin end up not only a Buddhist, but someone who publishes widely on Buddhist topics? It is quite mysterious, even to me, or perhaps it is more mysterious to myself than others. People sometimes discuss religious identity as if it were about choices that one makes or does not make. Some people would claim that a person committed to the religion into which they were born was "chosen by the religion, rather than making a personal choice," as a colleague recently put it to me. Her implication was that I, by contrast, had chosen my religion, much as I might choose a dress or a car.

But it doesn't feel that simple and straightforward to me. I did not decide to become a Buddhist. Rather, one day, in the midst of great personal pain, it overwhelmed me that the basic truths proclaimed by Buddhism are, indeed, *true.* So what should I do? Turn myself inside out trying to find the same clarifying and healing power in the religion I had been observing, as some would claim is the more appropriate course of action? Or follow my heart and my mind into Buddhism?

Obviously, I chose the later course, and in that sense one could say I *chose* to become a Buddhist. But the motivation for that choice was not the result of consulting some "consumers' guide" to religions, but of something that still feels as if it came to me. In Buddhist language, it would be said that I had a "karmic connection" with Buddhism, so that becoming Buddhist feels more like finally coming home than like choosing a new home. Indeed, many Western converts to Buddhism feel the same way. Granted, I already knew a lot about Buddhism when this experience happened. In fact, I was a college professor teaching university courses about Buddhism. But the fact that I studied about Buddhism for so long without ever considering becoming a Buddhist only strengthens my feeling that Buddhism came to me before I came to Buddhism.

Not that this has always been a romantic or an easy journey. I was and am very dissatisfied with the male dominance found in Buddhism throughout its history, even though I know that, in this regard, it is not unlike all other major religious traditions. I have not been silent on this point, but have written extensively about Buddhism and gender. Especially important are suggestions for changes that seem, to me and to many others, to be more reasonable, more sensible, and more in accord with Buddhism's basic values. This last point is especially important, for it is hard to justify male dominance on the basis of Buddhism's basic values and teachings. For this activity, I have been criticized by both Asian and Western Buddhists. But many, especially women, have also written to tell me that the work I have done has helped them remain within Buddhism. Such comments have not come only from Western women.

This is all part of the difficult and exciting work of transmitting the Dharma to "the West." At present, there is much controversy over how much Buddhism can or should adopt practices and values common to Western culture. Such controversies are to be expected in this first generation of widespread practice of Buddhism by people of European and other non-Asian origins. For though Buddhism has been practiced in North America for generations by Asian Americans, only in the past thirty years has Buddhism been widely adopted by other North Americans. For us, at least, this *is* the first generation of what feels like a momentous cultural shift. How better could I have spent my life than to be part of this shift? What fortunate karma!

RITA M. GROSS

Professor Emerita, Department of Philosophy and Religious Studies
University of Wisconsin–Eau Claire

---

thing that takes shape over many centuries, not just a few decades. The United States is still in the first stages of such a process, where there is the need for translations of texts and commentaries, the establishment and stabilization of valid practice lineages and other institutions, and the creation of Buddhist literary, artistic, and other cultural expressions. In this ongoing process leading to American Buddhism, as has been the case from the beginning, both Asian Americans and European Americans continue to have much to offer.

In fact, Asian American and convert Buddhist communities have provided balance and mutual enhancement for one another in the process of creating viable forms of American Buddhism. For example, Asian American communities tend to hold carefully to the Dharma and its practice as crafted in Asia over many centuries. They feel that Dharma and practice, so defined, have proven themselves by the fact that they produced so many enlightened lives, lasting institutions, inspiring writings, and great cultural expressions. As we shall see, convert communities have tended to bring the Dharma and its practice to bear on more social and political matters, such as poverty and social injustice, peacemaking and environmental issues, healing, and modern psychology. While the convert groups inspire Asian American communities to take these matters seriously, the latter also emphasize aspects of the Dharma and its practice that could become watered down by pursuing only secular goals.

Also, Asian American and convert communities are facing some of the same problems today as they try to live the Dharma in the West. For example, the children of the older immigrant generation often tend to disappear from the Buddhist temples of their parents. Convert Buddhists often are reluctant to pass on their Buddhism to their children, seeing their own involvement as a personal decision. In both cases, there is the problem of retaining new generations of members. However, there is also an important difference between the two groups. In the Asian American temples, some children continue to participate in a nonreligious manner. They find that such participation strengthens their identity as, for example, Thai, Chinese, Korean, Vietnamese, or Japanese Americans. This is not the case in the convert Buddhist communities. Members of both kinds of Buddhist communities in the West are finding it helpful to address together common problems on, for example, local and regional Saṅgha councils.

Authority and Gender Issues

A second issue that has emerged in the development of American Buddhism in the United States comes out of specific events that took place in some of the convert communities. During Buddhism's rise in popularity in the United States in the 1960s and 1970s, the countercultural influence on some convert Buddhist communities resulted in a disengaging of ethics from spiritual practice. This led to a number of scandals in the 1980s that resulted in crises of leadership. The extent of the scandals is unclear, but it included sexual improprieties and abuse of power. These scandals demonstrated not only the need for ethical standards but also the weaknesses of using an Asian male-dominated authoritarian hierarchy in modern Western society.

In response to this crisis in leadership, the San Francisco Zen Center established a democratic authority structure and a set of guidelines for proper student-teacher relations. Soon, other Buddhist organizations followed suit. In many communities today, teachers share authority with a lay board of directors. In the case of the San Francisco Zen Center, it now elects its abbot for a four-year term. While Asian monastics continue to be respected for their maturity in the Dharma and play mentor and teaching roles in communities, the unquestioned authority of monastics so common in Asia has given way in the West to models of leadership wherein all persons are held accountable for their actions. Today, scholars refer to this radical change toward a more egalitarian community structure as the "democratization of American Buddhism."

Another aspect of this democratization following the scandals of the 1980s has been an attempt to give men and women equal exercise of authority in Buddhist communities. For example, as of this writing, Zōketsu Norman Fischer and Zenkai Blanche Hartman share the leadership of the San Francisco Zen Center. Beyond this kind of structural change, some have also been more critical of traditional male-centered practice forms which can produce an atmosphere that is, at times, almost militant. As more women take leadership roles, new patterns of training are being developed that are more in line with women's spirituality. Similar changes are also taking place in communities with regard to gay and lesbian members. Buddhist gay and lesbian practitioners have in recent decades participated more in leadership roles in Buddhist communities. There are also more gay and lesbian practice groups, such as the New York Maitre Dorje and the Hartford Street Zen Center in San Francisco.

In recent decades, many Buddhist women have also taken creative leadership roles in organizations outside their specific Buddhist communities. For example, Paula Green founded the Karuna Center for Peacebuilding, which gives workshops based on Buddhist teachings. Her work has taken her to such places as Bosnia and Rwandan refugee camps in the Congo. Joan

Halifax, founder of the Upaya Institute in New Mexico, applies her Dharma teachings to caregiving for the dying. Herself influenced by Buddhist ideas and values, Melody Ermachild Chavis founded Strong Roots, a neighborhood gardening project working with "high-risk" youth in Berkeley. Virginia Straus, once an aide in Jimmy Carter's administration, now directs the Boston Research Center for the 21st Century in its work on behalf of the environment and world peace. Finally, one of the best-known Buddhist activist is Joanna Macy. Her "despair and empowerment" workshops based on Buddhist principles have inspired Buddhist and non-Buddhist activists for decades. The following are her words about the healing of self and world:

> It also helps a lot to remember that each one of us has been called into being at this time. I am convinced of that. We are not here by accident. Is it my imagination to think that we have chosen this? Is it not a privilege to be incarnating at a time when the stakes are really high, at a time when everything we've ever learned about interconnectedness, about trust, about courage, can be put to the test? Each one of us, I believe, is a gift the earth is giving to itself now, a unique gift. Every anguish, betrayal, disappointment can even help prepare us for the work of healing. You don't need to be extraordinary. If the world is to be healed through human efforts, I am convinced it will be by ordinary people, people whose love for this life is even greater than their fear, people who can open to the web of life that called us into being, and who can rest in the vitality of that larger body.[8]

Another leadership issue has to do with intellectual authority in American Buddhism. While "scholar-monastics" from Asia reside in Buddhist communities in the Untied States, the convert communities themselves are not producing scholar-monastics as is common in Asia. This is primarily because, as we have seen, Western Buddhism is mainly a lay phenomenon. However, academic departments and programs devoted to Buddhist Studies at American universities and colleges offer Buddhist communities a place to send their members in order to be trained to meet some of their educational needs. Also, within the discipline of Buddhist Studies itself are a number of "scholar-practitioners," who already do provide some intellectual leadership in various communities around the country. As long as Western Buddhism does not develop a monastic tradition, it may be that in the future scholar-practitioners will fulfill the leadership roles traditionally played by scholar-monastics in Asia.

Buddhist Ecumenism

Buddhists from all lineages are today finding various opportunities to meet together in Western pluralistic societies that were not available to them in Asia. For example, in the United States, local and regional Sangha councils provide forums in which Buddhists of various traditions can carry out ecumenical discussions, address common problems, and organize cooperative activities in pursuing shared goals. This emerging Buddhist ecumenism opens participants to more productive inter-Saṅgha relationships resulting in greater mutual understanding. This in turn creates a liberal environment in which historical divisions between Buddhist lineages are sometimes softened, and from which new Western forms of Buddhism may eventually emerge. Two active regional councils that have made progress in this regard are the Buddhist Saṅgha Council of Southern California and the Buddhist Council of the Midwest. A desire to establish this kind of ecumenical organization at the national level was behind the foundation of the American Buddhist Congress.

Besides these kinds of ongoing venues for ecumenical contacts, there have also been Buddhist ecumenical conferences in the United States. In 1987, Samu Sunim and Luis Gómez held the afore-mentioned Conference on World Buddhism in North America at the University of Michigan. At that meeting, representatives of Buddhist traditions in North America crafted the following "Statement of Consensus" in which they agree:

1. To create the conditions necessary for tolerance and understanding among Buddhists and non-Buddhists alike.
2. To initiate a dialogue among Buddhists in North America in order to further mutual understanding, growth in understanding, and cooperation.
3. To increase our sense of community by recognizing and understanding our differences as well as our common beliefs and practices.
4. To cultivate thoughts and actions of friendliness towards others, whether they accept our beliefs or not, and in so doing approach the world as the proper field of Dharma, not as a sphere of conduct irreconcilable with the practice of Dharma.[9]

This movement toward building a Buddhist ecumenism was reinforced by speakers ten years later at the 1997 Buddhism in America Conference in Boston. There, the hope was expressed that ecumenical endeavors toward Buddhist harmony and mutual enrichment can provide a rich resource at the local and regional levels for all Buddhist communities facing common issues and problems. Also during the same year, the Buddhist Saṅgha Council of Southern California and the American Buddhist Congress hosted an ecumenical meeting of Buddhist representatives at Hsi Lai Temple. There, participants established some guidelines for Buddhist ecumenical consensus-building that respect differences in the spirit of open-mindedness and tolerance.

On a more informal grassroots level, for some time now certain Buddhist teachers from convert communities in the West have been visiting one another and sharing their practices. In this practice-based ecumenism, teachers from one tradition have found that practices from another tradition may be healing or enriching to themselves and to members of their communities. Based on their personal contacts with one another, Buddhist teachers began to meet more formally with each other during the early 1990s to discuss the common challenges they were facing. This led to a meeting between Western Buddhist teachers from America and Europe and the Dalai Lama in Dharamsala, India, in 1993. There, participants discussed ways of adapting Buddhism in the West, given their concerns about such issues as integrating the Dharma with Western psychology, the possibility of a viable monasticism in the West, and the need to emphasize ethical precepts and gender equity. One result of this meeting was the conclusion that Buddhist sectarianism in the West can be countered by ecumenical contacts and discussions, a broader study of Buddhism as a whole, and more opportunities for shared practice.

Interfaith Dialogue

The same pluralistic situation in the West that has brought Buddhists closer together has also brought them into closer contact with persons of other religions. In the United States, the writings of persons like Thomas Merton in the 1960s led Christians to explore Buddhism while remaining faithful to their own traditions. This interfaith exploration eventually led to persons like Ruben Habito and Robert E. Kennedy, mentioned earlier, gaining Dharma transmission and becoming Christian Zen teachers. Buddhists have also found their interfaith relationship with Christians to be enriching. Since Western society has to a significant degree been formed by Judeo-Christian traditions, many Buddhists have found interfaith dialogue to be an aid to Buddhist inculturation as well as to interreligious understanding, appreciation, and collaboration concerning issues of mutual concern. Havanpola Ratanasara spoke about this interfaith goal in a talk to a group of Christian monastics:

> Religious differences have often been the most deeply rooted and destructive of all. If *we*, as representatives of two of the world's major religions, can show the rest of the world that we can communicate with each other, they just *might* come to realize that there is no reason why they cannot do the same. Here is the real and pressing task of interreligious dialogue today.
>
> In Buddhism, virtuous conduct (*sila*) includes "right speech." And by practicing the virtue of right speech in the context of dialogue, we will be setting an example for the larger world community to emulate. The many problems which beset our communities, indeed all humankind at the close of this century, include: the environment, international terrorism, human rights, urban violence, social justice, and the like. All of our religious communities are affected by these issues and are drawn into the fray. The only question is: Will we rise to the occasion? Will we choose the path of dialogue leading to a more united and peaceful world?[10]

Interfaith dialogue can also provide the context for Buddhism to formulate the Dharma in ways that speak to Western cultural and intellectual traditions. Kitarō Nishida, founder of the Kyoto School mentioned in Chapter 9, crafted his thought in conversation with the ideas of Western philosophers and Christian theologians. One of the recent figures in the Kyoto

School, Masao Abe is credited with helping to bring Nishida's philosophy to the attention of Western scholars in the United States and Europe. Abe's intercultural, interreligious engagement of Buddhist philosophy with Christian theology led him and John B. Cobb, Jr., to found the International Buddhist-Christian Theological Encounter in 1984. This annual encounter has brought Buddhist and Christian scholars together from Europe, Asia, and North America for dialogue on issues of mutual interest. At this writing, the Encounter is addressing the contemporary problems of social and environmental violence and their economic roots. The work of scholars like these demonstrate the intellectual promise that dialogue holds for Buddhism in the modern world.

Buddhist and Christian scholars in Asian countries have been engaged in dialogue for decades with very fruitful results. For example, in Japan, based on its dialogue with Buddhism, the Nanzan Institute in Nagoya has produced numerous translations of works by recent Japanese Buddhist scholars who engage Western philosophical and religious ideas in their writings. Also, Japanese Buddhist and Christian scholars involved in dialogue founded what is now named the Japan Society for Buddhist-Christian Studies in order to carry on their mutually enriching encounter. This kind of academic dialogue in Asia inspired Buddhist and Christian scholars in the United States to found the Society for Buddhist-Christian Studies in 1988. This society now has a large membership, a newsletter, and a respected academic journal entitled *Buddhist-Christian Studies* published by the University of Hawaii. It also holds annual meetings in conjunction with the American Academy of Religion and hosts large international conferences every four years. In 1996, scholars in Europe also founded the European Network of Buddhist-Christian Studies, with their own academic publications and conferences.

In 1977, the Catholic Benedictine monastic tradition established the Monastic Interreligious Dialogue (MID) in Europe and North America to stimulate, develop, and assist in exchanges and dialogues between Buddhist and Christian monastics. During the 1980s and 1990s, Zen and Tibetan monastics traveled to Christian monasteries in North America and Europe, while Christian monastics visited Zen and Tibetan monasteries in Asia. These contacts enabled MID to provide aid to Tibetan monastics in exile during the 1990s. Based on this decades-long friendship, in 1993 the Dalai Lama asked MID to hold an in-depth dialogue on the spiritual life at the Abbey of Gethsemani, home of his friend Thomas Merton. In 1996, MID held the now-historic Gethsemani Encounter with the Dalai Lama and other Buddhist spiritual masters from Sri Lanka, Thailand, Myanmar, Cambodia, Taiwan, Korea, Japan, and India, as well as the United States and Europe. The topics discussed included the practice of prayer and meditation, the stages of growth in the spiritual life, the role of the teacher and the community in spirituality, and the goals of spiritual and social transformation. Beyond the dialogue, Buddhist and Christian participants also practiced meditation together each day and experienced each other's religious rituals. A second Gethsemani Encounter will be held in 2002.

Another interfaith dialogue that has been fruitful for Buddhism has been with Judaism, due in large part to the many Jews who have leadership roles in Western Buddhist convert communities. Given this fact, and given that the American Jewish World Service assisted Tibetan exiles in the 1980s, the Dalai Lama met with Jewish rabbis and scholars in 1989. This first meeting led to a group of Jewish leaders going to Dharamsala, India, to meet with the Dalai Lama in 1990. This meeting was recorded in Rodger Kamenetz's 1994 book *The Jew in the Lotus: A Poet's Rediscovery of Jewish Identity in Buddhist India*. The Dalai Lama was interested in the comparison between Jewish Kabbalah and Tibetan Tantra. He was also interested in how Judaism kept its traditions alive during the Diaspora. In answer to Jewish concern about losing Jews to Buddhism, the Dalai Lama responded:

> In my public teachings I always tell people who are interested that changing religions is not an easy task. So therefore it's better not to change, better to follow one's own traditional religion, since basically the same message, the same potential is there.[11]

More recently, Kamenetz helped found the Seders for Tibet in order to foster Jewish-Tibetan relations. The Dalai Lama attended one of their seder services in 1997, hosted by Rabbi David Saperstein of the Religious Action Center in Washington, DC. At the closing of the service, those attending recited in Hebrew, "Next year in Jerusalem" and "Next year in Lhasa." Since Kameretz's book was published, other Jews have published books reflecting on their own inner dialogue as Jewish Buddhist practitioners. For example, in 1996, Sylvia Boorstein, a leader in the Insight Meditation movement, published *That's Funny, You Don't Look Buddhist: On Being a Faithful Jew and a Passionate Buddhist*. In that book, Boorstein explains how she has become a more prayerful Jew through understanding more deeply the Buddhist experience of the interdependence of life.

Social Engagement

In this final part, we want to introduce a number of significant socially engaged initiatives that have been successfully undertaken by Buddhists in the West, especially in the United States. In terms of peacemaking, the most influential Buddhist organization in the United States is the Buddhist Peace Fellowship (BPF). In 1977, Robert and Anne Aitken hosted a small meeting at their Maui *Zendō* to discuss ways of helping Buddhist practice centers and groups become involved in social and political issues. The result of this meeting was the eventual founding of the BPF as a nonsectarian Buddhist network drawing members from many Buddhist lineages in the United States. Today, that membership includes some four thousand persons, including persons of other faiths.

Recent literature of BPF states that while the *duḥkha* that pervades human existence can be addressed through personal practice, its social, political, and economic structures must also be addressed by collaborative efforts. These efforts are to be guided by the Buddhist experience of interdependence and the nonduality between oneself and other suffering beings. To this end, BPF has developed a five-point mission:

1. To make clear public witness to Buddhist practice and interdependence as a way of peace and protection for all beings;
2. To raise peace, environmental, feminist, and social justice concerns among North American Buddhists;
3. To bring a Buddhist perspective of nonduality to contemporary social action and environmental movements;
4. To encourage the practice of nonviolence based on the rich resources of traditional Buddhist and Western spiritual teachings;
5. To offer avenues for dialogue and exchange among the diverse North American and world sanghas.[12]

In terms of actual projects, BPF has funded such endeavors as medical aid for displaced Burmese people, loans to Tibetan exiles in India and Nepal, and peace walks led by Maha Ghosananda in Cambodia. In the United States, BPF has been involved in disarmament activities, anti–land mine campaigns, and prison work. In the 1980s, BPF sponsored lecture tours by Thich Nhat Hanh. The popularity of Nhat Hanh's engaged Buddhist spirituality led to the founding of the Community of Mindful Living, with its own forms of social engagement. The newest BPF project is the Buddhist Alliance for Social Engagement (BASE), suggested by Robert Aitken in 1992. BASE has organized volunteer corps–type programs responsive to local needs. In its first BASE program, lasting for six months in San Francisco in 1995, volunteers worked in local community programs and attended regular community meditation practice and processing sessions. By the end of the 1990s, BASE had expanded its volunteer program to other parts of the United States.

Robert Aitken expressed some of the ideals of BPF's work in relation to the Buddhist experience of dependent arising:

> We can begin our task . . . by meeting in informal groups within our larger sanghas to examine politics and economics from a Buddhist perspective. It will be apparent that traditional teachings of interdependence bring into direct question the rationale of accumulating wealth and of governing by hierarchical authority. What, then, is to be done?
>
> Something, certainly. Our practice of the Brahma Vihāras—kindliness, compassion, goodwill, and equanimity—would be meaningless if it excluded people, animals, and plants outside our formal sangha. . . . On the contrary, it is clear that we're in it together with all beings.
>
> [The] collaboration in networks of mutual aid would follow from our experience of *paticca-samuppāda*, interdependent co-arising. All beings arise in systems of biological affinity, whether or not they are even "alive" in a narrow sense. We are born in a world in which all things nurture us. As we mature in our understanding of the Dharma, we take responsibility for *paticca-*

samuppāda and continually divert our infantile expectations of being nurtured to an adult responsibility for nurturing others. . . . With careful, constant discipline on the Eightfold Path of the Dharma, greed becomes *dāna* [giving], exploitation becomes networking.

Paticca-samuppāda is not just a theory but the profound realization that I arise with all beings and all beings arise with me. I suffer with all beings; all beings suffer with me. The path to this fulfillment is long and sometimes hard; it involves restraint and disengagement from ordinary concerns. . . . Dharmic society begins and prevails with individuals walking this path of compassionate understanding, discerning the noble option at each moment and allowing the other options to drop away.[13]

A second important Buddhist mode of social engagement was begun by Bernard Tetsugen Glassman upon founding the Greyston Mandala in the 1980s. This organization dedicated to Zen social engagement includes their Greyston Bakery, which provides goods for hotels and restaurants and hires and trains homeless persons and the unskilled poor. Profits are used to purchase and renovate buildings in New York for a housing project for the homeless that also provides childcare and job training. In 1998, Glassman and his wife, Sandra Jishu Holmes, also founded the Zen Peacemaker Order. The members of this new order include religious leaders, social workers, and activists who are committed to its three tenets. These are "not knowing," as a letting go of ideas and prejudices; "bearing witness," as a sharing the pains and joys of others in need; and "healing" oneself and others, as a response to that shared experience. Specifically, the tenets are lived by going into situations of pain that society ignores, being there with openness united with those in need, witnessing to the interrelatedness of life, and finding therein a way to help bring healing to the situation.

A third form of social engagement has developed from Buddhist environmentalism. Sometimes called "Eco-centric Saṅgha" or "Green Dharma," this diverse movement has no organized structure. It includes individuals who address environmental concerns from the standpoint of the Buddhist experience of interdependence and such Buddhist values as mindfulness, compassion, nonharming, and serving all living beings. In 1969, Gary Snyder portrayed the connection between Buddhist practice and ecology in his Pulitzer Prize–winning *Turtle Island*. The following are selections from that book:

> Position: Man is but a part of the fabric of life—dependent on the whole fabric for his very existence. As the most highly developed tool-using animal, he must recognize that the unknown evolutionary destinies of other life forms are to be respected, and act as gentle steward of the earth's community of being.
>
> Situation: The human race in the last century has allowed its production and scattering of wastes, by-products, and various chemicals to become excessive. Pollution is directly harming life on the planet; which is to say, ruining the environment for humanity itself.
>
> Goal: Balance, harmony, humility, growth which is a mutual growth with Redwood and Quail: to be a good member of the great community of living creatures. True affluence is not needing anything.[14]

During the 1980s, BPF began to address the environmental crisis affecting so many living beings. In the 1990s, numerous books and articles were published on Buddhism and ecology, and conferences were held on the topic. One such conference was the Spirit and Nature conference in 1990 at Middlebury College with the Dalai Lama as keynote speaker. Since 1998, the International Buddhist-Christian Theological Encounter has also addressed the factors responsible for ecological violence in its annual meetings.

Concrete Buddhist ecological programs include, among others, Gary Snyder's Yuba River Institute; the San Francisco–based Buddhists Concerned for Animals; the Washington, DC–based Center for Respect of Life and the Environment; and the work done of the Boston Research Center for the 21st Century on behalf of the Earth Charter, a set of guidelines for human-earth relations. In most cases, what distinguishes Buddhist environmentalism is the cultivation through practice of the experience of interrelatedness that in turn becomes a basis both for insight into the importance of ecology and for addressing ecological issues. In this regard, Stephanie Kaza says,

> The Hua-yen School of Buddhism . . . placed particular emphasis on this principle, using the jewel net of Indra as a teaching metaphor. . . . To extend this metaphor, if you tug on any one of the lines of the net—for example, through loss of species or habitat—it affects all the other lines. Or, if any of the jewels become cloudy (toxic or polluted), they reflect the others less clearly. Likewise, if clouded jewels are cleared up (rivers cleaned, wetlands restored), life across the web is enhanced. . . . This, then, provides a principle of both explanation for the way things are, and a path for positive action.[15]

Buddhists are also finding ways of relating their mindfulness and meditation practices to psychology. As we can glimpse in the earlier quotation from Joseph Goldstein, the Insight Meditation movement has found that in their spirituality of mental culture, the inner journey that faces suffering and its causes in the mind and heart aids in the process of psychic healing and integration. Today, some health care professionals, such as those at the Cambridge Institute for Meditation and Psychotherapy, integrate mindfulness and meditation into their clinical practice. For over twenty years at the Stress Reduction Clinic at the University of Massachusetts Medical Center, Jon Kabat-Zinn has used mindfulness and Zen meditation in programs for pain management and for treating stress-related disorders. More recently, Kabat-Zinn and his colleagues have also founded the Center for Mindfulness in Medicine, Health Care, and Society in connection with the University of Massachusetts in order to apply their work to other settings such as prisons, schools, and the workplace.

Finally, a number of Buddhist prison ministry programs have been founded in the criminal justice system. During the 1960s and 1970s, Hogen Fujimoto of the Buddhist Churches of America presented Dharma sessions at San Quentin and Soledad prisons. Abbot John Daido Loori of the Zen Mountain Monastery in New York founded the Lotus Flower Zendo in Green

Haven Prison, and his ministry program now serves a number of New York prisons with meditation training, talks, and other services. In 1992, Kobutsu Kevin Malone and Liz Potter founded what has become the Dharma Song Zendo at Sing Sing. In 1994, Malone established the Engaged Zen Foundation to provide materials and training to Buddhist prison meditation groups. Today, the BPF's Prison Meditation Network provides volunteers to work in jails and prisons. Also, the Upaya Prison Program as part of the Zen Peacemakers Order teaches mindfulness, meditation, and peacemaking at a maximum-security penitentiary in Santa Fe.

These recent forms of Buddhist social engagement, along with the many other types of innovations introduced in this chapter, are some of the ways in which Buddhism is adapting its lineage forms to Western cultures. As this reformation takes new shapes in the ongoing experience of Buddhism in the West, we will eventually be able to see the emergence of new forms of Western Buddhism. This process of crafting Western Buddhism will most likely take a number of generations, if not centuries, to complete. At least this was the experience of Buddhism as it moved into new areas of Asia. But in the meantime, Buddhists are finding ways to inspire and nourish positive innovations in their communities, while at the same time working to address the pressing problems of contemporary society. As Buddhism re-creates itself through its experience in the modern Western world, it weaves new threads that add rich new textures to the 2500-year tapestry of Buddhist life. In so doing, Western Buddhism will certainly bring the Dharma to a fuller level of global expression. At the beginning of the twenty-first century, the story of Buddhism as a truly world religion, drawing on the West as well as the East, is only now beginning to be written.

NOTES

1. Edwin Arnold, *The Light of Asia* (Boston: Roberts Brothers, 1890), pp. 230–231.

2. Jack Kerouac, *Dharma Bums* (New York: Penguin Books, 1958), pp. 9–10.

3. Joseph Goldstein, *Insight Meditation: The Practice of Freedom* (Boston: Shambhala Publications, 1993), pp. 3–4.

4. Sogyal Rinpoche, *The Tibetan Book of Living and Dying*, Partick Gaffney and Andrew Harvey, eds. (San Francisco: HarperSanFrancisco), pp. 48, 49, 59, 61–62, 189, 198.

5. Samu Sunim, "Worldly Bodhisattvas: Zen Awakening and Social Transformation," in Donald W. Mitchell and James Wiseman, O.S.B., eds., *The Gethsemani Encounter: A Dialogue on the Spiritual Life by Buddhist and Christian Monastics* (New York: Continuum Publishing Co., 1997), pp. 143–146.

6. Shinryu Suzuki, *Zen Mind, Beginner's Mind*, Trudy Dixon, ed. (New York: Weatherhill, 1970), pp. 76–77, 79.

7. Charles S. Prebish and Kenneth K. Tanaka, eds., *The Faces of Buddhism in America* (Berkeley: University of California Press, 1998), p. 288.

8. Joanna Macy, "Schooling Our Intention," *Tricycle: The Buddhist Review* 3, no. 2 (Winter 1993), p. 51.

9. Eleanor Rosch, "World Buddhism in North America Today," *Vajradhatu Sun* 9, no. 1 (October–November 1987), p. 28.

10. Ven. Dr. Havanpola Ratanasara, "Dialogue and Unity: A Buddhist Perspective" in Mitchell and Wiseman, eds., *Gethsemani Encounter*, 14–15.

11. Rodger Kamenetz, *The Jew and the Lotus: A Poet's Rediscovery of Jewish Identity in Buddhist India* (San Francisco: HarperSanFrancisco, 1994), pp. 228–229.

12. Buddhist Peace Fellowship mailing, February 11, 1997.

13. Robert Aitken, *Original Dwelling Place* (Washington, DC: Counterpoint, 1997), pp. 138–142.

14. Gary Snyder, *Turtle Island* (New York: New Directions, 1969), pp. 91, 94, 97.

15. Stephanie Kaza, "To Save All Beings: Buddhist Environmental Activism," in Christopher S. Queen, ed., *Engaged Buddhism in the West* (Boston: Wisdom Publications, 2000), pp. 166–167.

SUGGESTIONS FOR FURTHER READING

Batchelor, Stephen. *The Awakening of the West: The Encounter of Buddhism and Western Culture*. Berkeley, CA: Parallax Press, 1994.

Boucher, Sandy. *Turning the Wheel: American Women Creating the New Buddhism*. Boston: Beacon Press, 1993.

Cobb, John B., Jr., and Christopher A. Ives, eds. *The Emptying God: A Buddhist-Jewish-Christian Conversation*. Maryknoll, NY: Orbis Books, 1990.

Coleman, James William. *The New Buddhism: The Western Transformation of an Ancient Tradition*. New York: Oxford University Press, 2000.

Fields, Rick. *How the Swans Came to the Lake: A Narrative History of Buddhism in America*. Boston: Shambhala Publications, 1992.

Gross, Rita M. *Buddhism after Patriarchy: A Feminist History, Analysis, and Reconstruction of Buddhism*. Albany, NY: SUNY Press, 1993.

Hammond, Phillip E., and David W. Machacek. *Sōka Gakkai in America: Accommodation and Conversion*. New York: Oxford University Press, 1999.

Kaza, Stephanie, and Kenneth Kraft, eds. *Dharma Rain: Sources of Buddhist Environmentalism*. Boston: Shambhala Publications, 2000.

Mitchell, Donald W., and James Wiseman, O.S.B., eds. *The Gethsemani Encounter: A Dialogue on the Spiritual Life by Buddhist and Christian Monastics*. New York: Continuum Publishing Co., 1997.

Morreale, Don, ed. *The Complete Guide to Buddhist America*. Boston: Shambhala Publications, 1998.

Prebish, Charles S. *Luminous Passage: The Practice and Study of Buddhism in America*. Berkeley, CA: University of California Press, 1999.

Prebish, Charles S., and Kenneth K. Tanaka, eds. *The Faces of Buddhism in America*. Berkeley, CA: University of California Press, 1998.

Queen, Christopher S., ed. *Engaged Buddhism in the West*. Boston: Wisdom Publications, 2000.

Seager, Richard Hughes. *Buddhism in America*. New York: Columbia University Press, 1999.

Tanaka, Kenneth K. *Ocean: An Introduction to Jōdo-Shinshū Buddhism in America*. Berkeley, CA: WisdomOcean Publications, 1997.

Tonkinson, Carole. ed. *Big Sky Mind: Buddhism and the Beat Generation*. New York: Riverhead Books, 1995.

Tweed, Thomas A. *The American Encounter with Buddhism, 1844–1912: Victorian Culture and the Limits of Dissent*. Bloomington, IN: Indiana University Press, 1992.

Tworkov, Helen. *Zen in America: Five Teachers and the Search for an American Buddhism*. New York: Kodansha America, 1994.

Williams, Duncan Ryuken, and Christopher S. Queen, eds. *American Buddhism: Methods and Findings in Recent Scholarship*. Richmond, UK: Curzon Press, 1998.

Glossary of Technical Terms

abhidharma (S) [P: abhidhamma]: "Higher Dharma"; collection of scholastic treatises in the Pali Canon that outline and classify Buddhist teachings; one of the three major divisions of the Pali Canon.

adosa (P): Nonhate; loving kindness and other positive motivations in relation to others.

āgama (S): Canonical texts corresponding to the *Nikāyas* of the Pali texts.

ahiṃsa (S): Nonhurting; nonkilling; nonviolence.

akṣobhya (S): "Immovable"; first celestial Buddha to be mentioned in Mahāyāna texts.

akuśala (S) [P: akusala]: Unwholesome; referring to defiling states of consciousness.

ālaya-vijñāna (S): "Storehouse consciousness"; Yogācāra concept of a depth of consciousness that contains impure seeds of karmic experience along with pure seeds of Awakening.

alobha (P): Nongreed; positive intentions toward others.

amala-vijñāna (S): Pure consciousness; innate pure consciousness that is identified with the nirvanic nature of reality.

amitābha (S) [C: o-mi-t'o; J: amida]: Celestial Buddha of the Western Paradise or Pure Land; Buddha worshiped by Pure Land schools of Buddhism.

amoha (S, P): Nondelusion; clarity of mind in relation to others.

anāgāmin (S, P): Non-returner; third advanced stage in early Buddhist path leading to being an *arhat*.

Note: Sanskrit (S), Pali (P), Tibetan (T), Chinese (C), Korean (K), Japanese (J), Thai (Th).

ananda (S): Happiness, joy.

anātman (S) [P: anattā]: No-self; denial of a permanent self or soul (*ātman*); denial of any permanent substantial nature of phenomena.

anitya (S) [P: anicca]: Impermanence; transiency that is characteristic of all phenomena.

anupadhiśeṣa (S): "Without remainder"; Nirvana without the Five Aggregates; *parinirvāṇa*.

arhat (S) [P: arahant]: "Worthy One"; person who is free from all defilements and has attained Nirvana; fourth and final stage of the advanced Theravāda path.

arūpa-loka (S, P): Formless realm; place of rebirth where deities have no shape or form, only mental existence.

asaṃskṛta (S) [P: asaṅkhāta]: Unproduced; unconditioned; quality of Nirvana.

āsrava (S) [P: āsava]: "Outflow"; mental "canker" that ferments defilements; usually defined as sensual desire, desire for continued existence, ignorance, and, sometimes, holding views that are not liberating.

āśraya-parāvṛtti (S): Yogācāra notion of the reversion or conversion of the basis of consciousness that brings insight into the essence of consciousness.

ātman (S) [P: attā]: Soul; permanent self; central notion in Upaniṣadic Hinduism.

avalokiteśvara (S) [C: kuan-yin; J: Kannon]: Bodhisattva of compassion.

avidyā (S) [P: avijjā]: Ignorance.

āyatana (S, P): Sense faculty.

bhāva (S, P): Being; becoming; existence.

bhāvanā (S, P): Mental culture; mental cultivation through meditation.

bhavaṅga (P): Subliminal life-continuum.

bhikṣu (S) [P: bhikkhu]: Monk; male Buddhist monastic.

bhikṣuṇī (S) [P: bhikkhunī]: Nun; woman Buddhist monastic.

bhūmi (S): Stage on the bodhisattva path to Buddhahood.

bīja (S): Seed.

bodhi (S, P): Awakening; enlightenment.

bodhicitta (S): "Thought of Awakening"; altruistic aspiration to attain Buddhahood for the sake of all living beings.

bodhisattva (S) [P: bodhisatta]: Person who seeks the wisdom and liberation of a Buddha; in Mahāyāna, one who seeks Buddhahood in order to deliver others from suffering.

bodhisattvayāna (S): Bodhisattva journey, course, or vehicle leading one to Buddhahood for the benefit of other beings.

bön (T): Religion of Tibet that has indigenous and Buddhist elements.

brahmā (S, P): Hindu deity; a type of deity who inhabits the higher heavenly realms according to Buddhism.

brahman (S): Ultimate Reality in Hinduism.

brahmā-vihāra (S, P): Four divine states cultivated in Buddhism: loving kindness, compassion, sympathetic joy, and equanimity.

buddha (S, P): Awakened One.

caitasika (S) [P: cetasika]: Mental states discussed in Abhidharma texts and various schools of Buddhism.

cetanā (S, P): Will; volition; willful states of mind forming karma.

ch'an (C) [K: sŏn; J: zen]: Meditation; from the Chinese *ch'an-na*, transliterating *dhyāna*, meaning meditation; school of Chinese Buddhism emphasizing the practice of meditation.

ch'eng-shih (C): School of Chinese Buddhism based on Sautrāntika and Mādhyamika; *Satyasiddhi* Treatise.

chên-yen (C) [J: shingon]: "True word"; Tantric school of Chinese Buddhism.

ching-t'u (C) [K: chŏng-t'o; J: jōdo]: Pure Land; Pure Land Buddhism in China.

chogye (K): Modern Korean Buddhist order.

chŏng-t'o (K): Korean Pure Land Buddhism.

ch'ŏnt'ae (K): Korean T'ien-t'ai School of Buddhism.

chü-shê (C): School of Chinese Buddhism based on Sarvāstivāda.

citta (S, P): Mind.

dalai lama (T): *Dalai* means "ocean," implying the Dalai Lama's wisdom is as deep as the ocean; title of the head of the Geluk School of Tibetan Buddhism; spiritual and temporal leader of Tibetan people.

dāna (S, P): Giving; donations to the Saṅgha; method of making merit.

daśabhūmi (S): Ten stages of the bodhisattva journey to Buddhahood.

deva (S): Deity; type of Hindu deity; deities that inhabit the lower heavenly realms according to Buddhism.

deva-yoga (S): Deity yoga; type of Tantric visualization practice whereby one becomes familiar with the qualities and consciousness of bodhisattvas, Buddhas, and their realms.

dhāraṇī (S): "That which sustains"; ritual formulas used to sustain religious life, in meditation, or to invoke deities.

dharma (S) [P: dhamma]: Teaching of the Buddha; ultimate truth taught by the Buddha; law that governs things; essence or nature of phenomena; ultimate mental and physical constituents of existence.

dharmadhātu (S): Realm of truth; realm of the *dharmas* as they truly are; totality of all phenomena; absolute foundation for all phenomena.

dharmakāya (S): "Body of the Dharma"; totality of the Buddha's qualities in early Buddhism; luminous and nirvanic essence of the Buddha in Mahāyāna; innate reality of Buddhahood.

dhyāna (S) [P: jhāna]: Meditation; meditative states of consciousness.

dosa (P): Hate; aversion.

duḥkha (S) [P: dukkha]: Dissatisfactory condition of human nature; suffering; the condition of transitory existence; first of the Four Noble Truths.

dzogchen (T): Nyingma meditation practice focusing on the essential pure and free nature of the mind.

ekayāna (S): One vehicle; notion in the *Lotus Sūtra* that refers to the essence or true practice behind all forms of Buddhism.

fa-hsiang (C) [J: hossō]: "Characteristics of the *Dharmas*"; Yogācāra School of Chinese Buddhism.

fo guang shan (C): Modern socially engaged Buddhist order in Taiwan.

garbha (S): Womb; embryo.

geluk (T): "Order of Virtue"; school of Tibetan Buddhism; the school of the Dalai Lama.

gohonzon (J): Great *maṇḍala*; *maṇḍala* used in Nichiren Buddhism.

guru (S): Teacher; spiritual master.

guru-yoga (S): Tantric practice of venerating one's guru as embodiment of wisdom and compassion of Buddhahood.

haedong (K): Korean sect based on teachings of Wŏnhyo.

haiku (J): Type of Japanese poetry.

hīnayāna (S, P): Small or lesser journey, course, or vehicle; a pejorative term used by Mahāyāna to denote all forms of early Buddhism that did not accept Mahāyāna teachings.

hossō (J): "Characteristics of the *Dharmas*"; Japanese school of Yogācāra Buddhism.

hōza (J): "Dharma sitting"; communal sharing practice of the Risshō Kōsei-kai in which members search together the *Lotus Sūtra* for aid in daily life.

hua-yen (C) [K: hwaŏm; J: kegon]: *Avataṃsaka*; "Flower Ornament"; School of Chinese Buddhism based on the *Avataṃsaka Sūtra*.

hwadu (K): "Critical phrase" in a *kongan* used in Korean Sŏn Buddhism to focus the mind in meditation.

hwaŏm (K): Korean school of Hua-yen Buddhism.

inka (J): Formal certification of Awakening and teaching approval in Zen.

irwŏn-sang (K): Unity circle symbolizing the *Dharmakāya* in Won Buddhism.

jātaka (S, P): Birth stories; collection of tales about the previous lives of Gautama Buddha.

jiriki (J): Self power; realizing Awakening by relying on one's own effort.

jīva (S): Soul.

jōdo (J): Pure land; Pure Land School of Buddhism in Japan founded by Hōnen.

jōdo shinshū (J): True School of Pure Land Buddhism; Pure Land Buddhism in Japan founded by Shinran.

jōjitsu (J): Japanese school of Ch'eng-shih Buddhism; *Satyasiddhi* Treatise.

kadam (T): "Bound to commands [of the Buddha]"; early school of Tibetan Buddhism.

kagyü (T): "Teaching lineage"; school of Tibetan Buddhism.

kāma-loka (S, P): Sense-desire realm; realms of hells, hungry ghosts, animals, humans, and lower gods.

kami (J): Spirits worshiped in Japanese Shintō religion.

kanjur (T): "Translation of Buddha's word"; division of the Tibetan Buddhist canon containing what is thought to be the Buddha's teachings.

karma (S) [P: kamma]: Action; intentional act; the effect such actions leave that influence the future of the actor; principle governing cause and effect.

karuṇā (S, P): Compassion.

kegon (J): Japanese Hua-yen School of Buddhism.

kenshō (J): "Seeing the nature"; enlightened insight in Zen Buddhism.

kleśā (S) [P: kilesa]: Defilement.

kṛtṣna (S) [P: kasiṇa]: Devices used as objects in meditation.

kṣānti (S): Patience.

kung-an (C) [K: kongan; J: kōan]: "Public legal case"; authoritative, paradoxical sayings and questions used in Ch'an, Sŏn, Zen practice.

kuśala (S) [P: kusala]: Wholesomeness.

kusha (J): Japanese Sarvāstivāda School.

kyeyul (K): Korean *Vinaya* School.

kyo (K): Doctrinal Schools of Buddhism in Korea.

lama (T): "Guru" in Sanskrit; spiritual teacher.

lamdre (T): "Path and fruit"; meditative practice of the Sakya School of Tibetan Buddhism.

li (C): Principle; inherent pure nature of existence.

lin-chi (C) [J: Rinzai]: School of Ch'an Buddhism that uses *kung-an* practice.

lobha (P): Greed; attraction.

lu (C): Chinese *Vinaya* School of Buddhism.

mādhyamika (S): Major school of Mahāyāna Buddhism in India that stresses emptiness.

mahāmudrā (S): "Great seal"; meditative system of practice associated with the Kagyü School of Tibetan Buddhism and used for the realization of the luminous and empty nature of existence.

mahāsaṅghika (S): "Great Assembly"; early school of Buddhism.

mahāyāna (S): Great vehicle, great course, or great journey; name of one of the major divisions of Buddhism wherein persons strive to become a Buddha rather than an *arhat*.

maitreya (S): Bodhisattva who will be the next human Buddha.

maitri (S) [P: metta]: Loving kindness; friendliness.

manas (S, P): Mind.

maṇḍala (S): Diagram or picture, often circular, used in meditative practice; Tantric diagram used for visualization of a Buddha's qualities and realm.

mañjuśrī (S): Bodhisattva associated with wisdom.

mantra (S): Ritual formula; verse used to invoke a deity or to gain protection; sound used for focus in meditation.

mantrayāna (S): Tantric Buddhism with its stress on the use of *mantras*.

mappō (J): Age of the Degenerate Dharma.

māra (S, P): Tempter; highest deity in the sense-realm, who uses sensuality to prevent people from gaining Awakening and thereby escape from his realm.

mārga (S) [P: magga]: Path; way.

māyā (S, P): Illusion.

mikkyō (J): "Esoteric practice"; Tantric Buddhist practice.

moha (S, P): Delusion; distortion of the truth.

mokṣa (S): Liberation.

muditā (S, P): Sympathetic joy.

mudra (S): "Seal"; hand ritual gesture.

mukti (S) [P: mutti]: Freedom; liberation.

nāma-rūpa (S, P): "Name-form"; the mental and physical constituents of existence.

nembutsu (J): "Recollection of Buddha"; Pure Land Buddhist practice of reciting the name of Amitābha Buddha; Japanese translation of the Chinese *nien-fo*.

nichiren (J): School of Japanese Buddhism based on the *Lotus Sūtra* and teachings of its founder, Nichiren.

nidāna (S, P): Link; cause.

nien-fo (C) [J: nembutsu]: "Recollecting Buddha"; chanting the name of the Buddha, primarily Amitābha Buddha in Pure Land Buddhism.

nikāya (S, P): "Collection"; text; group of early *sūtras* in the Pali canon; also called *Āgama*.

nirmāṇakāya (S): Manifestation body of the Buddha; emanation body used by a Buddha to help living beings and teach the Dharma.

nirodha (S, P): Cessation; cessation of *duḥkha* in the Four Noble Truths.

nirvāṇa (S) [P: nibbāna]: "Blowing out"; extinguishing a flame; goal of Buddhism; release from *saṃsāra* by attainment of Awakening.

nyingma (T): "Ancient school"; one of the four major schools of Tibetan Buddhism.

ōbaku (J): School of Japanese Zen Buddhism.

paramārtha-satya (S): Ultimate truth; truth found in wisdom insight into dependent arising of existence according to Mādyamika.

pāramitā (S, P): Perfection; virtue, of which there are six or ten traditionally in Buddhism.

paratantra (S): Interdependent nature of experience; experience of all phenomena as arising interdependently; category in Yogācāra Buddhism.

parikalpita (S): Imagined nature of ordinary experience; ordinary experience of phenomena as independent entities; category in Yogācāra Buddhism.

parinirvāṇa (S) [P: parinibbāna]: Complete or final Nirvana; utter release from *saṃsāra* achieved by a Buddha or *arhat* at the moment of death.

pariniṣpanna (S): Perfected nature of experience; purified consciousness recognizing that all phenomena are in essence consciousness only; category in Yogācāra Buddhism.

pŏpsang (K): Korean Yogācāra School of Buddhism.

prajñā (S) [P: paññā]: Wisdom; knowledge of truth associated with Awakening; liberating wisdom into the true nature of existence.

prajñā-paramitā (S): Perfection of wisdom; designation for early Mahāyāna *sūtras*, the Wisdom Literature.

prapañca (S): "Play of words"; meaningful conceptualization of the world through use of language; important notion in Mādyamika Buddhism.

prāsaṅgika (S): Sect of Mādhyamika Buddhism founded by Buddhapālita.

prātimokṣa (S) [P: pāṭimokkha]: Code of monastic precepts.

pratītya-samutpāda (S) [P: paticca-samuppāda]: Dependent arising; dependent origination; dependent co-arising of all phenomena.

pratyekabuddha (S): "Solitary Buddha"; person who attains Awakening with no help and never preaches to others.

preta (S) [P: peta]: Hungry ghost.

pudgala (S): Person.

pudgalavāda (S): Personalists; early school of Buddhism in India.

rinzai (J): School of Zen Buddhism that uses *kōans*, based on the Chinese Lin-chi School.

risshō kōsei-kai (J): Modern Buddhist lay movement in Japan based on the *Lotus Sūtra*.

ritsu (J): Japanese *Vinaya* school of Buddhism.

roshi (J): Zen master.

rūpa (S, P): Form; material element of existence.

rūpakāya (S, P): Form or material body of a Buddha.

rūpaloka (S, P): Realm of form; place of rebirth as higher Brahmā deity.

sādhana (S): Esoteric or Tantric practice.

sakṛdāgāmin (S) [P: sakadāgāmin]: "Once-returner"; second advanced stage of early Buddhist path leading to being an *arhat*.

sakya (T): One of the four major schools of Tibetan Buddhism.

sakyadhītā (S): "Daughters of the Buddha"; Association dedicated to Buddhist women's issues, especially full ordination of women monastics in Theravāda Buddhism.

samādhi (S, P): Concentration; Right concentration in the Noble Eightfold Path; deep state of meditation.

śamatha (S) [P: samatha]: Tranquillity; calmness; serenity; cessation of thoughts and desires in meditation.

sambhogakāya (S): Enjoyment or reward body of a Buddha; body of a celestial Buddha.

saṃjñā (S) [P: saññā]: Perception; one of the Five Aggregates.

saṃsāra (S, P): "Wandering"; process of birth, death, and rebirth; world of suffering.

saṃskāra (S) [P: saṃkhāra]: Mental formation; volition; one of the Five Aggregates.

saṃvṛti-satya (S): Conventional truth; truth given by ordinary sense perception and conceptualization according to Mādyamika.

saṅgha (S, P): "Community"; orders of men and women monastics; all Buddhist persons, lay and monastic.

san lun (C): "Three treatises"; school of Mādhyamika in China.

sanron (J): Mādyamika School of Buddhism in Japan.

sarvāstivāda (S): All-Exists School of Buddhism.

satori (J): Awakening; sudden enlightenment in Zen Buddhism.

sautrāntika (S): "Adherents to the *Sūtras*"; early school of Buddhism.

sesshin (J): Intensive Zen retreat.

shakubuku (J): Confrontational method of evangelizing in Nichiren Buddhism.

shih (C): Phenomena; phenomenal *dharmas*.

shikan-taza (J): "Just sitting"; quiet sitting practice in Sōtō Zen.

shingon (J): "True Word"; school of Tantric or esoteric Buddhism in Japan.

shinjin (J): Arising of faith; trust in the saving action of Amida Buddha.

shintō (J): "Way of the spirits"; indigenous religion of Japan.

shōdō (J): Holy Path; Pure Land Buddhist name for the path to liberation that demands one's own effort, and not relying on the grace of Amida Buddha.

siddhi (S) [P: iddhi]: Supernormal power or ability.

śīla (S) [P: sīla]: Precepts; morality.

skandha (S) [P: khandha]: Aggregate; the five kinds of constituents of existence: material form (*rūpa*), sensation (*vedanā*), perception (*saṃjña*), mental formation (*saṃskāra*), and consciousness (*vijñāna*).

smṛti (S) [P: sati]: Mindfulness; part of the Noble Eightfold Path.

sōka gakkai (J): Modern Nichiren lay movement.

sŏn (K): Meditation; Ch'an Buddhism in Korea.

sopadhiśeṣa (S): "With remainder"; Nirvana with the Five Aggregates.

sōtō (J): School of Zen Buddhism in Japan founded by Dōgen.

śramaṇa (S) [P: samaṇa]: Renunciate status present in India during the time of the Buddha.

śrāvaka (S): Disciple; term for disciple of the Buddha seeking to be an *arhat*.

śrāvakayāna (S): Term for the early Buddhist path leading to being an *arhat*.

srotāpanna (S) [P: sotāpanna]: "Streamwinner"; first of the advanced stages of early Buddhism leading to being an *arhat*.

sthavira (S) [P: thera]: Elder.

sthaviravāda (S) [P: Theravāda]: Way or teaching of the elders; school of early Buddhism.

stūpa (S, P): Memorial mound for the bones or remains of the dead; used as a shrine for the Buddha.

sukhāvati (S): Land of bliss; Pure Land of Amitābha Buddha.

śūnyatā (S): Emptiness; lack of substantial independence; fundamental Mahāyāna notion of ultimate reality.

sūtra (S) [P: sutta]: Text; scripture; collection of discourses by the Buddha in the Buddhist canon.

svabhāva (S): "Own-being"; substantial self-existence; that which enables a phenomenon to exist independently; attributed to the *dharmas* by some early Buddhist schools.

svabhāva-śūnya (S): "Emptiness of own-being"; notion in Mahāyāna that denies own-being of all *dharmas* in favor of emptiness, the dependence of existence.

svalakṣaṇa (S): "Own-characteristic"; distinguishing characteristic of a *dharma*.

svātantrika (S): Sect of Mādyamika Buddhism founded by Bhāvaviveka.

tantra (S): Esoteric tradition in Buddhism; esoteric texts in Buddhism.

tao (C): Way; Chinese term for ultimate reality that is the ground of all existence.

tariki (J): Other power; relying in Pure Land Buddhism on the power of Amida Buddha to gain liberation.

tathāgata (S, P): One who has "thus come" or "thus gone" to Awakening; epithet for the Buddha after his enlightenment; title for all Buddhas in Mahāyāna.

tathāgata-garbha (S): "Womb or embryo of the Buddha"; innate potential for Buddhahood; Buddha-nature.

tathatā (S): Suchness; thusness; true reality; such as things truly are.

tendai (J): Japanese school of Buddhism based on the Chinese T'ien-t'ai School and additional teachings by Saichō.

tenjur (T): Division of the Tibetan canon that contains commentaries.

terma (T): Hidden treasure; entities or teachings hidden in Tibet by spiritually advanced persons and discovered when helpful to the community; Nyingma practice.

tertön (T): Treasure finder; one who finds a *terma*.

theravāda (P): Way or teaching of the elders; early Buddhist school that became the major form in Buddhism in Sri Lanka and Southeast Asia.

t'ien-t'ai (C): "Heavenly terrace"; Chinese school of Buddhism based on the *Lotus Sūtra*.

trikāya (S): Three bodies of the Buddha: *Dharmakāya, Sambhogakāya,* and *Nirmāṇakāya*.

tripiṭaka (S) [P: tipiṭaka]: Three baskets; three divisions of the Pali canon: *Sūtra, Vinaya,* and *Abhidharma*; three parts of the Tibetan and East Asia comprehensive collection of Buddhist texts.

tṛṣṇā (S) [P: taṇhā]: Thirst; desire or craving; a root cause of *duḥkha*.

trisvabhāva (S): Three natures of experience; Yogācāra's three ways in which one experiences existence: *parikalpita, paratantra,* and *pariniṣpanna*.

ts'ao-tung (C): Sect of Chinese Ch'an Buddhism that stresses silent sitting; known as Sōtō Zen in Japan.

upādāna (S, P): Attachment; clinging.

upaniṣad (S): Texts from early Hinduism that posit the existence of an absolute ultimate reality (*Brahman*) and its identity with the soul (*Ātman*).

upāya (S): Skillful means.

upekṣā (S) [P: upekkhā]: Equanimity; equal treatment of all beings.

vairocana (S): "Shining out"; celestial Buddha associated with the totality of the cosmos.

vajra (S): "Diamond" or "thunderbolt"; Tantric symbol for the power of Tantrism, and the basis of Buddhahood.

vajrayāna (S): Diamond journey, course, or vehicle; path to Buddhahood based on Tantric practice.

veda (S): Early texts of Hinduism that teach about the many gods.

vedanā (S, P): Sensation; feeling; one of the Five Aggregates.

vibhajyavāda (S): Distinctionalist School of early Buddhism.

vihāra (S, P): Monastery.

vijñāna (S) [P: viññāna]: Consciousness; mental awareness and discrimination; one of the Five Aggregates.

vijñānavāda (S): School of mind or consciousness; Yogācāra Buddhism.

vijñaptimātra (S): Ideation only; mind or consciousness only; according to Yogācāra, the basis of physical and mental experience.

vinaya (S, P): Precepts; rules for proper conduct; monastic discipline; one of the Three Baskets of the Pali canon.

vipaśyanā (S) [P: vipassanā]: Insight; meditation that produces insight into reality.

visuddhimagga (P): Path of Purification associated with Theravāda Buddhism.

wat (Th): Monastic temple complex.

won (K): One; symbol of unity and the *Dharmakāya*; new movement in Korean Buddhism.

wu (C) [J: mu]: Nothingness; emptiness; void.

yathābhūtam (S): "Things as they truly are"; what one discovers in Awakening.

yogācāra (S): "Practice of yoga"; major Mahāyāna school of Indian Buddhism that emphasizes the nature of consciousness.

yoga-tantra (S): Tantric practice involving visualization of oneself as a Tantric deity.

yŏlban (K): Nirvana; school of Buddhism in Korea based on the *Nirvana Sūtra*.

zange (J): Repentance.

zazen (J): Seated meditation in Zen Buddhism.

zen (J): Meditation; Japanese School of Buddhism based on the Chinese Ch'an school.

zendō (J): Zen meditation hall.

Index